klin's life in 1769 was relatively
, but politics were stormy. The
es affair came to a crisis in the
g; the Grafton ministry was beset
troubles and nearing its end, and
North was emerging as the Duke's
successor. The colonial issue, much
e fore when the year opened, seemed
e moderating as time passed. The
nportation agreements in America
beginning to put pressure on the
sh mercantile community, which in
generated political pressure; when
ament recessed in the late spring,
Lord Hillsborough was saying that
ast some of the Townshend Acts
d be repealed in the next session.
klin was doing what he could to
g about total repeal, and by the end
ne year was ready for a sustained
paign in the press.

nwhile he was developing his ideas
t the whole colonial question. His
lvement in it was broadened during
ear by his assumption of the agency
he New Jersey Assembly and by his
asing contacts with Boston. Simul-
ously, it seems, he began to collect
read and annotate the pamphlets that
ented the British side of the quarrel.
nese marginalia he sometimes agreed
the author and more often argued
him, calmly or angrily; in the pro-
he hammered out his concept of the
nial position, even to the point of
icitly denying Parliament's sove-
nty in America. The nonimportation

agreements heartened him, for he saw in
them the means of stimulating manufacture in the colonies and thereby increasing their self-sufficiency. He was
coming to believe that they were not only
coequal with Great Britain constitu-
tionally, but also capable economically of
standing on their own feet.

THE PAPERS OF
BENJAMIN FRANKLIN

SPONSORED BY

The American Philosophical Society
and Yale University

The Duke of Grafton

THE PAPERS OF

Benjamin Franklin

VOLUME 16   *January 1 through December 31, 1769*

WILLIAM B. WILLCOX, *Editor*

Dorothy W. Bridgwater, Mary L. Hart, Claude A. Lopez,
Catherine M. Prelinger, and G. B. Warden, Assistant Editors

New Haven and London YALE UNIVERSITY PRESS, 1972

Library of Congress catalog card number: 59–12697
International standard book number: 0–300–01570–4

Designed by Alvin Eisenman and Walter Howe,
and printed by Cambridge University Press

Published in Great Britain, Europe, and Africa by
Yale University Press, Ltd., London.
Distributed in Canada by McGill-Queen's University
Press, Montreal; in Latin America by Kaiman & Polon,
Inc., New York City; in Australasia and Southeast
Asia by John Wiley & Sons Australasia Pty. Ltd.,
Sydney; in India by UBS Publishers' Distributors Pvt.,
Ltd., Delhi; in Japan by John Weatherhill, Inc., Tokyo.

Administrative Board

Thomas C. Cochran, University of Pennsylvania, *Chairman*
Whitfield J. Bell, Jr., American Philosophical Society Library
Carl Bridenbaugh, American Philosophical Society
Chester Kerr, Yale University Press
Edmund S. Morgan, Yale University
Walter M. Whitehill, Boston Athenaeum
William B. Willcox, Yale University, *Secretary*

Advisory Committee

Thomas Boylston Adams
Bromwell Ault
Samuel F. Bemis
Charles Braibant
Prince Louis de Broglie
Lyman H. Butterfield
Julien Cain
I. Bernard Cohen
Gaylord Donnelley
Morris Duane
Sir Frank C. Francis

Andrew Heiskell
Bernhard Knollenberg
Wilmarth S. Lewis
Henry R. Luce III
David C. Mearns
Sir Owen Morshead
Howard H. Peckham
John E. Pomfret
Clifford K. Shipton
Robert E. Spiller
S. K. Stevens

Since the previous volume was in press, the Advisory Committee has been reduced by the death of Messrs. Gilbert Chinard, Lawrence Gipson, Philip Hamer, and Lawrence Wroth. The loss, however deeply felt, of their service to the editors is overshadowed by the loss to the entire community of scholars.

Contents

xi

List of Illustrations

An engraving from the portrait by John Hoppner. August Henry
Fitzroy, third Duke of Grafton (1735–1811), served in the brief
Rockingham ministry and was a principal figure in that of Lord
Chatham. As the great ex-Commoner retired more and more into
seclusion, Grafton became the acting head of the government and,
after Chatham's resignation late in 1768, its nominal head. The Duke
was more moderate than most of his colleagues, particularly on the
colonial question, and his position grew more and more difficult until he
resigned in January 1770. He resumed office under Lord North but
refused a seat in the Cabinet; the purpose of his return, he said, was to
work against an open breach with America, and when that breach came
he resigned again. He was a man of liberal instincts and good judgment,
and developed into that rarity among dukes, a Unitarian; but he lacked
the qualities of the political leader.

An engraving by Thomas Hollaway after the portrait by Benjamin
West; reproduced by courtesy of the Yale University Library. The
Rev. Dr Richard Price, F.R.S. (1723–91), was perhaps the most distinguished dissenting minister of his day. His interests were wide; they
ranged from theology and morals to mathematics and statistics and
political theory. He had known Franklin during the latter's first English mission, when they had been fellow members of the Club of
Honest Whigs, and the friendship grew closer after Franklin's return
to England. Price was such an ardent defender of the American cause
that in 1778 Congress invited him to America. His sympathy with revolution did not cool as he grew older: in 1789 he delivered the sermon, inspired by events across the Channel, which drew from Edmund
Burke his famous reply, *Reflections on the Revolution in France*.

This specimen, selected at random from Allan Ramsay's pamphlet,
illustrates the way in which Franklin's mind and pen worked, and the
editorial problems of reproducing his comments in relation to the text.

Contributors to Volume 16

The ownership of each manuscript, or the location of the particular copy used by the editors of each rare contemporary pamphlet or similar printed work, is indicated where the document appears in the text. The sponsors and editors are deeply grateful to the following institutions and individuals for permission to print or otherwise use in the present volume manuscripts or other materials which they own.

INSTITUTIONS

American Philosophical Society
Amherst College Library
British Museum
Clements Library, University of
  Michigan
Fulham Palace Library
Haverford College Library
Historical Society of
  Pennsylvania
Library Company of Philadelphia
Library of Congress
Massachusetts Archives, Office
  of the Secretary of State

Massachusetts Historical Society
Pierpont Morgan Library
New York Public Library
New York State Library, Albany
Public Record Office
The Royal Society
Scottish Record Office
South Carolina Archives
  Department
Stanford University Library
University of Uppsala Library
Yale University Library

INDIVIDUALS

Mr. S. Hallock du Pont, Wilmington, Del.
Mr. Albert M. Greenfield, Philadelphia
Mr. Adinell S. Hewson, Bryn Mawr, Pa.

Method of Textual Reproduction

An extended statement of the principles of selection, arrangement, form of presentation, and method of textual reproduction observed in this edition appears in the Introduction to the first volume, pp. xxiv–xlvii. A condensation and revision of the portion relating to the method of reproducing the texts follows here.

Printed Material:

Those of Franklin's writings that were printed under his direction presumably appeared as he wanted them to, and should therefore be reproduced with no changes except what modern typography requires. In some cases, however, printers carelessly or willfully altered his text without his consent; or the journeymen who set it had different notions from his—and from each other's—of capitalization, spelling, and punctuation. Such of his letters as survive only in nineteenth-century printings, furthermore, have often been vigorously edited by William Temple Franklin, Duane, or Sparks. In all these cases the original has suffered some degree of distortion, which the modern editor may guess at, but in the absence of the manuscript can do nothing to remedy. We therefore follow the printed texts as we find them, and note only obvious misreadings.

We observe the following rules in reproducing printed materials:

1. The place and date of composition of letters are set at the top, regardless of their location in the original printing.

2. Proper nouns, including personal names, which were often printed in italics, are set in roman, except when the original was italicized for emphasis.

3. Prefaces and other long passages, though italicized in the original, are set in roman. Long italicized quotations are set in roman within quotation marks.

4. Words in full capitals are set in small capitals, with initial letters in full capitals if required by Franklin's normal usage.

5. All signatures are set in capitals and small capitals.

6. We silently correct obvious typographical errors, such as the omission of a single parenthesis or quotation mark.

7. We close a sentence by supplying, when needed, a period or question mark.

8. Longhand insertions in the blanks of printed forms are set in italics, with space before and after.

Manuscript Material:

a. *Letters* are presented in the following form:

1. The place and date of composition are set at the top, regardless of their location in the original.

2. The complimentary close is set continuously with the text.

3. Addresses, endorsements, and docketing are so labeled and printed at the end of the letter.

b. *Spelling* of the original we retain. When it is so abnormal as to obscure the meaning, we supply the correct form in brackets or a footnote, as "yf [wife]."

c. *Capitalization* we retain as written, except that every sentence is made to begin with a capital. When we cannot decide whether a letter is a capital, we follow modern usage.

d. Words underlined once in the manuscript are printed in italics; words underlined twice or written in large letters or full capitals are printed in small capitals.

e. *Punctuation* has been retained as in the original, except:

1. We close a sentence by supplying, when needed, a period or question mark. When it is unclear whether the sentence ends, we retain the original punctuation or lack of it.

2. Dashes used in place of commas, semicolons, colons, or periods are replaced by the appropriate marks; when a sentence ends with both a dash and a period, the dash is omitted.

3. Commas scattered meaninglessly through a manuscript are eliminated.

4. When a mark of punctuation is not clear or can be read as one of two marks, we follow modern usage.[1]

5. Some documents, especially legal ones, have no punctua-

1. The typescripts from which these papers are printed have been made from photocopies of the manuscripts, and marks of punctuation are sometimes blurred or lost in photography. It has often been impossible to consult the original in these cases.

tion; others have so little as to obscure the meaning. In such cases we silently supply the minimum needed for clarity.

f. *Contractions and abbreviations* in general are expanded except in proper names. The ampersand is rendered as "and," except in the names of business firms, in the form "&c.," and in a few other cases. Letters represented by the thorn or tilde are printed. The tailed "p" is spelled out as per, pre, or pro. Symbols of weights, measures, and monetary values follow modern usage, as: £34. Superscript letters are lowered. Abbreviations in current use are retained, as: Col., Dr., N.Y., i.e.

g. *Omitted or illegible words or letters* are treated as follows:

1. If not more than four letters are missing, we supply them silently when we have no doubt what they should be.

2. If more than four letters are missing, we supply them conjecturally in brackets, with or without a question mark depending on our confidence in the conjecture.

3. Other omissions are shown as follows: [*illegible*], [*torn*], [*remainder missing*], or the like.

4. Missing or illegible digits are indicated by suspension points in brackets, the number of points corresponding to the estimated number of missing figures.

5. Blank spaces are left as blanks.

h. *Author's additions and corrections.*

1. Interlineations and brief marginal notes are incorporated in the text without comment, and longer notes with the notation [*in the margin*].

2. Footnotes by the author, or by an earlier editor when significant, are printed with our notes but with a bracketed indication of the source.

3. Canceled words and phrases are in general omitted without notice; if significant, they are printed in footnotes.

4. When alternative words and phrases have been inserted in a manuscript but the original remains uncanceled, the alternatives are given in brackets, preceded by explanatory words in italics, as: "it is [*written above:* may be] true."

5. Variant readings of several versions are noted if important.

Abbreviations and Short Titles

Acts Privy Coun., Col.	W. L. Grant and James Munro, eds., *Acts of the Privy Council of England, Colonial Series, 1613–1783* (6 vols., London, 1908–12).
AD	Autograph document.[1]
ADS	Autograph document signed.
AL	Autograph letter.
ALS	Autograph letter signed.
Amer.	American.
APS	American Philosophical Society.
Autobiog.	Leonard W. Labaree, Ralph L. Ketcham, Helen C. Boatfield, and Helene H. Fineman, eds., *The Autobiography of Benjamin Franklin* (New Haven, 1964).
BF	Benjamin Franklin.
Bigelow, *Works*	John Bigelow, ed., *The Complete Works of Benjamin Franklin . . .* (10 vols., N.Y., 1887–88).
Board of Trade Jour.	*Journal of the Commissioners for Trade and Plantations . . . April 1704 to . . . May 1782* (14 vols., London, 1920–38).
Brigham, *American Newspapers*	Clarence S. Brigham, *History and Bibliography of American Newspapers, 1690–1820* (2 vols., Worcester, Mass., 1947).
Carter, ed., *Gage Correspondence*	Clarence E. Carter, ed., *The Correspondence of General Thomas Gage . . .* (2 vols., New Haven and London, 1931–33).
Cavendish's Debates	John Wright, ed., *Sir Henry Cavendish's Debates of the House of Commons during the Thirteenth Parliament . . .* [1768–71] (2 vols., London, 1841–43).

1. For definitions of this and other kinds of manuscripts, see above, I, xliv–xlvii.

Chron.	*Chronicle.*
Cobbett, *Parliamentary History*	William Cobbett and Thomas C. Hansard, eds., *The Parliamentary History of England from the Earliest Period to 1803* (36 vols., London, 1806–20).
Crane, *Letters to the Press*	Verner W. Crane, ed., *Benjamin Franklin's Letters to the Press, 1758–1775* (Chapel Hill, [1950]).
DAB	*Dictionary of American Biography.*
DF	Deborah Franklin.
DNB	*Dictionary of National Biography.*
DS	Document signed.
Exper. and Obser.	*Experiments and Observations on Electricity, made at Philadelphia in America, by Mr. Benjamin Franklin...* (London, 1751). Revised and enlarged editions were published in 1754, 1760, 1769, and 1774 with slightly varying titles. In each case the edition cited will be indicated, e.g., *Exper. and Obser.* (1751).
Gaz.	*Gazette.*
Geneal.	Genealogical.
Gent. Mag.	*The Gentleman's Magazine, and Historical Chronicle.*
Gipson, *British Empire*	Lawrence H. Gipson, *The British Empire before the American Revolution* (15 vols.: I–III, Caldwell, Idaho, 1936; IV–XV, N.Y., 1939–70; I–III, revised ed., N.Y., 1958–60).
Hist.	Historical.
Jensen, *Founding of a Nation*	Merrill Jensen, *The Founding of a Nation: a History of the American Revolution, 1763–1776* (New York, London, and Toronto, 1968).
Johnson Papers	James Sullivan, Alexander C. Flick, Almon W. Lauber, and Milton W. Hamilton, eds., *The Papers of Sir William Johnson* (14 vols., Albany, 1921–65).
Jour.	*Journal.*

Kammen, *Rope of Sand*	Michael G. Kammen, *A Rope of Sand: the Colonial Agents, British Politics, and the American Revolution* (Ithaca, N.Y., [1968]).
Lewis, *Indiana Co.*	George E. Lewis, *The Indiana Company, 1763–1798: a Study in Eighteenth Century Frontier Land Speculation and Business Venture* (Glendale, Cal., 1941).
LS	Letter signed.
Mag.	*Magazine.*
MS, MSS	Manuscript, manuscripts.
Namier and Brooke, *House of Commons*	Sir Lewis Namier and John Brooke, *The History of Parliament. The House of Commons 1754–1790* (3 vols., London and N.Y., 1964).
N.J. Arch.	William A. Whitehead and others, eds., *Archives of the State of New Jersey* (2 series, Newark and elsewhere, 1880–). Editors, subtitles, and places of publication vary.
N.Y. Col. Docs.	E. B. O'Callaghan, ed., *Documents relative to the Colonial History of the State of New York* (15 vols., Albany, 1853–87).
Pa. Arch.	Samuel Hazard and others, eds., *Pennsylvania Archives* (9 series, Philadelphia and Harrisburg, 1852–1935).
Pa. Col. Recs.	*Minutes of the Provincial Council of Pennsylvania...* (16 vols., Philadelphia, 1838–53). Title changes with Volume XI to *Supreme Executive Council.*
Phil. Trans.	The Royal Society, *Philosophical Transactions.*
PMHB	*Pennsylvania Magazine of History and Biography.*
Proc.	*Proceedings.*
Rev.	*Review.*
Sabine, *Loyalists*	Lorenzo Sabine, *Biographical Sketches of Loyalists of the American Revolution...* (2 vols., Boston, 1864).

Sibley's Harvard Graduates	John L. Sibley, *Biographical Sketches of Graduates of Harvard University* (Cambridge, Mass., 1873–). Continued from Volume v by Clifford K. Shipton.
Smyth, *Writings*	Albert H. Smyth, ed., *The Writings of Benjamin Franklin*... (10 vols., N.Y., 1905–07).
Soc.	Society.
Trans.	*Transactions.*
Trench, *Wilkes*	Charles C. Trench, *Portrait of a Patriot: a Biography of John Wilkes* (Edinburgh and London, [1962]).
Van Doren, *Franklin*	Carl Van Doren, *Benjamin Franklin* (N.Y., 1938).
Van Doren, *Franklin–Mecom*	Carl Van Doren, ed., *The Letters of Benjamin Franklin & Jane Mecom* (American Philosophical Society *Memoirs*, XXVII, Princeton, 1950).
Vaughan, *Miscellaneous Pieces*	Benjamin Vaughan, ed., *Political, Miscellaneous, and Philosophical Pieces*... *Written by Benj. Franklin*... (London, 1779).
Votes, N.J.	*Votes and Proceedings of the General Assembly of the Province of New-Jersey*... (New York, Woodbridge, etc., 1711–). A separate volume was published for each session and is so designated, e.g., *Votes, N.J.* (Oct.–Dec., 1769).
WF	William Franklin.
WTF, *Memoirs*	William Temple Franklin, ed., *Memoirs of the Life and Writings of Benjamin Franklin, LL.D., F.R.S., &c.*... (3 vols., 4to, London, 1817–18).
W&MQ	*William and Mary Quarterly.*

Introduction

Franklin's life in 1769 was relatively calm. He was as busy as usual, but less in the public eye; his letters to the press, for example, were far fewer than in either 1768 or 1770. He had time to pursue his scientific interests, by publishing at the beginning of the year the fourth edition of his *Experiments and Observations*,[1] by his usual extensive correspondence, by serving on a committee to recommend lightning rods for St. Paul's, and in the dog days of midsummer by a second visit with Sir John Pringle to Paris, where the two stayed long enough for Franklin to renew contact with his acquaintances there. But London, as always, was his focus; and he was never removed for long from the politics of the capital.

Politics were stormy throughout the year. In February John Wilkes was expelled a second time from the House of Commons, and the ensuing battle between the House and the voters of Middlesex led in May to the seating of his defeated opponent. This action, which was arrogantly illegal, brought a flood of petitions in protest; the opposition in Parliament was temporarily unified, and plunged into the congenial task of organizing public discontent with the Grafton administration. Although the Duke managed for the moment to weather this storm, his days in office were numbered. His Chancellor of the Exchequer, Lord North, had led the attack on Wilkes in the Commons, with an adroitness that had commended itself to the King; and by December negotiations were under way to form a new administration under North instead of Grafton.

Meanwhile the American issue, much to the fore when the year began, seemed as the months passed to be entering a more tranquil phase. At the end of 1768 news of events in the colonies—riots, petitions, the beginning of the nonimportation movement—had produced a strong reaction in Westminster: eight stern resolutions, introduced by Lord Hillsborough, had passed the House of Lords, together with an address to the King suggesting that he bring troublemakers from Massachusetts to stand trial in England for treason. When the House of Commons reconvened in January,

1. For a discussion of the various editions and the differences between them see above, III, 115–17.

1769, the resolutions and the address touched off a major debate on colonial affairs, which ended in victory for the strong line that the government was advocating. By the time Parliament recessed in the late spring, however, more moderate counsels were beginning to prevail. Franklin was of course working hard for that end, but a more powerful factor was the spread of the nonimportation movement, to which even the Philadelphia merchants agreed in March. By May Lord Hillsborough was changing his tune. He informed the colonial governors in a circular letter that no additional duties would be levied, and that in the following year some of the Townshend duties would be repealed. As the months wore on, Franklin did all he could to marshal support for repeal within the mercantile community and among members of the government, to whom in November he addressed his answers to William Strahan's prearranged queries.[2] By the end of December he was ready to open a full-scale campaign in the press.[3]

Meanwhile he was developing his ideas about the issues that underlay the whole question of taxation. His increasing contacts with Boston during the year, and his assumption of the agency for New Jersey, may well have broadened his view of the Anglo-American controversy, as they certainly broadened his involvement in it. The polemical pamphlets spawned in England by the quarrel caught his attention and made him, in the privacy of the study, polemical in turn. It was apparently at this time that he developed the habit of making marginal comments on the pamphlets he was reading, as he continued to do in 1770. These comments are often repetitive but never obscure. Sometimes he agreed with the author and sometimes argued calmly with him; sometimes he was angry, and then his language was sharper than anything he permitted himself even in private correspondence. His thinking, also, was in one major respect more radical: he reached the point of explicitly denying Parliament's sovereignty in America.[4] Through his marginalia he can be seen in his workshop, hammering out a concept of the economic and constitutional position of the colonies.

His other concerns during the year were, for the most part, re-

2. See below, Strahan to BF, Nov. [21–]22, BF to Strahan, Nov. 29.
3. The series of eleven essays in the *Public Advertiser*, "The Colonist's Advocate," which appeared in the early months of 1770.
4. See below, pp. 284–5, 300–1, 316–17, 325.

lated in one way or another to colonial prosperity. He kept harping on the point that the nonimportation agreements would lead to greater economic independence because they would encourage colonial manufactures.[5] This argument presumably had the dual purpose of heartening Americans and frightening Englishmen, but it drew its strength from his countrymen's firm resistance to the Townshend Acts. That resistance seems to have heightened his awareness of the American economic potential. His interest in canals, machinery, the culture of silk in the colonies, like his emphasis on the rapid rise in the population, was part of the same sense of a burgeoning economy. So, in a different area, was the campaign for a land grant in which he and others were involved. In 1769 the campaign became more ambitious than ever: by late spring Samuel Wharton and William Trent were in London, acting as agents for their group of land speculators; and within a remarkably short time the agents and others, Franklin among them, succeeded in forming the Grand Ohio or Walpole Company, to obtain and then exploit a vast grant in the trans-Allegheny west.[6] Franklin of course hoped to profit financially from this scheme, far more than from any of his other activities; but the hope was set in the larger context of his faith in endless expansion. Just as he was coming to believe that the colonies were subject only to the King, and hence politically coequal with Great Britain, so he was coming to believe that they were economically free-standing and capable, if let alone, of populating the wilderness.

5. See, for example, BF to Folger below, Sept. 29.
6. See below, pp. 163-8.

To Lord Kames

My dear Friend,   London, Jan. 1[-16]. 1769.

It is always a great Pleasure to me to hear from you, and would be a much greater to be with you, to converse with you on the Subjects you mention, or any other. Possibly I may yet one day enjoy that Pleasure. In the meantime we may use the Privilege that the Knowledge of Letters affords us, of conversing at a distance by the Pen.

I am glad to find you are turning your Thoughts to political Subjects, and particularly to those of Money, Taxes, Manufactures, and Commerce. The World is yet much in the dark on these important Points; and many mischievous Mistakes are continually made in the Management of them. Most of our Acts of Parliament for regulating them, are, in my Opinion, little better than political Blunders, owing to Ignorance of the Science, or to the Designs of crafty Men, who mislead the Legislature, proposing something under the specious Appearance of Public Good, while the real Aim is, to sacrifice that to their own private Interest. I hope a good deal of Light may be thrown on these Subjects by your Sagacity and Acuteness. I only wish I could first have engag'd you in Discussing the weighty Points in dispute between Britain and the Colonies: But the long Letter I wrote you for that purpose in February or March 1767 perhaps never reach'd your Hand, for I have not yet had a Word from you in Answer to it.[1]

The Act you enquire about[2] took its Rise thus. During the War, Virginia issued great Sums of Paper Money for the Payment of their Troops, to be sunk in a Number of Years by Taxes. The British Merchants trading thither receiv'd these Bills in Payment for their Goods, purchasing Tobacco with them to send home. The Crop of Tobacco one or two Years falling short, the Factors who were desirous of making speedy Remittance, sought to buy, with the Papermoney, Bills of Exchange. The Number of Bidders for these Bills rais'd the Price of them 30 per Cent above Par. This was deem'd so

1. For this letter, which was indeed lost, see above, XIV, 62–71.
2. The Currency Act of 1764, for which see above, XI–XIV, *passim*, and particularly XIV, 33, 76–7. See also Jack P. Greene and Richard M. Jellison, "The Currency Act of 1764 in Imperial-Colonial Relations, 1764–1776," *W&MQ*, 3d ser., XVIII (1961), 485–518; and Joseph A. Ernst, "The Currency Act Repeal Movement: a Study of Imperial Politics and Revolutionary Crisis, 1764–1767," *ibid.*, XXV (1968), 177–211.

much Loss to the Purchasers, and suppos'd to arise from a *Depreciation* of the Paper money. The Merchants on this Supposition founded a Complaint against that Currency to the Board of Trade. Lord Hillsborough then at the Head of that Board, took up the Matter strongly, and drew a Report which was presented to the King in Council against all Paper Currency in the Colonies. And tho' there was no Complaint against it from any Merchants but those trading to Virginia, all those trading to the other Colonies being satisfy'd with its Operations, yet the Ministry propos'd and the Parliament came into the Making a general Act, forbidding all future Emissions of Paper Money that should be a legal Tender in any Colony whatever. The Virginia Merchants have since had the Mortification to find, that if they had kept the Paper money a Year or two, the above mention'd Loss would have been avoided; For as soon as Tobacco became more plenty, and of course Bills of Exchange also, the Exchange fell as much as it before had risen. I was in America when the Act pass'd. On my Return to England, I got the Merchants trading to New York, Pensilvania, Maryland, Virginia, &c. to meet, to consider and join in an Application to have the Restraining Act repeal'd. To prevent this Application, a Copy was put into the Merchants Hands of Lord Hillsborough's Report, by which it was supposed they might be convinced that such an Application would be wrong. They desired my Sentiments on it, which I gave in the Paper I send you inclos'd.[3] I have no Copy by me of the Report itself; but in my Answer you will see a faithful Abridgment of all the Arguments or Reasons it contained. Lord Hillsborough has read my Answer, but says he is not convinc'd by it, and adheres to his former Opinion.[4] We know nothing can be done in Parliament that the Minister is absolutely against, and therefore we let that Point rest for the present. And as I think a Scarcity of Money will work with our other present Motives for lessening our fond Extravagance in the Use of the Superfluous Manufactures of this Country (which unkindly grudges us the Enjoyment of common Rights) and will tend to lead us naturally into Industry and Frugality, I am grown more indifferent about the Repeal of the Act; and if my Countrymen will be advis'd by me, we shall never ask it again.

There is not, as I conceive, any new Principle wanting, to ac-

3. The paper on currency printed above, xiv, 76–87.
4. See above, xv, 48–9.

count for all the Operations of Air and all the Affections of Smoke in Rooms and Chimneys; but it is difficult to advise in particular Cases at a Distance, where one cannot have all the Circumstances under View. If two Rooms and Chimneys are "perfectly similar" in Situation, Dimension, and all other Circumstances, it seems not possible that "in Summer when no Fire had been in either of them for some Months, and in a calm Day, a Current of Air should at the same time go up the Chimney of the one and down the Chimney of the other."[5] But such Difference may and often does take place from Circumstances in which they are dissimilar, and which Dissimilarity is not very obvious to those who have little studied the Subject. As to your particular Case, which you describe to be, that "after a whole Day's Fire, which must greatly heat the Vent, yet when the Fire becomes low, so as not to emit any Smoke, neighbour Smoke immediately begins to descend and fill the Room." This, if not owing to particular Winds, may be occasion'd by a stronger Fire in another Room communicating with yours by a Door, the outer Air being excluded by the outward Door's being shut, whereby the stronger Fire finds it easier to be supply'd with Air down thro' the Vent in which the weak Fire is, and thence thro' the communicating Door, than thro' the Crevices. If this is the Circumstance, you will find that a Supply of Air is only wanting that may be sufficient for both Vents. If this is not the Circumstance, send me if you please a compleat Description of your Room, its Situation, Connections, &c. and possibly I may form a better Judgment. Tho' I imagine your Professor of N. Philosophy Mr. Russel, or Mr. George Clark,[6] may give you as good Advice on the Subject as I can. But I shall take the Liberty of sending you by the first convenient Opportunity, a Collection of my Philosophical Papers lately publish'd, in which you will find something more relating to the Motions of Air in Chimneys.[7]

5. Kames had complained in the previous February of smoke from adjacent flues that was entering the rooms of his new house in Edinburgh; he had asked help of his "smoke Doctor," who had given him an explanation and advice. Above, XV, 50–1, 61–2. Although Kames's response has been lost, it clearly said that BF's attempts to solve the problem were wide of the mark.

6. For James Russell and George Clark, two of BF's Edinburgh acquaintances, see above, X, 22 n, 28 n, 386 n.

7. The fourth edition of *Exper. and Obser.*, which contains on pp. 284–318 an account of the Pennsylvania fireplace.

To commence a Conversation with you on your new Subject, I have thrown some of my present Sentiments into the concise Form of Aphorisms, to be examin'd between us, if you please, and rejected or corrected and confirm'd as we shall find most proper. I send them inclos'd.[8] With Thanks for your good Wishes, and with unalterable Esteem, I remain, my dear Friend, Affectionately yours,

B FRANKLIN

P.S. Jan. 16. The Paper on Currency having been lent out, I have been oblig'd to detain my Letter till I could get it home. As I have no other Copy, be so good as to return it when perus'd.

I shall be glad to learn by the least Line that this Packet is got safe to hand. Write more fully at your Leisure.

Lord Kaims.

From William Franklin

ALS (incomplete): American Philosophical Society

[c. January 2, 1769]

Many of your Friends, as well as myself, would be glad to have such a Bust of you. Pray what would be the Expence? That of Lord Halifax, I am told, was not cut in Marble first, but made of Clay, and from that the Casts in Plaister of Paris was made.[9] I am often ask'd for your Prints by your old Friends and Acquaintance, and I have given among them all I had except one.[1] All that Hall had to sell were sold immediately. If the Plate is good I should be glad you would have a 100 of them work'd off and sent to me. Coz. Davenport[2] says, he could sell any Number. I hope you will bring over

8. Probably a draft of "Positions to Be Examined," for which see below, April 4.

9. The idea of a bust may well have started with BF's mentioning that he had given one of Lord Chatham to Harvard; see below, Jan. 4. We have been unable to identify the bust of Halifax. In any case the sculptor who executed it does not seem to have done one of BF, of whom the earliest known bust dates from 1777. See Charles C. Sellers, *Benjamin Franklin in Portraiture* (New Haven and London, 1962), p. 236.

1. The mezzotint by Edward Fisher after Mason Chamberlain's portrait; see above, x, frontispiece.

2. BF's nephew, Josiah Franklin Davenport (C.12.4).

4

your Picture for me, or send it in the Spring.[3] I have been long expecting it with Impatience.

I saw my Mother and Sister well at Philadelphia last Week, and shall take the first Opportunity of shewing them your Letter respecting the King of Denmark.[4] I was much pleas'd with the Account of your Entertainment and Reception by that amiable Monarch. Mr. Bache is gone again to Jamaica.[5]

I publish'd an Extract of your last Letter relative to Wilkes in the Chronicle, as I thought it might have a good Effect; for all the Nonsense about No. 45 is almost as much attended to in the Colonies as in England.[6]

Betsy has had no Letter yet from young Mr. Allen since his Marriage, but we are much pleas'd that he has done so well for himself, and heartily wish him and his Wife every Felicity.[7]

I hope young Temple continues well.[8] I should be glad to know your Sentiments about bringing him over with you. He might then take his proper Name, and be introduc'd as the Son of a poor Relation, for whom I stood God Father and intended to bring up as my own. But this I submit. If he was to come I could, I think, prevail on Mr. Odell[9] to educate him. He knows him well, and speaks highly of him.

Coz. Ben. Mecom is starving at Philadelphia, and would have been, I suppose in Gaol by this Time, if it had not been for the Assistance my Mother and I have afforded him and his Family. Goddard would have given 35 s. a Week to him if he would have work'd as other Journeymen do, but he insisted on coming and going just as he pleas'd, on which Goddard and he quarrel'd and parted. He has likewise been at work at some other Printing Offices in Phila-

3. Probably the copy of his portrait that BF had commissioned from Mason Chamberlain in 1763 as a gift for WF's new home, and that seems to have been subsequently destroyed in a fire. See Sellers, *op. cit.*, p. 220.

4. Above, XV, 225–7.

5. *Ibid.*, p. 259 n.

6. *Ibid.*, p. 224. The extract printed in the *Pa. Chron.* of Dec. 26, 1768–Jan. 2, 1769 is our basis for dating the present letter.

7. *Ibid.*, pp. 183–5, 186–7.

8. WF's illegitimate son, a six-year-old at the time.

9. Jonathan Odell, a surgeon and Anglican clergyman, whom the Society for the Propagation of the Gospel had sent as a missionary to Burlington, N.J. See above, XIII, 508 n.

delphia but cannot agree with any Body, and is I believe now without any Employ. His Pride and Laziness are beyond any Thing I ever knew, and he seems determin'd rather to sink than to strike a Stroke to keep his Head above Water. He has had Seventeen Pounds of me, and what of my Mother I know not. He has got it in his Head that you intend to set him up in a Printing Office on your Return, and therefore seems determin'd to idle away his Time till your Arrival. In short I look upon him to have a Tincture of Madness.[1] I have likewise assisted his Brother John with Money, who has turn'd out as bad as Ben, and gone and quarter'd himself and Wife on his Mother at Boston.[2] I sometimes hear from Aunt Mecom, and have sent her some Barrels of Flour at different Times, for which she is always very thankful and I heartily wish it was in my Power to do more for her. She lives better than ever, I am told, since her Husband's Death, and I expect her here on a Visit in the Spring, if you return.[3]

Betsy sends her Duty, and joins me in wishing you many happy New Years. I am Honoured Sir, your ever dutiful Son

W. F.

PS. I have no Time to copy or even read this.

From Harvard College

Reprinted from William C. Lane, "Harvard College and Franklin," Colonial Society of Massachusetts *Publications*, X (1907), 236.

At a Meeting of the Presdt. and Fellows of Harvard-College
Jany 4. 1769.

1. The vicissitudes of Benjamin Mecom have been writ large in the previous volumes. William Goddard, the publisher of the *Pa. Chron.* (above, XII, 287 n), was only one of those who found Mecom unemployable; and WF's guess of insanity was later borne out. *DAB*.

2. John Mecom (C.17.7) and his wife had arrived in Boston the previous November, but they did not stay long. John was soon back in New Jersey, where he died the following year. Van Doren, *Franklin-Mecom*, pp. 107, 111, 113–14.

3. Edward Mecom, a Boston saddler, had died in 1765. His widow visited her nephew in the late autumn, when she went on to Philadelphia and stayed with DF. Van Doren, *op. cit.*, pp. 111, 113.

Voted 4. That the Thanks of this Board be given to Dr. Benja. Franklin for his very acceptable Present, of a fine Bust of that great Assertor of American Liberties, Lord Chatham.[4]

Pennsylvania and Nonimportation

Reprinted from Verner W. Crane, ed., *Benjamin Franklin's Letters to the Press, 1758–1775* (Chapel Hill, N.C., [1950]), p. 152.

Franklin had just received a memorial from the Philadelphia merchants, dated November 1, 1768, and addressed to the manufacturers and merchants of Great Britain, protesting against the Townshend Acts and threatening the renewal of nonimportation.[5] In order to bring the memorial before the public he wrote the ostensible inquiry that follows. The printer, by what he made to sound like a coincidence, had on hand the means to provide an answer, in the form of the memorial and a covering letter to the British merchants; and he published these in the same issue of the *Public Advertiser* that carried Franklin's inquiry.[6]

To the Printer of the Public Advertiser.

Sir,   [January 5, 1769]

When we were first informed by your Paper of the proposed Combination in North America to take no more of our Manufactures till the Colonies were restored to their antient Privileges, we understood at the same Time that a Stop was put to that Combination by the Pensylvanians not acceding to it. A Rumour now prevails that it was a Delay only; that they are now likely to agree with the rest; and that 'tis probable the Resolution will become general, the Colonies being universally irritated by our sending Troops to Boston, and by their Behaviour there. If you have received any authentic Advices relating to this Matter, I wish you would communicate them. It may be of Use to the Manufacturers of this King-

---

4. The bust was presumably a copy of the only one known from this period, that executed by Joseph Wilton in 1759, for which see Margaret Whinney, *Sculpture in Britain, 1530 to 1830* (Harmondsworth, Middlesex, 1964), pp. 137–41. Harvard had ordered a scientific instrument through BF, which was completed in the previous September (above, XV, 166–7); the bust was doubtless part of the same shipment.

5. For the merchants' covering letter to BF and a discussion of the memorial see *ibid.*, pp. 266–7.

6. See Crane, *Letters to the Press*, pp. 151–2 and n. 1.

dom to know the State of the Case, that they may regulate their Business accordingly; and among others it will oblige Yours &c.
A LONDON MANUFACTURER.

To Michael Hillegas[7]

Reprinted from *The Historical Magazine*, III (1859), 212.

Sir: London, Jan. 5, 1769.
I received yours of Nov. 3, and was very sorry to find you had been disappointed of your Glasses by their being broken in going over.[8] I have given Orders to have the Loss repair'd, agreeable to the Directions in your Letter, and hope it will not be long before they are executed. Make no Apology as if you gave me Trouble, for I assure you it is a Pleasure to me, when in my Power to do a Friend any little Service. With great regard, I am, Sir, Your most obedient, Humble Servant,   B. FRANKLIN.

Mr. Hillegas.

To Charles Thomson and Thomas Mifflin[9]

ALS: Amherst College Library

Gentlemen,   London, Jan 5. 1769
I received yours with two Bills of Exchange enclos'd, for £150 Sterling, with a Catalogue of Books to be procur'd for the Library Company, which I have given Orders for Collecting immediately, and hope they will be ready to send by Budden or the next Ship. I am not acquainted with the Work intitled British Zoology, but shall enquire its Character of some knowing Friends. Be pleased to

7. Hillegas (1728–1804), a wealthy Philadelphia merchant of German extraction, later became the first treasurer of the United States. He was a member of the Pennsylvania Assembly (1765–75) and had recently been elected to the APS. *DAB*. He was one of the group of speculators, to which BF belonged, that was seeking settlers for lands in Nova Scotia; see his answer to this letter below, April 15.

8. The glasses were for his armonica, which BF must have had made for him in London. *Ibid.* For the instrument that BF had designed see above, X, 116–30.

9. In reply to their letter of Nov. 5, 1768, which explains the substance of this one. Above, XV, 257–8; see also BF's second reply below, Jan. 27.

present my Respects to the Directors, and assure them that I shall have a Pleasure in obeying their Orders. With great Esteem, I am, Gentlemen, Your most obedient humble Servant   B FRANKLIN

Messrs. Thomson and Mifflin.

To John Bartram

> Reprinted from William Darlington, ed., *Memorials of John Bartram and Humphry Marshall* (Philadelphia, 1849), pp. 402–3.

My Dear old Friend: London, January 9, [–28], 1769.

I received your kind letter of November 5, and the box directed to the King is since come to hand.[1] I have written a line to our late dear friend's son,[2] (who must be best acquainted with the usual manner of transacting your affairs here,) to know whether he will take charge of the delivery of it; if not, to request he would inform me how, or to whom, it is to be sent for the King. I expect his answer in a day or two, and I shall when I see him, inquire how your pension is hereafter to be applied for and received; though I suppose he has written to you before this time.

I hope your health continues—as mine does, hitherto; but I wish you would now decline your long and dangerous peregrinations, in search of your plants, and remain safe and quiet at home, employing your leisure hours in a work that is much wanted, and which no one besides is so capable of performing—I mean the writing a Natural History of our country. I imagine it would prove profitable to you, and I am sure it would do you honour.

My respects and best wishes attend Mrs. Bartram, and your family.[3] With sincere esteem, I am, as ever, Your affectionate friend,   B. FRANKLIN.

P.S. January 28. The box is delivered, according to Mr. Michael Collinson's directions, at Lord Bute's. Mr. Collinson takes it amiss that you did not write to him.

1. See above, xv, 256–7.
2. For Michael Collinson (1727–95) see *ibid*.
3. Ann Mendenhall Bartram was his second wife, and the family by the two marriages was a large one. The most distinguished of the sons was William Bartram (1739–1823), the traveler and naturalist whom the Indians christened "the flower-hunter." *DAB*.

I have sent over some seed of Naked Oats, and some of Swiss Barley, six rows to an ear. If you would choose to try some of it, call on Mrs. Franklin.

To Joseph Galloway

ALS: Clements Library

Dear Sir,   London, Jan. 9. 1769

I have now before me your several Favours of Oct. 15, 17, and 20, and of Nov. 6.

I am much oblig'd to the Assembly for the Honour they have done me in a new Appointment.[4] Be pleased to present my respectful Thanks to the House, and assure them of my best Service.

I have bespoke the Telescope they have ordered, and hope it will be done in time.[5] The Workmen have promised it, but it should have been thought of sooner; for they have so much upon their Hands by Orders from different Parts on the same Occasion, that I think it rather doubtful.

I am glad to hear that Matters were yet quiet at Boston, but fear they will not continue long so. Some Indiscretion on the part of their warmer People, or of the Soldiery, I am extreamly apprehensive may occasion a Tumult; and if Blood is once drawn, there is no foreseeing how far the Mischief may spread. I much doubt the Presence of Soldiers there may occasion more Mischief than it could prevent.

As to the State of Things here, we have for some time had a Ministry not well united among themselves. The Duke of Grafton, to avoid, as some suppose, their Opposition to his intended Divorce from his Dutchess, has admitted so many of the Bedford Party, that

4. The renewal of his agency for the Pennsylvania Assembly; see above, XV, 228–9.

5. Galloway, as speaker, had sent BF £100 for a telescope with which the APS hoped to observe the transit of Venus. *Ibid.*, p. 228 n. BF ordered from Edward Nairne a reflecting telescope with two small speculums, two sets of tubes with eyeglasses, a brass frame with smoked glasses, and "an additional frame to swing to set the Telescope Equatorial," along with a micrometer. The instruments were completed and shipped in March at a total cost, including mahogany boxes and crating and shipping charges, of £104 18s. 6d. From Nairne's bill, receipted March 24, 1769, in the Franklin Papers in the APS, Vol. LXVII, No. 3.

they are now almost too strong for him and his Friends.[6] The Ministers have been to Appearance, a good deal embarras'd and puzzled how to act with America. The Bedford People have been all along for violent Measures; the others for milder, whom we have spar'd no Pains to confirm in this Disposition. The Majority really wish the Duty Acts had never been made; they say they are evidently inconsistent with all sound Commercial and Political Principles, equally prejudicial to this Country as to America; But they think the National Honour concern'd in supporting them, considering the Manner in which the Execution of them has been oppos'd. They cannot bear the Denial of the Right of Parliament to make them, tho' they acknowledge they ought not to have been made. They fear being despis'd by all the Nations round if they repeal them; and they say it is of great Importance to this Nation that the World should see it is Master of its Colonies, otherwise its Enemies on a Conceit of its Weakness, might be encourag'd to insult it. On the other Hand, they are really afraid of provoking the Colonies too far, lest a Rupture should become inevitable, and the old Enemies of the Nation take Advantage of it. It is therefore they give out that they actually had an Intention of Repealing, till the ill Behaviour of America made it improper and at present impracticable; and that if Matters should remain quiet a Year or perhaps two, tho' they would not be understood to promise the Repeal, they say 'tis highly probable it will take place. I have represented to them, that tho' the Right has been deny'd, the Payment of the Duties has nevertheless been every where submitted to; that the Riot occasion'd by the Seizure of a Vessel at Boston, had no Relation to the Act about Paper, Glass, &c. That the Honour of Parliament and of the Nation, is best maintain'd by rectifying what it has done improperly as soon as it can be convinc'd of it, and not by being

6. Grafton's divorce could scarcely have antagonized the Bedford faction because his second wife, whom he married almost immediately, was the Duchess of Bedford's niece. The divorce did, however, stir up a mare's nest of bickering that complicated Grafton's position; see Wilmarth S. Lewis and A. Dayle Wallace, eds., *Horace Walpole's Correspondence with the Countess of Upper Ossory* (3 vols., New Haven, 1965), III, 241–2. The Duke's political troubles were worse than ever: in the previous October Chatham had finally resigned, and Shelburne had perforce followed him; Grafton, Chatham's erstwhile lieutenant, now had little support against the pressure for a strong line toward America from the Bedfordites whom he had admitted to office a year before.

obstinate in the Wrong: That in a Country so frequent in mischievous Mobs and murderous Riots as this is, 'tis surprizing to find such Resentment of a trifling Riot in Boston;[7] and strange that it should be thought just to punish all the Colonies, by continuing an oppressive Act affecting the Whole, for the Offence only of one of them: That Government is not establish'd merely by *Power*; there must be maintain'd a general Opinion of its *Wisdom* and *Justice*, to make it firm and durable. I have also us'd and enforc'd all the Arguments in the Committee's Letter of Sept. 22.[8] which indeed I think have had some Weight with many. But a few Days before the Recess, Lord Hillsborough made a long Speech in the House of Lords, aggravating every Indiscretion of the Americans, and declaring that tho' he always thought the Duty Acts ought not to have been made, yet he was absolutely against Repealing them, and should not only oppose any Motion that should be made for that purpose, but if carried would protest against such Repeal. We had been told that he was to propose some thundering Resolutions against the Colonies, and this Speech was to introduce them. But when they were read, I was surpriz'd to find so little in them. They seem to be mere *bruta Fulmina*, calculated chiefly to obtain Parliamentary Approbation of the Steps he had already taken as a Minister, on which he had been attack'd in the House of Commons at the Opening of the Session. I send a Copy of them to the Committee. The Address, which was mov'd by the Duke of Bedford, is of the same Stamp. The Lords agreed to them with little Opposition, the Duke of Richmond only speaking against them, and he is not a very good Speaker. Lord Shelbourne said he should reserve himself as to American Affairs, to another Occasion, when the Relation between the two Countries and their mutual Rights must come into Discussion. What that Occasion would be, he did not explain. Lord Egmont, tho' our Friend, gave no Opposition to the Resolves.[9] But I had a long Conversation with him at Court the

7. The disturbance occasioned by the seizure of John Hancock's sloop, *Liberty*, in June, 1768.

8. See above, xv, 210–14.

9. For the resolutions introduced by Hillsborough on Dec. 15 and the address to the King, condemning Massachusetts and upholding the government's policy of coercion, see Cobbett, *Parliamentary History*, xvi (for 1765–71), 476–80. The resolutions were published in the *N.-Y. Gaz.* (Gaine), March 20, and the *Pa. Chron.*, March 20–27. Charles Lennox, third Duke of Richmond

Sunday before, in which he told me he was sorry to find we were gone off the Distinction we formerly made of external and internal Taxes, which was Ground he thought we could better have maintain'd than that we were on at present. That formerly when he was in the House of Commons, and it was propos'd to include Ireland in a Duty on Glass then about to be laid by an Act of Parliament, he had objected to the Mention of Ireland in that Clause, as it was laying an internal Tax there, which Parliament had never before done; and propos'd instead of it, that as Britain had undoubtedly in its rightful Possession the *Turnpike of the Sea*,[1] she should content herself with preventing Ireland's rivalling and underselling her in foreign Markets, by bringing untax'd Glass to Sale there; and should only forbid the Exportation of that Article from Ireland; which the House agreed to. His Lordship on the whole seem'd to think, that we ought not to have deny'd the Right of laying Duties on the Manufactures of this Country exported, but have oppos'd them on other Principles. I will not trouble you with all the Observations I made to his Lordship on this Opinion. But one was, that if we allow'd the Right of Britain to lay what Duties she pleas'd on her own Commodities exported to us, we must then call in question her Right of forbidding us to go to a better and cheaper Market whenever we could find it; for those Rights exercis'd together might be most intolerable Oppression; and this would strike at her Navigation Acts. But his Opinion seem'd fix'd, that while Britain by her Naval Force had the Sovereignty of the Sea, she had all the Powers and Rights annext to such Sovereignty, of which that was one. The Resolves pass'd the Lords, and were sent down to the Commons for their Concurrence. They did not pass there so readily as was expected, but the Consideration of them was postpon'd till after the Holidays, and I hear there will be strong Opposition to them. But if the pre-

---

(1735–1806), was an ineffective politician who had the rare distinction of being a radical; he championed the American cause and later, for a while, the cause of Parliamentary reform. For Egmont, an acquaintance of BF of some years' standing, who had been for a time joint postmaster general and then First Lord of the Admiralty, see above, x, 286 n.

1. If this telling phrase was not original with Egmont, we have been unable to trace its origin. It reversed a comment of Grotius, that the sea was the highway of nations and should be free to all; for *turnpike*, which had hitherto meant a barrier, was coming to mean a road that was barriered for collecting tolls.

sent Ministry continue, 'tis more than probable they will pass.[2] If Lord Rockingham should again come in, which now begins to be talk'd of, probably they will be thrown out, and the Acts also repealed. So uncertain is everything here: In the meantime we are doing all we can. The Memorial of the Merchants, which is well written, came over very seasonably.[3] Lord H. had flattered himself, and said it to every body, that the Colonies could never agree in a Resolution to import no more Goods, for that Pensilvania would not come into it, and her Refusal would soon occasion a Dissolution of the Agreements of any others. Now he has seen the Memorial, he appears extreamly angry with Pensilvania, and exclaims against both that and our Petitions, saying that of all the Provinces we have the least Pretence to claim an Exemption from Parliamentary Duties, having settled there under a clear Stipulation in our Charter, by which the Right of laying such Duties was expressly reserved.[4] I wrote to you before that our Petition to the King was delivered, the Answer I am told is sent to the Governor, as all other Answers of Petitions to the King now are, the Plan here at present being, to have as little to do with Agents as possible. That to the Commons was offered, but not received, which I must explain to you, because the Manner of presenting Petitions to Parliament differs something from ours. Here the Member who has the Petition to present, first stands up in his Place, and opens the Contents and Purport of the Petition, or, with leave, reads it, which Reading is only understood as an Opening of it, and then asks Leave to bring it up to the Table and present it. If the House do not like to receive such a Petition, the Leave to present it is not given, and then there is no mention of it in the Minutes; because the Petition has only been *offered* but not *presented*. If Leave to present it is given, he then goes to the Bar of the House, and from thence up to the Table, where he delivers it, and then 'tis read by the Clerk. In our Case, no Member could be found for some time who would venture

2. BF was right on both counts. The resolution and the address encountered strong opposition in the House of Commons when they came before it on Jan. 25, but after long debate were passed by a large majority. See BF to Galloway below, Jan. 29; Cobbett, *Parliamentary History*, XVI, 485–510.

3. The memorial dated Nov. 1 from the Pennsylvania merchants to the manufacturers and merchants of Great Britain, for which see the headnote above, p. 7.

4. See above, XV, 211 n.

to offer it, Mr. Jackson thinking what he intended to say in support of it, would have more weight if it was *offered* by another. At length Mr. Huske undertook it;[5] but to guard against the Displeasure of the House, which any Member might apprehend, who should offer a Petition denying a Right that they imagine they have so firmly established by a solemn Act of Parliament, he took the Precaution, after slightly mentioning its purport, of asking Leave to *offer* it; which being given, he then ask'd Leave and was allow'd to read it by way of opening it. Mr. Wellbore Ellis[6] then call'd for the Declaratory Act to be read, which being done, he endeavour'd to show from thence that 'twas impossible for the House to receive a Petition which directly impugn'd the Right of Parliament declar'd by that Act. Lord North[7] said he had such a Regard for Pensilvania, which had behav'd so well in all the late Disturbances in America, and had shown such a dutiful Obedience to Parliament in the Billeting Affair, that it would be with the utmost Pain if he should find himself oblig'd to vote for rejecting any Petition from that Province, and therefore hoped the Member would not urge its being received, but withdraw it. Several others spoke against receiving it, and some for it; but finally Mr. Huske perceiving that it would certainly be rejected if he insisted on presenting it, told them that he could not consent absolutely to withdraw it, but having fully opened it to the House, he should withdraw it for the present, only to give the House an Opportunity of considering more maturely the Consequence of rejecting a Petition from the only Colony that had paid them the Respect of Petitioning on this Occasion, and if this Petition was rejected, it would probably be the last ever offered them from any Colony on any Occasion; concluding that he should offer it again on some future day. I suppose you know, that no Government of New England has made any kind of Application to Parliament, but to the King only; and that tho' the Virginians have apply'd

5. Richard Jackson was of course BF's co-agent for Pennsylvania. For John Huske see *ibid.*, pp. 249, 286–8.

6. Welbore Ellis (1713–1802) was a thoroughly undistinguished placeman, whose power of endurance brought him eventually to the peerage. At the time he was M.P. for Petersfield, and in 1782 he became the last in the series of Secretaries of State for the American Colonies that began with Hillsborough.

7. Frederick North, the eldest son of the Earl of Guilford and soon to be the King's first minister, had succeeded Charles Townshend as Chancellor of the Exchequer in Oct., 1767.

to King, Lords, and Commons, the Application to the King is the only one called a *Petition*; that to the House of Lords is stiled a *Memorial*, and that to the House of Commons, a *Remonstrance*, in which they say, they do not ask the Repeal of the Acts as a Favour, they claim it as a Right.[8] No Lord or Commoner has yet been found hardy enough to offer either the Memorial or Remonstrance. I am told by all the Members I have spoken to about it, that if Mr. Huske offers our Petition again, the Royal Charter of Pensilvania will be call'd for, and those Clauses read which reserve Parliamentary Duties, and it will infallibly be rejected on the Principle that by settling under that Charter we contracted to submit to such Duties. I am not myself of that Opinion, but have never been able to reason any other Person out of it. And I think it would have been better if Maryland instead of Pensylvania had stood foremost in such a Contest with Parliament, their Charter being full and clear, if I remember right, in an Exemption from all Duties whatsoever;[9] and an Exemption appearing clear in their Case, might have been suppos'd in the others, but the contrary may happen by the Discussion of our Charter first, especially by such partial, prejudiced and interested Judges. All our Friends advise the not offering it again. They say, that it having been deliberately read by the Member in a full House, it has thereby already made all the Impression to be expected from it; and the urging it farther against the Grain of the House can answer no good End. This is Mr. Jackson's Opinion at present. Possibly something may arise changing this Opinion, and therefore it still lies open under Consideration. As to our Petition to the Lords, it has not yet been presented. Mr. Jackson had it a considerable time in his Hands, in order to get some Lord of his Acquaintance to present it, but finally return'd it to me, saying he could not find any one Lord that was proper and willing to present and support it, and wish'd me to try Lord Egmont; but as I know his declar'd Sentiments to be contrary with Regard to the Right of laying Duties, I cannot think it proper or decent to ask him, nor could it be expected that he would support such a Petition. I have therefore let it lie for the present till I see what will become of that

8. See Gipson, *British Empire*, XI, 167–9.

9. The Maryland House of Delegates had already sent a petition to the King in which it strongly asserted its charter right to be exempt from taxation. *Ibid.*, pp. 177–8 and n. 34.

16

to the Commons, as it will afterwards be time enough to offer the other to the Lords. A Pamphlet has lately been published here in our Behalf, which seems to make some Impression. As it contains many Sentiments and Arguments that I have occasionally thrown out, in Conversation, I think I know the Author, one of the Rockingham Party, and I have distributed a Number of them where I thought they might do good, gratis. It handles the Argument concisely, and yet with great Clearness and Force. Towards the Conclusion, indeed, some Consequences are drawn from a Concession of Mr. Otis's, which perhaps we may hereafter think too extensive;[1] but if Britain satisfy'd with the Reservation of that Claim, should at present be willing to give up the Rest, *Hereafter* will take care of itself.[2] Of late a Cry begins to arise, Can no body propose a Plan of Conciliation? Must we ruin ourselves by intestine Quarrels? I was ask'd in Company lately by a noble Lord if I had no Plan of that kind to propose? My Answer was, 'Tis easy to propose a Plan; mine may be express'd in a few Words; *Repeal* the Laws, *Renounce* the Right, *Recall* the Troops, *Refund* the Money, and *Return to the old Method of Requisition.* I have no Objection, says he, to repealing the Laws and recalling the Soldiers; and as to refunding the Money, I believe it may be easily done; for I suppose what we have receiv'd amounts to no great Matter: But why would you insist on our Re-

1. The new pamphlet was *The Case of Great Britain and America, Addressed to the King and Both Houses of Parliament* (London, 1769). It is attributed to Gervase P. Bush and George P. Butler; it was summarized in the *London Chron.*, Jan. 10–12, 1769, and reprinted almost in its entirety in the *Pa. Chron.*, April 3–10, 10–17, 1769. Otis' two "concessions," quoted in the pamphlet from *The Rights of the British Colonies Asserted and Proved* (Boston, 1764), are that Parliament has the power to legislate for the empire as a whole in matters affecting the general good, and to prohibit the colonies from trading in a given commodity.

In the *St. James Chron.* of Feb. 11, 1769, appeared a letter, signed "A Briton," which endorsed and expanded the argument of *The Case of Great Britain and America.* The pseudonym was one that BF had used (above, XV, 132, 237, 244); Verner Crane once suggested that the letter might have been by him. "Certain Writings of Benjamin Franklin on the British Empire and the American Colonies," Bibliographical Soc. of America *Papers,* XXVIII, part I (1934), 20 n. But the style and the method of argument, we believe, are not BF's.

2. As Verner Crane points out in *Letters to the Press,* pp. 232–3 and n. 6, BF here foreshadows the idea that he developed four years later in his "Infallible Method to Restore Peace and Harmony."

nouncing the Right? How can you expect it when you see your own little Assemblies think themselves above *rescinding*? I do not insist upon that, says I; if continuing the Claim pleases you, continue it as long as you please, provided you never attempt to execute it: We shall consider it in the same Light with the Claim of the Spanish Monarch to the Title of King of Jerusalem.[3] This growing Desire of finding some conciliating Measure, I think a favourable Token that we are about to come right again. With great Esteem, I am, Dear Sir, Your most obedient humble Servant   B FRANKLIN

Joseph Galloway Esqr

"A Horrid Spectacle to Men and Angels"

AD (draft): American Philosophical Society

This emotional outpouring cannot be precisely dated. Verner Crane assigns it to January, 1769, because some of the ideas that it contains were elaborated in Franklin's two letters printed in the *Public Advertiser* on January 17. Hays, on the other hand, assigns it to *c.* 1775.[4] But that date is virtually ruled out by the reference to Corsica. In May, 1768, the Genoese had abandoned their prolonged effort to maintain sovereignty over the island and had sold it to France; for the next year the Corsicans under Pasquale Paoli held out against this new and mightier enemy, but by the summer of 1769 the French had gained firm control. Franklin's wording strongly suggests that the struggle was still going on. If so he must have been writing in 1768 or 1769, and we believe that the most likely date is just before the letters printed on January 17.

[Before January 17, 1769?]

A horrid Spectacle to Men and Angels is now about to be exhibited on the Stage of this Globe. Two great and Powerful Nations are employing their Forces in the Destruction of Civil LIBERTY, that heavenly Blessing without which Mankind lose half their Dignity

3. A bit of genealogical fantasy, like the claim of King George to the throne of France: the last crowned King of Jerusalem was the Emperor Frederick II, from whom the title descended through the Houses of Aragon and Hapsburg to the Bourbon Kings of Spain. The vanished kingdom was also claimed by most of the monarchs of Europe, not to mention the Pope and the Republic of Venice.

4. Crane, *Letters to the Press*, p. 160; I. Minis Hays, *Calendar of the Papers of Benjamin Franklin*... (5 vols., Philadelphia, 1908), III, 501.

and Value! one in oppressing and enslaving a handful of Men the last brave Assertors of it within the Bounds of the old Roman Commonwealth; the other crushing in its Infancy, the first Appearance of it in the Western World. The former seems to have lost Sight of its antient Name and State, *Franks* from the *Freedom* it once enjoy'd;[5] the latter, while it boasts of enjoying Freedom itself, would ruin others for vindicating their common Right to it. The first is acting a cruel, a mean and unmanly Part, thus to use its vastly superior Force against People so unable to resist it; but is however *more excusable* than the latter as the People to be oppress'd and enslav'd, are NOT her *own Children*!

The 4 refused Petitions[6]

Calculation of the time necessary to subdue the Colonies[7]

Instructions to dissolve Assemblies.[8]

A Purported Letter from Paris

Printed in The Public Advertiser, January 17, 1769

Extract of a Letter from Paris to a Gentleman in London, dated Dec. 23.[9]

You English consider us French as Enemies to Liberty: You reproach us for endeavouring to reduce Corsica to our Obedience,[1] and say, that if we heard of a Freeman on the other Side of the Globe, you suppose we should hasten thither to make a Slave of him. How easy it is for Men to see the Faults of others, while blind to their own! The Corsicans are not so remote from us as the Americans are from you; they never enriched us by their Labour and their Commerce; they never engaged in our Wars, and fought as Brothers, Side by Side

5. An often accepted but erroneous etymology.

6. Presumably the petitions against the Townshend Acts, one from Virginia, one from Pennsylvania, and two from Massachusetts.

7. See "An Account Stated against G. G." below, Jan. 17.

8. Presumably Lord Hillsborough's instructions to the colonial governors to dissolve assemblies that received the circular letter from Massachusetts denouncing the Townshend Acts.

9. As Crane explains in *Letters to the Press*, p. 160, the extract is completely fictitious. The date is invented along with the contents; hence we assign the letter to the date of its publication in the *Public Advertiser*.

1. See the headnote to the preceding document.

with us, and for us, bleeding in the same Cause; they never loved and honoured us; they are not *our* Children. But all this your American Colonists have been and are to you! Yet at this very Moment, while you are abusing us for attempting to reduce the Corsicans, you yourselves are about to make Slaves of a much greater Number of those British Americans; depriving them of their Property by the Authority of your Laws; taking away the Right of giving their own Money; arbitrarily dissolving their Parliaments, and dragooning their Citizens. In short, you appear to have no true Idea of Liberty, or real Desire to see it flourish and increase: All the Liberty you seem to value, is the Liberty of abusing your Superiors, and of tyrannizing over those below you.

Defense of American Placeholders

Printed in The Gazetteer and New Daily Advertiser, *January 17, 1769*

In his two roles of colonial agent and royal official, Franklin was particularly vulnerable to charges in America that he was betraying the first, and in England that he was betraying the second. Criticism in the London press of him and other Americans in royal service continued as long as he remained in England, but this is his only public reply. It requires little editorial annotation because Verner Crane, with his usual thoroughness, has explained the journalistic attacks that elicited this defense.[2]

To the Printer.

Your correspondent *Machiavel* tells us, that "Nothing can be a greater burlesque on Patriotism, than the conduct of the Americans, who affect discontent at being taxed, and therefore not only petition and remonstrate, but are continually writing pamphlets, filling newspapers, and consecrating Trees to Liberty; when, at the same time, many of them are writing to administration how to enforce the collection of such duties as are imposed, &c. &c. with a view to obtain offices and pensions under the Crown, in America." And then he gives us a list of fifteen Americans, whom he charges with having been successfully guilty of this baseness.[3] The whole ap-

2. *Letters to the Press*, pp. 153–5.
3. Machiavel's letter appeared in the *Gazetteer*, Jan. 13, 1769; BF's name was at the top of the list, which also included WF and BF's sometime associates, John Temple, Jared Ingersoll, and David Colden.

parently with a view of lessening any concern the friends of Liberty here may have for the injured people of that country, and of discountenancing any endeavours for their relief, by thus rendering them both contemptible and odious.

But, methinks it should be considered,

1. That if not only *fifteen*, but fifteen hundred, out of three millions, had been seduced by corruption, to betray the interests of their country, the proportion is not so great as to judge of the rest by them, to conclude that therefore they might be oppressed without injury, stripped of their rights without remorse; their petitions and remonstrances disregarded; their constitution dissolved; their towns insulted and dragooned; their real patriots hanged as traitors, not for any disloyalty to their King, but merely for doubting the power of parliament, in particular cases, or, perhaps, only thwarting the views of a wrong-headed, pertinacious minister.

2. That being loyal subjects to their sovereign, the Americans think they have as good a right to enjoy offices under him in America, as a Scotchman has in Scotland, or an Englishman in England; and that they may equally hold them consistent with honour; since they have never yet been taught to believe that the interests of their King and his subjects are so contrary and incompatible, that an honest man cannot serve the one without betraying the other.

Let me farther add, that, among the gentlemen in his list, I know some, who, far from receiving the offices they hold, as the wages of corruption, rose in them gradually and regularly, in a course of years; others had been conferred as rewards of public service, by sea and land, during war; others enjoyed their offices many years before any dispute arose, or was dreamt of, between the two countries; and have yet, throughout those disputes, been firm to the cause of their country, at all hazards. If there are any of them who are known, or even, on probable grounds, suspected, to have betray'd it, such are in universal odium among their virtuous compatriots; and therefore their country ought not to be censured upon their account. To defend it from such indiscriminate censure, is the chief end of my giving you this trouble.

Your correspondent adds, "Behold how true it is, that *every* man has his price." In a former paper [Dec. 19.]⁴ he had told us, (speak-

4. Brackets in the original. The letter of that date in the *Gazetteer*, signed "Machiavel the Second," was much the same but shorter, and named only nine

ing of mankind) "We are honest as long as we thrive by it; but if the Devil himself gives better wages, we change our party." For the honour of my species, as well as of my country, I cannot but suppose these maxims much *too general*. But as this writer has professedly adopted them in their full extent, I must conclude they may be true *so far at least as relates to himself*, since it is plain *he knows of no exception*.   AN AMERICAN

An Account Stated against G. G.

Reprinted from Verner W. Crane, ed., *Benjamin Franklin's Letters to the Press, 1758–1775* (Chapel Hill, N.C., [1950]), pp. 156–9.

To the Printer of the PUBLIC ADVERTISER.

Sir,   [January 17, 1769]

I thank you for the Information you so readily gave at the Request of the *Manufacturer of London*, relating to the Agreement *going forward* in America not to use more of our Manufactures.[5] The Memorial you published in your Paper of the 13th inst. from the Merchants of Philadelphia, addressed to the Merchants and Manufacturers of Great Britain, makes the Point sufficiently clear. And as, by what I can otherways learn, there is not the smallest Probability of an Accomodation while the present A—n M—r continues in that Department, nor the least Prospect of his being removed; but on the contrary all his rash ill-judged Measures are to be approved confirmed and pursued; and even the first Projector of the Mischief, Mr. G. G. is to be brought in again, to assist in compleating it,[6] I think 'tis Time to state an Account, in order to form some kind of Estimate what we are like to be Gainers or Losers by quarreling with our best Friends and greatest Customers. For a Quarrel I see it will be! Depriving them of their Privileges for no Offence, and

---

men. Among them, but not in the later list, was Lieut. Gov. Hutchinson. Hence BF was defending, among others, a man who was in fact urging strong measures against Massachusetts, and whose views BF later helped to expose.

5. See "Pennsylvania and Nonimportation" above, Jan. 5. We have not collated this essay with BF's earlier writings because Crane, as cited above, has already done so in his excellent annotation.

6. The American Minister was of course Hillsborough, and G. G. was George Grenville.

sending Soldiers to insult them, strengthens their Determination to take no more of our Goods, and makes that Determination more general: *This* will provoke us to use them with more Severity; *that* more alienates and exasperates *them*; till, driven to Despair, an open Rupture becomes unavoidable, and the cordial Amity so much to the Advantage of both, which has hitherto subsisted between the two Countries, comes to be converted into the most implacable mutual Hatred, such as we see at this Day, between the Spaniards and Portuguese, the Genoese and the Corsicans, which arose originally from the *very same* Misconduct in the governing Countries.[7] By this we are to lose a greatly growing Trade, at present worth Five Millions a Year, which our Enemies will gain sooner or later, and so to us make the Difference double; and we are to turn Three Million of Friends into so many mortal Enemies, another double Diminution of our comparative Strength. And what is all this for? Is it that we [may] obtain *by Force* much *less* than we might have had from them by *voluntary Grant?* And how comes it about? A wrong-headed, short-sighted Financier imagined that he should make a great Figure in opening his Budget, and appear to have wonderful Abilities, if he could shew how a new Tax might be raised, which none who heard him should either pay or feel. America was then no longer to *give*; but what we wanted was to be *taken* from her by our Almighty Power. The Measure was found impracticable, and therefore soon dropt. An inconsiderate Successor, from the same Motives, renewed the Attempt in another Shape.[8] Just or unjust, politic or impolitic, constitutional or unconstitutional, are with such Statesmen Points entirely out of the Question. The first disappointed and displaced Projector harbours inveterate Malice to the Americans for murdering his Child. He and his Scribblers are thence continually endeavouring to exasperate the Nation against them, and urging every Step that may provoke them to such Acts as may justify the Character he gives of them. We are told indeed sometimes that the People of America would generally be quiet, if it were not for their factious Demagogues, and that the

---

7. Portugal was under Spanish rule, thinly disguised as a dynastic union, for almost sixty years before 1640, and did not make good its independence until 1668. For Corsica see the headnote above, p. 18.

8. The references are to George Grenville and the Stamp Act, and to Charles Townshend and the Townshend Acts.

whole Mischief is owing only to two or three restless Spirits there; that the Contest really is between Messrs. *Otis, Cushing* and *Adams*[9] on the one Part, and the whole People of England on the other. This is merely to countenance the Proposition of sending for these Men in order to hang them, which some seem to have much at Heart; though from the Blood of those three, probably would spring three hundred more. But in Truth, the Parties are G.G. L——d H. and the D. of B.[1] on the one Side, and on the other all our Fellow-Subjects in America. The People of England have no other Concern in the Dispute but that of being immense Losers by it's being started and persisted in, or infinite Gainers by it's being dropt. I talked of stating in Account: For Distinctness sake, I will state two: the first of what our Stockholders *have lost already*, the second of what the Nation will probably lose; in doing which I shall not pretend to mathematical Precision, for the Premises will scarce admit of it, they being partly assumed upon probable Conjecture. I only put them into the Form of Accounts for the sake of more distinctly viewing the Subject.

Dr. the Right Hon. G. G. *Esq*; *and* Co. *in Account with the Stockholders of* Great Britain.

	£
To the Loss of Five per Cent. on their Capital Stock of 145 Millions by the Fall occasioned by the late American Measure, amounting to	7,250,000

Supra .... Cr.

By the Stockholders Share of the neat Duties received in America, in Alleviation of British Taxes	3,500
Balance due from the said G. G. and Co.	7,246,500
	7,250,000

In this I have stated the Loss of Five per Cent. as so much Loss to the Stockholders only; and this already incurred. What their future Loss will be, if the Rupture hitherto only apprehended shall take Place, is impossible to estimate, as no one can foresee how low the Stocks will then fall. If it should be, as probably it may be, Thirty per Cent more, their Loss will exceed FORTY MILLIONS. But it will besides be accompanied with a proportionate Loss to the

9. The Bostonian trio of James Otis, Thomas Cushing, and Samuel Adams.
1. Grenville, Hillsborough, and Bedford.

Nation by the Fall of Public Credit, since the State must of course give so much more for Money wanted.

Now to form my other Account, I will make several immediate Suppositions. First, I will suppose no other Nation shall take Advantage of our Embroil in America, to fall upon us while we are subduing her. Secondly, that a War of ten Years, in which Twenty-five Thousand of Land Forces only are to be kept up and employed, with twenty Frigates, and Five Thousand Seamen, shall be sufficient to finish the Business by reducing the whole fifteen Colonies; though it cost us five Years in the last War to reduce but one of them, with the Help of all the rest, and double the Number of Men.[2] Thirdly, that after they are reduced, they shall be in the most perfect Good-humour with us, retain no Resentment of the Injuries we have done them, be as fond of us, and of our Fashions and Manufactures as ever they were, and that it will be therefore quite unnecessary to keep up an equal or indeed any Army to continue and secure the Subjection we have reduced them to. The Account will then stand thus:

Dr. The Hon. G.G. *Esq*; *and* Co. *in Account with* Great-Britain.

	£
For the Transport Service in carrying over 25,000 Men, with the Stores, &c. at the Rate of £10 per Man, including all Charges	250,000
The above to be repeated three Times more in the ten Years to keep up the Number; an Army in actual Service always requireing a Number of Recruits equal to the whole in every three Years	750,000
For the Recruiting Service and Bounty Money of 100,000 Men to be spent in this War	500,000
For the Pay, Cloathing and Subsistence of 25,000 Men ten Years at £20 per Man, including also Arms, Ammunition, &c.	5,000,000
For the Sea Service, 5000 Men, their Pay, Subsistence, Wear and Tear of Ships, &c. &c. &c. at £200,000 per Ann.	2,000,000
For the Loss of our Trade with those Countries during the ten Years, at 5,000,000 per Ann.	50,000,000

2. See above, xv, 192.

	£
For weakening the British Empire by all the Damage done it's Subjects, in obstructing or destroying their Improvements, Buildings, Ships, Trade with Foreigners, &c. and throwing all the Commerce they used to carry on for us into the Hands of our Rivals or Enemies	50,000,000
For the Blood spilt on both Sides, we charge	000
	108,500,000

Supra .... *Cr.*
By the Honour and Glory of having made Slaves
of Three Millions of Freemen 000

Thus stand the Accounts; and yet this same G.G. the Root of the whole Evil, sets up for an OEconomist. I am, Sir, Your humble Servant,   ANOTHER MANUFACTURER OF LONDON.

From Lord Kames

Extract: reprinted from Jared Sparks, ed., *The Works of Benjamin Franklin...* (10 vols., Boston, 1836–40), VII, 432 n.

Edinburgh, January 21st, 1769.
The letter you mention, about American affairs, never came to hand.[3] I have an essay on the subject of your Queries, and you shall hear from me soon about our agreeing or differing.[4] I have a great fund of political knowledge reduced into writing, far from being ripe, but fit for your perusal. If you will come to my aid, I know not but that we shall make a very good thing of it. If not, it may be lost to the world, and what a loss will that be!

3. See BF to Kames above, Jan. 1, to which this letter is a reply.
4. The wording suggests that BF had sent his friend a copy of his "Queries" to those advocating a strong line against the Americans, published the previous summer; see above, XV, 187–9. It is possible, alternatively, that Kames is referring to the enclosure in BF's letter of Jan. 1, which we conjectured was a draft of "Positions to Be Examined"; in that case, however, Kames's essay must have been written in remarkably short order.

26

To Charles Thomson and Thomas Mifflin[5]

ALS: Amherst College Library

Gentlemen, London, Jan. 27. 1769.

Enclos'd is Bill of Lading and Invoice of the Books you order'd, which I wish safe to hand, and am, Gentlemen Yours and the Company's most obedient Servant B FRANKLIN

P.S. On looking over your Letter I see that I am desir'd to add other Books if the List does not amount to your Money. Now that I have receiv'd the Invoice and find it amounts to so little,[6] I shall look out

5. This letter is on the back of the same sheet as, and hence clearly a postscript to, BF's letter to Thomson and Mifflin of Jan. 5.

6. The minutes of the Library Company of Philadelphia contain the invoice from William Strahan of the books that he shipped for BF on the *Pennsylvania Packet*, Capt. Falconer; the invoice is dated Jan. 24 and comes to only £37 7s. out of the £150 that BF had received and acknowledged in his letter of Jan. 5. Most of the books can be definitely identified from the catalogue published soon after the merger of the Library and Union Library Companies, *The Charter, Laws and Catalogue of Books . . .* (Philadelphia, 1770). Some identifications are doubtful, because the duplicates produced by the merger were sold before the catalogue was made; see Edwin Wolf, II, "The First Books and Printed Catalogues of the Library Company of Philadelphia," *PMHB*, LXXVIII (1954), 52–4. The list can be reconstructed with unusual accuracy, nevertheless, and it is worth reproducing as an index of the taste, or what the Library assumed would be the taste, of the Philadelphia reading public at that moment in time. Two points that are particularly striking are the range of subject matter represented and the absence of any work in a foreign language, classical or modern.

The books were as follows: [Thomas Amory], *The Life of John Buncle, Esq. . . .* (2 vols., London, 1763–66); Giuseppe M. A. Baretti, *An Account of the Manners and Customs of Italy: with Observations on the Mistakes of Some Travellers . . .* (London, 1768); [Cesare B. Beccaria], *An Essay on Crimes and Punishments, Translated from the Italian; with a Commentary attributed to Mons. de Voltaire, Translated from the French . . .* (London, 1767); [Francis Blackburne], *The Confessional; or a Full and Free Inquiry into the Right, Utility, Edification, and Success, of Establishing Systematical Confessions of Faith and Doctrine in Protestant Churches* (2d ed., London, 1767); William Blackstone, *Commentaries on the Laws of England* (3d ed., 3 vols., London, 1768); James Boswell, *An Account of Corsica; the Journal of a Tour to That Island; and Memoirs of Pascal Paoli . . .* (2d ed., London, 1768); *British Liberties; or the Free-Born Subject's Inheritance . . .* (2d ed., London, 1767); [James Burgh], *Crito; or Essays on Various Subjects* (2 vols., London, 1767), and *The Dignity of Human Nature, or a Brief Account of the Certain and Established Means for Attaining the True End of our Existence . . .* (probably 2d ed., 2 vols., London, 1767); [John Bush], *Hibernia Curiosa; Being a Letter from a Gentleman in Dublin, to His Friend at*

27

for some valuable Books to send you per Storey, or to bring with me for you.

Dover in Kent...(London, n.d.); George Colman, trans., *The Comedies of Terence, Translated into Familiar Blank Verse* (2d ed., 2 vols., London, 1768); *A Complete Collection of the Lords' Protests, from the First upon Record, in the Reign of Henry III, to the Present Time*...(2 vols., London, 1767); Alexander Cumming, *The Elements of Clock and Watch-Work; Adapted to Practice*... (London, 1766); James Steuart Denham, *An Inquiry into the Principles of Political Œconomy*...*by Sir James Steuart* (2 vols., London, 1767); [William Falconer], *The Ship-Wreck*... (new ed., London, 1764); Adam Ferguson, *An Essay on the History of Civil Society* (2d ed., London, 1768); James Fordyce, *Sermons to Young Women* (5th ed., 2 vols., London, 1768); [James] Hampton, trans., *The General History of Polybius*... (2d ed., 2 vols., London, 1761) and probably *Two Extracts from the Sixth Book of Polybius*...*to Which Are Prefixed Some Reflections*...*Concerning the Natural Destruction of Mixed Governments, with an Application of It to the State of Britain* (London, 1764); John Harrison, *The Principles of Mr. Harrison's Time-keeper, with Plates of the Same* ...(London, 1767); John Hawkesworth, trans., *The Adventures of Telemachus, the Son of Ulysses*...[by François de Salignac de la Mothe-Fénelon] (London, 1768); John Jones, *Free and Candid Disquisitions Relating to the Church of England, and the Means of Advancing Religion therein*...(2d ed., London, 1750); William Lewis, *Commercium philosophico-technicum; or, The Philosophical Commerce of Arts*...(London, 1763); [Henry Lloyd], *The History of the Late War in Germany*... (Vol. 1, London, 1766); George Lyttleton, *The History of the Life of King Henry the Second*... (2d ed., 3 vols., London, 1767); Catharine Macaulay, *The History of England, from the Accession of James I to the Elevation of the House of Hanover*... (4 vols., London, 1767); Thomas Major, *The Ruins of Paestum*... (London, 1768); Jean François Marmontel, *Moral Tales*... (perhaps the Edinburgh ed., 3 vols., 1768); *The Nautical Almanac and Astronomical Ephemeris*...*for the Year 1767* (London, 1766); *A New Collection of Voyages, Discoveries and Travels*... (7 vols., London, 1767); John Ogilvie, *Poems on Several Subjects*... and *Providence, an Allegorical Poem* (both London, 1764); *The Present State of Great Britain and North America*... (London, 1767), generally attributed to Dr. John Mitchell of Virginia; Joseph Priestley, *The History and Present State of Electricity, with Original Experiments* (London, 1767); probably a volume of the *Proceedings* of the Royal Dublin Society; [William Robertson], *An Attempt to Explain the Words Reason, Substance, Person, Creeds, Orthodoxy, Catholic-Church, Subscription, and Index Expurgatorius*... (3d ed., London, 1767); Samuel Sharp, *Letters from Italy; Describing the Customs and Manners of That Country*... (3d ed., London, n.d.), and *A View of the Customs, Manners, Drama, etc. of Italy*...*as They Are Described*...*by Mr. Baretti*... (London, 1768); Adam Smith, *The Theory of Moral Sentiments, to Which Is Added a Dissertation on the Origin of Languages* (3d ed., London, 1767); Laurence Sterne, *A Sentimental Journey through France and Italy, by Mr. Yorick* (new ed., 2 vols., London, 1768); Jonathan Swift, *Letters, Written by the Late Jonathan Swift D.D....and Several of His*

To Joseph Galloway

ALS: Clements Library

Dear Friend,   London, Jan. 29. 1769

The within was written to go by Budden, then expected to sail every Day.[7] But as he still continues here, I now send it per Falconer.

The Parliament has since come together after their Recess. The Lords Resolutions were to have been taken into Consideration last Monday by the Commons. They had before determin'd to let none be present that were not Members. I got a Member to endeavour obtaining Leave for the Agents from America at least, as the Matter was of such Importance to that Country; and I attended the House to be ready for going in if it might be done; but it was deny'd. The Affair however was not debated that Day, but postpon'd to Wednesday. Then the Question came on in a Committee of the whole House, and the Debate continu'd 'till three a Clock the next Morning; the Friends of America signalizing themselves, and beating the Ministry out of every Argument they advanc'd in support of the Resolves, so that it was for a while thought they would have been thrown out. But finally on a Division, there was a Majority for agreeing to the Resolutions, and to the Address.[8] I am promis'd by a Member a full Account of the Debate, which he intends to draw out at length from his own short Notes; and therefore as I hope to have it to send by Story, I will not attempt to give you one from the Scraps I have been able to collect here and there, which must be very imperfect. The Ministry however, tho' they carry'd their Point, were so stagger'd, that tho' they had intended to report the next Morning, and obtain the Agreement of the House to the Opinion of the Committee; yet knowing that a Number of Members,

---

Friends, From the Year 1703 to 1740... (John Hawkesworth, ed.; new ed., 3 vols., London, 1766); Floyer Sydenham, *A Synopsis, or General View of the Works of Plato* (London, 1759); Bonnell Thornton, trans., *The Comedies of Plautus; Translated into Familiar Blank Verse* (2 vols., London, 1767); Ferdinando Warner, *The History of Ireland* (London, 1763), and probably *The History of the Rebellion and Civil War of Ireland* (2d ed., London, 1768); Bulstrode Whitelocke, *Whitelockes Notes upon the King's Writt for Choosing Members of Parliament...* (2 vols., London, 1766).

7. The "within" was the letter to Galloway above, Jan. 9, to which the present letter is, as BF remarks later on, "only a kind of separate postscript." Capt. Budden was delayed by an accident to his eyes. *PMHB*, XI (1887), 98.

8. See Cobbett, *Parliamentary History*, XVI, 485–94.

some of Weight, had not spoken in the Committee by reason of the lateness of the Hour, but had reserv'd themselves for the Report, and fearing the Event, they postpon'd Receiving the Report for ten Days. It is now to come on again on Friday next, when there will be another Struggle; but tho' our Friends are evidently increasing, such is ministerial Influence in that House, one can scarce expect the Determination will be against the Resolves: If it should, the Ministers must quit the Reins to abler Hands: and in case of a Change, we hope for our old Friends again of the Rockingham Party, who will probably repeal the offensive Laws, and restore Harmony between the two Countries. The Merchants have consulted that Party to know whether they think it time to bring in Petitions from the manufacturing Towns, &c. in order to make a Push for obtaining the Repeal: That Party have had a Meeting on it; and have given it as their unanimous Opinion, that 'tis better to wait a little longer. This to your self only. I intended writing to the Committee. But I cannot be so free on Affairs here in a Letter that must lie on the Table, subject to be copied, and Parts of it perhaps sent back hither. In writing to you I am not under that Restraint; because you can keep to yourself all Passages that would embroil me with Government here and hurt my Negociations. I shall however write to them per Story. Enclos'd I send you a Copy of the Resolutions and Address as propos'd by the Lords;[9] they have receiv'd some Alterations I hear in the Commons, which I have not yet got, but they are said not to be very material. I send you also my rough Draft of Observations on them; they were made at the Request of a Member who was to speak against the Resolves.[1] My Son, who knows my Scrawl, will transcribe the Paper for you if you cannot make it out.

In my Letter (this is only a kind of separate Postscript) I omitted telling you a Passage that happen'd in the House of Lords upon the first proposing of the Resolutions and Address by Lord Hillsborough

9. A copy of the address, contributed by a correspondent—very likely Galloway—who said that he had just received it from London, was printed in the *Pa. Chron.*, March 27–April 3, 1769.

1. Verner Crane identifies the M.P. as Thomas Pownall, the former governor of Massachusetts and BF's old friend, and adds that Pownall used the material supplied him for his speech in the House on Jan. 26. *Letters to the Press*, p. 200. We agree on the identification but not the speech, which we believe was that of Feb. 8, reported at length in Cobbett, *Parliamentary History*, XVI, 494–507.

and the Duke of Bedford. I omitted it there as I thought it rather too light for a serious Letter, but here you may have it. Lord Temple[2] stood up immediately after they were read, and said he had come to the House that Day, *tho' not very well*, in hopes of hearing some effectual Plan propos'd for reducing America to Obedience; but this he found was no Plan at all, the Resolutions were perfectly nugatory; and therefore as he did not think them worth a Moment's Consideration, he should enter into no Debate about them. And so saying he turn'd on his Heel and went abruptly and hastily out of the House. Upon which one in the Ministry said to one of the Opposition who sat next him, 'Tis pity Lord Temple ventur'd to come abroad in such Circumstances; he says he is not well, and by his abrupt Departure he has certainly *taken Physick*. If that's the Case, reply'd the other, *I wish he had taken the Resolutions with him.*

The House will probably sit till June or perhaps July, and it is thought here, that if News can come of all the Colonies having join'd in the Determination to buy no more British Goods, the Acts must be repeal'd before they rise. It is impossible to say such must be the Effect. But perhaps 'tis the only way in which we can yet contend with this powerful People with any Prospect of Success. Frugality and Industry is not, like War, a Waste of Treasure, but the Means of increasing it. And the Losing our Commerce must certainly weaken this Country. Possibly they may think of some equal Means of hurting us; but something must be try'd and some Risque run, rather than sit down quietly under a Claim of Parliament to the Right of disposing of our Properties without our Consent. Yours affectionately   B F

From Thomas Gilpin

Extract: reprinted from "Memoir of Thomas Gilpin," *Pennsylvania Magazine of History and Biography,* XLIX (1925), 302–3.

This letter is the first surviving one in a correspondence that continued, insofar as it is extant, until November, 1770. Thomas Gilpin belonged to a wealthy Quaker family; although he had estates in Maryland and Dela-

2. Richard Grenville-Temple, Earl Temple (1711–79), George Grenville's brother, was the brother-in-law of Chatham, who had quarreled long and violently with him; the two had been reconciled only a few months before. Temple was arrogant and an intriguer, given to dirty fighting; but he was also generous enough to pay Wilkes's legal expenses. *DNB.*

ware, his principal residence was Philadelphia. His fortune allowed him to indulge his hobbies, which were varied: he was a naturalist, a mathematician and surveyor, an engineer with a particular interest in building canals and bridges, and the inventor of a hydraulic pump. He was a member of the two organizations that merged in 1769 to form the American Philosophical Society;[3] he submitted an essay on the pump and a model of it to the Society and subsequently sent the model to Franklin, who was delighted by it and expected great things of it.[4] In 1777, on the eve of the British capture of Philadelphia, Gilpin was among the Quakers who were first imprisoned by the state authorities and then exiled to Virginia, where he died soon afterward.[5]

Janry. 29th 1769

The sentiments of our Sovereign and disposition of Parliament received by the last advices[6] affect the people here with great surprize and increasing suspicion. I hope and trust they will not determine in a desperate opposition, but be firmly and coolly met as an arbitrary advance; they will however occasion great alarm; demands made without consultation or even our knowing the object of them can only be considered in a desperate light; I wish sincerely ministerial wisdom may present some more favorable measures, otherwise both our trade and affections will be lost; we are denied the right of complaining, it is even looked upon as idle and contemptuous in us to do so. The debts and expences of England are certainly very great, but who are the creditors and who the debtors, who the burthened and who impose the burthens? Will not the expensive and lucrative plan of the nation itself bear correction and ought it not to be attempted before the weight is imposed upon us?

3. See above, XV, 259–61.
4. See below: Gilpin to BF, May 16, and BF to Gilpin, July 10.
5. "Memoir of Thomas Gilpin," *PMHB*, XLIX (1925), 289–328; Carl and Jessica Bridenbaugh, *Rebels and Gentlemen: Philadelphia in the Age of Franklin* (New York, [1942]), pp. 345–9; [Thomas Gilpin, Jr., ed.], *Exiles in Virginia: with Observations on the Conduct of the Society of Friends during the Revolutionary War...* (Philadelphia, 1848), pp. 210–12.
6. The King's speech at the opening of Parliament and the addresses in reply from the two Houses were printed in *Pa. Chron.*, Jan. 2–9, 16–23, 1769.

To Jean-Baptiste LeRoy[7]   ALS: Pierpont Morgan Library

Dear Sir,   London, Jan. 31. 1769.
I received your obliging Favour of Nov. 15. I presented your
Compliments to Sir John Pringle, who was glad with me to hear of
your Welfare, and desired me to offer his best Respects whenever I
wrote to you.[8] The Farmers Letters were written by one Mr. Dickinson of Philadelphia, and not by me as you seem to suppose. I only
caus'd them to be reprinted here with that little Preface,[9] and had
no other hand in them, except that I see some of my Sentiments
formerly publish'd are collected and interwoven with those of
others and his own, by the Author: I am glad they afforded you any
Amusement. It is true as you have heard, that Troops are posted in
Boston, on the Pretence of preventing Riots and protecting the
Custom house Officers; but it is also true, that there was no Intention among the People there to oppose the Landing of those Troops,
or to resist the Execution of the Law by Arms. The Riots talked of,
were sudden unpremeditated things, that happened only among a
few of the lower sort. Their Plan of making War on this Country is
of a different kind. It is to be a War on the Commerce only, and
consists in an absolute Determination to buy and use no more of
the Manufactures of Britain till the Act is repeal'd. This is already
agreed to by four Provinces, and will be by all the rest in the ensuing
Summer. Eleven Ships now here from Boston and New York, who
would have carried, one with another, £50,000 Sterling each in
Goods, are going away in their Ballast, as the Parliament seems
determin'd not to repeal.[1] I am inclined to think however, that it

7. The French physicist and member of the Académie des sciences, whom
BF had seen during his visit to Paris in 1767 and with whom he had since been
corresponding. See above, x, 61 n; xv, 82, 204–6. Although LeRoy's most
recent letter has been lost, its contents can be inferred from BF's reply.

8. BF had dined at Sir John's four days before, in company with his old friend
William Strahan, David Hume, the Duc de la Rochefoucauld, and others.
PMHB, xi (1887), 100.

9. See above, xv, 110.

1. BF was anticipating events in saying that the merchants in four provinces
had agreed to nonimportation, for only those in Boston and New York had yet
done so; hence the empty ships. He was correct, however, in predicting that the
others would follow suit; the first to take action were Pennsylvania in February
and Maryland in March, 1769. See Jensen, *Founding of a Nation*, pp. 283–5, 305–
6.

will alter its Mind before the End of the Session. Otherwise it is to be fear'd the Breach will grow wider by successive Indiscretions on both sides.

The Subject you propose to me, the Consequences of allowing a free Exportation of Corn, the Advantages or Disadvantages of the *Concurrence*,[2] &c. is a very extensive one; and I have been and am at present so much occupy'd with our American Affairs, as that if I were ever so capable of handling it, I have not time to engage in it at present to any purpose. I think however with you, that the true Principles of Commerce are yet but little understood, and that most of the Acts of Parliament, Arrets and Edicts of Princes and States, relating to Commerce, are political Errors, solicited and obtained by Particulars for private Interest under the Pretext of Public Good.

The Bearer of this, Capt. Ourry, is a particular Friend of mine, who now only passes thro' Paris for Lyons and Nice, but in his Return may stay in your City some time.[3] He is a Gentleman of excellent Character and great Merit, and as such I beg Leave to recommend him to your Civilities and Advice, which may be of great Service to him as he is quite a Stranger in Paris. With the greatest Esteem and Respect, I am, Dear Sir Your most obedient and most humble Servant   B FRANKLIN

Your English is extreamly good; but if [it] is more easy for you to write in French, do not give yourself the Trouble of Writing in English, as I understand your French perfectly well.

M. LeRoy

From William Franklin

ALS (perhaps incomplete): American Philosophical Society

[January 31, 1769[4]]
The last Packet, which left England about the Middle of Novr.

2. Literally competition, but the context suggests that LeRoy may have had in mind free competition on the international market, as the means of establishing for commodities what the physiocrats called "le bon prix."

3. Capt. Lewis Ourry, an old friend of the Franklins, had returned to England from America in 1765. See the references to him in Vols. VII, XII, XIV, and XV.

4. The letter lacks place, date, and salutation. In the corner of the MS appears in an eighteenth-century hand "Janry 31, 17 9," and internal evidence leaves no doubt of the year.

brought no Letter from you, that I can hear of, except one to the Committee of Correspondence. I imagine your Time must be almost wholly engross'd in attending on the publick Business at this important Crisis, and in writing for the Press. I see a Number of Pieces in the Chronicle which I am sure have you for their Author, particularly Two sign'd *A Briton*, and one sign'd F.B. which has a State of the Trade between England and the Colonies. This latter Bradford has printed in his last Journal, which I send you enclosed, that you may see an Extract of a Letter from London which he has likewise publish'd, wherein you are said to have spoke in a large Company against the *Right* of Parliament to tax the Colonies.[5] This, no doubt, will do you great Credit in the Colonies, but as Bradford is known to have always carefully avoided publishing any thing that might have that Tendency, and readily printed every Thing that might injure your Reputation, it is thought that his publishing this Letter from London is from no friendly Motive, but with Hopes of its incensing the Ministry or Parliament against you, for denying the Right of the latter when they had so fully and repeatedly asserted it.

I likewise send you the last Chronicle which contains two Pieces sign'd *Amor Patriae*, said to be wrote by one Crawley in London, who is thought to be a little crack'd. He has sent me several of his Pieces, and desired me to publish them in our *New Jersey Gazette*.[6]

I send you also a Copy of Lord Hillsborough's last Letter, enclosing the King's Speech, and the Addresses. My Answer I trans-

5. The three essays in the *London Chron.* were the two "Arguments Pro and Con" and "The State of the Trade with the Northern Colonies," for which see above, xv, 233–7, 241–4, 251–5. William Bradford, BF's old enemy since the days of the Stamp Act, had published "The State of the Trade" in the *Pa. Jour.*, Jan. 26, 1769, along with the extract that WF mentions. The key sentences in the latter, which were also printed in the *Pa. Chron.*, Jan. 30–Feb. 6, 1769, were: "Doctor Franklin is indefatigable in his endeavours to serve his country. I heard him say, a few days ago, in a large company 'Britain has no right to tax the Colonies and never had any such right, and I trust never will have it.'"

6. For Thomas Crowley see above, xv, 238–41. His letter and proposals for imperial federation, first published in the *Public Advertiser*, were reprinted in the *Pa. Chron.*, Jan. 23–30, 1769. There was no *N.J. Gaz.* (which may be one reason why WF thought Crowley a little cracked); New Jersey had no newspaper until 1777: James M. Lee, *History of American Journalism* (Boston, 1917), pp. 59–60. In 1773 BF, in writing to WF, echoed his son's remark that Crowley was "rather a little cracked." WTF, *Memoirs*, II, 200.

mit herewith, which, if you approve of, please to seal and forward; otherwise write another and make use of the enclosed *Subscription*, in the manner I desired you in my last Letter.[7]

I suppose the Success which has attended the Measure of Sending Troops to Boston, that is, in putting a Stop to the Riots, and preventing any Opposition to the late Acts of Parliament, will be a means of establishing Lord H———h in the Administration, and I don't doubt but he exults greatly on the Occasion. The same Spirit however, still prevails in the Colonies, as did before, and nothing can make them acknowledge the Right of Parliament to tax them, tho' they may at present acquiesce in it.

Mr. Foxcroft is gone to Virginia, where he goes frequently to endeavor to collect in some Debts he has owing to him, but generally without Success. He intends for England, I am told, in April next. I do assure you that I never did say to any one that you continued in England this Winter "at *the Sollicitation* of the Duke of G[rafto]n." Nor do I believe Mr. Foxcroft heard that I had said any thing of the kind, notwithstanding what he says in his Letter to you. He was up at my House the other Day, when I ask'd him to tell me who it was that gave him such Information (repeating the Words he wrote you that he had heard) and he deny'd that he had wrote you any Thing of the kind, but upon my Taking out your Letter and reading the Paragraph he seem'd much confounded, said you had quite mistook him, and endeavoured to explain it away, but did it

7. For Hillsborough's letter of Nov. 15, 1768, see 1 *N.J. Arch.*, x, 60–2; for WF's reply see *ibid.*, pp. 99–102. The reply was scarcely controversial, at least by comparison with WF's earlier letter to the Minister; and for that reason his handling of it is all the more remarkable. He submits it to his father's judgment, with *carte blanche* to amend it as BF sees fit; so much is clear from the text. What is less clear is the particular method which BF was to use, and which WF had spelled out in his previous letter—presumably a missing section of the incomplete one printed above, *c.* Jan. 2.

Our conjecture is that he had said he would enclose, and in this later letter did enclose, a blank sheet with his signature at the bottom; subscription means, *inter alia*, a piece of paper that is signed. If BF had exercised his option of redrafting the letter, he would presumably have had it copied by a clerk (to conceal the hand) in such a way as to end with WF's genuine signature. But what about the seal? An official letter from the Governor of New Jersey to a principal Secretary of State would scarcely have gone without WF's signet. Did BF have a copy of it, or was he expected to seal the letter with plain wax? The whole episode bristles with unanswered questions.

in so confused and awkward a Manner as betray'd a Consciousness of having done what he ought not to have done.[8]

I see Governor Pownal has publish'd a new Edition of his Administration of the Colonies.[9] I should be glad that you would send it to me, with some of the Reviews and Magazines, and other new Publications, for I am out of the way of seeing every Thing of that kind in Burlington, and they would afford me some Amusement.

I recommended Mr. Stockton to Lord Hillsborough to be appointed one of the Council, and he acquainted me some time ago that my Letter was referr'd by His Majesty to the Board of Trade. By the last Packet I receiv'd a Letter from his Lordship enclosing one for Mr. Stockton, which it seems contain'd his Mandamus but not a Syllable was said of the Matter in his Lordship's Letter to me, which was using me very unpolitely, to say no worse, as I had recommended Mr. Stockton.[1] Perhaps, he did not chuse that I should think the Appointment was in Compliance with my Request, as I am at present out of Favour. There is a Meanness in this kind of Conduct extremely unbecoming one in his Station. Another trifling Matter of the like Nature, hardly worth mentioning, is his having ever since his famous Letter No. 13, to me,[2] omitted the usual Words at the Conclusion of all his and former Secretary's Letters, viz *"I am with great Truth and Regard, Sir,* &c. and only says "I am, Sir," &c.

I hear nothing now a Days of Mr. Hughes, except that he shuns all his old Friends and Acquaintance, lives entirely upon his Farm and continues writing his Letters of Advice to the Ministry. Coz.

---

8. By his own account John Foxcroft had gone to Virginia to put the affairs of the Post Office in good order before he returned to England on leave; see his letter to BF below, Feb. 21, in which he avoided all mention of WF's taking him to task. In any case the matter was a tempest in a teapot, for BF had in fact received tentative suggestions, which he thought originated with Grafton, of a public appointment if he would stay in England. See above, xv, 159–62.

9. Thomas Pownall, *The Administration of the Colonies*... (4th ed., London, 1768).

1. For WF's letter and Hillsborough's reply see 1 *N.J. Arch.*, x, 44–5, 58–60. For Richard Stockton and his subsequent career see above, xii, 78 n.

2. Of Aug. 16, 1768, in which Hillsborough angrily and rudely berated WF for his conduct in office. 1 *N.J. Arch.*, x, 45–8. For WF's reply, defending his actions at great length, see *ibid.*, pp. 64–95.

Davenport, however, in a Letter just receiv'd, says, "I met Mr. Jno. Hughes on the Lancaster Road last Thursday, who enquired much about your Father and you, and desired to be remembered."[3]

Pray have you receiv'd the Four Guineas of Mr. Swinton?[4] I have not made you any Remittance of late, as I have been for some Time expecting you Home, and now I must beg your Patience a little longer till I have got my Land patented.

I have desired Mr. Jackson to introduce Mr. Wharton to Mr. Cooper,[5] lest any thing should happen to prevent your doing it.

I have not Time to copy this Scrawl. Betsy sends her Duty. I am, Honored Sir, Your dutiful Son   WM. FRANKLIN

From Thomas Gordon   ALS: American Philosophical Society

Worthy Sir   Philada, Feby. 5th. 1769

It is a Tax on Superior Merrit and Benevolence, to be troubled with Importunities of every kind of People, who want Assistance. Your kindness formerly to my own Son,[6] Encourages me now to Apply in behalf of my Son in Law Henry Benbridge, a very Deserving youth who has been Several Years in Italy for his improvement in Painting, and is now going to London for Business.[7] As I am

3. John Hughes, BF's old political ally, had been unpopular ever since he had been forced to resign as a stamp distributor in 1765. He moved to New Hampshire in 1769, then to Charleston, S.C. See above, VI, 284 n. Josiah Franklin Davenport (C.12.4) was BF's nephew.

4. John Swinton, a Scottish lawyer, was receiving help from WF in litigation about his land claims in New Jersey. See the frequent references to him in Vols. XII, XIII, and XV.

5. Richard Jackson was BF's co-agent for Pennsylvania, and Grey Cooper was secretary to the Treasury. Samuel Wharton and William Trent were preparing to leave for England to press the claims of the "suffering traders" to lands ceded by the Indians at Fort Stanwix the previous autumn. WF was collecting introductions to ease Wharton's path. See 1 *N.J. Arch.* X, 97–8; WF to Strahan, Jan. 29, 1769, Pierpont Morgan Library.

6. For Thomas Gordon, a Scottish merchant of Philadelphia, and his son Alexander see above, VII, 392–3. The son had run out of money in England in 1758 and had appealed successfully to BF for help.

7. Henry Benbridge (1744?–1812), Gordon's stepson and a relative of BF's friends the Benjamin Wests, had been in Italy for some four years; he was coming to England via Corsica with a portrait of Pasquale Paoli that he had painted on commission from James Boswell. *DAB.*

Sensable your Acquaintance must be large, and of the best fashion, Pardon me Sir, for Begging you'll be kind enough (if he has merit in his Profession) to Recommend him to such of your Acquaintance as you think may be likely to employ him: and I hope my Son will always have the Gratitude properly to Acknowledge with me the obligation Confer'd on us both. I am Sir with the greatest Esteem and Regard your most obedient humble Servant To Command.

THOS GORDON

Addressed: To Benjamin Franklin Esqr

From Thomas Gilpin[8]

Extracts: reprinted from "Memoir of Thomas Gilpin," *Pennsylvania Magazine of History and Biography*, XLIX (1925), 303.

Febry. 6th. 1769

Our last advices of ministerial and parliamentary measures has revived the motion of a non-importation of manufactures from Great Britain; for myself I should have rather preferred to confine it to particular articles suited to the convenience of each colony which would have sufficiently established the principles we acted upon and proclaimed the exigency we complain of but such is the alarm the attempt to abridge our liberties has given that nothing can arrest it. Laws without representation are rejected and held in abhorrence, in every shape they are presented: a fair representation of the colonies with an influence according to their magnitude and pecuniary requisitions made of them seem at this time to be considered as vague and idle attempts foreign to our rights and abilities, but should some reasonable measures be proposed and the choice in some degree left to ourselves there is no doubt we should act correctly.

[February 6, 1769]

This day a non importation resolution has been adopted[9] and it now

8. See his letter to BF above, Jan. 29.

9. See Merchants of Philadelphia to BF below, April 18. The merchants, meeting on Feb. 6, produced something short of a nonimportation agreement: they canceled all orders for goods not shipped from Britain by April 1, and promised to order no more until March 10, when they would reconsider the matter. Arthur M. Schlesinger, *The Colonial Merchants and the American Revolution, 1763–1776* (New York, 1918), pp. 128–9.

seems that nothing will ever open the connection again but an exemption from the burthens attempted to be laid on us unless they are done by those whom we may chuse.

To Joseph Galloway

ALS: Yale University Library

Dear Friend,   London, Feb. 7. 1769

I wrote to you pretty fully per Falconer,[1] since which nothing material has pass'd relative to American Affairs. The Grand Committee was to have reported on them[2] last Friday; but Wilkes had taken up so much of their Time, the House sitting four Nights successively till three in the Morning, that they were oblig'd to postpone it for another Week. He is expell'd, but sets up and will be chosen again; if the House do not first disqualify him by an Act.[3] I inclose you some Papers by which you will see the Temper of the Times here. There will be another tough Battle before the House agrees with the Committee, but there is little doubt that finally the Report will be approved and the Resolutions agreed to. I have not yet obtained the Account I promis'd you of the Debate. I can now only tell you another little Anecdote of a Passage in it. Mr. Grenville speaking of the Inefficiency of the present Ministry, compar'd them to two raw Sailors who were got up into the round Top, and understanding nothing of the Business, pretended however to be very busy. *What are you doing there, Jack,* says the Boatswain. *Nothing* says Jack. *And pray what are you about, Tom? I,* says Tom, *am helping him.* On this Story one of the Members observ'd, that it would have been much better for the Nation, if that honourable Gentleman and his Friends, had, during their Administration, been employ'd only in helping one another to do *nothing.* I have sent you the last Votes per Capt. Reed: and am, with sincerest Esteem, Yours affectionately   B FRANKLIN

Joseph Galloway Esqr

1. Above, Jan. 29.
2. BF has underlined the word, inserted above it "A Affairs," and lined this and the following sentence in the margin, presumably for an extract. The debate on America in the House of Commons was resumed on Feb. 8.
3. Wilkes was expelled from the House on Feb. 3, re-elected for Middlesex on Feb. 16, and expelled again the next day. Trench, *Wilkes,* pp. 240–3.

To Smith, Wright, & Gray[4] ALS: American Philosophical Society

Friends, Cravenstreet, Feb. 13. 69

Be so kind as to procure a Letter of Credit on Paris for Dr. Benjamin Rush,[5] a young Physician from Pensylvania, of excellent Character, and a particular Friend of mine; the Sum Two Hundred Pounds. He sets out to-morrow. I will be answerable to you for what he may take up there on such Letter.

I inclose a Bill of £100 for which please to send me a Receipt per Bearer. Mr. Galloway, in whose favour the Bill was drawn has omitted to indorse it, but I suppose that on sight of his Letter, which I send with it, Messrs. Barclay[6] may accept it.

Send me by the Bearer, Mr. Coombe,[7] Twenty Guineas, one in Silver. I am, very respectfully, Yours, &c B FRANKLIN

Addressed: To / Messrs Smith, Wright & Gray / Bankers / Lombard street

To Smith, Wright, & Gray ALS: Yale University Library

Gentlemen Feb. 14. 69

Enclos'd is Dr. Rush's Signature[8] which you desired. I thank you for so readily furnishing the Letter of Credit. Yours &c

B FRANKLIN

Addressed: To / Messrs. Smith, Wright & / Gray, / Bankers / Lombard street

From Joseph Priestley

ALS (fragmentary copy): American Philosophical Society

Leeds 14th. February 1769.

[A few lines at the end of a letter, which convey Priestley's best

---

4. For this London banking firm see above, x, 350 n, and XI, 179–80.

5. Benjamin Rush had come to London after receiving his medical degree from the University of Edinburgh in 1768; he stayed at Mrs. Stevenson's and continued his medical studies. In February, 1769, he left for a month's visit to Paris. George W. Corner, ed., *The Autobiography of Benjamin Rush...* ([Princeton], 1948), pp. 43, 52–73.

6. For David Barclay & Sons see above, IX, 190 n; XIV, 256 n.

7. Thomas Coombe, for whom see above, XV, 53.

8. See the preceding document.

wishes "for the success of your laudable endeavours in the cause of *science, truth, justice, peace,* and, which comprehends them all, and everything valuable in human life, LIBERTY."]

From James Parker   ALS: American Philosophical Society

Honoured Sir   New York, Feb 17. 1769
This covers one of a Set of Bills of Exchange, which I just received from Mr. Hubbart of Boston, for £60 13*s.* 9*d.* Sterling on John Blackburn, Esq. London:[9] The first of this Set I sent down to Mr. Foxcroft, who is gone to Virginia,[1] and I apprehend he will send it to you, but very probably this will come to your Hand first, and of this I have advised him, by Letter therewith.

Tho' in general we had a mild Winter here, yet for a few Weeks past, and at present, we have what may be called Severe Weather. For a Year or two past, we have endeavoured to make every Rider keep and sound Horns on their Way; in which Exercise for want of Skill or Care, many have lost their Horns, or got them broke, so that we are in Want of some, and if it be consistent with the Service, I wish you would send me some; and tho' we hath hitherto found the Horns, yet if they wantonly destroy them, we must oblige them to pay for them, so that if you please to let me know the Price also when you send them.

I suppose Mr. Foxcroft wrote you per last Packet of his going to Virginia, he tells me, he purposes to be back the latter End of March: This Opportunity happens by a Merchantman, that I just now heard of.

I have not had the Pleasure of one Line from you this great While: I have now the worst Fit of the Gout, that I have had these three Years, when I was at Burlington.[2] Now 6 Weeks, but I flatter myself I am getting better. The last News I had from Philadelphia

9. Tuthill Hubbart, the stepson of BF's brother John, had been postmaster of Boston since 1756; above, V, 118 n. John Blackburn was a London merchant with offices near the corner of Bush Lane and Cannon Street.

1. For John Foxcroft's visit to Virginia, to settle Post Office business before returning to England on leave, see his letter to BF below, Feb. 21.

2. He means since his attack at Burlington three years before, for which see above, XII, 407–9. His current attack was so severe, according to him, that it incapacitated him for two months and often made him "doubtful of any recovery." Parker to James Balfour, March 4, 1769, APS.

and Burlington, they were all well. We momentarily expect the December Packet, and a Report prevails that she is at the Hook; she must have had a hard Spell on the Coast, if it be her. With Respect to Business it is much as it used to be. We have a dear Place to live in, and not much Work; tho' I have such a Number of Customers, as would have well supported me 15 Years ago, yet every Thing here being so much raised, whilst our Work is the same, that it will be hard Work to make both Ends meet. Weyman you know is dead: but a young Scotch man has got his Tools and set up here, and tis said, in the Spring will publish a News-paper, I don't know his Capacity, but we shall soon see what it is.[3] Holt yet continues without any Settlement, but I purpose soon to offer him all the Advantages I can, to get him to it, that I may at last settle with Hamilton and Balfour of Edinburgh:[4] I have a hard Trial, but I will Strive to Struggle thro'. Mean while, with all our Respects I am Your most obliged Servant   JAMES PARKER.
To Dr. Franklin

Addressed: For / Dr Benjamin Franklin / Craven-Street / London

From the Selectmen of Boston

LS (incomplete): American Philosophical Society

Between February 16 and 24, 1769, the Selectmen twice exchanged letters with the Governor, Francis Bernard, on the subject of false representations made to London about the riots of the previous year and about the convention held in September to protest the Townshend Acts. One of the Selectmen's letters took specific exception to *ex parte* depositions, which were of course calculated to present the case against the town without possibility of rebuttal. When Bernard refused to give them satis-

3. William Weyman, Parker's former partner, died on July 25, 1768: above, XIV, 322 n; *Pa. Chron.*, July 25–Aug. 1, 1768. For his successors, James and Alexander Robertson, see above, XV, 270.

4. Parker's earlier letters have been full of his troubles with John Holt and his disputed debt to Hamilton and Balfour. In the letter to Balfour just cited (n. 2), he outlined the present situation: he had sold the remaining books at auction for a little more than £40, or about £30 sterling (which he subsequently amended to £25); those he had previously disposed of had brought in £12 to £14; the remainder were Holt's responsibility. Parker had had writs out for him for two years, he told Balfour, and feared Holt would go bankrupt "not only with your Effects but twice as much or more of mine." See also Parker's letters to BF below, March 20, 29.

faction on this or any other point, the Selectmen decided to publish the exchange and to make their side of the case known in England by writing to a number of people there, Franklin among them. On March 13 a town meeting thanked them for doing so.[5] Hence this letter was sent at some time between the beginning of the altercation and the day of the meeting; in accordance with our usual practice we are assigning it to the earliest likely date, which is that of Bernard's reply to the protest about depositions.

[Between February 18 and March 13, 1769]

With respect to depositions taken ex parte, to the prejudice of the town which we apprehend has been a practise here, his Excellency has not thought propper to be explicit in his reply to our address upon that head. 'Tis a proceeding so contrary to the plain rules of law, and the principles of natural Justice, that it must be held in the utmost detestation, and contempt: And we are perswaded that your regard to equity will induce you to emply your influence to prevent any ill consequences, that may arrise to the towns from so illegal and dangerous a practice. This town Sir, professes to be firmly attached to his Majestys person, family and government, A character which we think cannot fairly be impeached: And they have not been inferior to [any] of their fellow subjects in a regard to peace and good order: of all which were they called, we trust they could give satisfactory evidence [to] the world: But they think they have the right of all other subjects to complain and petition when they are aggrieved. Like all true British subjects they have an invinsible attachment to constitutional liberty, and they will always in decency assert it: their attachment to liberty is construed by those who would build their fortune upon its ruin, a spirit of rebellion—Their complaints under grievances and oppression, a contempt of lawful Authority—such colourings have our enemies given to transactions which if impartially, and clearly view'd would appear to be not only innocent but laudable. Hence appears the necessity the town is under of friends on your side of the water to discover the secret machinations of interested and designing men. We desire no friends, but such as are friends of truth and liberty; and as we es-

5. W. H. Whitmore *et al.*, eds., *Reports of the Record Commissioners of the City of Boston* (30 vols., Boston, 1881–1909), [XVI,] 272–3; [XXIII,] 6–9. Copies of the Selectmen's first letter to the Governor and his reply must have been enclosed, for they are among BF's papers.

teem you as such, we beg your attention to our interest and remain
Sir Your Most Obedient humble Servants[6]

JOSHUA HENSHAW
JOSEPH JACKSON
JOHN RUDDOCK
JOHN HANCOCK
SAML. PEMBERTON
HENDERSON INCHES

Benjamin Franklin Esq
Endorsed: Boston

From Moses Franks[7]

ALS: American Philosophical Society

Sir   Great Russel Street Monday 20 feby / 69
I must entreat you to deliver to Mr. Dagge[8] the Account and
Papers relative to the Sufferers by Indian Depredations in 1754.

6. The signers in order of their appearance were: Joshua Henshaw (1703–
77), who served frequently as selectman and justice of the peace between 1752
and 1770, and in 1770–71 was a member of the Governor's Council; Joseph
Jackson (1707–74), a distiller, who had recently been colonel of the Boston
militia regiment; John Ruddock (1713–72), a former shipwright and tax-
collector, who was a leader of the Boston Caucus, the first urban political
machine in America; John Hancock (1737–93), the son of a poor minister, who
had been raised by a wealthy uncle, had recently inherited the richest estate in
Boston, and yet, because of Samuel Adams's influence, favored the popular
party as selectman, representative, and in 1772–74 as a member of the Governor's Council; Samuel Pemberton (1723–79), who was a Mason like Hancock
and Jackson, and served as selectman for four years after 1768; Henderson
Inches (1726–80?), Joseph Jackson's son-in-law, who began his political
career in 1763 as an overseer of the poor and was a selectman for the same four-
year term as Pemberton. For further information see Robert C. Seybolt, *The
Town Officials of Colonial Boston, 1634–1775* (Cambridge, Mass., 1939), pp.
330–63; Lyman H. Butterfield *et al.*, eds., *The Diary and Autobiography of John
Adams* (4 vols., Cambridge, Mass., 1961), I, 238, 270, 333, 343; II, 45–6, 61, 65,
82–93, 135; III, 321–4; *Sibley's Harvard Graduates*, XIII, 325, 416–46; Anne R.
Cunningham, ed., *Letters and Diary of John Rowe, Boston Merchant, 1759–
1762, 1764–1779* (Boston, 1903), pp. 78, 153, 163, 165–6, 172, 187, 192, 196.
7. Moses Franks (1718–89), a merchant in London, was the brother of David
Franks; see above, X, 73 n, 409 n.
8. Henry Dagge became the London lawyer for Trent and Wharton. See
Lewis, *Indiana Co.*, pp. 149–50.

There being particular occasion for them; being requested by the legal representatives of those Sufferers to solicit compensation.[9] You were troubled formerly by Mr. Levy on the subject,[1] and Mr. Dagge having just told me he is to meet you this morning, I would most willingly have done myself the pleasure of attending him but other necessary engagements prevent it. I have the Honor to be, sir Your most Obedient Servant   MOSES FRANKS.

Addressed: To Benjamin Franklin Esqr

To Lord Kames   ALS: Scottish Record Office

My dear Friend   London, Feb. 21. 1769.

I received your excellent Paper on the preferable Use of Oxen in Agriculture, and have put it in the way of being communicated to the Public here.[2] I have observed in America that the Farmers are more thriving in those Parts of the Country where Cattle are used, than in those where the Labour is done by Horses. The latter are said to require twice the Quantity of Land to maintain them, and after all are not good to eat, at least we don't think them so. Here is a Waste of Land that might afford Subsistance for so many more of the human Species. Perhaps it was for this reason that the Hebrew Lawgiver, having promis'd that the Children of Israel should be as numerous as the Sands of the Sea, not only took care to secure the Health of Individuals by regulating their Diet that they might be

9. For the complicated affairs of the "suffering traders" see above, XV, 265 n. Many of the papers relating to their claims were published in Kenneth P. Bailey, *The Ohio Company Papers, 1753–1817* (Arcata, Calif., 1947), pp. 200–20; see also Jack M. Sosin, *Whitehall and the Wilderness . . .* (Lincoln, 1961), pp. 181–2.

1. This may have been Levi Andrew Levy, for whom see above, X, 373 n; he was deeply involved in the affairs of the traders. It may equally well have been Benjamin Levy, one of a Philadelphia group that claimed to be the only legal representatives of the traders, and that had written Moses Franks a few weeks before to offer him, for his services, one-ninth of whatever land might be acquired, Bailey, *op. cit.*, pp. 211–13.

2. BF did not succeed, as far as we have been able to discover, in having the paper published; it presumably became the section on "Farm-Oxen" in Kames's *The Gentleman Farmer: Being an Attempt to Improve Agriculture . . .* (Edinburgh, 1776).

fitter for Procreation, but also forbid their using Horses, as those Animals would lessen the Quantity of Subsistence for Men. Thus we find, that when they took any Horses from their Enemies, they destroy'd them; and in the Commandments, where the Labour of the Ox and the Ass is mention'd and forbidden on the Sabbath, there is no mention of the Horse, probably because they were to have none.[3] And by the great Armies suddenly rais'd in that small Territory they inhabited it appears to have been very full of People.

Food is *always* necessary to *all*, and much the greatest Part of the Labour of Mankind is employ'd in raising Provisions for the Mouth. Is not this kind of Labour therefore the fittest to be the Standard by which to measure the Values of all other Labour, and consequently of all other Things whose Value depends on the Labour of making or procuring them? May not even Gold and Silver be thus valued. If the Labour of the Farmer in producing a Bushel of Wheat be equal to the Labour of the Miner in producing an Ounce of Silver, will not the Bushel of Wheat just measure the Value of the Ounce of Silver?[4] The Miner must eat, the Farmer indeed can live without the Silver, and so perhaps will have some Advantage in settling the Price. But these Discussions I leave to you as more able to manage them. Only I will send you a little Scrap I wrote sometime since on the Laws prohibiting foreign Commodities.[5]

I congratulate you on your Election as President of your Edinburgh Society. I think I formerly took Notice to you in Conversation, that I thought there had been some Similarity in our Fortunes, and the Circumstances of our Lives. This is a fresh Instance; for by Letters just received, I find that I was about the same time chosen

3. BF is apparently importing his own ideas into the Old Testament. It contains no prohibition on the use of horses but, on the contrary, abounds in chariots and mounted men. Although Joshua did once hamstring the mounts of his defeated enemies, on instructions from the Lord (Jos. 11:6–9), this shows nothing about the Hebrews' attitude. See the famous paean to the horse in Job 39:19–25.

4. BF is here repeating, almost verbatim, the labor theory of value that he had paraphrased from Sir William Petty forty years before. See above, I, 149. He subsequently elaborated his ideas for public consumption in "Positions to Be Examined," for which see below, April 4.

5. Probably a copy of his "Note Respecting Trade and Manufactures" above, XIV, 211–12.

President of our American Philosophical Society established at Philadelphia.[6]

I have sent by Sea to the Care of Mr. Alexander a little Box containing a few of the late Edition of my Books for my Friends in Scotland.[7] One is directed for you, and one for your Society, which I beg that you and they would accept as a small Mark of my Respect. With the sincerest Esteem and Regard, I am, my dear Friend, Yours most affectionately   B Franklin

p.s. I am sorry my Letter of 1767, concerning the American Dispute, miscarried.[8] I now send you a Copy of it from my Book. The Examination mention'd in it, you have probably seen. Things daily wear a worse Aspect, and tend more and more to a Breach and final Separation.

Lord Kaims

From John Foxcroft[9]   ALS: American Philosophical Society

Dear Sir   Williamsbg. Febry 21st. 1769

Immediately on my receiving your favour by the Genl. Gage Captain Kemble (enclosing me Mr. Todds Letter Signifying to me that their Lordships had been pleased to grant me leave of absence for a few Months) I set out for this Colony, in order to put the Riders on such a footing that no stopages might happen during my absence, which I think I have Effectually done; and at the same time, have by this new Regulation, Saved near One Hundred Pounds per Annum to the Revenue, in the Riding work between this place and Annapolis, a perticular Account of which I shall lay before you when we meet. You have my Dear Sir laid me under an

6. Kames had just been elected president of the Philosophical Society of Edinburgh; see Alexander F. Tytler, Lord Woodhouselee, *Memoirs of the Life and Writings of the Honourable Henry Home of Kames* . . . (3 vols., Edinburgh, 1814), I, 256–9; II, 116. For BF's election to the presidency of the newly resurrected American Philosophical Society see above, XV, 261–2.

7. For Robert Alexander, Edinburgh merchant and banker, see above, VIII, 444 n. The box contained copies of the fourth edition of BF's *Exper. and Obser.*, which had appeared in January; see above, XV, 293 n.

8. See above, XIV, 62–71.

9. Joint deputy postmaster general, with BF, for the northern district of North America.

additional obligation in the part you have taken in obtaining me leave to visit my Native Country for the last time, if it please God I arrive safe, and am bless'd with a sight of an Aged Parent which I have not seen for upwards of Sixteen Years I can quit England and spend the Remainder of my Days in America very happily.

I am a good deal Uneasy at present on finding by Mr. Todds Letter of Novr. 2d. which I received from Philada. by the last Post that I have fallen under the Displeasure of our Honoured Masters, occasion'd by my writing to Mr. Colden at New York that I could not agree to the Packett's sailing before Her usual Day, and that if She was dispatch'd it must be at his own perrill. It was certainly an Errour of Judgement in me, and the good of the Revenue was the sole motive of my writing that Letter to Mr. Colden. I got Mr. Coldens Letter (giving an Account that the Genl. had order'd the Packet to Sail on Monday Morning) on Saturday Night a little after Eleven o Clock on Sunday Morning I had many Applications from different Merchants that the Packet might not Sail untill Her usual Day, which as well as I can remember was about Eight or Ten Days to it—and on my having recourse to the Secretarys Letter to us of the 12th. of March 1763 I thought and so did one or two of your Friends that the Genl. had nothing to do with the Packets in time of Peace; and I was very sure that not one Letter, could possibly go by Her from the Southard of New York; was She to sail agreeable to the Generals orders.[1]

I hope my Dear Friend that you will be able to prevent any disagreable consequences taking place from this unfortunate mistake and that if you are apprehensive of such a thing, that you would give my Brother timely Information that He may use his Intrest with His Friends on the Occasion.[2] Perhaps I may be able on my

1. Gage's orders for the packet to sail had been in letters to Alexander Colden, the New York postmaster, on Sept. 24 and 26, 1768. Anthony Todd, the secretary of the Post Office, had told Foxcroft in a letter of Nov. 2 that his objections had been overruled at home; and on Nov. 15 Hillsborough had told Gage the same thing. Carter, ed., *Gage Correspondence*, II, 78 n. 4, 79–80. Foxcroft was on firm ground, nevertheless, for Todd's letter in 1763 had assured him and BF that in time of peace the packets were solely under the direction of the Post Office and not subject to orders from the Commander in Chief. Above, x, 218.

2. The only brother of whom we have record is Thomas, who had arrived in Philadelphia from England in 1765 and become postmaster there in the following year. Above, x, 77. Why he should have had more influential friends than

coming over to set the Matter in a fairer light to their Lordships[3] than it stands at present.

I had a Letter from Philada. by the last post your Family was well, I shall set out on my return in a few Days, and purpose embarking from philada. or New York the begining of April. I am and ever shall be my Dear Friend yours most affectionately

JOHN FOXCROFT

To Ben: Franklin Esqr.

To Jane Mecom

ALS: American Philosophical Society

Dear Sister,   London, Feb. 23. 1769

I have received your kind Letters of Sept. 26. Oct. and Nov. 7.[4] That of Sept. 26. is directed to my Wife, but she sent it to me, I suppose that I might see your Opinion of Mr. Bache: I am glad you approve the Choice they have made. I write a few Lines to Mr. Leadly: I cannot say much on that Subject till I see Mr. Foxcroft, whom I now expect daily.[5] I am glad Major Small call'd on you. He is a Man I much esteem, as I do his Brother with whom I am intimately acquainted here.[6] My best Respects to him.

Your Political Disputes I have no Objection to if they are carried on with tolerable Decency, and do not become outrageously abusive. They make People acquainted with their Rights and the Value of them. But your Squabbles about a Bishop I wish to see speedily ended. They seem to be unnecessary at present, as the Design of sending one is dropt; and if it were not dropt, I cannot think it a matter of such Moment as to be a sufficient Reason for Division

---

John, and how BF was supposed to know who they were, are questions that we cannot answer.

3. Le Despencer and Sandwich, the Postmasters General.

4. Only the letter of Nov. 7 has survived: above, XV, 263.

5. Hugh Ledlie, a soldier, police officer, and land speculator, often lodged with Jane when in Boston. He was trying to promote a new road from Hartford to Boston. Carl Van Doren, *Jane Mecom* ... (New York, 1950), p. 46, and *Franklin-Mecom*, p. 108. The road was of obvious interest to the Post Office, and was presumably what BF expected to discuss with Foxcroft when the latter arrived in England on leave.

6. Major John Small was with the British troops who had arrived in Boston the previous autumn. His brother Alexander was an army surgeon living in London. *Ibid.*; above, IX, 110 n; XII, 42 n.

among you, when there never was more need of your being united. I do not conceive that "Bishops residing" in America, would either be of such Advantage to Episcopalians, or such Disadvantage to Anti-episcopalians as either seems to imagine.[7] Each Party abuses the other, the Profane and the Infidel believe both sides, and enjoy the Fray; the Reputation of Religion in general suffers, and its Enemies are ready to say, not what was said in the primitive Times, *Behold how these Christians love one another*,[8] but, *Mark how these Christians* HATE *one another!* Indeed when religious People quarrel about Religion, or hungry People about their Victuals, it looks as if they had not much of either among them.

The Money you sent Mrs. Stevenson by Capt. Foulger came safe to hand.[9] You have given no fresh Orders for Goods, or she would have comply'd with them. And she does not care to send any on her own Guess, especially as the late Proceedings here against America, may possibly strengthen the Resolutions of your People against wearing the Trumpery Finery of this Country, and make such Goods as *you* us'd to write for (if *Goods* they may be called) unsaleable. But as I had before discharg'd your Account for you, you may look on this Money as so much of yours in her Hands, and order it in what you please.

You will see by the inclos'd that your Town and Province has still some Friends in P——t.[1] But their Endeavours have hitherto been attended with little Success. My best Wishes attend you, being ever Your affectionate Brother   B FRANKLIN

7. The campaign for a resident colonial episcopate, which aroused such fears and antagonism in other denominations, was based in part on practical considerations. In the absence of an American bishop all those seeking ordination had to go to England, which not only involved time and expense but also, when the candidates were unknown in London, often precluded careful scrutiny of their qualifications. For an example of what could happen in consequence see the case of George Spencer above, xv, 199 n. The tone of BF's comments to Jane strengthens the suggestion, implicit in his recommending Spencer, that he paid little attention to the quality of Episcopal clergymen.

8. Tertullian, *Apologeticus*, c. 39.

9. For Timothy Folger, the Nantucket ship captain and BF's first cousin twice removed, see above, xv, 223 n, 246–7.

1. BF presumably enclosed a copy of the speech by Thomas Pownall, former governor of Massachusetts, in the House of Commons on Jan. 26. Pownall had the speech privately printed and gave BF some copies; see BF to Galloway below, March 9.

P.S. There has lately been a new Edition of my philosophical Papers here. I send Six Copies to you, which I desire you would take care to have delivered as directed.[2] There is one for your Trouble.

To Samuel Cooper[3]   ALS: British Museum

Dear Sir,   London, Feb. 24. 1769

I received your Favour by Mr. Jefferies.[4] I should have been glad if in any thing I could have serv'd him here. The Part I took in the Application for your Degree,[5] was merely doing Justice to Merit, which is the Duty of an honest Man whenever he has the Opportunity. I did that Duty indeed with Pleasure and Satisfaction to myself, which was sufficient: But I own the Pleasure is greatly increas'd by finding that you are so good as to accept my Endeavours kindly.

I was about to return home last Summer, and had some Thoughts of doing it by way of Boston; but the untoward Situation of American Affairs here, induc'd my Friends to advise my staying another Winter. I should have been happy in doing any Service to our Country. The Tide is yet strong against us; and our Endeavours to turn it have hitherto had but little Effect. But it must turn; if your frugal and industrious Resolutions continue. Your old Governor Mr. Pownall appears a warm and zealous Friend to the Colonies in

2. The fourth edition of *Exper. and Obser.* One copy was for Harvard, one for John Winthrop, and one for James Bowdoin. Jane's copy, the only book of hers that has survived, eventually belonged to Carl Van Doren: *Franklin-Mecom*, p. 108.

3. The Rev. Samuel Cooper, minister of the Brattle Square Church in Boston from 1743 till his death in 1783, took a keen interest in politics. See above, IV, 69 n.

4. John Jeffries (1745–1819), the son of the town treasurer of Boston, had been practicing medicine there since 1766, and had come to England—apparently with a letter of introduction from Cooper to BF—to pursue his studies. He received his M.D. from Aberdeen in 1769, became a surgeon in the British navy and then army, and in later life was an ardent balloonist. After his Channel crossing by balloon in Jan., 1785, he dined with BF at Passy. *Sibley's Harvard Graduates*, XV, 419–20; *DAB*.

5. See above, XIV, 218–19.

Parliament, but unfortunately he is very ill-heard at present.[6] I have been in constant pain since I heard of Troops assembling at Boston, lest the Madness of Mobs or the Insolence of Soldiers, or both, should, when too near each other, occasion some Mischief difficult to be prevented or repaired, and which might spread far and wide. I hope, however that Prudence will predominate and keep all quiet.

A great Cause between the City of London and the Dissenters was decided here the Year before last, in the House of Lords; no Account of it has been printed but one having been taken in Writing, I obtain'd a Copy of it, which I send you supposing it may afford you [and] your Friends some Pleasure.[7]

Please to present my respectful Compliments to Mrs. Cooper and to Mr. Bowdoin[8] when you see him. With sincere and great Esteem, I am, Reverend and dear Sir, Your affectionate and most obedient humble Servant   B FRANKLIN

Revd Dr. Cooper

Endorsed: From D. Franklin By Capt Freeman.[9]
Receiv'd Apr. 19. –69.

6. The resolutions were of course those for nonimportation; Thomas Pownall's position had been expressed in a number of speeches in the House of Commons, most recently on Feb. 8.

7. The case of Allan (or Allen) Evans was important in the history of dissent. The Corporation of London passed a bylaw whereby anyone nominated to a civic office who declined to run for election was subject to a heavy fine. The Lord Mayor then nominated dissenters, who paid the fine rather than plead nonconformity, which was still held to be a crime under the Test Act. Evans refused to pay. The case was carried on appeal to the House of Lords, which after an eloquent speech by Lord Mansfield pronounced nonconformity to be no crime. The legal position of a dissenter who accepted any one of a great variety of offices remained, nevertheless, highly unsatisfactory. See Anthony Lincoln, *Some Political & Social Ideas of English Dissent, 1763–1800* (Cambridge, 1938), pp. 45–6, 240–1.

8. For a brief biographical sketch of James Bowdoin see above, IV, 69 n.

9. Presumably not Isaac Freeman, BF's and Jane Mecom's friend, whose death in the Grenadines was reported in the *Boston Chron.*, March 6–9, 1769, but another Freeman, whose arrival from London was noted in *ibid.*, April 23–24, 1769.

Draft of a Petition from the Colonial Agents to the House of Commons

Copy: Charles Garth Letterbook, South Carolina Archives Department

The fate of the petition that follows illustrates the difficult position of the colonial agents. In the late winter they had, or thought they had, indications that the mounting excitement in America might induce the administration to repeal the Townshend Acts if there were some way to cover its retreat. The problem was to find a basis for repeal that was acceptable to both sides: the government clearly would not concede the claim of the colonies that Parliament had no right to tax them; would the colonists settle for anything less than this concession? The agents hoped that the issue could be obscured if they petitioned for repeal on other grounds, and they deputed to Franklin the delicate task of drawing up a document that would give the ministry an excuse to act and yet would not antagonize their American constituents. He composed a brief draft that neither asserted nor denied the colonial claim of right, although it contained a few words implying, he thought, that the right existed. The agents at first approved his draft, and then at a later meeting had second thoughts. The attitude of the administration seemed to them to be hardening, so that the small chance of success was decreasing. Many of them had come to doubt, furthermore, that their constituents would countenance any move that seemed to withdraw from the assertion of right.[1] The upshot was that they dropped the whole idea. The episode reveals how little they could now do to bridge the widening gap between the colonies and the mother country.

[Between February 24 and March 7, 1769[2]]
The Petition of the Agents of the Plantations and Colonies of the Massachusets Bay, Rhode Island, Connecticut, New York, New Jersey Pennsylvania, the Counties of New Castle, Kent and Sussex upon Delaware, Virginia, Maryland, South Carolina and Georgia, whose Names are hereunto subscribed.
Humbly Sheweth
That the Act of Parliament passed in the Seventh Year of His

1. See BF to Galloway below, March 9.
2. The colonial agents held three meetings on this draft petition. The first, on Feb. 24, authorized Franklin to draw it up; the second discussed it; the third, on March 7, rejected it. Although it was finished before March 7, we have been unable to date the second meeting and thereby narrow the period of possible composition.

present Majesty's Reign. "for granting certain Duties in the British Colonies and Plantations in America &c." is complained of as an Aggrievance by the Inhabitants of the said Colonies, for the following *among other* Reasons.[3]

FIRST, for that the said Duties are made payable only in Silver Money, which in some of the Colonies is not to be had in sufficient Quantity, whereby the Merchant is discouraged from dealing in Commodities that expose him to such Difficulty, and in most of the Colonies the Current Proportion of Silver Money is so exceeding small and so absolutely necessary for the Trade of the Country, more especially since the Restrictions laid here upon their Paper Currency, that the Collecting the Silver in Duties and carrying it away, disturbs and obstructs the common Course of Commerce, and greatly distresses all concerned in Trade.

SECONDLY. for that the appropriation by the Act of the Money to be raised, vizt. "for making a more certain and adequate Provision for the Charge of the Administration of Justice, and the support of Civil Government in such of the said Colonies and Plantations where it shall be found necessary" appears inequitable and unjust; all of the Old Colonies, each for itself, having from their Infancy provided, and continuing to provide, for the Charge of the Administration of Justice, and the support of civil Government without any Expence to the Crown, or to any neighbouring Colony, and yet by the Operation of this Act, they are moreover to be burthened with the payment of great Salaries to public Officers, in new Provinces wherein they have no Concern.

The Petitioners therefore, and because the said Act hath occasioned great Discontents in the Colonies, and much ill Humour between the Inhabitants of Great-Britain and them, which if continued, may be prejudicial to their mutual Commerce and Common Interest, do pray that the said Act may be Repealed.

And your Petitioners as in Duty bound &ca.

To the Honorable the Commons House of Great Britain in Parliament Assembled.

3. BF's remark in his letter to Galloway (cited in n. 1), that "I used some Words that should imply what they would not allow us to mention," must apply to this seemingly innocuous phrase.

From Joseph Priestley

ALS: American Philosophical Society

Dear Sir   Leeds 24 Feb 1769.
  I sincerely ask your pardon for the trouble I gave you with my last. The dedication was written, and sent to you, before I had taken time to reflect upon it.[4] I shall confine myself to the *inscription* I first proposed, and shall be obliged to you if you will throw the *dedication* into the fire without showing it to any person whatever. I am, Dear Sir your most obliged humble Servant   J PRIESTLEY

Addressed: To | Doctor Franklin | at Mrs Stephenson's Craven-Street | in the Strand | London

From Joseph-Étienne Bertier[5]

ALS: American Philosophical Society

Monsieur   à Paris ce 27 fev. 1769
  Vous m'avéz fait grand plaisir de m'adresser M. le Capitaine Houry.[6] Vous m'avéz donné l'occasion de vous marquer ma reconnoissance, mon attachement, et mon estime, et de rendre les services dont je suis capable à un homme de merite, et bien aimable. Pour couroner l'oeuvre, il faudroit faire encore un voyage en france. C'est votre pays autant que l'Angleterre, vous y seriés au milieu des franklinistes. Un Père est dans son pays, quand ce pays est habité par ses enfans. Continués, je vous en prie, de m'adresser des gens de merite, et de m'honorer de vos commissions. Je suis avec respect votre très humble et obeissant serviteur
                                    BERTIER FRANKLINISTE

J'etois frankliniste sans le savoir, maintenant que je le sais je ne manqueray pas de citer l'auteur de ma secte Monsieur.

Endorsed: Pere Berthier Paris

4. Of Priestley's earlier letter only the concluding lines survive, as noted above under Feb. 14. Among his many publications in 1769 we have been unable to locate any that contains an "inscription," let alone a dedication, with which BF might have been concerned. We therefore have no idea what Priestley was talking about.
5. For Père Bertier see above, XV, 33.
6. For Lewis Ourry and his visit to Paris see BF to LeRoy above, Jan. 31.

To Deborah Franklin
ALS: American Philosophical Society

My dear Child,   London, March 1. 1769

I received yours of Jan. 3. per Packet, and one from Sally. I wrote to you very fully by the late Ships. This is only to let you know I am well, and particularly that my Arms, which you enquire after, have perfectly recover'd their Strength. Your Account of Mr. Coleman's fresh Disorder, grieves me exceedingly.[7] I have had a Visit from Mr. Bache's Sister, who appears a very agreable, genteel, sensible young Woman.[8] My Love to Sally and our other Children. Remember me affectionately to Mr. Rhoads, Roberts[9] and other Friends. Send word to Billy that I have receiv'd his Letter of Jan. 4. which I shall answer fully per Sparks. I am as ever, my dear Debby, Your affectionate Husband   B FRANKLIN

I received Sally's little Letter with yours and enclose one from Miss Bache for her.

Addressed: To / Mrs Franklin / Philadelphia / via N York / per Packet / B Free Franklin

From James Parker
ALS: American Philosophical Society

Honoured Sir   Newyork. March 1. 1769

By Mrs. Franklin's Desire, I now send by this Opportunity, two small Kegs of Keskatomas Nuts,[1] one is a Firkin the other a small Quarter Cask: They contain very near a Bushel and a half. I hope they may come safe and sound to your Hands: As I have been now a great while confined by the Gout, I could not go out about them; but as the Second Mate, is a near Neighbour's Son, and long Ac-

7. Judge William Coleman, BF's old friend, had come to England in the spring of 1768 for an operation, apparently for cancer, and had returned in the autumn; he died on Jan. 11, 1769. See above, XV, 139, 174 n.

8. Richard Bache had several sisters, one of whom, Martha, was living with her mother in Preston, Lancs., a few years later: Mrs. Mary Bache to BF, Feb. 5, 1772, APS.

9. For Samuel Rhoads and Hugh Roberts see above, respectively, II, 406 n; V, 11 n.

1. Hickory nuts.

quaintance, I have committed them to his Care, and he is a worthy young Man.

The Packet's Letters may probably reach you before this, as she is to be discharged three Days hence: As your Business so engages all your Attention, that I presume not to hope the Pleasure of any Letters from you, not having had one these many Months; I will not intrude farther on your Time, than just to add, humble Complements from Your most obliged Servant   JAMES PARKER.

PS. I sent a 2d Bill of a Set of Ex[change] by Capt. Arnold to you about 10 Days ago, the first of which I sent to Mr. Foxcroft, who is gone down to Virginia, I have not received the Third. It was from Mr. Hubbart for £60 Sterl. some Shillings.[2] And I shall send by the Packet A Bill for £100 Sterl. more, which I have just received: Would have sent one of them now, but have received only one of the Set yet.

Addressed: For / Dr Benjamin Franklin / Craven Street / London / Per Capt. Kemble / Newspapers

From William Franklin   ALS: American Philosophical Society

Honored Father,   Burlington March 2d. 1769
The Mail which [left?] England in December is arriv'd, but I have not [heard?] from you, nor had I one by the November Mail. I apprehend that it must be owing either to the Letters being detain'd at the Post Office in London, or else to their being intercepted by some impertinently curious Person between New-York and here. At first I was apprehensive that you might be indisposed, and not able to write, but I have just had the Pleasure of hearing from Mr. Galloway that he has receiv'd a Letter from you by the last Mail.[3] Perhaps Lord H. may have given Orders to the Postmasters General to stop your Letters to me, for I have heard from good Authority, that Secretarys of State frequently do things of [this?] kind, which occasion'd me to write *Office Account* [in the?] Manner I did upon a Cover of the Packet I sent you in January—in hopes that, if it was stopt, they would, upon seeing that Indorsement, ex-

2. The sentence refers to the second bill; see Parker to BF above, Feb. 17.
3. See BF to Galloway above, Jan. 9.

amine no further. My Packet of London Chronicles which came by the two last Mails were both broke open and several of them stole, which I think must have been done either by the Posts or Postmasters between this and New York, and possibly your Letters, if you wrote any to me, are gone the same Way. Should this be the Case, it would be best for the future, when you write to me by the Packet, to enclose your Letter to Parker, or Colden, and desire him to send it under a Cover of his own directed to the Postmaster at Burlington.[4]

I sent you a Copy of Lord H—'s last Letter to me, No. 16, by Mr. Wharton, and I now send you a Duplicate of it, and of my Answer; the latter of which, if you have no Objection to it, please to fo[r-ward in] any way you think proper to his Lordship. If you receiv'd and altered the Original perhaps it may not be necessary to send a Duplicate.[5] I have receiv'd no Letters from him since the above-mentioned. I likewise send a short one to him (No. 16) which should be seal'd and forwarded.

Nothing new of a public Nature has occurr'd since my last, except what you will see in the Papers. The Boston People continue their Attacks on Governor B[ernar]d and the Commissioners and have lately begun, in their *Journal of Occurrences*,[6] to attack the Military, which seems very impolitic, (as the Officers are as little fond of the Governor as the Bostonians themselves are) and probably will be productive of some ill Blood among them.

The Piece sign'd *Francis Lynn*, in Answer to Crawley's Letter is much admir'd,[7] and has been reprinted, I believe, in all the Papers on the Continent. Every Body attributes it to you, and some have had Sagacity enough to discover that the Signature is a Pun

4. WF was invoking the aid of officialdom: James Parker was comptroller and secretary of the Post Office for the northern district, and Alexander Colden was the New York postmaster.

5. For WF's remarkable arrangement to have his official correspondence edited by his father see above, p. 36.

6. A daily account of happenings in Boston, Sept. 28, 1768, to Aug. 1, 1769, probably written by Samuel Adams, Samuel Cooper, Benjamin Edes, and other radicals. It was sent to local newspapers and those in New York and Philadelphia, and reprinted elsewhere in America and in England. See Oliver M. Dickerson, ed., *Boston under Military Rule*... (Boston, [1936]), *passim*; Philip Davidson, *Propaganda and the American Revolution, 1763–1783* (Chapel Hill, N.C., 1941), pp. 236–7.

7. See "Reply to Thomas Crowley" above, xv, 238–41.

on the real Name of the Author. I fancy Mr. Crawley will not be fond of continuing the Correspondence.

I lately saw at a Gentleman's House, Priestly History of Electricity, in which very honorable Mention is made of your Experiments:[8] Pray who is Dr. Priestly. I find he writes upon a great Variety of Subjects, and as far as I can judge from some Extracts which I have seen in the Reviews, &c he seems a Man of great Ability. A new Edition of your Experiments is advertised, with Corrections and Additions, which I long much to see.[9] It is surprizing how you could find Time to attend to T[hings?] of that Nature a[mid all?] your Hurry of public Business, and Variety of other Engagements.

I have employ'd a good deal of my Time lately in reading Books of Husbandry, as I am soon to be put in Possession of my Farm; and I have engaged an English Farmer to act as Overseer, who is strongly recommended to me as a Person every way qualified for that Employment. The worst on it is, that he has no Knowledge of the Drill or New Husbandry[1] (as it is called) which, from some Trials lately made, promises to succeed well in America. I have a first Vol. of Mills's Husbandry belonging to you, and I have a Notion that you had one or more Volumes of that Work, and lent them to Mr. Bartram, but am not certain.[2] I understand that there are in all 5 Volumes of that Work, and should be glad to have them complete, as they are said to contain almost all that is valuable in the best Books on the Subject. If there is any Likelihood of their being a Second Edition publish'd soon, I would rather wait for that, as new Discoveries and Improvements in Agriculture are making every Day. I send you enclosed a List of several other Books, which

8. Joseph Priestley, *The History and Present State of Electricity* (London, 1767).

9. BF could scarcely have neglected to send WF a copy of *Exper. and Obser.* (4th ed., London, 1769), which he had broadcast among his friends; see above, XV, 293.

1. Drill husbandry involved the use of a machine for digging holes or furrows in which the seed was planted. The first such machine that was practical had been invented by Jethro Tull early in the century, but drilling had not yet become popular except in planting turnip seeds. See Mabel E. Seebohm Christie, *The Evolution of the English Farm* (London, [1927]), pp. 304, 308–9.

2. For John Bartram, the Quaker farmer and botanist, see above, II, 378 n. The work that he had supposedly borrowed was a massive one: John Mills, *A New and Complete System of Practical Husbandry*... (5 vols., London, 1762–65).

I shall be much oblig'd to you, if you would purchase for me, and charge to my Account.

In the Gentleman's Magazine for Janry. 1767, is a Description of a new invented Plough for Cutting Trenches and making Drains; for the constructing of which the Inventor receiv'd a Premium of 50 Guineas from the Society for the Encouragement of Arts. There are likewise some Improvements in it proposed by the Editor of the Magazine, which make it a much more simple Instrument. A Plough of this kind would be one of the most useful Things that could be introduced int[o this? cou]ntry, where Labor is so dear. I wish you would make some Enquiry concerning it, and if you think it will answer have one constructed in the best Manner for me, and sent over.[3] Perhaps some farther Improvements may occur to you, or some of your Friends, on seeing it.

Pray what is become of the Machine for Pulling [stumps] by the Roots. Was it ever so improv'd in England as to answer the Purpose? I have some Thoughts of trying whether I can't pull them down by applying the Power of a Screw, such as they have in the Timber Wheels in Philadelphia. I have likewise thought of a Windlas, and have had the Model of one made, on a new Construction, the Axis turning in a Gudgeon like that of a Wheelbarrow, whereby the Friction is much less than in the common Way; but I think if [I can] contrive a Method of fixing the Screw, so that I can turn it with Levers, I shall be able to exert a much greater Force. Had I your Genius for Mechanics I should not doubt of Success. I likewise want a good Hand-Mill, and should be glad to know whether any of those communicated to the Society of Arts are got into general Use?[4]

3. See *Gent. Mag.*, XXXVII (1767), 25–6, and for the Society for the Encouragement of Arts, Manufactures, and Commerce above, VI, 186–9. The inventor was Cuthbert Clarke, who subsequently published works on agriculture and mechanics. *DNB*. BF acted promptly on his son's request: his Journal contains an entry on May 15 of £7 10s. for a plough for WF.

4. The Royal Society of Arts had offered a prize for an efficient handmill, with which poor families could grind their own grain; between 1757 and 1761 a number of awards were made. See William Bailey, *The Advancement of Arts, Manufactures, and Commerce*... (2 vols., London, 1776–79), I, 175–8; and Derek Hudson and Kenneth W. Luckhurst, *The Royal Society of Arts, 1754–1954* (London, [1954]), pp. 110–11. BF spent £5 5s. for a handmill for WF; Journal, July 11, 1769.

I make no Apology for troubling you with Things of this Nature, as I know you love to encourage whatever has a useful Tendency.

Young Dunlap has publish'd an Edition of the *Sermons to Asses*, and to give them a Sale, has had the Impudence to attribute them to you. I am told Mein the Bookseller at Boston has done the same.[5]

I send you enclosed one of Mr. Odell's Poems on Liberty.[6]

If Mr. Wharton is arriv'd, please to acquaint him that I have lately wrote to him via Bristol.[7]

Betsy sends her Duty; and desires to know if you receiv'd a Letter from her during my Absence? I am always Honored Sir, Your dutiful and obliged Son   WM. FRANKLIN

From James Parker   ALS: American Philosophical Society

[March 4, 1769. Repeats the substance of his letters of February 17 and March 1, printed above. Adds that he has received another bill of exchange from Postmaster Hubbart for £100, drawn by Nathaniel Rogers[8] on a London merchant. The worst of the winter was in February, which is unusual. He hopes his gout will not lose him his place.]

To Joseph Galloway   LS: Clements Library

Dear Sir   London March 9. 1769
    I wrote a few Lines to you per Packet, in which I mention'd that at a late Meeting of the Agents they had agreed to join in a Petition

5. *Sermons for Asses*, a satirical work by James Murray (1732–82), was first published in London in 1768. For Dunlap (1747–1812) see *DAB*; he was the nephew of William Dunlap, the printer-turned-postmaster-turned-cleric, for whom see above, XIII, 84–7, 176. WF was right about Mein, the printer of the *Boston Chron.*, which in its issue of June 13–20, 1768, attributed the first sermon to BF. For this skillful and combative Tory journalist see John Alden, "John Mein: Scourge of Patriots," Col. Soc. of Mass. *Publications*, XXXIV (1942), 571–99.

6. For a biographical sketch of WF's rector at Burlington see above, XIII, 508 n. The sketch does not mention Odell's greatest claim to fame in later years, which was as a Tory satirist in verse. We have not found that he had published anything as early as 1769; he may have been only beginning to try his poetical wings.

7. For Samuel Wharton's visit to England see above, p. 38 n.

8. For Rogers see BF to Winthrop below, March 11.

for the Repeal of the Duty Act. I was desir'd to make a Draft, which I did. The Proposition came from Mr. Garth, who is a Member of Parliament and Agent for S. Carolina.[9] The Opinion was that the Ministry might probably wish to get rid of that Act if they had a fair Opportunity given them; that they could not do it on any of the Petitions that had been offer'd, because those Petitions denied the Right of Parliament and therefore could not be receiv'd: And if we were to petition, giving other Reasons, our Petition must be receiv'd, and would give Government an Opening to relieve itself and America if so disposed. I accordingly drew a Petition of which I send you the Copy, wherein, tho' we did not mention the Right, we avoided saying anything that might be construed as a Relinquishing of it; and I used some Words that should imply what they would not allow us to mention.[1] The Draft was approv'd at our next Meeting by all present; but two being absent it was agreed to shew it to them before we proceeded farther, and to meet again as last Tuesday.[2] At this Meeting their Minds began to change, from an Apprehension that their Constituents might think the not mentioning the Right was a tacit relinquishing of it, and be offended with them for taking such a Step;[3] and that even Government here might pretend so to construe it. After debating it some time, and one declaring that his Instructions were express not to ask for a Repeal on any other Foundation than the Incompetency of the Right, it was found that no one car'd to sign it unless it was to be sign'd by all; and being besides assur'd that the Ministry were absolutely determin'd to do nothing farther in the Affairs of America this Session, we broke up, concluding to drop the Petition. Mr. Jackson

---

9. For Charles Garth, the agent for the Maryland assembly as well as for South Carolina, see above, XII, 30 n; Kammen, *Rope of Sand, passim.* The idea of petitioning for repeal of the Townshend Acts was first considered at a meeting of the agents on Feb. 24; see BF's draft of the petition above under that date.

1. The implication was, to put it mildly, well veiled: *ibid.*

2. *I.e.,* March 7, the third meeting; the second we have been unable to date.

3. The agents' fears were amply borne out in the case of Charles Garth, who had suggested the move. When the Commons House of South Carolina heard what he had proposed, it voted unanimously to disapprove it and to express its shock that he had considered consenting to a proposal that did not expressly assert the colony's right to be taxed only by its own representatives. Joseph W. Barnwell, ed., "Garth Correspondence," *South Carolina Hist. and Geneal. Mag.,* XXXI (1930), 59–60.

however privately told me, he intended to move for the Repeal in the House on the Grounds of the Petition, tho he had no Prospect of Success; but it would give an Opportunity for some Debates which might be of Use.[4]

Gov. Pownall has taken the Part of being a warm Friend for the Colonies in Parliament. I sent you with the Votes his Speech against the Resolutions: He had it printed to communicate privately to his Friends among the Members, that they might see what they could not hear; for the Court Party kept a continual Talk during the whole time of his Speaking, to prevent his being heard. He has given me some Copies, and I send you herewith another. If it should be publish'd with you, his Name must not be mention'd.[5]

On the whole it is my clear Opinion that nothing will bring on a Change of Measures here but our unanimous Resolution to consume no more of their Goods, while these Acts are continued: We mention'd but one in the Petition, leaving the other for a future Attempt, as apprehending we might by asking too much at once fail of getting anything. If our People enter into such Engagements, I could wish it were not among the Members only, but all the Inhabitants. The Clamours of the Manufacturers here are the most likely thing to bring the American Minister to his Senses.[6] But

4. Richard Jackson, M.P. for New Romney and BF's co-agent for Pennsylvania, apparently decided against raising the issue himself. When Gov. Pownall tried unsuccessfully in April to secure a debate on repeal, Jackson supported him in a brief speech that is the last he is known to have made on the American question. Namier and Brooke, *House of Commons*, II, 671.

5. The speech of Jan. 26 in which Pownall attacked the resolutions, introduced by Hillsborough in the House of Lords the month before, that were under debate in the House of Commons. No copy of this printing seems to have survived. Pownall made a second speech, on Feb. 8, on a somewhat different aspect of the American question. The two speeches were subsequently run together and printed in London as a single pamphlet, without place, date, or sign of authorship to avoid the Parliamentary ban on the publication of debates; there is considerable evidence that BF had William Strahan print this pamphlet for him. Crane, *Letters to the Press*, xlix–l; Thomas R. Adams, *American Independence, the Growth of an Idea* (Providence, R.I., 1965), pp. 54–5. The combined speeches, by then identified as a single one, were reprinted in America in April and May in the *Boston Chron.* and the *Pa. Chron.*, and as a separate pamphlet in Boston.

6. Complaints about the decline in American trade and the consequent threat of unemployment at home had recently come from London, Southwark,

whether the Acts are ever repeal'd or not, the Frugality and Industry will work greatly to our Advantage, and make Money plenty among us, tho we should never be allow'd to issue Paper. I am Dear Sir Your most obedient humble Servant   B FRANKLIN

In Franklin's hand: I have been oblig'd by Hurry to make use of Help in Copying. But it is a faithful trusty Hand, tho' not a neat one.   B F.

Jos. Galloway, Esqr

To John Winthrop   ALS: American Philosophical Society

Dear Sir,   London, March 11. 1769
At length after much Delay and Difficulty I have been able to obtain your Telescope that was made by Mr. Short before his Death. His Brother, who succeeds in the Business, has fitted it up and compleated it. He has followed the Business many Years at Edinburgh, is reckon'd very able, and therefore I hope every thing will be found right; but as it is only just finish'd, I have no time left to get any philosophical or astronomical Friends to examine it as I intended, the Ship being on the Point of sailing, and a future Opportunity uncertain. Enclos'd is his Direction Paper for opening and fixing it. I have not yet got the Bill of the Price: it is to be made from the deceased Mr. Short's Book of Memorandums of Orders, in which he enter'd this Order of ours and as it is suppos'd the Price: I do not remember, it is so long since, whether it was £100 or 100 Guineas; and the Book is in the Hands of the Executors, as I understand; When I have the Account, I shall pay it as I did Bird's for the Transit Instrument, which is 40 Guineas, and then shall apply for the whole to Mr. Mauduit.[7] By the way, I wonder that I have not heard from you of the Receipt of that Instrument, which went from

Birmingham, Sheffield, and Manchester. *Lond. Chron.*, Feb. 9–11, Feb. 28–March 2, 1769.

7. For James Short, John Bird, and the telescope see above, xv, 166–7. For Jasper Mauduit, the former Massachusetts agent who was now acting for Harvard, see above, xii, 13 n. On May 29 he paid BF £147, and on June 14 BF paid £100 for the telescope to a man named Atkinson; see BF's Journal under those dates. Atkinson was clearly Short's successor, and may have been his half-brother or brother-in-law.

hence in September per Capt. Watt. I hope it got safe to hand, and gave Satisfaction: The Ship was the same that Mr. Rogers went in, who I hear is arriv'd, and by him too I sent the Philosophic Transactions, with a Number of Copies of your Paper as printed separately.[8] But I have no Letter from you since that by the young Gentleman you recommended to me, Grandson to Sir Wm. Pepperell,[9] which I think was dated about the Beginning of October, when you could not have receiv'd them.

By a late Ship, I sent your College a Copy of the new Edition of my Philosophical Papers; and others I think for yourself and for Mr. Bowdoin.[1] I should apologize to you for inserting therein some part of our Correspondence with out first obtaining your Permission: But as Mr. Bowdoin had favour'd me with his Consent, for what related to him; I ventur'd to rely on your Good Nature as to what related to you, and I hope you will forgive me.

I have got from Mr. Ellicot the Glasses, &c. of the long Galilean Telescope which he presents to your College. I put them into the Hands of Mr. Nairne, the Optician, to examine and put them in

8. For Winthrop's *Cogitata de Cometis* see above, xv, 168 n. Nathaniel Rogers, the bearer of the book and offprints, was a Boston merchant (*c.* 1736–70) who had spent a year in England. A few months after his return, when he hoped to become secretary of Massachusetts, he cited the Pownall brothers, Hillsborough, and BF as men who would vouch for him in England; he was known in Boston as a government man, he added, and had suffered accordingly. *Copy of Letters Sent to Great-Britain, by His Excellency Thomas Hutchinson, the Hon. Andrew Oliver, and Several Other Persons, Born and Educated among Us* (Boston, 1773), pp. 38–40. Rogers' sufferings were soon exacerbated: in May, 1769, he was cited as a violator of the nonimportation agreement; in January, 1770, the Committee of Inspection visited his store; in the following May he went to New York, where the Sons of Liberty hanged him in effigy. The next day he left town, and died in Boston in August. *New England Hist. and Geneal. Register*, xii (1858), 340; Oliver M. Dickerson, ed., *Boston under Military Rule* . . . (Boston, [1936]), p. 100; Charles M. Andrews, "The Boston Merchants and the Non-Importation Agreement," Col. Soc. of Mass. *Publications*, xix (1918), 232, 233 n.

9. William Pepperell Sparhawk (1746–1816), who inherited the estate and took the name of his grandfather after the latter's death in 1759, was himself made a baronet in 1774. After graduating from Harvard in 1766 he visited England, and returned there as a loyalist refugee in 1775. See Cecil H. C. Howard, *The Pepperells in America* (Salem, Mass., 1906), pp. 36–7; Sabine, *Loyalists*, ii, 168–76.

1. See the postscript of BF to Jane Mecom above, Feb. 23.

Order.[2] I thought to have sent them by this Ship, but am disappointed; they shall go by the next if possible.

There is nothing new here in the philosophical Way at present. With great and sincere Esteem, I am, Dear Sir, Your most obedient and most humble Servant   B FRANKLIN

P.S. There is no Prospect of getting the Duty Acts repeal'd this Session if ever. Your steady Resolutions to consume no more British Goods may possibly if persisted in have a good Effect another Year. I apprehend the Parliamentary Resolves and Address will tend to widen the Breach. Inclos'd I send you Governor Pownall's Speech against these Resolves; his Name is not to be mention'd. He appears to me a hearty Friend to America; tho' I find he is suspected by some on Account of his Connections.[3]

John Winthrop Esqr

From James Parker   ALS: American Philosophical Society

Honoured Sir   New-York, March 20, 1769

Inclosed in this comes a Bill of Exchange for Fifty-five pounds Sterl. on Messrs. Sargent, Chambers & Co.[4] which from a presumption of your Goodness, I have troubled you with on the following Occasion: Having collected up all that I could of Mr. Balfour of Edinburg's Books, I got them sold at Auction, which produced as much Money as purchased £25 Sterl. but as I could not get a single Bill so small, and Mr. Relfe, (now in our Jail) being desirous of purchasing a Bill for £30 Sterl. to send to one Mr. Bird of London,[5] the Person who tried to get a Bill for him, found it also

2. For John Ellicott, the London clockmaker and scientist, and Edward Nairne, the electrician and instrument-maker, see above, X, 171 n, 248 n. A Galilean telescope is refracting, with a concave eyeglass.

3. For Pownall's speech see the preceding document. The Governor may have been suspect because he was corresponding with Lieut. Gov. Hutchinson, but more probably because of his older brother John, who had been for more than a decade the secretary of the Board of Trade and hence was associated with Hillsborough.

4. See above, XIII, 295 n.

5. For Parker's complicated involvement with Hamilton & Balfour see his letter to BF above, Feb. 17. The jailbird may have been the Philadelphia merchant, John Relfe, who had gone bankrupt in 1767 (above, XIV, 279 n), although

not practicable, as Nobody would draw under £50 Sterl. so we at last agreed to join the Stock, and purchase the inclosed. And to this purpose I have given an Order of this same Day's Date, to Mr. Relfe for him to send to Mr. Bird, to call upon you for the £30 which I am sure you will pay, when you receive it: but if this Bill should not be accepted or paid, and so protested you will not pay that Money, as he must run that Part of the Risk as well as I. I have also sent another Order to Mr. Balfour, acquainting him with the same Matter, and don't doubt, but the same Measures will be taken in Regard to him: and if Charges shall accrue on this Affair, I must see you paid them.

I have also sent you the second of a Bill of £100, I received from Mr. Hubbart, the first of which I sent you by the Packet, the 5th of this Instant, which I hope you will have received. I will write again per next Packet. Mean while I am Your most obliged Servant

JAMES PARKER.

Addressed: For / Dr Benjamin Franklin / Craven-Street / London

To Deborah Franklin   AL: American Philosophical Society

My dear Child,   London, March 21. 1769

By Capt. Sparks Mrs. Stevenson sent you a large square Case, containing the Things mentioned in the inclos'd Invoice; it was marked *Stores for Mrs. Franklin Philadelphia*, and carried on board by our Porter, who says he deliver'd it to the Mate, but he brought back no Receipt. The Mate told him he liv'd not far from you, and knew us both. I hope there has been no Mistake, and that he has not put it on board a wrong Ship.

Mrs. Stevenson now sends you per Capt. Creighton a little Trunk marked with brass Nails SB containing the Things mentioned in the other Paper, which she bought; and also 1/2 a Dozen Caudle Cups and Saucers of my Choice for Sally; they cost 3 Guineas, are in my Opinion great Beauties.[6] I hope they will get safe and whole to hand.

why he should have been imprisoned in New York we cannot guess. Mr. Bird was perhaps the London bookseller and liveryman of the Company of Stationers mentioned above: IX, 13.

6. The first reference to the impending arrival of Benjamin Franklin Bache, who was born in the following August. The chest marked with Sally's initials

Mrs. Stevenson sends her Love to you and Sally, says she is always willing and ready to *do* every thing for you, but cannot write; rejoices that you are so happy with your Son and Daughter living with you; hopes you will soon be a happy Grandmother, and wishes she could come and kiss the Child, &c. &c. &c. and keeps talking as much as would fill [*missing*] My Love to Sally [*missing*] Thanks

Addressed: To / Mrs Franklin / at / Philadelphia per Capt. Creighton / with a small / Trunk, marked / S.B.

To Joseph Galloway

ALS: Clements Library

Dear Sir   London, March 21. 1769

Inclos'd is a Bill of Lading for the Telescope; I hope it will get safe to hand, and give Satisfaction.[7] I have not yet got the Maker's Account. It was with great Difficulty got done to go by this Ship.

We have been greatly alarmed last Week by a Project of Lord Barrington's (Secretary at War) to bring in a Clause to be added to the American Mutiny Bill, impowering Military Officers in America to quarter their Troops in private Houses. He had very insidiously conceal'd his Intention, in order to surprize the House into it when the Bill was gone thro' and just ready for engrossing: But we made such a Clamour about it, that the Ministry disclaim'd the Measure. Mr. Barré roasted him on it very severely; and the House would not come into it.[8] I was so taken up in running about on this Occa-

---

may have contained presents for her and the baby; the caudle-cups were for her alone. Caudle is a warm drink, made of wine or ale, bread, sugar, spices, and sometimes eggs, given to a woman in childbed and her visitors.

7. See above, xv, 228 n, and BF to Galloway, Jan. 29.

8. William Wildman Barrington, second Viscount Barrington in the peerage of Ireland, had served as secretary at war from 1755 to 1761, and in 1765 had resumed the position at the King's express wish. He continued in it until 1778 and, although conscientious, never distinguished himself. The secretary at war was a relatively minor official, who was in effect the King's military secretary, with no direct voice in policy-making; his principal Parliamentary concern was with the finances of the army. Barrington's intervention in the matter of quartering troops was unusual, which may partly account for the clamor it raised from the opposition. Col. Isaac Barré (1726–1802), M.P. for Lord Shelburne's borough of Chipping Wycombe, was one of the most redoubtable

sion for two or three days, that I could not attend to examine the Telescope: but as it is made by the best Workman we now have, and a very honest Man, I rely on its being good, and well pack'd up.

Inclos'd is an additional Clause for the Mutiny Bill as propos'd by Mr. Pownall; part of it is adopted with some Variations; I cannot yet say precisely what they are;[9] but you shall know per next Packet. With great Esteem, I am, Sir, Your most obedient humble Servant   B FRANKLIN

P.S. The Session hastens to a Conclusion, and no Probability yet appears that the Acts will be repealed.

Jos. Galloway Esqr

To Daniel Burton[1]   ALS: Fulham Palace Library, London

The note of recommendation printed below, like Franklin's recommendation of George Spencer a year earlier,[2] raises a question about his judgment in sponsoring candidates for the Anglican priesthood. Theodorus Swaine Drage grew up in England, where he is said to have been a schoolmate of Lord Hillsborough. He emigrated to Pennsylvania, if Franklin is correct in his dates, in 1753 or before, and became a partner first of George Croghan and then of John Hughes, trading on the frontier. In 1769 he returned to England, and on April 17 he wrote Burton to request, on the basis of this note from Franklin, one from Burton himself, and other testimonials, that he be ordained and sent as a missionary to North

members of that opposition, and such an outspoken champion of America that his name, a few months later, was combined with that of John Wilkes for the christening of Wilkes-Barre, Pa.; Barre, Vt., was also named after him in 1793. For a brief description of the episode in the House of Commons that BF is describing see Cobbett, *Parliamentary History*, XVI, 605–7.

9. Pownall offered two proposals: that the Quartering Act (*i.e.*, the Mutiny Bill) should not apply to any colony that had itself made appropriate provision for the troops, and that where the Act was not specific the commanding officer and local magistrates might agree on how the soldiers were to be quartered. Both proposals, after some slight amendment, were accepted. *Ibid.*, col. 606. The whole problem of quartering was under review at this time because of the difficulties encountered in housing the troops sent to New York in 1767 and to Boston in the autumn of 1768.

1. Secretary of the Society for the Propagation of the Gospel in Foreign Parts; see above, XIII, 483, 508.

2. See above, XV, 199 n.

Carolina, where he could use his knowledge of the frontier. The Bishop of London ordained him in late May, and by November he was installed in a back-country parish at Salisbury, N.C.

What sort of person was he? On this point the evidence is meager, but it certainly does not substantiate Franklin's good opinion of him. When Samuel Wharton learned in London in early April about the impending ordination, he wrote Croghan that Drage would be a disaster as a missionary; and the new clergyman did run into almost immediate trouble with his parishioners, whether or not through his own fault. The vestry, according to provincial law, was elected by all freeholders with title deeds, and among these the Presbyterians predominated; they had no taste for an Anglican priest, and chose a vestry pledged not to meet at all. In 1773 Drage, thus deprived of his salary, was driven to find another parish in Camden, S.C., where he died the following year.[3]

The only other information about him is that he claimed to have written a work on the Northwest Passage, which is also credited to Charles Swaine.[4] One modern scholar concludes that Drage's claim was spurious and brands him a liar.[5] Another argues that he and Swaine were one and the same person, but we do not find the argument convincing;[6] we incline to the view that Drage was indeed lying. Whether he was or not, what is known of his career leaves a doubt about Franklin's wisdom in sponsoring him.

Reverend Sir   Craven street, March 26. 1769.
At the Request of the Bearer Mr. Drage I beg Leave to inform you, that I have known him well for these Sixteen Years past, during

3. Howard N. Eavenson, *Map Maker & Indian Traders* . . . (Pittsburgh, 1949), pp. 85–109, 207–13; Gipson, *British Empire*, XV, 261; Drage to BF below, March 2, 1771, the only extant letter between them.

4. For further references to this controversy see above, IV, 381 n; X, 95 n. The work in question was *The Great Probability of a Northwest Passage* (London, 1768); and there is evidence that WF, presumably following BF, believed that Drage was the author. In July, 1769, BF sent his son a collection of prints and books. Among the latter were "Ten of *Drage's* Books," WF wrote later, which he consigned for sale in Philadelphia. "Remarks on B. Franklin's Account. . . April 20, 1771," APS.

5. Howard N. Eavenson, *Swaine and Drage* . . . (Pittsburgh, 1950).

6. Percy C. Adams, "The Case of Swaine versus Drage: an Eighteenth-Century Publishing Mystery Solved," in Heinz S. Bluhm, ed., *Essays in History and Literature Presented by Fellows of the Newberry Library to Stanley Pargellis* (Chicago, 1965), pp. 157–68. The extensive evidence that the author amasses does not, in our opinion, outweigh the striking differences in the handwriting of the two men.

which time he has lived very reputably in or near Philadelphia, and ever maintained the Character of an honest Man. With great Respect, I am, Reverend Sir, Your most obedient and most humble Servant   B FRANKLIN

Dr. Burton

From James Parker   ALS: American Philosophical Society

Honoured Sir   N York, March 29. 1769
    This Day yours of the 22d December and 4th January via Philadelphia, came to Hand. And tho' I had determined not to trouble you with long Epistles, yet at this Time I think I shall tire your Patience: if so, lay the Letter by, till you have more Leisure.
    My Son arrived here the Beginning of January, when I had been laid up with the Gout five or 6 Days. He knew not of his Wife's Death till he came within the Hook.[7] After sauntering about the Town, a whole Week, our Election was to come on, and several little Jobs offering, and I unable myself, I asked him to go to Work;[8] he pretended to be very willing and desirous to do so; He was in the Office some Days, but not so much Work done as I should have thought—and the News was much behind-hand on the Sunday at Noon, and tho' he saw it, and I had only two poor Prentices, he went off, and I saw him no more till Tuesday Morning. My two poor Boys stood it out all Night, and happily accomplished it by Monday Morn. Tuesday Morn I received a Note from him telling me he had a Mind to go down to Woodbridge.[9] I told him he might go where he pleased forever; for I could put no Dependance on him. He went. That Week more electioneering Jobs presenting: and I being just able to crawl, I ventured myself and work'd two Days, and in that Week with my Boys did as much Work as they

7. Samuel Franklin Parker, of whom his father had long taken a dim view, was returning from a visit to England; his wife Sarah had died in October, 1768. See above, XV, 131, 159, 233.
    8. The election was precipitated by the Governor's dissolving the Assembly in January, 1769. The campaign meant activity for the *N.-Y. Gaz.*, which Parker had resumed printing in 1766; and he himself was incapacitated for the two months by the attack of gout he mentions.
    9. Woodbridge, N.J., was James Parker's birthplace, home for many years, and headquarters of the northern postal district, of which he was the comptroller.

had done the Week before, but at the same time knock'd myself up, to such a Degree, that I could not move a Fortnight after: He staid there about 3 Weeks and then wrote me several Supplicating Letters, that if I would give him Encouragement he would come, and be diligent; I told him, unless he could resolve to act rationally and to be depended on, he need never to come. He came however, and the third Day, he went out in the Forenoon, at a Time he saw the Boy that work'd, taken from Work to carry in some Wood, and the Work standing still. A few Hours after a small Job came in, and we were obliged to let the Wood lye till Night, and set the Boy about the Job, which being wanted in Haste gave me double Pain in not having a Hand capable of doing it speedily: he never came near us, till Night, when I told him, I was sorry he attempted to come; for I found he was a broken Reed, and wish'd him to leave me forever; for he only would ruin me, and himself also; upon which he went off again. While he was at Woodbridge, he had contracted another Acquaintance with a young Woman, to whom he went, and immediately married again.[1] It is one small Comfort, that she was a Woman of good Character, and has with her only Sister, a Small Plantation worth about £700, or perhaps £800, which I suppose he will try to attain, to enable him to spend more of his Days in Idleness and Dissipation. You may remember I had a Brother who went to North-Carolina, whose Children by his first Wife, were lost, with my other Brother at Sea.[2] This Brother got married again, and being a Ship-Carpenter by Trade, he had purchased a Tract of Cedar Land on the Banks of Currituck Inlet in North Carolina, where he made a Living by getting Ship Timber and selling it. It pleased God to take him away the 27th of December, 1767, leaving a Wife with 7 young Children, and his Wife pregnant with the 8th. On his Death Bed he saw he should leave his Wife destitute of the Means of living: and he could only recommend them to the Care of Hea-

1. The bride was Mary Moore: 1 *N.J. Arch.*, XXII, 297.
2. There were four Parker brothers, Samuel, John, James, and Elisha. N.J. Hist. Soc. *Proceedings*, new ser., VIII (1923), 194. Elisha probably went to North Carolina, because a man of that name was married there in 1752: William M. Clemens, *North and South Carolina Marriage Records from the Earliest Colonial Days to the Civil War* (New York, 1927), p. 215. In that case Elisha was the uncle Samuel visited in 1765 (see above, XIII, 412, 455, 491), but of the fate, or even identity, of Elisha's brother, wife, and children nothing is known.

ven, and to me: As I was not born for myself, and all I have is the Gift of God, who has made me Steward only of it, when he Calls, I should obey: therefore looking on this as one of the Calls of Heaven, I sent for her, with a View to place them at my House in Woodbridge, where the Children might have some Education, to enable them to be something more than Savages. As she was with Child she could not come till she was delivered And accordingly she was delivered in the Summer following, and arrived here with all her Infants the 5th Day of October last, two Days before Sammy's Wife died. Full of Trouble on every Quarter, I blessed God, it was no Worse: I carried the Corps to Woodbridge to inter with her Family: at the same Time carried my poor Sister and her Children down there: There is House-Room enough: She is a good sort of a Woman, the two eldest are Daughters, whom I employ there in spinning, the 6 young ones are Boys, the youngest but a few Months old, and having not been named yet, I directed her to call it Franklin, in Remembrance of my Friend and Patron: The Boys I send to School: they are good-looking Children, brave and hearty, and I flatter my self they may possibly become good Members of the Community in Time, if it please God to spare my Life and give me Ability to support them till they can help themselves: My Son's Misconduct, and my own Infirmities, make this Load the heavier: but I am determined to struggle on, and never give out while I have Life: and tho' the Hand of God seems often heavy on me, I trust it is for wise Ends, and that in his Providence, I shall not be forsaken, whilst I continue to do my possible, which I will do, as long as I can. I keep my Press and Letter yet at Woodbridge, and as I still have the Jersey Work, I chuse to keep it there, and go down thither, when I have publick Work to do:[3] Soon after my Son was married, he begged of me, to let him live in that House, as that belonging to his Wife was leased out, and to work with the Materials, if any Work offered; but I assured him, I would not suffer him to insult or abuse his Aunt, nor to let him into the House without her Leave and Consent: but that he readily got: and he now promises to reform: How far, or how honest his Pretensions may be, God only knows, but I have told him, I would not trust him with any Thing, till he had given better Proofs than he has hitherto done, of being trust-

3. For more than a decade Parker had been public printer for the province of New Jersey.

worthy: In this State they stand at present. There is little or no Work to be had there, only at the Time of the Assembly sitting, unless its forced, as I have experienced for 12 or 13 Years. The Times are really distressing here: and yet every Thing very dear, much more so than ever I knew it: I print full 30 Quire of News-papers, but they will not subsist me, tho' 16 Year ago, Money might be saved at that: Provisions being here more than double what they were then: My Sickness prevents me from working much myself, and I am chiefly a Sufferer by not being able to go out to collect News: I have but one Journey man, and he is not capacitated for such Work, and three Boys, neither of which are good for such a Business. I have tried to get a suitable one, but hither to not able: Lewis Jones left me soon after he was free, and went to work with a new Printer just set up, who had got Mein & Fleeming of Boston's Plan for a Newspaper which they have published, but murdered in the Publication: but they are going to publish a New York Chronicle, large as Goddard's.[4] I don't think them equal to the Task, as I had the Trial of the best Hand, and never had a Worse. They are Scots Lads: and if they be *fortunate Fools*, they will have no Need of Wisdom, otherwise they will fall through. I hear they have a tolerable Run of Subscribers, as the Plan is specious, if they are capable of executing it but This Time must shew. Lewis now works with Gaine, and I hear is married.[5]

But enough of these Matters, I come now to one that gives me some pain to relate; tho' it is done to prevent any Misrepresentations taking place with you, and what I say shall be strictly Truth.

You may remember, when Benny Mecom surrendered up at New York, and quitted the Place, he went to New-Haven: I had offered him that Place in the following Manner: He should go up and see it, and if we could agree for the Rent he should have it: My Words were this, That Goddard had given Green for the Press and Letter

4. For the sad history of Lewis Jones see above, x, 344 n. His new employers were James and Alexander Robertson, who were just starting their newspaper; see above, xv, 270 n. The plan that John Mein and John Fleeming had implemented at the beginning of the year in the *Boston Chron.* was for a folio newspaper issued semi-weekly; Goddard's *Pa. Chron.* had been a large folio until early in 1768, when it had been reduced to a quarto. Brigham, *American Newspapers*, I, 276; II, 929.

5. For Hugh Gaine, the New York printer, see above, XIII, 344 n. Lewis had married Mary Bennett on Jan. 11, 1769.

at Providence 100 Dollars per An.[6] that I thought that was too much by one Half; but that if he thought one Half too much, he should make his own Proposal: I shall pass by the Difficulties I had to move him: but he went, he saw, he liked, and wrote me word, that if I would consent, he would be willing to allow me 20 Dollars for the first Year, 30 for the 2d—40 for the 3d—and 50 for the 4th—which would be 35 on an Average, if I would engage it for 4 Years. I told him, content, on Condition, I own'd it so long: for as I was probably to dispute it with Holt or Col. Hunter,[7] I could not absolutely promise so long; but if not his first Years were low. The whole Time elapsed, without a Copper of Rent, tho' I trusted him also on his going up with about £10 of Paper: He had the Post-Office, and he fell short with that, and is so still, and on my scolding at him about that, he resigned it, saying it did him more Harm than Good. When his 4 Years were out, and I could get Nothing, I told him, I could not afford to support him any longer, nor trust him with the Materials any more: And as Green came to New Haven, and set up in Opposition to him, and gained Ground on him[8] I told him, that I did not think he would ever do as a Master: for that he had not Courage or Spirit enough to drive himself: but that I believed he would do better as a Journey man, and as he had try'd Boston and New York, there did not appear good Prospects there: but inasmuch as Goddard had both wrote to me, and advertised for Hands, I believed he might do the [work?]. Accordingly he went first thither, and agreed with Goddard for 35s. per Week (higher Wages than ever I had or could give) and then went back, and took his Wife and Family. I believe would he have been careful and diligent, he might have there done well: but Goddard says he found he could place no Dependance on him, while Benny says he was slack in paying his Wages: they parted, and Ben's Distresses I suppose touch'd Mrs. Franklin, and she lays all the Blame on me:[9] Now, Sir, I dare appeal

6. When William Goddard set up his printing shop in Providence in 1762 he bought, for £120, type and at least one press from Thomas Green, who was then taking over Parker's shop in New Haven. Ward L. Miner, *William Goddard, Newspaperman* (Durham, N.C., 1962), p. 20.

7. For Col. John Hunter and his role in the Parker-Holt dispute see above, VI, 223 n; XIII, 301 n.

8. Green and his brother were publishing the *Conn. Jour.* in competition with Mecom's *Conn. Gaz.*

9. WF would certainly have disagreed with DF on this point: he echoed

to you, if I were to blame; I was unable to support him any longer, My Tools were worn out, and if ever I came to Account about them, I must allow all his Rent. I have since had part of the Letters brought here, and hired the Press and Letter to Green, at the Rate of 30 Dollars per An. the first Year's Rent he has paid me since Benny's Absence. Benny owes the Post-Office yet a good Sum, which I believe he will never be able to pay. I would do all I could for him, but it was hard for me to bear him, when I had so many other Pressures.

By Capt. Townsend who saild a few Days ago, I sent the first of a Bill of Exchange for £55 Sterl. the 2d comes with this. Of that Bill £30 belongs to Mr. Relfe, now in Jail here, to be paid by you on his Account to one John Bird of London: the other £25 is for Mr. John Balfour, of Edinburgh, being the Amount of all the remaining Books I could find of his, which I got sold at Auction: I hope you will receive it, and pay it as desired: Our Reason for it, was I could not get a small Bill, so join'd with him for this: I have sent to each of them respectively by Townsend, an Order on you for the Sum: but if Townsend should be lost, you can pay them without and take their Receipt which will answer the same End. I sent also by Townsend, the 2d Bill of a Set I had from Boston, the first of which I sent by the last Packet.[1]

After your Post-Office Suit[2] was determin'd at New Haven the Money was paid, and the Attachment on Holt's House and Land taken off. I immediately attach'd it on my own private Account, on Holt's Bond I had. I got Judgment last April, on Condition of Stay of Execution till November, as Holt pleaded he did not owe me much, if Accounts were settled, and he would get them done before November. The Time came, but no Settlement. Execution was delay'd till January, when no Accounts appearing the Place was apprized [appraised], and Execution writ[;] the Place I was by their Laws obliged to take at the Appraisement—but it leaves near £70 unpaid on the Bond and Judgment. These were appraised at some-

---

Parker's version of the parting with Goddard, and expressed a far stronger view of Mecom's worthlessness, in his letter to BF above, c. Jan. 2.

1. The substance of this paragraph repeats what Parker had already said in his letters above of Feb. 17, March 1, 4, and 20.

2. The suit was BF's only because it was brought by the Post Office; see above, XIV, 98 n and *passim*.

thing more than £350 our Money, and as the Title is now in me, I will try to sell them. So far, so good. No Accounts yet settled: I hitherto have had Writs out for Holt, but I this Day made him Propositions, which I hope he will accept—and tho' I do not expect much more of him, being apprehensive he is really on the decline, yet I will try to dye in Peace with him: Not that I doubt but he would fall in my Debt, but I will be placable and forgiving.

You'll say, what an Itch of Scribbling this tedious Fellow has. What Nonsense! Dear Sir, consider its all I can do just now. Mr. Foxcroft is daily expected here from Virginia. All my Family desires their respectful Complements. They are all well. My little Grand-Daughter is with me. My Daughter single yet[3] so I have told you all, except what I have often told you, that I am Your most obliged Servant   JAMES PARKER

PS With Regard to the Custom-House, I have been confined near 3 Months, and fear they'll turn me out for Non-Attendance;[4] if they do, let them, but I won't resign without, as I have stood the first Brunt, the Unpopularity wear off: tho' if they don't turn me out, I shall continue till further orders.

To Noble Wimberly Jones[5]

Reprinted from Allen D. Candler, ed., *The Colonial Records of the State of Georgia* (26 vols., Atlanta, Ga., 1904–16), xv, 26–7.

Sir   London April 3d[-21] 1769
I received duely your favour of December 24th with the Address of your Commons House of Assembly to the King.[6] I directly waited on Lord Hillsborough Secretary of State for American Affairs, and delivered it to him to be presented to his Majesty, which he assured me he would do immediately, and I understand

3. The granddaughter was Mary, Samuel Parker's child by his first marriage; the daughter was Jane, who subsequently married Gunning Bedford, Jr.

4. He had been a land waiter in the New York customs house since 1766: above, XIII, 262 n.

5. The Speaker of the Georgia Commons House of Assembly. On Nov. 7, 1769, he presented to the House this letter and the later one from BF printed below, June 7, together with various enclosures.

6. See above, XV, 294.

he has transmitted the Answer to your Governor this is the present Channel of Communication chosen by his Lordship who seems to think Agents unnecessary (perhaps troublesome) and says all applications from the Colonies to Government here ought to be thro' the hands of the Respective Governors, and thro' the same hands The Assemblies should receive the Answers. But I apprehend America, will in many Cases find this new Mode inconvenient and perhaps not readily come into it. As your Address was on Business of a Publick and very important kind, it was necessary it should be communicated to the Secretary of State and by him be laid before the King, I could not with propriety present it my Self as I might have done if it had been meerly an Address of Compliment.

The Resolutions and Address proposed by his Lordship and by the Duke of Bedford of which I send you a Copy passed both Houses and the King in his Answer to the address has promised to give the Orders they request of him. They did not pass without opposition in the Commons, several of our Friends spoke warmly against them,[7] some of the arguments used you will see in a printed Speech, of which I send you a copy.[8]

It was as well that you did not send Petitions to the Lords and Commons, they would not have been received if they Contained any Expressions denying the right of Parliament to tax us. Pensilvania, and New York, are the only Provinces who have Petitioned Parliament, and their Petitions have been refused.

The Agents however, have done their utmost by Seperate Sollicitations to Obtain a Repeal of the Injurious Acts, but hitherto in vain And we are told, it is not to be expected this Sessions. Hints are indeed given, that if every thing remains quiet in America, possibly, they may be repealed next Year and probably none of the like Kind will ever be made hereafter, but the Possibilities and Probabilities are not much relyd on by our Friends who think that if we bear without Complaining another Year, it will be supposed that we may bear forever, and all thoughts of repealing will be dropt.

Certainly nothing can be of more Importance to the Welfare of

7. Edmund Burke, Alderman Trecothick, Col. Barré, George Johnstone, and Thomas Pownall; see Gipson, *British Empire*, XI, 234–8.

8. Probably Pownall's printing of his speech of Jan. 26, but perhaps the pamphlet combining that and his speech of Feb. 8; see BF to Galloway above, March 9.

the whole British Empire than what you recommend, a Restoration of that Harmony which heretofore subscribed [sic] between the Mother Country and its Colonies. The Agents earnestly wish it and will endeavour it by all possible means consistent with the just rights and essential Privileges of their Constituents.

The Secretary at War, on occasion of continuing the Act for Quartering Troops in America talk'd of proposing a Clause for enabling the Officers in case of Necessity to quarter the Soldiers in private Houses. This alarmed us greatly as it would always be in the Power of the Military to create the Necessity by bringing more Troops to any Place they had a mind to distress, than the Publick Houses, or Barracks could accomodate. We therefore opposed it so strongly that the Ministry disownd the Measure, and the Secretary was obliged to give it up. On the other Hand the Act is made rather more favourable than it was being declared not to extend to any Colony, that has or shall make such Provision by Acts of its own for Quartering the Troops as shall have received the Kings Assent, and even leaving the Mode open to be varied by an Agreement between the Magistrates and Officers.⁹ I enclose a Copy of the Act as it passed.

I send you also a Pamphlet which I think very well written in our Favour, and therefore have distributed many of them the author is yet unknown.¹ Be pleased to present my best respects to your Assembly when you have one, and assure them of my most faithful Services. I am with great Regard Sir Your most Obedient and most humble Servant   B. FRANKLIN

PS. April 21. The Ships not being sailed, I have an opportunity of informing you, that, on Wednesday last, a Motion was mad [sic] in the House of Commons for repealing the Duty Acts, which was supported by Gen. Conway, Sir George Saville, and a number of our Friends, but not carried.² An Act, however, will pass, for granting a Bounty, during 21 Years, on all raw Silk imported from

9. See BF to Galloway above, March 21.
1. Probably *The Case of Great Britain and America*, for which see BF to Galloway above, Jan. 9.
2. The motion was that of Gov. Pownall on April 19 for a debate on repeal; see Gipson, *British Empire*, XI, 242–4. For Henry Seymour Conway see above, XII, 209 n; XV, 15 n. Sir George Savile (1726–84), a scion of the great Yorkshire family, was a sturdy independent; he belonged to no faction and aspired to no

the Colonies, of £25 for every £100 value during the first Seven Years £20 for Do. during the next Seven Years, and £15 for Do. during the last Seven Years. The Act permitting the exportation of Rice from Carolina and Georgia to more Southern Parts of America is also Continued.[3]

From Richard Price: "Observations on the Expectations of Lives, the Increase of Mankind, the Influence of Great Towns on Population, and Particularly the State of London with Respect to Healthfulness and Number of Inhabitants. In a Letter...to Benjamin Franklin, Esq; LL.D. and F.R.S."

Printed from the Royal Society, *Philosophical Transactions*, LIX (for 1769; London, 1770), 89–125.

The document that follows is only in form a letter to Franklin. Price addressed it to him, presumably as a way of acknowledging the latter's work on population;[4] Franklin transmitted it to the Royal Society, where it was read on April 27 and May 4 and subsequently printed in the *Transactions*. How fully he recognized the importance of what he was transmitting no one can say. Although he doubtless appreciated Price's use of his own findings, he may well have found the rest of the paper hard going; for he was not the mathematician that his friend was.

For some years Price had been concerned with mathematical probability. He had recently been asked for advice on annuity systems, which were of crucial importance in the rise of benefit societies; annuities had led him into the problem of life expectancy as a particular form of probability, and he had mastered the literature on the subject. The paper that follows was his first contribution to the field, but far from his last: another appeared in the *Transactions* in 1770 and was followed almost at once by his *Observations on Reversionary Payments*... (London, 1771). The book, which went through a number of editions, established him as an authority on what was then the infant science of vital statistics, and hence

---

office and was, within limits, a friend of America; see Namier and Brooke, *House of Commons*, III, 405–9.

3. The two acts were both 9 Geo. III, respectively c. 38 and c. 4. For silk-growing in America see BF to Evans below, 200 and n. 2.

4. Verner Crane's plausible conjecture in "The Club of Honest Whigs: Friends of Science and Liberty," *W&MQ*, 3d ser., XXIII (1966), 224. For BF's work on population see in particular above, IV, 225–34; IX, 77–85; XIII, 367–8.

on the theory of life insurance and annuities.[5] Franklin's transmission of this paper to the Royal Society, in other words, marked the beginning of a major development.

Dear Sir,   Newington-Green, April 3, 1769.

I beg leave to submit to your perusal the following observations. If you think them of any importance, I shall be obliged to you for communicating them to the Royal Society. You will find that the chief subject of them is the present state of the city of London, with respect to healthfulness and number of inhabitants, as far as it can be collected from the bills of mortality. This is a subject that has been considered by others; but the proper method of calculating from the bills has not, I think, been sufficiently explained.

No competent judgment can be formed of the following observations, without a clear notion of what the writers on Life Annuities and Reversions have called the *Expectation of Life*. Perhaps this is not in common properly understood; and Mr. De Moivre's manner of expressing himself about it is very liable to be mistaken.[6]

The most obvious sense of the *expectation* of a given life is, "That particular number of years which a life of a given age has an equal chance of enjoying." This is properly the time that a person may reasonably *expect* to live; for the chances *against* his living longer are greater than those *for* it; and, therefore, he cannot entertain an *expectation* of living longer, consistently with probability. This period does not coincide with what the writers on Annuities call the *expectation of life*, except on the supposition of an uniform decrease in the probabilities of life, as Thomas Simpson[7] has observed in his *Select Exercises for Young Proficients in the Mathematicks* (London, 1752), p. 273. It is necessary to add, that, even on this supposition,

5. See James H. Cassedy, *Demography in Early America: Beginnings of the Statistical Mind* (Cambridge, Mass., 1969), pp. 183–6; Carl B. Cone, *Torchbearer of Freedom: the Influence of Richard Price on Eighteenth Century Thought* (Lexington, Ky., [1952]), pp. 37–45; Roland Thomas, *Richard Price: Philosopher and Apostle of Liberty* (London, 1924), pp. 51–63.

6. Abraham de Moivre, or Demoivre (1667–1754), a French Protestant who fled to England in 1688, was one of the most distinguished mathematicians of his day, a friend of Newton and Halley, and a pioneer in the study of probability and life-contingencies. *DNB* under Moivre.

7. For Simpson (1710–61), a weaver, astrologer, and mathematician, see *DNB*. We have expanded and amended Price's references, both in the text and in his own footnotes, to conform to modern usage and our abbreviated titles.

Richard Price

it does not coincide with what is called the *expectation of life* in any case of joint lives. Thus, two joint lives of 40 have an even chance, according to Mr. De Moivre's hypothesis,[8] of continuing together only $13\frac{1}{2}$ years. But the *expectation* of two equal joint lives being (according to the same hypothesis) always a *third* of the *common complement*, it is in this case $15\frac{1}{3}$ years. It is necessary, therefore, to observe, that there is another sense of this phrase which ought to be carefully distinguished from that now mentioned. It may signify "The *mean continuance* of any given *single, joint,* or *surviving* lives, according to any given table of observations:" that is, the number of years which, taking them one with another, they actually enjoy, and may be considered as sure of enjoying, those who live or survive *beyond* that period, enjoying as much *more* time in proportion to their number, as those who *fall short* of it enjoy *less*. Thus, supposing 46 persons alive, all 40 years of age, and that, according to Mr. De Moivre's *hypothesis*, one will die every year till they are all dead in 46 years, half 46 or 23 will be their *expectation of life*: that is, The number of years enjoyed by them all will be just the same as if every one of them had lived 23 years, and then died; so that, supposing no interest of money, there would be no difference in value between annuities payable for life to every single person in such a set, and equal annuities payable to another equal set of persons of the same common age, supposed to be all sure of living just 23 years and no more.

In like manner, the *third* of 46 years, or 15 years and 4 months, is the *expectation* of two joint lives both 40; and this is also the *expectation* of the survivor. That is, supposing a set of marriages between persons all 40, they will, one with another, last just this time, and

8. [*Author's note:*] Mr. De Moivre's hypothesis, here referred to, supposes (as is well known to those who have studied the subject of Life Annuities) an equal decrement of human life through all its stages. That is, it supposes that out of any given number alive at a given age, the same number will die every year till they are all dead. Thus 86 Mr. De Moivre makes the utmost probable extent of life. The number of years which any given life wants of 86 he calls the *complement* of that life. 56, therefore, is the *complement* of 30; and supposing 56 persons alive at this age, *one* will die every year till, in 56 years, they will be all dead. The like will happen to 46 at 40, to 36 at 50, and so on, for all other ages. This is an excellent *hypothesis*. It eases exceedingly the labour of calculating the values of lives. It is remarkably agreeable to Dr. Halley's Table of Observations; and, as far as it implies an equal decrement of life, is, in a great measure, confirmed by other Tables.

the survivors will last the same time; and annuities payable during the continuance of such marriages would, supposing no interest of money, be of exactly the same value with annuities to begin at the extinction of such marriages, and to be paid, during life, to the survivors. In adding together the years which any great number of such marriages and their survivorships have lasted, the sums would be found to be equal.

One is naturally led to understand the *expectation* of life in the first of the senses now explained, when, by Mr. Simpson and Mr. De Moivre, it is called, *the number of years which, upon an equality of chance, a person may expect to enjoy*; or, *the time which a person of a given age may justly expect to continue in being*; and, in the last sense, when it is called, *the share of life due to a person*.[9] But, as in reality it is always used in the last of these senses, the former language should not be applied to it: and it is in this last sense that it coincides with the *sums* of the *present* probabilities that any given single or joint lives shall attain to the end of the 1st, 2d, 3d, &c. *moments* from this time to the end of their possible existence; or, in the case of survivorships, with the sum of the probabilities that there shall be a survivor at the end of the 1st, 2d, 3d, &c. *moments*, from this time to the end of the possible existence of survivorship. This coincidence every one conversant in these subjects must see, upon reflecting, that both these senses give the true present value of a life-annuity secured by land, without interest of money.[1]

9. [*Author's note:*] See Abraham De Moivre, *Annuities on Lives* . . . (4th ed., London, 1752), p. 65, &c.; and Simpson's *Select Exercises*, pp. 255, 273.

1. [*Author's note:*] The *sum* of the probabilities that any given lives will attain to the end of the 1st, 2d, 3d, &c. *years* from the present time to the utmost extremity of life (for instance, $\frac{45}{46} + \frac{44}{46} + \frac{43}{46}$, &c. to $\frac{1}{46} = 22\frac{1}{2}$ for lives of 40, by the *hypothesis*) may be called their *expectation*, or the number of payments due to them, as *yearly annuitants*. The sum of the probabilities that they will attain to the end of the 1st, 2d, 3d, &c. *half years* (or, in the particular case specified, $\frac{91}{92} + \frac{90}{92} + \frac{89}{92} + \frac{88}{92}$, &c. $= \frac{91}{2}$ *half* years, or $22\frac{3}{4}$ *years*) is their expectation as *half yearly annuitants*. And the sums just mentioned of the probabilities of their attaining to the end of the 1st, 2d, 3d, &c. *moments* (equal in the same particular case to 23 years) is properly their *expectation of life*, or their *expectation* as annuitants secured by land.

Mr. De Moivre has concealed the demonstrations of the rules he has given for finding these *expectations* of life, and only intimated, in general, that he discovered them by a calculation deduced from the method of fluxions, p. 66, of his *Treatise on Annuities*. It will, perhaps, be agreeable to some to see how

This period in *joint* lives, I have observed, is *never* the same with the period which they have an equal chance of enjoying; and in

---

easily they are deduced in this method upon the hypothesis of an equal decrement of life.

Let $\dot{x}$ stand for a moment of time and n the *complement* of any assigned life. Then $\dfrac{n-\dot{x}}{n}, \dfrac{n-2\dot{x}}{n}, \dfrac{n-3\dot{x}}{n}$, &c. will be the *present* probabilities of its continuing to the end of the 1st, 2d, 3d, &c. moments; and $\dfrac{n-x}{n}$ the probability of its continuing to the end of x time. $\dfrac{n-x}{n} \times \dot{x}$ will therefore be the *fluxion* of the sum of the probabilities, or of an *area* representing this sum, whose *ordinates* are $\dfrac{n-x}{n}$, and *axis* x. The *fluent* of this expression, or $x - \dfrac{x^2}{2n}$ is the sum itself for the time x; and this, when $x = n$, becomes $\frac{1}{2}n$ and gives the *expectation* of the assigned life, or the sum of all the probabilities just mentioned for its whole possible duration. In like manner: Since $\dfrac{\overline{n-x^2}}{n^2}$ is the probability that two equal joint lives will continue x time $\dfrac{\overline{n-x^2}}{n^2} \times \dot{x}$ will be the *fluxion* of the sum of the probabilities. The *fluent* is $x - \dfrac{x^2}{n} + \dfrac{x^3}{3n^2}$, which when $n = x$ is $\dfrac{n}{3}$ the expectation of two equal joint lives. Again: Since $\dfrac{n-x}{n} \times \dfrac{2x}{n}$ is the probability that there will be a survivor of two equal joint lives at the end of x time, $\dfrac{n-x}{n} \times \dfrac{2x}{n} \times \dot{x}$ will be the *fluxion* of the sum of the probabilities; and the *fluent*, or $\dfrac{x^2}{n} - \dfrac{2x^3}{3x^2}$ is (when $x = n$) $\frac{1}{3}n$, or the *expectation* of survivorship between two equal lives, which therefore appears to be equal to the *expectation* of their joint continuance. The expectation of two *unequal* joint lives found in the same way is $\dfrac{m}{2} - \dfrac{m^2}{6n}$, m being the *complement* of the oldest life, and n the *complement* of the youngest. The whole *expectation* of survivorship is $\dfrac{n}{2} - \dfrac{m}{2} + \dfrac{m^2}{3n}$. The expectation of survivorship on the part of the oldest is, $\dfrac{m^2}{6n}$; and the expectation on the part of the youngest is, $\dfrac{n}{2} - \dfrac{m}{2} + \dfrac{m^2}{6n}$. It is easy to apply this investigation to any number of joint lives, and to all cases of survivorship.

I have above endeavoured to shew distinctly how the *expectations* of *single* lives may be found, agreeably to any Table of Observations, without having recourse to any principles, except such as are plain and common.

single lives, I have observed, they are the same only on the supposition of an uniform decrease in the probabilities of life. If this decrease, instead of being always uniform, is *accelerated* in the last stages of life, the former period, in single lives, will be *less* than the latter; if *retarded*, it will be *greater*.

It is necessary to add, that the number expressing the former period, multiplied by the number of single or joint lives whose expectation it is added annually to a society or town, gives the whole number living together, to which such an annual addition would in time grow. Thus, since 19, or the third of 57, is the *expectation* of two joint lives whose common age is 29, or common *complement* 57, twenty marriages every year between persons of this age would, in 57 years, grow to 20 times 19, or 380 marriages always existing together. The number of *survivors* also arising from these marriages, and always living together, would, in twice 57 years, increase to the same number. And, since the *expectation* of a single life is always half its *complement*, in 57 years likewise 20 single persons aged 29, added annually to a town, would increase to 20 times 28.5 or 570; and when arrived at this number, the deaths every year will just equal the accessions, and no further increase be possible.

It appears from hence, that the particular proportion that becomes extinct every year, out of the whole number constantly existing together of single or joint lives, must, wherever this number undergoes no variation, be exactly the same with the *expectation* of those lives at the time when their existence commenced. Thus, was it found that a 19th part of all the marriages among any body of men, whose numbers do not vary, are dissolved every year by the deaths of either the husband or wife, it would appear that 19 was, at the time they were contracted, the *expectation* of these marriages. In like manner, was it found in a society, limited to a fixed number of members, that a 28th part dies annually out of the whole number of members, it would appear that 28 was their common expectation of life at the time they entered. So likewise, were it found in any town or district, where the number of births and burials are equal, that a 20th or 30th part of the inhabitants die annually, it would appear that 20 or 30 was the *expectation* of a child just born in that town or district. These *expectations*, therefore, for all *single* lives, are easily found by a *Table of Observations*, shewing the number that die annually at all ages, out of a given number alive at those ages; and the general rule for this purpose is "to divide the sum of all the living in the Table at the age whose expectation is required, and at all greater ages, by the sum of all that die annually at that age, and above it; or, which is the same, by the number in the Table of the living at that age; and half subtracted from the quotient will be the required *expectation*." Thus, in Dr. Halley's[2] Table, the sum of all the living at 20 and upwards is 20,724. The number living at that age is 598; and the former number divided by the latter, and half unity[3] subtracted from the quotient, gives 34.15 for the *expectation* of 20. The expectation of the same life by Mr. Simpson's Table, formed from the bills of mortality of London, is 28.9.

These observations bring me to the principal point which I have had all along in view. They suggest to us an easy method of finding the number of inhabitants in a place from a *Table of Observations*, or the *bills of mortality* for that place, supposing the yearly births and burials equal. "Find by the Table, in the way just described, the *expectation* of an infant just born, and this, multiplied by the number of yearly births, will be the number of inhabitants." At Breslaw, according to Dr. Halley's Table,[4] though half die under 16, and therefore an infant just born has an *equal chance* of living only 16 years,

2. The fame of Edmond Halley (1656–1742) as an astronomer has been perpetuated by the comet named after him. But he was also an antarctic explorer, oceanographer, translator from the Arabic, professor of geometry at Oxford, and "the virtual originator of the science of life-statistics." *DNB*. Price is referring to Halley's "An Estimate of the Degrees of Mortality of Mankind, Drawn from Curious Tables of the Births and Funerals at the City of Breslau; with an Attempt to Ascertain the Price of Annuities upon Lives," *Phil. Trans.*, XVII (1693), 596–610.

3. [*Author's note:*] This subtraction is necessary, because the *divisor* ought to be made as much greater than the number dying annually given in the Table, as the *expectation*, with ½ unity added, is greater than the *expectation*, on account of the number that will die, in the course of the year, out of those who are continually added, in order to preserve the number of the living the same.

In other words: If we conceive the *recruit* necessary to supply the *waste* of every year to be made always at the *end* of the year, the *dividend* ought to be the *medium* between the numbers living at the *beginning* and the *end* of the year; that is, it ought to be taken *less* than the sum of the living in the Table at and above the given age, by *half* the number that die in the year; the effect of which *diminution* will be the same with the *subtraction* I have directed.

4. [*Author's note:*] See John Lowthorp, *The Phil. Trans. and Collections to the End of the Year 1700, Abridg'd and Dispos'd under General Headings* (2d ed., 3 vols., London, 1716), III, 669.

yet his *expectations*, found by the rule I have given, is near 28 years; and this, multiplied by 1238 the number born annually, gives 34,664, the number of inhabitants. In like manner, it appears from Mr. Simpson's Table, that, though an infant just born in London has not an *equal chance* of living 3 years, his *expectation* is 20 years; and this number, multiplied by the yearly births, would give the number of inhabitants in London, were the births and burials equal. The medium of the yearly births, for the last 10 years, has been 15,710. This number, multiplied by 20, is 314,200, which is the number of inhabitants that there would be in London, according to the bills, were the yearly burials no more than equal to the births: that is, were it to support itself in its number of inhabitants without any supply from the country. But for the last 10 years, the burials have, at an average, been 22,956, and exceeded the christenings 7,246. This is, therefore, at present, the yearly addition of people to London from other parts of the kingdom, by whom it is kept up. Suppose them to be all, one with another, persons who have, when they remove to London, an *expectation* of life equal to 30 years. That is, suppose them to be all of the age of 18 or 20, a supposition certainly far beyond the truth. From hence will arise, according to what has been before observed, an addition of 30 multiplied by 7,246, that is 217,380 inhabitants. This number, added to the former, makes 531,580; and this, I think, at most, would be the number of inhabitants in London were the bills perfect. But it is certain that they give the number of births and burials too little. There are many burying-places that are never brought into the bills. Many also emigrate to the navy and army and country; and these ought to be added to the number of deaths. What the deficiencies arising from hence are, cannot be determined. Suppose them equivalent to 6000 every year in the births, and 6000 in the burials. This would make an addition of 20 times 6000 or 120,000 to the last number, and the whole number of inhabitants, would be 651,580. If the burials are deficient only two thirds of this number, or 4000, and the births the whole of it, 20 multiplied by 6000, must be added to 314,290 on account of the defects in the births: and, since the excess of the burials above the births will then be only 5,246, 30 multiplied by 5,246 or 157,380, will be the number to be added on this account; and the sum, or number of inhabitants will be 591,580. But if, on the contrary, the burials are deficient 6000, and the births only 4000, 80,000 must be added to 314,290, on account of the deficiencies in the births, and 30 multiplied by 9,246, on account of the excess of the burials above the births, and the whole number of inhabitants will be 671,580.

Every supposition in these calculations seems to me too high. *Emigrants* from London are, in particular, allowed the same *expectation* of continuance in London with those who are born in it, or who come to it in the firmest part of life, and never afterwards leave it; whereas it is not credible that the former *expectation* should be so much as half the latter. But I have a further reason for thinking that this calculation gives too high numbers, which has with me irresistible weight. It has been seen that the number of inhabitants comes out less on the supposition, that the defects in the christenings are greater than those in the burials. Now it seems evident that this is really the case; and, as it is a fact not attended to, I will here endeavour to explain distinctly the reason which proves it.

The proportion of the number of births in London, to the number who live to be 10 years of age, is, by the bills, 16 to 5. Any one may find this to be true, by subtracting the *annual medium* of those who have died under 10, for some years past, from the *annual medium* of births for the same number of years. Now, tho', without doubt, London is very fatal to children, yet it is incredible that it should be so fatal as this implies. The *bills*, therefore, very probably, give the number of those who die under 10 too great in proportion to the number of births; and there can be no other cause of this, than a greater deficiency in the *births* than in the *burials*. Were the deficiences in both equal, that is, were the *burials*, in proportion to their number, just as deficient as the *births* are in proportion to *their* number, the proportion of those who reach 10 years of age to the number born would be right in the *bills*, let the deficiencies themselves be ever so considerable. On the contrary, were the deficiencies in the *burials* greater than in the *births*, this proportion would be given too great; and it is only when the former are least that this proportion can be given too little. Thus, let the number of annual *burials* be 23,000; of *births* 15,700; and the number dying annually under 10, 10,800. Then 4,900 will reach 10 of 15,700 born annually; that is, 5 out of 16. Were there no deficiencies in the *burials*, and were it fact that only *half* die under 10, it would follow, that there was an annual deficiency equal to 4,900 subtracted from 10,800, or 5,900 in the *births*. Were the *births* a third part too little, and the *burials* also a third part too little, the true number of *births*, *burials*, and of *children dying under* 10, would be 20,933, 30,666 and 14,400; and, therefore, the number that would live to 10 years of age would be 6,533 out of 20,933, or 5 of 16 as before. Were the *births* a third part, and the *burials* so much as two-fifths wrong, the number of *births*, *burials*, and children dying under 10 would be 20,933, 32,200 and 15,120; and, therefore, the number that would live to 10 would be 5,813 out of 20,933, or 5 out of 18. Were the *births* a 3d part wrong, and the *burials* but a 6th, the foregoing numbers would be 20,933—26,833—12,600; and, therefore, the number that would live to 10 would be 8,333 out of 20,933, or 5 out of 12.56: and this proportion seems as low as is consistent with any degree of probability. It is somewhat less than the proportion in Mr. Simpson's Table of *London Observations*, and near *one half* less than the proportion in the Table of *Observations* for Breslaw, where it appears that above 9 of 16 live to be 10, and that *one half* live to be 16. The deficiencies, therefore, in the *births* cannot be much less than double those in the *burials*;[5] and the least numbers I have given must, probably, be nearest to the true number of inhabitants. However, should any one, after all, think that it is not improbable that only 5 of 16 should live in London to be 10 years of age, or that above *two thirds* die under this age, the consequence of admitting this will still be, that the foregoing calculation has been carried too high. For it will from hence follow, that the *expectation* of a child just born in London cannot be so much as I have taken it. This *expectation* is 20, on the supposition that half die under 3 years of age, and that 5 of 16 live to be 29 years of age, agreeably to Mr. Simpson's Table. But if it is indeed true, that *half* die under 2 years of age, and 5 of 16 under 10, agreeably to the *bills*, this expectation must be less than 20, and all the numbers before given will be considerably reduced.

Upon the whole, I am forced to conclude from these observations, that the second number I have given, or 651,580, though short

5. [*Author's note:*] One obvious reason of this fact is, that *none* of the *births* among *Jews*, *Quakers*, *Papists*, and the *three denominations of Dissenters* are included in the bills, whereas *many* of their *burials* are. It is further to be attended to, that the abortive and stillborn, amounting to about 600 annually, are included in the burials, but never in the births. If we add these to the christenings, preserving the burials the same, the proportion of the born, according to the bills, who have reached ten for the last sixteen years will be very nearly one *third* instead of *five sixteenths*.

of the number of inhabitants commonly supposed in London, is, very probably, *greater*, but cannot be much *less*, than the true number. Indeed, it is in general evident, that in cases of this kind numbers are very much overrated. The ingenious Dr. Brakenridge, 14 years ago, when the bills were lower than they are now, from the number of houses, and allowing six to a house, made the number of inhabitants 751,800.[6] But his method of determining the number of houses is too precarious; and, besides, six to a house is, probably,[7] too large an allowance. Many families now have two houses to live in. The magistrates of Norwich, in 1752, took an exact account of both the number of houses and individuals in that city.[8] The number of houses was 7,139, and of individuals 36,169, which gives nearly 5 to a house. Another method which Dr. Brakenridge took to deter-

6. [*Author's note:*] See William Brakenridge, D.D., F.R.S., "A Letter... Concerning the Number of Inhabitants within the London Bills of Mortality," *Phil. Trans.*, XLVIII, pt. 2 (1754), 788–800.

7. [*Author's note:*] If this is true, Dr. Brakenridge has also over-rated the number of people in England. The number of houses rated to the window tax he had, he says, been certainly informed was 690,000. The number of cottages not rated was not, he adds, accurately known; but from the accounts given in it appeared, that they could not amount to above 200,000; and, allowing 6 to a house, this would make the number of people in England 5,340,000. But if 5 to a house should be a juster allowance, the number will be 4,450,000. The number of people in Scotland he reckons 1,500,000, and in Ireland 1,000,000. See "A Letter... Concerning the Present Increase of the People in Britain and Ireland," *ibid.*, XLIX, pt. 2 (1756), 877–90.

8. [*Author's note:*] See *Gent. Mag.*, XXII (1752), 347; Thomas Short, *Comparative History of the Increase and Decrease of Mankind in England, and Several Countries Abroad*... (London, 1767), p. 38. In page 58 of this last work the author says, that, in order to be fully satisfied about the number of persons to be allowed to a family, he procured the true number of families and individuals in 14 market towns, some of them considerable for trade and populousness; and that in them were 20,371 families, and 97,611 individuals, or but little more than 4¾ to a family. He adds, that, in order to find the difference in this respect between towns of trade and country parishes, he procured from divers parts of the kingdom the exact number of *families* and *individuals* in 65 country parishes. The number of *families* was 17,208; *individuals* 76,284; or not quite 4½ to a family. In the place I have just referred to, in the *Gentleman's Magazine*, there is an account of the number of *houses* and *inhabitants* in Oxford exclusive of the colleges, and in Wolverhampton, Coventry, and Birmingham, for 1750. The number of persons to a house was, by this account, 4⅘ in the two former towns, and 5⅘ in the two latter. It seems, therefore, to appear that 5 persons to a house is an allowance large enough for London, and too large for England in general.

mine the number of inhabitants in London was from the annual number of burials, adding 2000 to the bills for omissions, and supposing a 30th part to die every year. In order to prove this to be a moderate supposition he observes that, according to Dr. Halley's Observations, a 34th part die every year at Breslaw. But this observation was made too inadvertently. The number of annual burials there, according to Dr. Halley's account, was 1174, and the number of inhabitants, as deduced by him from his Table, was 34,000, and therefore a 29th part died every year.[9] Besides, any one may find, that in reality the Table is constructed on the supposition, that the whole number born, or 1238, die every year; from whence it will follow that a 28th part died every year. Dr. Brakenridge, therefore, had he attended to this, would have stated a 24th part as the proportion that dies in London every year, and this would have taken off 150,000 from the number he has given. But even this must be less than the just proportion. For let three fourths of all who either die in London or migrate from it, be such as have been born in London; and let the rest be persons who have removed to London from the country or from foreign nations. The *expectation* of the former, it has been shewn, cannot exceed 20 years, and 30 years have been allowed to the latter. One with another, then, they will have an *expectation* of $22\frac{1}{2}$ years. That is, one of $22\frac{1}{2}$ will die every year.[1] And,

9. [*Author's note:*] Care should be taken, in considering Dr. Halley's Table, not to take the first number in it, or 1000, for so many just born. 1238, he tells us, was the annual medium of births, and 1000 is the number he supposes all living at one year and under. It was inattention to this that led Dr. Brakenridge to his mistake.

1. [*Author's note:*] The whole number of inhabitants in Rome, in the year 1761, was 157,452; of whom 90,239 were males, and 67,213 females. And the annual medium of births, for 3 years from 1759 to 1761, was 5,167, and of burials 7,153. According to this account, therefore, a 22d part of the inhabitants die in Rome every year. See Short, *Comparative History*, pp. 59–60. In Berlin, as the same author relates, p. 69, in six years, from 1734 to 1740, the annual medium of births was 3,504, of burials 3,639, and the number of inhabitants was 68,197; males 32,990, and females 35,207. A 19th part, therefore, of the inhabitants of Berlin are buried every year. As numbers taken by actual survey are generally too little, suppose, in the present instance, an error committed in reckoning the number of inhabitants, equal to a 10th of the whole number, or to the whole number of children under 5; and suppose likewise no omissions in the burials. The consequence will be, that about 1 in 21 are buried at Berlin every year. At Dublin, in the year 1695, the number of inhabitants was found, by an exact survey, to be 40,508; see *Phil. Trans.*, XXII (1700–01), 518. I find

consequently, supposing the annual recruit from the country to be 7000, the number of *births* 3 times 7000 or 21,000, and the *burials* and *migrations* 28,000 (which seem to be all high suppositions), the number of inhabitants will be 22½ multiplied by 28,000, or 630,000.

I will just mention here one other instance of exaggeration on the present subject.

---

no account of the annual burials just at that time; but from 1661 to 1681, the medium had been 1613; and from 1715 to 1728 it was 2123. There can, therefore, be no material error in supposing that in 1695 it was 1800; and this makes 1 in 22 to die annually. In 1745 the number of *families* in the same city appeared, by an exact account laid before the Lord Mayor, to be 9,214. It is probable, this number of families did not consist of more than 50,000 individuals. Suppose them, however, 55,000; and, as at this time the medium of annual burials appears to have been 2,360, 1 in 23 died annually: see Short, *Comparative History*, p. 15, and *New Observations, Moral, Civil, and Medical, on the City, Town, and Country Bills of Mortality*... (London, 1750), p. 228. I know not how far these facts may be depended on. If they come at all near the truth, they demonstrate that I have been very moderate in making only 1 in 22½, including emigrants, to die in London annually. In 1631 the number of people in the *city and liberties* of London was taken, by order of the Privy Council, and found to be 130,178. This account was taken five years after a plague that had swept off near a quarter of the inhabitants; and when, therefore, the town being full of recruits in the vigour of life, the medium of annual burials must have been lower than usual, and the births higher. Could, therefore, the medium of annual burials at that time, within the walls and in the 16 parishes without the walls, be settled, exclusive of those who died in such parts of the 16 parishes without the walls, as are not in the *liberties*, the proportion dying annually obtained from hence might be depended on, as rather less than the common and just proportion. But this medium cannot be discovered with any accuracy. Graunt estimates that two thirds of these 16 parishes are within the *liberties*; and, if this is right, the medium of annual burials in the *city and liberties* in 1631, was 5,500, and 1 in 23¾ died annually; or, making a small allowance for deficiencies in the bills, 1 in 22. William Maitland, in his *History and Survey of London from Its Foundation to the Present Time*... (2 vols., London, 1756), II, 744, by a laborious, but too unsatisfactory, investigation, reduces this proportion to 1 in 24½; and on the suppositions, that this is the true proportion dying annually, *at all times*, in London, and that the deficiencies in the burials amount to 3,038 annually, he determines that the number of inhabitants within the bills was 725,903 in the year 1737.

The number of burials not brought to account in the bills is, probably, now much greater than either Dr. Brakenridge or Mr. Maitland suppose it. I have reckoned it so high as 6000, in order to include emigrants, and also to be more sure of not falling below the truth.

Mr. Corbyn Morris,[2] in his *Observations on the Past Growth and Present State of the City of London*... (London, 1751), supposes that no more than a 60th part of the inhabitants of London, who are above 20, die every year, and from hence he determines that the number of inhabitants was near a million. In this supposition there was an error of at least one half. According to Dr. Halley's Table, it has been shewn, that a 34th part of all at 20 and upwards, die every year at Breslaw. In London, a 29th part, according to Mr. Simpson's Table, and also according to all other Tables of London Observations. And in Scotland it has been found for many years, that of 974 ministers and professors whose ages are 27 and upwards, a 33d part have died every year. Had, therefore, Mr. Morris stated a 30th part of all above 20 as dying annually in London, he would have gone beyond the truth, and his conclusion would have been 400,000 less than it is.

Dr. Brakenridge observed, that the number of inhabitants, at the time he calculated, was 127,000 less than it had been. The bills have lately advanced, but still they are much below what they were from 1717 to 1743. The medium of the annual *births*, for 20 years, from 1716 to 1736, was 18,000, and of *burials* 26,529; and by calculating from hence on all the same suppositions with those which made 651,580 to be the present number of inhabitants in London, it will be found that the number then was 735,840, or 84,260 greater than the number at present. London, therefore, for the last 30 years, has been decreasing; and though now it is increasing again, yet there is reason to think that the additions lately made to the number of buildings round it, are owing, in a great measure, to the increase of luxury, and the inhabitants requiring more room to live upon.[3]

2. Corbyn Morris (d. 1779) was an able statistician and a prolific pamphleteer on economic subjects; he had been an F.R.S. since 1757 and a commissioner of the customs since 1763. *DNB*.

3. [*Author's note:*] The medium of annual burials in the 97 parishes within the walls was,

From 1655 to 1664,	3264
From 1680 to 1690,	3139
From 1730 to 1740,	2316
From 1758 to 1768,	1620

This account proves, that though, since 1655, London has doubled its inhabitants, yet, *within the walls*, they have decreased; and so rapidly for the last 30 years as to be now reduced to one half. The like may be observed of the 17

It should be remembered, that the number of inhabitants in London is now so much less as I have made it, than it was 40 years ago, on the supposition that the proportion of the omissions in the *births* to those in the *burials* was the same then that it is now. But it appears that this is not the fact. From 1728, the year when the ages of the dead was first given in the *bills*, to 1742, near five-sixths of those who were born died under 10, according to the *bills*. From 1742 to 1752 three quarters; and ever since 1752 this proportion has stood nearly as it is now, or at somewhat more than two-thirds. The omissions in the *births*, therefore, compared with those in the *burials* were greater formerly; and this must render the difference between the number of inhabitants now and formerly less considerable than it may seem to be from the face of the bills. One reason why the proportion of the amounts of the *births* and *burials* in the bills comes now nearer than it did to the true proportion, may, perhaps, be that the number of Dissenters is considerably lessened. The Foundling Hospital also may have contributed a little to this event, by lessening the number given in the bills as having died under 10, without taking off any from the *births*; for all that die in this hospital are buried at Pancrass church, which is not within the *bills*. See the preface to *A Collection of the Yearly Bills of Mortality from 1657 to 1758 Inclusive...* (Thomas Birch, ed.; London, 1759), p. 15.

I will add, that it is probable that London is now become less fatal to children than it was; and that this is a further circumstance which must reduce the difference I have mentioned; and which is likewise necessary to be joined to the greater deficiencies in the births, in order to account for the very small proportion of children who survived 10 years of age, during the two first of the periods I have specified. Since 1752, London has been thrown more open. The custom of keeping country-houses, and of sending children

---

parishes immediately without the walls. Since 1730 these parishes have been decreasing so fast, that the *annual burials* in them have sunk from 8,672 to 5,432, and are now lower than they were before the year 1660. In Westminster, on the contrary, and the 23 out-parishes in Middlesex and Surrey, the *annual burials* have, since 1660, advanced from about 4000 to 16,000. These facts prove that the inhabitants of London are now much less crowded together than they were. It appears, in particular, that *within the walls* the inhabitants take as much room to live upon as double their number did formerly. The very same conclusions may be drawn from an examination of the *christenings*.

to be nursed in the country, has prevailed more. But, particularly, the destructive use of spirituous liquors among the poor has been checked.

I have shewn that in London, even in its present state, and according to the most moderate computation, half the number born die under *three* years of age; and I have observed that at Breslaw half live to 16. At Edinburgh, if I may judge from such of its bills as I have seen, almost as great a proportion of children die as even in London. But it appears from Graunt's[4] accurate account of the births, weddings, and burials in three country parishes for 90 years; and also, with abundant evidence, from Dr. Short's collection of observations in his *Comparative History*, and his treatise entitled, *New Observations...on the City, Town, and Country Bills of Mortality*;[5] that in country villages and parishes, the major part live to mature age, and even to marry.[6] So great is the difference, especially to children, between living in great towns and in the country. But nothing can place this observation in a more striking light than the curious account given by Dr. Thomas Heberden, and published in the *Philosophical Transactions* (LVII [1767], 461–3), *of the increase and mortality of the inhabitants of the island of Madeira*.[7] In this island,

4. [*Author's note:*] See John Graunt, *Natural and Political Observations...Made upon the Bills of Mortality* (London, 1662).

5. [*Author's note:*] The public is much obliged to this author for the pains he has taken in collecting observations on the mortality and increase of mankind, in different countries and situations. In his *New Observations*, p. 309, he mentions an ingenious parish clerk, in the country, who, by a particular account which he took, found that of 314, who had been baptized in his parish in one year, 80, or nearly a quarter part, died under four years of age. Forty-six died the first year; thirteen the second; sixteen the third; and five the fourth. After four, life grows more stable, and at ten acquires its greatest stability; and in this case it cannot be reckoned that above a 10th, or, at most, an 8th more than the quarter that died under four, would die under age; and therefore, probably, near two-thirds arrived at maturity.

6. John Graunt (1620–74) has a strong claim to be considered the founding father of what came later to be known as statistics; *Natural and Political Observations* was a pioneering work. Thomas Short (1690?–1772), a physician of Sheffield, published voluminously on medical and demographic subjects. *DNB*.

7. Thomas Heberden was the older brother of the eminent William Heberden and, like him, was a doctor and F.R.S.; the only other information we have about him is that he died on Madeira. Audley C. Buller, *The Life and Works of* [William] *Heberden...* (London, 1879), App. A.

it seems, the weddings have been to the births, for 8 years, from 1759 to 1766, as 10 to 46.8; and to the burials as 10 to 27.5. Double these proportions, therefore, or the proportion of 20 to 46.8, and of 20 to 27.5 are the proportions of the number marrying annually, to the number born and the number dying. Let 1 marriage in 10 be a 2d or 3d marriage on the side of either the man or the woman, and 10 marriages will imply 19 individuals who have grown up to maturity, and lived to marry once or oftener; and the proportion of the number marrying annually the first time, to the number dying annually, will be 19 to 27.5, or near 3 to 4. It may seem to follow from hence, that in this island near three-fourths of those who die have been married, and, consequently, that not many more than a *quarter* of the inhabitants die in childhood and celibacy; and this would be a just conclusion were there no increase, or had the births and burials been equal. But it must be remembered, that the general effect of an increase, while it is going on in a country, is to render the proportion of persons marrying annually to the annual deaths *greater*, and to the annual births *less* than the true proportion marrying out of any given number born. This proportion generally lies between the other two proportions, but always nearest to the first;[8] and, in the

8. [*Author's note:*] In a country where there is no increase or decrease of the inhabitants, and where also life, in its first periods, is so stable, and marriage so much encouraged, as that half all who are born live to be married, the *annual* births and burials must be equal, and also *quadruple* the number of weddings, after allowing for 2d and 3d marriages. Suppose in these circumstances (every thing else remaining the same) the *probabilities of life*, during its first stages, to be improved. In this case, more than *half* the born will live to be married, and an increase will take place. The births will exceed the burials, and both fall below *quadruple* the weddings; or, which is the same, below *double* the number annually married. Suppose next (the *probabilities of life* and the *encouragement to marriage* remaining the same) the *prolifickness* only of the marriages to be improved. In this case it is plain, that an increase also will take place; but the *annual* births and burials, instead of being *less*, will now both rise above *quadruple* the weddings, and therefore the proportion of the born to that part of the born who marry (being by supposition two to one) will be less than the proportion of either the *annual* births or the *annual* burials to the number marrying *annually*. Suppose again (the *encouragement to marriage* remaining the same) that the *probabilities of life* and the *prolifickness of marriages* are both improved. In this case, a more rapid increase will take place, or a greater excess of the births above the burials; but at the same time they will keep nearer to *quadruple* the weddings, than if the latter cause only had operated, and produced the same increase. I should be too minute and tedious, were I to explain these obser-

present case, it is sufficiently evident that it cannot be much less than two-thirds.

In London, then, *half* die under three years of age, and in Madeira about *two-thirds* of all who are born live to be married. Agreeably to this, it appears also from the account I have referred to, that the *expectation* of a child just born in Madeira is about 39 years, or double the expectation of a child just born in London. For the number of inhabitants was found, by a survey made in the beginning of the year 1767, to be 64,614. The annual medium of *burials* had been, for eight years, 1293; of *births* 2201. The number of inhabitants, divided by the annual medium of *burials*, gives 49.89, or the *expectation* nearly of a child just born, supposing the *births* had been 1293, and constantly equal to the *burials*, the number of inhabitants remaining the same. And the same number, divided by the annual medium of *births*, gives 29.35, or the *expectation* of a child just born, supposing

---

vations at large. It follows from them that, in every country or situation where, for a course of years, the *burials* have been either *equal to* or *less* than the *births*, and both under *quadruple* the marriages; and also that wherever the burials are *less* than quadruple the annual marriages, and at the same time the births *greater*, there the major part of all that are born live to marry. In the instance which I have considered above, and which occasions this note, the annual births are so much *greater* than *quadruple* the marriages, and at the same time the annual burials so much *less*, that the proportion that lives to marry of those who are born can scarcely be much less than I have said, or two-thirds.

I have shewn how the allowance is to be made for 2d and 3d marriages; but it is not so considerable as to be of any particular consequence; and, besides, it is, in part, compensated by the natural children which are included in the births, and which raise the proportion of the births to the weddings higher than it ought to be, and therefore bring it nearer to the true proportion of the number born *annually*, to those who marry annually, after deducting those who marry a 2d or 3d time.

In drawing conclusions from the proportion of *annual* births and burials in different situations, some writers on the increase of mankind have not given due attention to the difference in these proportions arising from the different circumstances of increase or decrease among a people. One instance of this I have now mentioned; and one further instance of it is necessary to be mentioned. The proportion of *annual* births to weddings has been considered as giving the true number of children derived from each marriage, taking all marriages one with another. But this is true only when, for many years, the births and burials have kept nearly equal. Where there is an excess of the births occasioning an increase, the proportion of *annual* births to weddings must be less than the proportion of children derived from each marriage; and the contrary must take place where there is a decrease.

the burials 2201, the number of births and of inhabitants remaining the same; and the true *expectation* of life must be somewhere near the mean between 49.89 and 29.35.

Again: A 50th part of the inhabitants of Madeira, it appears, die annually. In London, I have shewn, that above twice this proportion dies annually. In smaller towns a smaller proportion dies, and the births also come nearer to the burials. At Breslaw, I have observed, that, by Dr. Halley's Table, a 28th part dies annually; and the annual medium of births, for a complete century, from 1633 to 1734, has been 1089; of burials 1256. At Norwich,[9] the annual medium of births, dissenters included for four years, from 1751 to 1754, was 1150; of burials 1214. And as the number of inhabitants was at that time 36,169 (see p. 103 [p. 91 above]), a 30th part of the inhabitants died annually. In general, there seems reason to think that in towns (allowing for particular advantages of situation, trade, police, cleanliness, and openness, which some towns may have), the excess of the burials above the births and the annual deaths are more or less as the towns are greater or smaller. In London itself, about 160 years ago, when it was scarcely a fourth part of its present bulk, the births were nearly equal to the burials. But in country parishes and villages the births almost always exceed the burials; and I believe it seldom happens that so many as a 30th, or much more than a 40th part of the inhabitants die annually.[1] In the four provinces of New

9. [*Author's note:*] See Short's *Comparative History*, p. 63; John Martyn *et al.*, *Phil. Trans. Abridged* (10 vols. in 11; London, 1734–56), VII, pt. 4, 46. During the five years on which Dr. Halley has founded his Table, or from 1687 to 1691, the births happened a little to exceed the burials.

1. [*Author's note:*] In 1738 there was an account taken of the number of families and inhabitants in the Prussian dominions. The number of inhabitants was 2,138,465. The medium of annual births, weddings, and burials was nearly 84,000, 21,000, and 55,481. Near a 40th part, therefore, died every year. See Short, *op. cit.*, p. 69; Martyn, *loc. cit.* The proportion of weddings and burials to the births shews that, in these countries, there was a quick increase, notwithstanding the waste in the cities. In the year 1733 a survey was taken of the inhabitants of the parish of Stoke Damerel in Devonshire, and the number of men, women, and children, was found to be 3361. The *christenings* for the year were 122—the *weddings* 28—*burials* 62. No more, therefore, than the 54th part of the inhabitants died in the year. In part of this year an epidemical fever prevailed in the parish. See Martyn, *op. cit.*, IX, 325. According to Graunt's account of a parish in Hampshire, not reckoned, he says, remarkably healthful, a 50th part of the inhabitants had died annually for 90 years. Graunt, *op. cit.*, chap. xii.

England there is a very rapid increase of the inhabitants: but, not-withstanding this, at Boston, the capital, the inhabitants would decrease were there no supply from the country: for, if the account I have seen is just, from 1731 to 1762, the burials have all along exceeded the births.[2] So remarkably do towns, in consequence of their unfavourableness to health, and the luxury which generally prevails in them, check the increase of countries.

Healthfulness and Prolifickness are, probably, causes of increase seldom separated. In conformity to this observation, it appears from comparing the births and weddings, in countries and towns where registers of them have been kept, that in the former, marriages, one with another, seldom produce less than four children each, generally between four and five, and sometimes above five. But in towns seldom above four, generally between three and four, and sometimes under three.[3]

I have sometimes heard the great number of old people in London mentioned to prove its favourableness to health and long life. But no observation can be much more erroneous. There ought, in reality, to be more old people in London, in proportion to the number of inhabitants, than in any smaller towns, because at least one quarter of its inhabitants are persons who come into it, from the country, in the most robust part of life, and with a much greater probability of attaining old age, than if they had come into it in the weakness of infancy. But, notwithstanding this advantage, there are much fewer persons who attain to great ages in London than in any other place where observations have been made. At Vienna, of 22,704 who died in the four years 1717, 1718, 1724, 1725,[4] 109 reached 90 years, that is, 48 in 10,000. But in London, for the last 30

2. [*Author's note:*] See a particular account of the births and burials in this town from 1731 to 1752 in *Gent. Mag.*, XXIII (1753), 413.

3. [*Author's note:*] Any one may see what evidence there is for this, by consulting the accounts in Dr. Short's two books already quoted, and in Martyn, *op. cit.*, VII, pt. 4, 46. In considering these accounts, it should not be forgotten that allowances must be made for the different circumstances of increase or decrease in a place, agreeably to the observation at the end of the note in p. 103 [above p. 91].

4. [*Author's note:*] See Martyn, *loc. cit.* It appears also that more than three-fifths of all who died in these years at Vienna were boys and girls, by whom, I suppose, are meant persons under 16. About the same proportion dies under 16 at Berlin.

years, only 35 of the same number have reached this age. At Breslaw it appears, by Dr. Halley's Table, that 41 of 1238 born, or a 30th
part, live to be 80 years of age. In the parish of All-saints in North-
ampton,[5] an account has been kept for many years of the ages at
which all die; and, I find, that of 1377, who died there in 13 years,
59 have lived to be 80, or a 23d part. According to Mr. Kersseboom's
Table of Observations, published at the end of Abraham De Moivre,
The Doctrine of Chances ... (3rd ed., London, 1756), a 14th part of
all that are born live to be 80; and, had we any observations in
country parishes, this, probably, would not appear to be too high a
proportion.[6] But in London, for the last 30 years, only 25 of every
1000 who have died, have lived to be 80, or a 40th part, which may
be easily discovered by dividing the sum of all who have died
during these years at all ages, by the sum of all who have died above
80.

Among the peculiar evils to which great towns are subject, I
might further mention the PLAGUE. Before the year 1666 this dread-
ful calamity laid London almost waste once in every 15 or 20 years;
and there is no reason to think that it was not generally bred within
itself. A most happy alteration has taken place, which, perhaps, in
part, is owing to the greater advantages of cleanliness and openness, which London has enjoyed since it was rebuilt, and which
lately have been very wisely improved.

The facts I have now taken notice of are so important that, I
think, they deserve more attention than has been hitherto bestowed
upon them. Every one knows that the strength of a state consists
in the number of people. The encouragement of population,
therefore, ought to be one of the first objects of policy in every
state; and some of the worst enemies of population are the luxury,

5. [*Author's note:*] In this town, as in most other towns of any magnitude,
the births, including Dissenters, fall short of the burials; and the greater part
die under age.

6. [*Author's note:*] This, however, will appear itself inconsiderable, when
compared with the following account: "In 1761, the burials in the district of
Christiana, in Norway, amounted to 6,929, and the christenings to 11,024.
Among those who died, 394, or 1 in 18, had lived to the age of 90; 63 to the age
of 100, and seven to the age of 101. In the diocese of Bergen, the persons who
died amounted only to 2,580, of whom 18 lived to the age of 100; one woman
to the age of 104, and another woman to the age of 108." *The Annual Register,
or a View of the History, Politicks, and Literature* ..., IV (1761), 191.

the licentiousness, and debility produced and propagated by great towns.

I have observed that London is now increasing.[7] But it appears that, in truth, this is an event more to be dreaded than desired. The more London increases, the more the rest of the kingdom must be deserted; the fewer hands must be left for agriculture; and, consequently, the less must be the plenty and the higher the price of all the means of subsistence. *Moderate* towns, being seats of refinement, emulation, and arts, may be public advantages. But *great* towns, long before they grow to half the bulk of London, become checks on population of too hurtful a nature, nurseries of debauchery and voluptuousness; and, in many respects, greater evils than can be compensated by any advantages.[8]

7. [*Author's note:*] This increase is greater than the bills shew, on account of the omission in them of the two parishes which have been most encreased by new buildings; I mean Marybone and Pancrass parishes. The former of these parishes is, I suppose, now one of the largest in London.

8. [*Author's note:*] The mean annual *births, weddings,* and *burials* in the following towns, for some years before 1768, were nearly,

	Births.	Weddings.	Burials.
At Paris,	19,200	4,300	19,500
Vienna,	5,600		6,800
Amsterdam,	4,500	2,400	7,600
Copenhagen,	2,700	868	3,100

In the Paris bills there is, I am informed, an omission of all that die in the Foundling Hospital, amounting to above 2000 annually. The excess, therefore, of the burials above the births is greater than the bills shew. This excess, however, is much less than could have been expected in so large a town. I am not sure to what cause this ought to be ascribed; but I cannot wonder at it, if it be indeed true, that a fifth of all born in Paris are sent to the Foundling Hospital, and that a third of the inhabitants die in *hospitals,* and also that all married men are excused from serving in the militia, from whence draughts are made for the army. These are encouragements to marriage and population, which no other city enjoys; and it is strange that in this kingdom some policy of the same kind with that last mentioned should not be pursued. A further singularity in the state of Paris is, that the births in it are above four times the weddings, nothing like which is the case in any other town whose bills I have seen. It may seem, therefore, that here, as well as in the most healthful and increasing country parishes, each marriage produces more than four children; but this is a conclusion which, in the present case, cannot be depended on. It should be considered that, probably, some who leave the country to settle at Paris, come to it already married; and that no small proportion of the births may be illegitimate. These causes, however, may only balance the allowance to be made for the second

Dr. Heberden observes that, in Madeira, the inhabitants double their own number in 84 years. But this (as you, Sir, well know) is a very slow increase compared with that which takes place among our colonies in AMERICA. In the back settlements, where the inhabitants apply themselves entirely to agriculture, and luxury is not known, they double their own number in 15 years; and all through the northern colonies in 25 years.[9] This is an instance of increase so rapid as to have scarcely any parallel. The births in these countries must exceed the burials much more than in Madeira, and a greater proportion of the born must reach maturity. In 1738, the number of inhabitants in New Jersey was taken by order of the government, and found to be 47,369. Seven years afterwards the number of inhabitants was again taken, and found to be increased, by procreation only, above 14,000, and very near one *half* of the inhabitants

---

and third marriages among the annual weddings; and, if it is indeed fact, that the people at Paris are so prolific as they appear to be in the bills, it will only prove more strongly that, like other great towns, it is very unfavourable to health; for the more prolific a people are, the greater must be the mortality among them if they do not increase. Let us suppose the true number of deaths at Paris, including emigrants and such as die in the Foundling Hospital, to be 21,000; the number married annually 2 × 4,300 or 8,600; and the births, as before, 19,200. 1,900 then will be the number of annual recruits from the country. Of these let only 1,200 be supposed to marry: and 8,600 lessened by 1,200, or 7,400, will be the number of those born at Paris who marry annually; and 11,800, or above *three-fifths* will be the number dying in childhood and celibacy. This, though it gives an unfavourable representation of Paris when compared with the country, makes it appear to advantage when compared with some other great towns. I am not sufficiently informed of the state of Paris to know how near this calculation comes to the truth. Every such doubt would be removed, were the ages of the dead given in the Paris bills. It is much to be wished this was done. The births and burials here come so near to one another, that there can scarcely be a properer place for such bills; and a Table of Observations might be formed from them that would give the values of lives much more exactly than the London Tables.

I cannot help adding that, excepting the omission I have mentioned in the burials, the Paris bills are complete; but it is well known that the London bills are extremely otherwise. London, therefore, must be much larger in comparison of Paris than it appears to be in the bills.

9. [*Author's note:*] See Ezra Stiles, *A Discourse on the Christian Union* (Boston, 1761), pp. 103, 109, &c. See also [BF], *The Interest of Great Britain Considered....with Regard to Her Colonies. To Which Are Added, Observations Concerning the Increase of Mankind, Peopling of Countries, etc.* (2nd ed., London, 1761), p. 35 [or above, IX, 87].

were found to be under 16 years of age.[1] In 22 years, therefore, they must have doubled their own number, and the births must have exceeded the burials 2000 annually. As the increase here is much quicker than in Madeira, we may be sure that a smaller proportion of the inhabitants must die annually. Let us, however, suppose it the same, or a 50th part. This will make the annual burials to have been, during these seven years, 1000, and the annual births 3000, or an 18th part of the inhabitants. Similar observations may be made on the much quicker increase in Rhode Island, as related in the preface to Dr. Birch's *Collection of the Bills of Mortality*, and also in the valuable pamphlet, last quoted, on *The Interest of Great Britain with Regard to Her Colonies*, p. 36 [above, IX, 87–88]. What a prodigious difference must there be between the vigour and the happiness of human life in such situations, and in such a place as London? The original number of persons who, in 1643, had settled in New England, was 21,200. Ever since it is reckoned, that more have left them than have gone to them.[2] In the year 1760 they were increased to half a million. They have, therefore, all along doubled their own number in 25 years; and, if they continue to increase at the same rate, they will, 70 years hence, in New England alone, be four millions; and in all North America[3] above twice the number of in-

1. [*Author's note:*] According to Dr. Halley's Table the number of the living under 16 is but a *third* of all the living at all ages; and this may be nearly the case in all places which just support themselves in the number of their inhabitants, and neither increase or decrease.

2. [*Author's note:*] See Ezra Stiles, *op. cit.*, p. 110, &c.

3. When Price reprinted this essay fourteen years later, he substituted "all the colonies" for "North America" and appended an interesting note: "In the original letter to Dr. Franklin, containing these observations, and communicated by him to the Royal Society (in April 1769), the following words were here added: 'Formerly an increasing number of FRIENDS, but now likely to be converted, by an unjust and fatal policy, into an increasing number of ENEMIES.' This reflexion was occasioned by the discontents which were then prevalent in the colonies, and which had been produced first by the Stamp Act, and after the repeal of that act, by the duties laid in America on tea, paper, glass, &c. When read to the Royal Society, it was softened by the omission of the words 'unjust and fatal policy'; but, notwithstanding this, it gave offence; and was suppressed in all the former publications of these Observations. I need not say how dreadfully the apprehensions expressed by it have been since verified." *Observations on Reversionary Payments, . . . to Which Are Added Four Essays on Different Subjects in the Doctrine of Life-Annuities and Political Arithmetick* (4th ed.; 2 vols., London, 1783), I, 284 n.

habitants in Great-Britain.[4] But I am wandering from my purpose in this letter. The point I had chiefly in view was, the present state

4. [*Author's note:*] The rate of increase, supposing the procreative powers the same, depends on two causes: The "encouragement to marriage;" and the "*expectation* of a child just born." When one of these is given, the increase will be always in proportion to the other. That is; As much *greater* or *less* as the *ratio* is of the numbers who reach maturity, and of those who marry to the number born, so much *quicker* or *slower* will be the increase. Let us suppose the operation of these causes such as to produce an annual excess of the *births* above the *burials* equal to a 36th part of the whole number of inhabitants. It may seem to follow from hence, that the inhabitants would double their own number in 36 years; and thus some have calculated. But the truth is, that they would double their own number in much less time. Every addition to the number of inhabitants from the births produces a proportionably greater number of births, and a greater excess of these above the burials; and if we suppose the excess to increase annually at the same rate with the inhabitants, or so as to preserve the *ratio* of it to the number of inhabitants always the same, and call this *ratio* $\frac{1}{r}$, the period of doubling will be the *quotient* produced by dividing the logarithm of 2 by the *difference* between the logarithms of $r + 1$ and r, as might be easily demonstrated. In the present case, r being 36, and $r + 1$ being 37, the period of doubling comes out 25 years. If r is taken equal to 22, the period of doubling will be 15 years. But it is certain that this ratio may, in many situations, be greater than $\frac{1}{22}$; and, instead of remaining the same, or becoming less, it may *increase*, the consequence of which will be, that the period of doubling will be shorter than this rule gives it. According to Dr. Halley's Table, the number of persons between 20 and 42 years of age is a third part of the whole number living at all ages. The prolific part, therefore, of a country may very well be a 4th of the whole number of inhabitants; and supposing four of these, or every other marriage between persons all under 42, to produce *one* birth every year, the annual number of births will be a 16th part of the whole number of people; and, therefore, supposing the burials to be a 48th part, the annual excess of the births above the burials will be a 24th part, and the period of doubling 17 years. The number of inhabitants in New England was, as I have said from Dr. Stiles's pamphlet, half a million in 1760. If they have gone on increasing at the same rate ever since, they must be now 640,000; and it seems to appear that in fact they are now more than this number. For, since I have writ the above observations, I have seen a particular account, grounded chiefly on surveys lately taken with a view to taxation and for other purposes, of the number of males, between 16 and 60, in the four provinces. According to this account, the number of such males is 218,000. The whole number of people, therefore, between 16 and 60, supposing 14 males to 13 females, must be nearly 420,000. In order to be more sure of avoiding excess, I will call them only 400,000. In Dr. Halley's Table the proportion of all the living under 16 and above 60, to the rest of the living, is 13·33 to 20; and this will make the number of people now living in the four

of London as to healthfulness, number of inhabitants, and its influence on population. The observations I have made may, perhaps, help to shew how the most is to be made of the lights afforded by the London bills, and serve as a specimen of the proper method of calculating from them. It is indeed extremely to be wished that they were less imperfect than they are, and extended further. More parishes round London might be taken into them; and, by an easy improvement in the parish registers now kept, they might be extended through all the parishes and towns in the kingdom. The advantages arising from hence would be very considerable. It would give the precise law according to which human life wastes in its different stages, and thus supply the necessary *data* for computing accurately the values of all *life-annuities* and *reversions*. It would, likewise, shew the different degrees of healthfulness of different situations, mark the progress of population from year to year, keep always in view the number of people in the kingdom, and, in many other respects, furnish instruction of the greatest importance to the state. Mr. De Moivre, at the end of his book on the doctrine of chances, has recommended a general regulation of this kind; and observed, particularly, that at least it is to be wished, that an account was taken, at proper intervals, of all the living in the kingdom, with their ages and occupations; which would, in some degree, answer most of the purposes I have mentioned. But, dear Sir, I am

---

provinces of New England to be 666,000. But, on account of the rapid increase, this proportion must be considerably greater in New England, than that given by Dr. Halley's Table. In New Jersey, I have said the number of people under 16 was found to be almost equal to the number above 16. Suppose, however, that in New England, where the increase is somewhat slower, the proportion I have mentioned is only 16 to 20, and then the whole number of people will be 720,000.

I cannot conclude this note without adding a remark to remove an objection which may occur to some in reading Dr. Heberden's account of Madeira, to which I have referred. In that account 5945 is given as the number of children under seven in the island, at the beginning of the year 1767. The medium of annual births, for eight years, had been 2201; of burials 1293. In six years, therefore, 13,206 must have been born; and if, at the end of six years, no more than 5945 of these were alive, 1210 must have died every year. That is; almost all the burials in the island, for six years, must have been burials of children under seven years of age. This is plainly incredible; and, therefore, it seems certain, that the number of children under seven years of age must, through some mistake, be given, in that account, 3000 or 4000 too little.

sensible it is high time to finish these remarks. I have been carried in them far beyond the limits I at first intended. I always think with pleasure and gratitude of your friendship. The world owes to you many important discoveries; and your name must live as long as there is any knowledge of philosophy among mankind. That your happiness in this, and every other respect, may continually increase, is the sincere wish of, Sir, Your much obliged, and very humble servant, RICHARD PRICE.

Positions to Be Examined   MS (copy): Yale University Library[5]

Franklin had long advocated a labor theory of value,[6] and in correspondence with Lord Kames and the French physiocrats he refined his ideas of the relation between labor, agriculture, manufacturing, and commerce. The brief paper below seems to have been a development of the "aphorisms," as he called them, that he had sent to Lord Kames early in the year.[7] His position relates, at least by implication, to his often expressed views on the dangers to the empire that were inherent in British commercial policies, and to the potential benefits of the nonimportation agreements to American manufacturing. He was not yet ready, however, to abandon the mercantilist system in favor of the theory of free trade then being discussed in France[8] and developed in Scotland by Lord Kames's protégé, Adam Smith.

April 4. 1769

Positions to be examined.

1 All Food or Subsistence for Mankind arise from the Earth or Waters.

2 Necessaries of Life that are not Foods, and all other Conveniencies, have their Values estimated by the Proportion of Food consumed while we are employed in procuring them.

5. The copy, though dated, is in an unidentifiable hand; we cannot tell, therefore, whether it was made before or after the first publication of the paper, which was in *De Re Rustica; or, the Repository for Select Papers on Agriculture, Arts, and Manufactures*, 1 (1769), 350–2.

6. See for example above, 1, 141–57; IX, 77–100.

7. See BF to Kames above, Jan. 1, and Kames's reply, Jan. 21.

8. See BF to LeRoy above, Jan. 31. "Positions to be Examined" was subsequently published in French in *Ephémérides du citoyen, ou bibliothèque raisonée des sciences morales et politiques*, X (Oct., 1769), 6–16.

3 A small People with a large Territory may subsist on the Productions of Nature, with no other Labour than that of gathering the Vegetables and catching the Animals.

4 A large People with a small Territory finds these insufficient, and, to subsist, must labour the Earth to make it produce greater Quantities of vegetable Food, suitable for the Nourishment of Men, and of the Animals they intend to eat.

5 From the Labour arises a *great Increase* of vegetable and animal Food, and of Materials for Clothing, as Flax, Wool, Silk, &c. The Superfluity of these is Wealth. With this Wealth we pay for the Labour employed in building our Houses, Cities, &c. which are therefore only Subsistence thus metamorphosed.

6 *Manufactures* are only *another Shape* into which so much Provisions and Subsistence are turned as were *equal in Value* to the Manufactures produced. This appears from hence, that the Manufacturer does not in fact, obtain from the Employer, for his Labour, *more* than a mere Subsistence, including Raiment Fuel and Shelter; all which derive their Value from the Provisions consumed in procuring them.

7 The Produce of the Earth, thus converted into Manufactures, may be more easily carried to distant Markets than before such Conversion.

8 *Fair* Commerce is where equal Values are exchanged for equal the Expence of Transport included. Thus if it costs A. in England as much Labour and Charge to raise a Bushel of Wheat as it costs B. in France to produce four Gallons of Wine then are four Gallons of Wine the fair Exchange for a Bushel of Wheat. A and B meeting at half Distance with their Commodities to make the Exchange. The Advantage of this fair Commerce is, that each Party increases the Number of his Enjoyments, having, instead of Wheat alone or Wine alone, the Use of both Wheat and Wine.

9 Where the Labour and Expence of producing both Commodities are known to both Parties Bargains will generally be fair and equal. Where they are known to one Party only, Bargains will often be unequal, Knowledge taking its Advantage of Ignorance.

10 Thus he that carries 1000 Bushels of Wheat abroad to sell, may not probably obtain so great a Profit thereon as if he had first turned the Wheat into Manufactures by subsisting therewith the Workmen while producing those Manufactures: since there are

many expediting and facilitating Methods of working, not generally known; and Strangers to the Manufactures, though they know
pretty well the Expences of raising Wheat, are unacquainted with
those short Methods of working, and thence being apt to suppose
more Labour employed in the Manufactures than there really is,
are more easily imposed on in their Value, and induced to allow
more for them than they are honestly worth.

11 Thus the Advantage of having Manufactures in a Country,
does not consist as is commonly supposed, in their highly advancing
the Value of rough Materials, of which they are formed; since,
though sixpenny worth of Flax may be worth twenty shillings when
worked into Lace, yet the very Cause of it's being worth twenty
shillings is, that besides the Flax, it has cost nineteen shillings and
sixpence in Subsistence to the Manufacturer. But the Advantage of
Manufactures is, that under their shape Provisions may be more
easily carried to a foreign Market; and by their means our Traders
may more easily cheat Strangers. Few, where it is not made are
Judges of the Value of Lace. The importer may demand Forty, and
perhaps get Thirty shillings for that which cost him but twenty.

12 Finally, there seem to be but three Ways for a Nation to ac-
quire Wealth. The first is by *War* as the Romans did in plundering
their conquered Neighbours. This is *Robbery*. The second by *Commerce* which is generally *Cheating*. The third by *Agriculture* the only
honest Way; wherein Man receives a real Increase of the Seed
thrown into the Ground, in a kind of continual Miracle wrought by
the Hand of God in his Favour, as a Reward for his innocent Life,
and virtuous Industry.   B F

From John Bartram   ALS: American Philosophical Society

April the 10th 1769
My much Respected ould and Constant Friend
I received with great pleasure my dear friends letter of January
the 9th 1769 and am much obliged to him for his kindness in takeing
care of the Box for the King. I should have wrote to Michael Colin-
son Last fall but I did not know then his name alltho I asked several
that had frequented his fathers house but towards the spring I received a very kindly expresed letter from him dated September the

22 wherein he gave me a perticular account of his father's death and the friendship that had subsisted between us but mentioned nothing of our Correspondent affairs how thay stand.[9] I allso by the same Vesail received a kind letter from Dr. Fothergil[1] who ofered to do me what kindness he could consistant with his great hurry of business. But stil I am at A loss to know whether I must send any more plants or seeds to his Majesty and whether he is pleased to continue his bounty to me or not. I wrote to Mr. Collinson and the Doctor by the first opertunity after I received thairs and desired Mr. Collinson to let me know how our accounts stands (which I expect is Considerable) and whether he inclines to Correspond with me as his father did for upwards of thirty years. I am at present in good health but hath been afflicted all winter with sore ancles one is healed and the other is mending occationed by a small bruise which turned to painfull ulcers so that my travails as to any distant provinces is at an end. I sent my Journal thro the Carolinas Georgia and florida wherein I wrote my observations daly of the perticular soils rivers and natural vegetable productions with which our friend Peter expresed Much satisfaction[2] but there was no artificial curiosities in those provinces as temples, theaters, piramids palaces bridges catacoms oblisks picturs and different methods of government and customs to be discribed; which fills up the greatest part of all our modern travailers Journals alltho thay have been ten times near as well or better related many years before.

We have had the appearance of the Borealis twice last winter one the most vivid the last of february and lately two severe thunder storms with allmost continual flashes of lightning for near two hours the streams of which ran in a horizontal direction generaly.

My dear beloved friend thy kind letter moved me much it was not

9. For the matters under discussion see above, Bartram to BF, XV, 256–7, and BF to Bartram, Jan. 9, 1769.

1. His and BF's old Quaker friend John Fothergill, for whom see above, IV, 126 n.

2. Bartram sent Peter Collinson the journals of most of his travels; few have survived, but the one to which he refers is among them. It was printed in part in William Stork, *An Account of East-Florida, with a Journal, Kept by John Bartram of Philadelphia...* (London, [1766]), and reprinted in Francis Harper, ed., *Diary of a Journey through the Carolinas, Georgia, and Florida from July 1, 1765, to April 10, 1766*, APS, *Trans.*, XXXIII, pt. 1 (Philadelphia, 1942).

for want of respect that I did not write to thee before but supposeing that thy publick afaires for the Provincial good took up so much of thy time as an hour was not to be spared to read or write a letter to thy ould friend JOHN BARTRAM

PS I am much obliged to thee for the barley and naked oats and I expect tomorow to receive some naked barley brought from Carolina.[3]

Addressed: To / Dr Benjamin Franklin in / London

From James Parker
ALS: American Philosophical Society

[Philadelphia, April 14, 1769. John Foxcroft has summoned him there. Encloses a second bill for £60 13s. 9d., the first of which he had sent from New York on February 13. This Foxcroft had returned to him to send to Franklin. Is in poor health but hopes to recover.]

From Michael Hillegas
ALS: American Philosophical Society

Sir   Philad. April 15th, 1769.
    Yours of the 5th January was handed me by Capt. Falconer, am much Obliged to you for having given the Orders for the making the Glasses for my Armonica—hope they will meet a better fate than the others you were pleased to send.[4]
    The Nova Scotia Adventurers will now soon be expecting your Letter in Answer to ours, and for which will be under Obligation.[5] I am Sir with unfeigned Esteem Your most Obedient Humble Servant   M. HILLEGAS

Addressed: To / Dr. Benja. Franklin / Craven Street / London / per favour of / Capt. Falconer

Endorsed: Hillegas

3. Naked oats and barley are particular varieties. For the grain that BF had sent see above, xv, 248, 292–3.
4. They had broken in transit: BF to Hillegas above, Jan. 5.
5. Neither the letter nor BF's answer, if he wrote one, has been found; but for his current involvement with the speculators see above, xv, 121.

From Thomas Coombe[6]

ALS: American Philosophical Society

Dear Sir, Philadelphia April 17th, 1769

Your favour of the 5th January, I receiv'd per Cap. Falconer. The Book you was pleased to send me, I also received, and accept as a mark of the Authors Friendship, tho the Instances of the very extraordinary kindness shewn my Son and your Assurances of it's continuance, together with the Pleasure you are pleased to express in my recommending him to you, are too strong to need any other.[7] For which my Dear Friend, please to accept the acknowledgments of a most grateful Heart, as a Tribute. The good opinion you are pleas'd to entertain of him, affords me much Joy, especially when I consider it is, that of *Dr. Franklin's*.

My warmest wishes for your Health and Happiness shall ever accompany you, and believe me to be with sentiments of the sincerest esteem and affection Dear Sir, Your affectionate Friend and humble Servant T COOMBE

Verte

P.S. Please to direct Cap. Falconer, where to get a Couple of those Tubes, mention'd in the 60th Letter of your Philosophic Works, also those described by Priestly in the 571 Page of his Compilation, which is for exhibiting the Phaenomenon of Elec[tricity] in *Vacuo*, and called *Canton's Aurora Borealis*.[8] T C

To Dr. Franklin

Addressed: To | Benjamin Franklin Esqr | at his House in Craven Street | London | per | Cap Falconer | QDC.

Endorsed: Coombe

6. For the little that is known about Thomas Coombe, Sr., see above, XI, 107 n. The letter that follows makes clear that he shared BF's scientific interest and that the two were friends of long standing, but no other correspondence between them has come to light.

7. The book was *Exper. and Obser.* (4th ed., London, 1769), which BF had been sending to many friends. For his hospitality to young Thomas Coombe in London see above, XV, 53, 286 n, 293.

8. BF's tubes were the pulse glasses mentioned in his letter to Winthrop above, XV, 170; the letter was printed in the edition of *Exper. and Obser.* that he sent to Coombe, pp. 485–92. In Priestley's tubes was a Torricellian vacuum, in which could be observed the phenomenon named for John Canton, the famous electrical experimenter: Joseph Priestley, *The History and Present State of Electricity* (London, 1767), p. 571.

Pennsylvania Assembly Committee of Correspondence to Benjamin Franklin and Richard Jackson

LS: Library of Congress

Gentlemen, Philada. April 18th. 1769

Being desirous of preventing any ill Effects which may ensue from a Misrepresentation of the Conduct of the Inhabitants of the Province at this Critical Juncture, We think it necessary to give you a brief account of a Riot lately committed in this City, by a few of the lower kind of the People, That, if any mention should be made of it, on your side of the Water, to the disadvantage of the Province, you may have it in your Power to do us Justice, by Stating the Facts in a true Light.

Several Pipes of Madeira Wine being siezed by the Collector of this Port, in a Store on the River, a number of Disorderly Persons on the First day of this Month, enter'd into a Combination to carry them off. The Collector hearing of their intentions went to the place, where he received some abuse and ill treatment, but did not succeed in preventing the Execution of their design. About Midnight several of the same People as it is suppos'd, passing through the Street, broke his Window's and behaved in a disorderly manner.

On application to the Mayor and other Majestrates of the City, they exerted themselves on the Occasion, and immediately sent the Constables to the Collectors assistance; But the Rioters having boats ready to carry off the Wines, they were too late to be of Service. However, on Complaint to the Mayor, several of the Rioters who were known, were apprehended, Indicted and fin'd by the Court which sat soon after. And every thing was done by the Officers of Justice that the Officers of the Customs required, and a laudable disposition appeared manifest in the former to suppress all illegal attempts against the latter in the performance of their Duty.

The Merchants and many reputable Inhabitants of the City discovered great concern on these lawless Transactions, and altho' they do not approve of the Acts imposing the Duties for which these Wines were seized, yet we can assure you, that they were neither privy to, aiding in, or by any means giving Countenance to them. But, on the Contrary, resolved to discourage such Illegal and Dangerous proceedings in future. A number of them met the next Day at the Coffee house, and were instrumental in prevailing on the Owner or Factor of the Wines (who is a Person who has not been long a resident in the Province) to redeliver them at the Store from whence they were taken, which was required by the Custom House Officers; This we understand has been since done, but whether to the full satisfaction of the Officers of the Customs, we are not Certain.[9]

At the last January sitting a Number of Laws, some of them of Public Importance were passed in Assembly. We conclude they will be presented by the Proprietarys as usual for the Royal Dissent or Approbation. Should any objections be made to them, we doubt not, your Attention and Utmost endeavours will be made use of to support them. Within the last Three Years many Laws have been Transmitted by the Governor to the Proprietarys, but whether presented, approved, or repeal'd, we have received no Account. It will therefore be agreeable to the House, to know how these Laws stand, whether approv'd or repeal'd, and we desire you to transmit per first opportunity an Account thereof as has been heretofore usual. We are Your respectful Friends[1]

> Jos. GALLOWAY Speaker
> Jas. PEMBERTON
> Jos. RICHARDSON

To Richard Jackson and Benja. Franklin Esqrs. London

Addressed: To / Richd. Jackson and Benja. Franklin Esqrs. / in / London

Endorsed: 1769

9. On orders from John Williams, the Inspector General of the customs, and brother of Jonathan, Sr., almost fifty pipes of madeira were seized by the customs collector, John Swift, on the charge that the consignee was evading the duty; seizure consisted of padlocking the building in which the wine was stored. When Swift tried belatedly to remove the pipes for safekeeping, he was prevented by force; the mob then removed them and sent them up river by boat. The owner knew where they were, and the merchants ostensibly prevailed upon him to return them to the building; what he actually delivered was another wine, less in quantity and worse in quality, or so one of the customs officers reported to the Commissioners in Boston. The officer added that he had been beaten and threatened until he fled for his life. George P. Donehoo, ed., *Pennsylvania: a History* (7 vols., New York and Chicago, 1926), II, 1038; Mass. Hist. Soc. *Collections*, 4th ser., x, 611–17.

1. For identification of the signers see above, xv, 23 n.

From the Philadelphia Merchants

LS: American Philosophical Society

Much Esteemed Friend,   Philada. 18th April 1769.

We are favoured with thy letter of the 19th January, and observe with pleasure the Steps thou hast taken to Serve the Cause of America, which we cannot forbear considering as the Cause of Liberty.

The Committee of Merchants in London inform us of an Application they had made to the proper Department in Administration. But the Answer they received is so very unfavourable, that we have but little prospect of Redress in a way that will put an End to the Dispute between Great Britain and the Colonies.[2]

We observe that both the Merchants and Minister confine themselves to the Act imposing Duties on Glass, Paper, &c. which they agree is Inexpedient, upon the Principles of impropriety in laying Duties on their own Manufactures, but they take no Notice of the other Acts passed for the purpose of raising a Revenue in America.[3] From this we are apprehensive that the Ministry, if pushed, intend only a partial Redress of American Grievances, and though they may suffer the Act laying a Duty on British Manufactures to be repealed, upon a principle of Inexpediency, yet they mean to continue the other Acts; in order to establish the Right of Parliament to tax the Colonies. Now as we are persuaded the Americans will

2. The letter from the London Committee of Merchants has apparently not survived, but some of its contents can be reconstructed from the answer of the Philadelphia merchants on April 8, printed in *PMHB*, XXVII (1903), 84–7. The Londoners reported that they had seen Hillsborough, who had told them that the act imposing duties on British manufactured goods was inexpedient, but that the reaction in America had been so unjustifiable as to preclude immediate repeal; the administration would not yield to threats. If, however, the colonial attitude changed and the merchants petitioned a later session of Parliament for repeal on the sole basis of expediency, Hillsborough added, there was every reason to suppose that the petition would be granted. An extract from this letter, or from another from London that covered part of the same ground, was printed in the *Pa. Gaz.*, March 30, 1769.

3. There were three Townshend Acts. The first created the board of Commissioners of the Customs in America; the second imposed duties on manufactured goods and tea entering American ports, and stipulated that the revenue so raised would be used for colonial defense and civil government; the third reduced the price of tea imported into America. Gipson, *British Empire*, XI, 111–12.

never admit this Right, nor give up the Privilege of solely taxing themselves, we can have little expectation of a cordial Union between both Countries, untill there is an alteration in the Sentiments of Administration.

Untill the Prospect mends the Merchants of this City have agreed to decline the Importation of Goods from Great Britain.

We take the liberty to inclose thee a copy of the Agreement and our Answer to the Committee of Merchants in London.[4]

We have no doubt of thy sincere Wishes for the Welfare of both Countries, nor of thy unremitted Endeavours to bring about a cordial Union between them; to effect which nothing in our Power shall be wanting. We are, with due regard, Thy assured Friends,[5]

JEREAH: WARDER	WM. WEST
WILLIAM FISHER	JAMES MEASE
ABEL JAMES	ROBT MORRIS
HENRY DRINKER	JOHN COX Junr.
ALEX HUSTON	TENCH FRANCIS
JOHN RHEA	THOMAS MIFFLIN
JOHN GIBSON	CHA THOMSON
JOSEPH SWIFT	GEO: ROBERTS
CONYNGHAM & NESBITT	

4. In February the Philadelphia merchants had adopted a tentative non-importation agreement; see Thomas Gilpin to BF above, Feb. 6. On March 10 they confirmed this agreement and made it binding until the duties were repealed. The two agreements and their preambles, and the letter of April 8 to the London Committee, are among BF's papers: APS.

5. Swift, Warder, Drinker, and West were the only members of the group who had signed the letter to BF the previous autumn, for which see above, XV, 266–7. William Fisher was a Quaker, a member of the Common Council (1767–70), and later an alderman and mayor of Philadelphia: *PMHB*, XVI (1892), 105. All that is known of John Rhea is that he was a merchant on Market Street, and of John Gibson that he was mayor of the city in 1772–73. For James Mease, who founded the shipping firm of Mease & Caldwell, see John H. Campbell, *History of the Friendly Sons of St. Patrick and of the Hibernian Society for the Relief of Emigrants from Ireland* (Philadelphia, 1892), pp. 121–2. Robert Morris needs no identification; see *DAB*. John Cox, Jr., may well have been the mysterious figure who led a faction of the "suffering traders"; above, XV, 265 n. The remaining signers have been identified or at least mentioned above, as follows: Abel James, XI, 436 n; Alexander Huston, XI, 472, 484; Conyngham & Nesbitt, VIII, 424 n; Tench Francis, Jr., XIV, 160 n; Thomas Mifflin, XI, 78 n; Charles Thomson, VII, 266 n; and George Roberts, IX, 116 n.

From Harvard College

Reprinted from William C. Lane, "Harvard College and Franklin," Colonial Society of Massachusetts *Publications*, X (1907), 237.

At a Meeting of the President and Fellows of
Harvard College April 25. 1769.

Vote 8. That the Thanks of this Board be given to Dr. Franklin for his many very obliging acts of friendship; particularly for his care in procuring several valuable Instruments for the Apparatus,[6] and that he be desired to continue his kind regards to the College.

To Samuel Cooper[7]

ALS: British Museum

Dear Sir, London, April 27. 1769

I received your Favour of Feb. 27. per Capt. Carver, and thank you for giving me an Opportunity of being acquainted with so great a Traveller.[8] I shall be glad if I can render him any Service here.

The Parliament remain fix'd in their Resolution not to repeal the

6. The instruments mentioned above, XV, 166–7, and probably also the telescope that BF had recently sent; see his letter to John Winthrop above, March 11. Five ships had just arrived after a one-month crossing; *Boston Chron.*, April 17–20, 1769.

7. For the Rev. Samuel Cooper see above, IV, 69 n. He circulated this letter among friends, and extracts were made for the delectation of the Boston merchants. BF's name was omitted, and the extracts were changed slightly in their wording to make them appear to be from various friends of America in England. In this altered and condensed form BF's letter, entitled "Intelligence...from London," found its way into the American press, first in the *Boston Gaz.* of June 12, 1769, and subsequently in other papers. See Cooper to BF below, Aug. 3; Crane, *Letters to the Press*, pp. 161–2. The sections that appeared in print are indicated by footnotes.

8. Jonathan Carver (1710–80) served in the French and Indian War and rose to be captain. He then made a 7000-mile journey to what is now Wisconsin and Minnesota, where a county and town and river bear his name. He made charts and kept a journal that he intended to publish, and early in 1769 he left his wife and children and went to England to find a publisher. Instead he found another wife, by whom he raised another family. When he eventually succeeded in having his work printed, *Travels through the Interior Parts of North-America in the Years 1766, 1767, and 1768* (London, 1778) was a great popular success. *DAB* and *DNB*, which differ markedly in details.

Duty Acts this Session, and will rise next Tuesday.⁹ I hope my Country-folks will remain as fix'd in their Resolutions of Industry and Frugality till those Acts are repeal'd. And if I could be sure of that, I should almost wish them never to be repeal'd; being persuaded that we shall reap more solid and extensive Advantages from the steady Practice of those two great Virtues, than we can possibly suffer Damage from all the Duties the Parliament of this Kingdom can levy on us. They flatter themselves that you cannot long subsist without their Manufactures; they believe that you have not Virtue enough to persist in such Agreements; they imagine the Colonies will differ among themselves, deceive and desert one another, and quietly one after the other submit to the Yoke and return to the Use of British Fineries: they think that tho' the Men may be contented with homespun Stuffs, the Women will never get the better of their Vanity and Fondness for English Modes and Gewgaws. The ministerial People all talk in this Strain, and many even of the Merchants!¹ I have ventur'd to assert, that they will all find themselves mistaken; and I rely so much on the Spirit of my Country as to be confident I shall not be found a false Prophet, tho' at present not believed.

I hope nothing that has happened or may happen will diminish in the least our Loyalty to our Sovereign, or Affection for this Nation in general. I can scarcely conceive a King of better Dispositions, of more exemplary Virtues, or more truly desirous of promoting the Welfare of all his Subjects. The Experience we have had of the Family in the two preceding mild Reigns, and the good Temper of our young Princes so far as can yet be discovered, promise us a Continuance of this Felicity. The Body of this People too is of a noble and generous Nature, loving and honouring the Spirit of Liberty, and hating arbitrary Power of all Sorts. We have many very many Friends among them. But as to the Parliament!—tho' I might excuse That which made the Acts, as being surpriz'd and misled into the Measure; [I] know not how to excuse This,² which under the fullest Conviction of its being a wrong one, resolves to continue it. It is decent indeed in your publick Papers to speak as you do of the "*Wisdom* and the *Justice* of Parliament"; but now that

9. *I.e.*, May 2. Parliament was actually prorogued a week later.
1. The paragraph to this point was the first extract.
2. The Parliament elected in the spring of 1768.

the Subject is more thoroughly understood, if this new Parliament had been really *wise* it would not have refused even to *read* a Petition against the Acts; and if it had been *just*, it would have repealed them and refunded the Money. Perhaps it may be *wiser* and *juster* another Year, but that is not to be depended on.

If under all the Insults and Oppressions you are now exposed to, you can prudently, as you have lately done, continue q[uiet,] avoiding Tumults, but still resolutely keeping up your Claims and asserting your Rights, you will finally establish them; and this military Cloud that now blusters over you, will pass away, and do you no more Harm than a Summer Thunder Shower. But the Advantages of your Perseverance in Industry and Frugality will be great and permanent: Your Debts will be paid; your Farms will be better improv'd and yield a greater Produce: Your real Wealth will increase in [a] Plenty of every useful home Production and all the true Enjoyments of Life, even tho' no foreign Trade should be allow'd you.[3] And this handicraft shopkeeping State will for its own [sake?] learn to behave more civilly to its Customers.

Your late Governor, Mr. Pownall, appears a hearty Friend to America. He moved last Week for a Repeal of the Acts, and was seconded by General Conway, Sir George Saville, Mr. Jackson, Mr. Trecothic and others, but did not succeed.[4] A Friend has favour'd me with a Copy of the Notes taken of Mr. Pownall's Speech, which I send you, believing it may be agreable to you and some other of our Friends to see them.[5] You will observe in some

3. The paragraph to this point was the second extract.

4. On April 19 Pownall made a long speech against the Townshend Acts, ending with a motion that the House of Commons debate their repeal. The administration succeeded, after considerable discussion, in having the issue postponed until the next session. *Cavendish's Debates*, I, 391–401. For the speakers who supported Pownall see Namier and Brooke, *House of Commons*, as follows: Conway, II, 244–7; Saville, III, 405–9; Jackson, II, 669–72; Trecothick, III, 557–60.

5. Cooper was actively corresponding with Pownall as well as with BF. Pownall's letters to Cooper have been printed in Frederick Griffin, *Junius Discovered* (Boston and London, 1854), pp. 204–300, and the other side of the correspondence in Frederick Tuckerman, ed., "Letters of Samuel Cooper to Thomas Pownall, 1769–1777," *Amer. Hist. Rev.*, VIII (1902–03), 301–30. On July 12 Cooper assured Pownall that the notes BF had sent were being handled with the greatest discretion: Speaker Cushing and some other friends were circulating them as they thought best; nothing was being copied, however, let alone

Parts of it the Language a Member of Parliament is obliged to hold on American Topicks, if he would at all be heard in the House. He has given Notice that he will renew the Motion next and every Session.

All Ireland is strongly in favour of the American Cause. They have reason to sympathize with us.[6] I send you four Pamphlets written in Ireland or by Irish Gentlemen here, in which you will find some excellent well said Things.[7] With the greatest Esteem, I am, my dear Friend, Yours most affectionately   B FRANKLIN

Revd Dr Cooper.

To Jane Mecom

ALS: American Philosophical Society

Dear Sister,   London, April 27. 1769.

I received your kind Letter of Jan. 30. Mrs. Stevenson has executed your Order, and sends the Things in a Bandbox directed to you, in the Care of Mr. Jefferies your Neighbour.[8] A new-fashion'd something that was not ready when the Box was pack'd up, is inclos'd in her Letter.

I am now grown too old to be ambitious of such a Station as that which you say has been mention'd to you. Repose is more fit for me, and much more suitable to my Wishes. There is no Danger of such a thing being offer'd me, and I am sure I shall never ask it. But even if it were offer'd, I certainly could not accept it, to act under such

---

printed, lest "thro the Baseness of the Times it might be improv'd to your Disadvantage." *Ibid.*, p. 309. This consignment from BF, in other words, was treated very differently from his later consignment of the Hutchinson letters.

6. This and the preceding sentence concluded the extract.

7. The four pamphlets may well have been the following, all of which were by Irishmen and were published by the time BF was writing: William Knox, *The Present State of the Nation*... (London, 1768); Edmund Burke, *Observations on a Late State of the Nation*... (London, 1769); Sir Hercules Langrishe, *Considerations on the Dependencies of Great Britain*... (London, 1769); and *The Case of Great Britain and America, Addressed to the King and Both Houses of Parliament* (London, 1769), which is attributed to Gervase P. Bush and George P. Butler.

8. Either David Jeffries, the treasurer of Boston, or his son Dr. John, who landed on June 9, 1769, after his sojourn in England. See BF to Cooper above, Feb. 24; *Sibley's Harvard Graduates*, XV, 420.

Instructions as I know must be given with it.⁹ So you may be quite easy on that head.

The Account you write of the growing Industry, Frugality and good Sense of my Country-women gives me more Pleasure than you can imagine: For from thence I presage great Advantages to our Country. I should be sorry that you are engag'd in a Business which happens not to coincide with the general Interest, if you did not acquaint me that you are now near the End of it.¹

You guess'd right upon the Similitude with Mrs. Blount's Letter.² But hold your Tongue. Love to your Children, from Your affection-ate Brother   B FRANKLIN

By Peter Hinrich Tesdorpf:³ Poem in Eulogy of Franklin

MS translation from German: American Philosophical Society

Lubek A[pril?]⁴ 1769
Upon the unvaluable Contrivance, of Mr. Francklin, k:
to carry of the Lightening.

9. Jane's missing letter had doubtless mentioned a rumor that BF might be offered the governorship of Massachusetts; see below, pp. 129–30. The rumor perhaps grew from vague overtures to BF in 1768: above, XV, 159–62.

1. BF is referring to Jane's modest millinery business.

2. Presumably a letter from Miss Dorothea Blunt, Polly Stevenson's friend; the reference is now incomprehensible.

3. This outpouring of the Germanic muse was undoubtedly the work of an odd businessman-turned-poetaster-and-naturalist. Tesdorpf (1712–78) was the scion of a prominent Lübeck family; he was trained in Hamburg, traveled widely in western Europe, and returned to banking in his native town in 1737. Thereafter he devoted himself more and more to indulging his scientific inter-ests, developing a wide correspondence with European savants, amassing a col-lection of natural curiosities, and composing his *magnum opus*, a long didactic poem on hummingbirds. He also wrote numerous other verses, on a par with this, and as he grew older became more and more of an eccentric. For his career see Oscar L. Tesdorpf, *Mittheilungen über das Tesdorpf'sche Geschlecht* (Munich, 1887), pp. 54–75. The German original has apparently not survived, and it is charitable to suppose that it suffered in translation.

The author could conceivably have been Tesdorpf's son of the same name (1751–1832). But the boy was scarcely old enough at the time, was more likely to have written in French than German, had no hobby of versifying, and did not share his father's interest in natural science. See *ibid.*, pp. 84–98.

4. The single letter could of course stand for August, but according to our practice we choose the earlier of two equally possible dates.

Hail! thou art blessed! said lately the Moon to the Earth, Thy
Wish was for a Francklin, and Heaven granted him to be. He arose,
that Godlike Man, and delivered thy Seat, like the Happiness of the
Angels from the danger of Lightening. He surmounts the limits to
make discoveries, and fetters Nature, when Lightening and Thunder are roaring in the Clouds. Mankind having been hitherto discouraged by doubts, had never reflected seriously enough upon the
importance of the Matter, till at last thy FRANCKLIN chosen by God
for that purpose, has executed the greatest action, that ever was
done upon Earth! What dost thou wish more, to fulfill thy Wishes?
What can be added to the removal of thy Trouble? Nothing, replied the Earth, but still one Francklin more, to secure us for the
Power of Death.   by PETER HENRY TESDORPF

[*In another hand:*] Translation of German Verses

Ezra Stiles: Memoir and Conjecture

AD (draft): Yale University Library

This brief memorandum on Franklin reveals a suspiciousness that Stiles
never openly expressed. On the surface he was all admiration for his old
friend. He wanted a copy of Franklin's Oxford diploma, listed his other
honors, hoped he would be made a baronet, and asked to perpetuate his
own name by editing for posterity the works of "my dear Maecenas."[5]
But Stiles was almost obsessed with British honorary degrees, and thinking about them led him indirectly to a quite different view of the person
through whom he had received his own from Edinburgh. As soon as it
reached him he asked, in order to find out about the company he kept,
what other Americans had similar degrees. Franklin sent him a list, which
has not survived; on the back of the letter Stiles listed the Episcopalians
who had been so honored. This suggests that he was wondering about
the distribution of degree-holders among the different denominations;[6]
if so, a natural next step would have been to wonder about the group of
Presbyterian and Congregational ministers who had been awarded de-

5. Above, XIII, 175; see also X, 267, 309–11.
6. Above, XIII, 174–5; XIV, 244–5. Our predecessors were unable to explain
this episode, and our explanation is highly conjectural; we envy the assurance
with which Stiles deduced another man's motivation.

grees, and about Franklin's motives in recommending the awards—the question with which the memorandum begins. As Stiles set out to answer the question his dear Maecenas became, at least for the moment, a wily politician who used whatever came to hand, denominational rivalries or honorary degrees, to further his own interests.

May 1 1769.

Q. How came Dr. Benja. Franklin to procure several Doctorates for american presbyterian Ministers, himself being an Episcopalian and a Crown officer of 5 or £600. Sterling yearly?

Facts

1. He was born in Boston in New England, and educated a Congrega[tionalist].

2. Removing to Philad[elphi]a in Disgust about the printing office[7] became a churchman; but truely read himself almost into Deism: seldom went to church.

3. His real Idea has been coalition of all parties, being true Friend to America and gaining honor from all: till he conceived the Scheme of dethroning the proprietary Gov[ernmen]t in Pensylvania: unexpectedly the presb[yterians] there who joyned with him at first, opposed this upon finding they were less Loosers by proprietary than royal Gov[ernmen]t. Franklin joyned the Quakers a Majority in the House only because [he needed?] a Majority in order to dethrone proprietary Gov[ernment]. The house refused to protect the Frontiers, under pretext of not fighting, but truly because they were presb[yterians] and Germans. Fr[anklin] labored for Militia Bill for their Defence. This excited the presb[yterians] to petition for augment[ation] of Members in proportion to people, this would have exceeded Quaker Interest——as they were not a third of the province and yet engrossed Two Thirds of the Representa[tives].[8] Deserted by Assembly, the Frontiers put their Lives in their own hands and determined to defend and revenge themselves for the Death and Captivity of their Fathers Brethren and Sisters: and rose on a body of Indians resident among the English in frontiers and

7. Or more accurately about the printer, his brother James. See Van Doren, *Franklin*, pp. 32–3.

8. For the Mutiny Bill of 1755 see above, VI, 266–73. The demand for reapportionment was first raised not as a result of that bill but in the disturbances of 1764: above, XI, 81–2, 123–5.

killed sundry. They alledged they *knew* that several of these Indians assisted Enemy Indians in Intelligence &c. This was doubtless Fact. But Dr. Franklin and the Quakers thot otherwise. The Dr. wrote a piece against these paxton Boys, painting forth an atrocious Crime and calling for prosecution.[9] Instead of Intimidating the Frontiers came down armed [in] a Body, and alledged their Reasons justifying and declaring Resolution for future Defending themselves against Indians——and further demanding Increase [in] Representatives &c. The proprietary Gov[ernor] to mortify the Quakers who by agent Franklin was pursuing the Ruin of Penn Gov[ernment] joyned the presb[yterians]. This so augmented the prop[rietar]y Interest, that when Dr. Franklin had procured Subscrip[tions] of Freeholders to petition to King for royal Gov[ernment] the Gov[ernor] procured another against it: Franklin got 3500, Penn 15,000.[1]

The Crown officers with whom F[ranklin] was in Connexion meditated the Dissolution of 3 New England Charters, the prop[rietary] Gov[ernment] of Maryland with Pensylvania. This was a great Stroke. Franklin rather believed than wishd this; he would have been against it could he have killed Penn singly. However he expected this Revolution and would have been pleased to spend his old age in New England and even Rhode Island especially after his unsuccess[fulness] with Penn. He liked New England and would have preferred the Gov[ernment] of Rhode Island to Penn[sylvania] or Jersey.

By recomm[endin]g Hughes as Stamp Officer his Credit suffered.[2] He well knew New England and America, and valued his Fame in American Ages above his European Fame. He was in great Anxiety——in 1766 within 3 months after he sollicited the appointment of Hughes he boldly appeared against Stamp Act and by his Evidence in Parl[iamen]t[3] in part he retreived his Char[acter] with us. It is lost in Pensylvania he intends to establish it among New E[ngland] Presb[yterians] and the rest of America.

9. Above, XI, 42–69.
1. *Ibid.*, pp. 145–7, 406.
2. Above, XII, 145 n.
3. Above, XIII, 124–62.

Events produced by principles.
1. In March 1765 at Time passing Stamp Act, and when he forsaw certain revoca[tion of] Charters in which Case had been glad to be Governor Rhode Island——Diploma E. Stiles, by him.[4]
2. After repeal and still doubtful period, tho' rather prospect Loss Charters, in 1767 Dr. Coopers Diploma procured by him.[5] This at Boston.
3. In 1768, Dr. Rogers Diploma procured also by him New York. At same Time conciliating his son Governor Franklin to Dr. With[erspoon] and Jersey College.[6] This had great Effect with the Synods, and reduce Presb[yterian] oppos[ition] to him to only the Clergy of Pens[ylvania] with perhaps but a third of Synod.
4. They pleased all New England Cong[regationalists] and whole presb[yterians] Int[erest], except Dr. Alison[7] and the Min[isters] of Pennsylvania. These perhaps he will gratify also.

From Charles Thomson and Thomas Mifflin

Copy: Minutes of the Library Company of Philadelphia

Sir   Philada: 3d. May 1769
Since we had the Pleasure of writing to you an Union has taken place between the principal Librarys in Town.[8] In Consequence of

4. Above, XII, 69–70, 80–1, 98–9, 165, 195–6, 384–5.
5. Above, XIV, 218–19.
6. For the degree awarded the Rev. John Rodgers at Whitefield's instigation see above, XV, 286, 290. Rodgers, who opposed an American episcopacy, was elected in 1765 a trustee of the College of New Jersey, later Princeton. *DAB*. The Rev. John Witherspoon (1723–94) had recently arrived from Scotland to assume its presidency, and his biographer alludes to unspecified efforts by WF to Anglicanize the institution. Varnum L. Collins, *President Witherspoon: a Biography* (2 vols., Princeton, 1925), I, 76, 85. But we cannot guess what role Stiles assigned to BF in "conciliating" his Anglican son and the Presbyterian Witherspoon or what connection, if any, he saw between this rapprochement and Rodgers' degree.
7. Stiles's old friend and BF's old enemy, the Rev. Francis Alison, for whom see above, IV, 470 n.
8. The Union Library Company, organized in 1746, had already absorbed by merger the Amicable and Association Libraries, and in April, 1769, had

which the Directors have ordered a Review of the Books. And as it is not yet fully known what we have or what we want, The Directors have ordered us to write and request the Favour of you, if you have not laid out our Money not to purchase any Books till you hear from them which will be in a short Time. What you have purchased they desire you will please to forward by the first Opportunity. Among them we hope for the Pleasure of seeing your Works and Robertsons History of Charles 5th.[9] We are, Sir with the greatest Esteem and Respect Your Obedient humble Servants.

CHARLES THOMSON
THOMAS MIFFLIN

From William Franklin

ALS:[1] American Philosophical Society

Honoured Father,   Burlington May 11th, 1769

A few Days ago I was favoured with your Letter of the 20th. of March by Capt. Creighton. The Packet which left England the 7th. of March is since arrived, but I had no Letter by her from any one. I suppose (tho' you do not mention it) that you have wrote to me before relative to the Letters I sent you by the January Mail;[2] perhaps by Sparks who is not yet arriv'd. I wait impatiently for the Arrival of the April Packet, as I do not think it proper to convene the Assembly till I have Answers to some Letters I have wrote to the Ministry.[3]

Mr. Galloway has sent me (agreeably to your Desire) Copies of the Clauses added to the last Mutiny Act.[4] I am very glad that they

---

agreed to unite with the Library Company of Philadelphia. See George M. Abbot, *A Short History of the Library Company of Philadelphia* (Philadelphia, 1914), p. 10; E. V. Lamberton, "Colonial Libraries of Pennsylvania," *PMHB*, XLII (1918), 193–207.

9. BF's *Exper. and Obser.* (4th ed., London, 1769); William Robertson, *The History of the Reign of the Emperor Charles V* . . . (3 vols., London, 1769).

1. Portions of the letter which are now illegible have been silently supplied from the text printed in [William Duane, ed.,] *Letters to Benjamin Franklin, from His Family and Friends. 1751–1790* (New York, 1859), pp. 41–5.

2. None of this correspondence has survived except part of one letter from WF, for which see above under Jan. 2.

3. These certainly included WF's letter to Hillsborough of Jan. 28, 1769, inquiring about the government's attitude toward the issuance by New Jersey of £100,000 in bills of credit, for which see 1 *N.J. Arch.*, X, 99–102.

4. See BF to Galloway above, March 21.

have pass'd, as I am convinced our Assembly would not have re-
ceded from the former Mode of providing Necessaries for the
Troops in Quarters; and consequently Altercation and Confusion
must have ensued.

I have wrote Col. Croghan[5] what you mention concerning his
Affair. I hope the Application will be attended with Success.

Capt. Trent met with some unexpected Delays[6] but I suppose is
by this Time arrived in England. I hear that Sir Wm. has a Letter
from Lord H. mentioning that His Majesty entirely approves of all
the transactions of the Treaty,[7] so that I imagine Capt. Trent will
meet with no Difficulty in his Application. Indeed it is necessary
to our Friend W's[8] affairs that he should finish his Business in England in a short Time for those with whom he has left the Care of his
Affairs find a good a deal of Difficulty in keeping Matters quiet with
some of his Creditors during his Absence.

I have entered far into the Spirit of Farming, and have lately
made a considerable Addition to my Farm, on very reasonable
Terms. It is now altogether a very valuable and pleasant Place. I
must beg you not to omit sending me the *Drain-Plough* I wrote to
you for, invented and made by *Wm. Knowles* at Newport in the Isle
of Wight. I observe by his Advertisement that he is to be heard of
at Mr. Bailey's Register of the Society for the Encouragement of
Arts.[9] I likewise want a *Rotheran or Patent Plough*, as it is called.

5. For George Croghan, the Indian trader and land speculator, see above, V,
65 n, and subsequent volumes.

6. William Trent and Samuel Wharton had been expecting to go to England
together as emissaries of the "suffering traders." When Trent was delayed by
his efforts to straighten out his involved legal affairs, Wharton sailed without
him. Lewis, *Indiana Co.*, pp. 70–2.

7. WF's wish must have been father to the supposed letter: what Hillsborough
actually wrote to Sir William Johnson was merely that the Board of Trade had
not yet reported its opinion of the treaty with the Indians concluded at Fort
Stanwix in the previous autumn. *Johnson Papers*, VI, 668. For the treaty see
above, XV, 264–5, 275–9.

8. Samuel Wharton.

9. WF was expanding and improving Franklin Park, in Burlington County,
N.J. In his letter to BF above, March 2, he had asked for a plough invented by
Cuthbert Clarke; now he wanted one by Knowles, who had, like Clarke, recently received a prize for his invention. Robert Dossie, *Memoirs of Agriculture, and Other Œconomical Arts* (3 vols., London, 1768–82), I, 12–13, 79–80.
William Bailey was registrar, or register, of the Royal Society of Arts from
1766 until his death in 1773.

There is a Draft of one in Mills's Husbandry, and in the Select Transactions of the Edinburgh Society,[1] but I can't get our Workmen here to make one by it. They understand the Making of no other Ploughs but what are in common Use here. I was thinking to request to get Knowles to make me one of this kind also (as he advertises making all Sorts of Ploughs on the best mechanical Principles) but since I have learnt that he lives in the Isle of Wight I am at a loss to know how it or the Drain Plough can be sent without a great Expence, as I believe none of our Vessels in Time of Peace touch at Portsmouth, and to send it to London (if by Land) will make it come very dear. If however there are Opportunities of sending them by Water to London, or some other Seaport from whence Vessels sail to Philad. the Expence may not perhaps be worth minding.

I have not yet seen Mr. Caiger, who was recommended to you by Mr. Small and Mr. More, nor heard of his Arrival in America.[2] Should it be in my Power to serve him in what he requests I shall readily do it.

Mr. Morgan, our Secretary is in Canada. I had a very polite Letter from him last Week in which he mentions his Intention of being here some Time this Month or the next. Mr. Reed, our Deputy Secretary has, I understand let his House at Trenton, and intends soon for England to marry DeBerdt's Daughter. He has not, however, mentioned his Intentions to me, and perhaps will not think it necessary. He never comes here but at the Time of the Courts, leaving his Business of Secretary entirely to Clerks both here and at Amboy. Mr. Morgann intimates as if he had a Design of changing his Deputy, but it is a Matter I don't chuse to interfere in; all that I

1. The Rotherham plough, based on a Dutch design, had come into use in England almost half a century earlier: E. Mingay, *The Agricultural Revolution, 1750–1880* (New York, 1966), pp. 69–70. In his letter of March 2 WF had complained of having only the first volume of Mills's *Practical Husbandry*; his other source for the plough was Robert Maxwell, ed., *Select Transactions of the Honourable the Society of Improvers in the Knowledge of Agriculture in Scotland...* (Edinburgh, 1743).

2. Mr. Caiger remains in obscurity, but the two who recommended him to BF were almost unquestionably Alexander Small, the Scottish surgeon and agricultural enthusiast, and Samuel More (d. 1799), who was secretary of the Society of Arts from 1769 to 1799. See above, IX, 110 n, and Derek Hudson and Kenneth W. Luckhurst, *The Royal Society of Arts* (London, [1954]), pp. 31–2, 172.

shall desire is that whoever he appoints may be obliged to reside here and may be properly qualified to execute the Business.[3]

Publick Affairs remain much the same on this Side of the Water as when I wrote to you last. The Members of the New York Assembly are differing greatly among themselves. Col. Schuyler and Mr. Walton went out to fight a Duel but thought better of the Matter when they got on the Ground, and settled their Differences amicably.[4] Col. Lewis Morris is expell'd for not being a Resident in the Borough of West Chester for which he was elected, tho' he has a considerable Estate in the Borough. Mr. Livingston, their late Speaker, is like to be expelled on the same Account.[5] By the Resolves of the House they allow Non Residents have a Right to elect but not to be elected. Parties run very high among them.

The Boston Writers have attack'd Governor Barnard on his Letters, and on his being created a Baronet. They worry him so much that I suppose he will not chuse to stay much longer among them.[6] There is a Talk that a new Governor is shortly to be ap-

3. Maurice Morgann, a former undersecretary of state for the Southern Department, had recently been appointed secretary of New Jersey; see above, XIII, 430 n. His deputy was Joseph Reed (1741–85), whose brother-in-law and protégé, Charles Pettit, succeeded him in October, 1769. Reed did not get to England until 1770 to marry Esther DeBerdt, the daughter of the colonial agent for Massachusetts. See *DAB* under Reed and 1 *N.J. Arch.*, x, 132–5.

4. Philip Schuyler (1733–1804) took a strong antiministerial stand as soon as he was elected to the Assembly in 1768. Jacob Walton (173?–82), a New York merchant and representative of the city, differed with him on almost all questions; only the intervention of friends prevented the duel. Don R. Gerlach, *Philip Schuyler and the American Revolution in New York, 1733–1777* (Lincoln, Neb., 1964), 170–2.

5. These expulsions were part of the feud between the Livingston and De Lancey factions, and helped to break the power of the former. Lewis Morris (1726–98), representing Westchester, was unseated in April for nonresidency; Philip Livingston (1716–78), who had just been defeated for re-election in New York City and then elected in Livingston Manor, was unseated in May because he was not a resident of the family appanage. Roger Champagne, "Family Politics versus Constitutional Principles: the New York Assembly Elections of 1768 and 1769," *W&MQ*, 3d ser., xx (1963), 75–9.

6. For Francis Bernard see above, x, 353 n. His letters to officials at home were procured by William Bollan, agent for the Massachusetts Council, who sent them to Boston; the first reference to them was a list in the *Boston Chron.*, April 7–10, 10–13, 1769. Although Bernard was created a baronet on April 5, word of the impending honor had reached Boston months before; see the ex-

pointed. Many of the principal People there wish you to be the Man, and say that you would meet with no Opposition from any Party, but would soon be able to conciliate all Differences.

Our Supreme Court is Sitting, and I am a good deal engaged and hurried.

Betsy joins me in Duty. I am, as ever, Honored Sir Your dutiful Son WM. FRANKLIN

From James Parker

ALS: American Philosophical Society

Honoured Sir Newyork, May 12. 1769

Before this reaches you, I hope Mr. Foxcroft will be safe arrived with you, as he sail'd from Philadelphia the 20th of last Month.[7] This covers the first of a Set of Bills for £100 Sterling which I purchased here with Money sent me by Mr. Vernon of Rhode-Island, who I have press'd hard for Payment.[8] His Accounts, tho' kept in Sterling when he sends Cash will not in general procure Sterling tho' at this Time it has. The 2d Bill I shall send next Week by a Merchant Ship. Mr. Foxcroft will acquaint you with the Affair of Mr. Robinson,[9] to whom I have by his Order paid Twenty Guineas, he is about to embark in a Week or two, but I am not certain yet what Vessel he goes in. I purpose to write fuller by him.

Mr. Foxcroft having given me Locks and Keys, with Orders to have them put upon all the Mails,[1] I accordingly have sent them: but find both those from this City for Boston are neither good Portmanteau's, or big enough, or have either Chains or Rings, in short,

---

tract of a letter from London in the *Boston Chron.*, Jan. 26–30, 1769, and a later report in *ibid.*, April 24–27. The Governor was soon recalled, ostensibly for consultation; he left Boston on August 1 and never returned.

7. For John Foxcroft's leave see his letter to BF above, Feb. 21.

8. Thomas Vernon was postmaster at Newport; see above, V, 451 n. Now that BF and Foxcroft were both absent, the northern district had no resident deputy postmaster general; and Foxcroft had clearly left Parker in charge of its affairs.

9. Robinson appears in three subsequent letters from Parker, but our best efforts have produced no information about him.

1. In the Post Office accounts discussed below under Jan. 3, 1770, BF noted a payment of £28 18s. in October, 1768, for "horns, locks, and mails."

they were absolutely unfit, and the Riders carry the Mails chiefly in Saddle Bags; upon which I have ordered two new Portmanteau's to be made with Chains and Rings fitting, as it is impracticable to carry on the King's Service to good purpose without. On my writing to Albany, I received the inclosed Letter about it;[2] and Major Skene, who lives near Crown-point,[3] being down here, he told me, he was ashamed to see the Couriers have Nothing but an Ozenbrigs[4] Bag to carry the Letters in, which could not screan them from wet, as he was a Friend to the Business, he thinks he had wrote to Mr. Foxcroft about it. But as I am assured this is the Truth, I have ordered two more Portmanteaus to be made here, One for Montreal, the other for Quebeck, which being absolutely necessary for the Good of the Service, and the Benefit of the Revenue, I hope it will be allowed me. I did not do this to shew any Authority, but purely because I think it just and reasonable, and flatter myself you will think so too, as I find others careless and dilatory about the Matter, tho' at the same time dissatisfied.

Some Merchant Vessels sail in 10 or 12 Days hence, by whom I shall write again. I have only respectful Compliments, &c. from Your most obliged Servant   JAMES PARKER.

Addressed: For / Dr Benjamin Franklin / Craven-Street / London / per Packet

Endorsed: Parker

2. From John Monier, the Albany postmaster, dated May 1 (APS). He acknowledged the receipt of a key to lock the mail bags to New York, and wished that similar provision had been made for the bags to Canada. The latter went open, and the newspapers that were always a major part of the contents were sometimes lost.

3. Philip Skene, owner of a vast tract of land between Lake Champlain and the Hudson, founded the town of Skenesborough and —as a result of his interest in postal affairs, to which Parker refers—became its postmaster in 1771. See above, v, 452 n. Subsequently Skene, as a loyalist, played a prominent part in assisting Burgoyne's advance during the Saratoga campaign.

4. Osnaburg, a kind of coarse linen cloth originally made in Osnabrück.

From Thomas Gilpin[5]

Reprinted from "Memoir of Thomas Gilpin," *Pennsylvania Magazine of History and Biography*, XLIX (1925), 304.

Worthy Friend   Philadelphia May 16th. 1769.

By the brig Ketly Capt. Osborne I have sent you the model of a machine the result of a thought occurring to me some time ago which I have realised in the present form. It is that of an horizontal windmill applied to three pumps——this application as one of the most useful for raising water from lands, draining mines or pumping ships in distress at sea; but if the first movement be found effective it may be applied to all the various uses of other windmills, without the inconvenience of turning the house or frame to the wind. I could mention some further objects that have occurred to me on the subject but I daresay they will present themselves to you; when you have examined the model if you think the invention of sufficient importance I would thank you to have it shewn to the Society of Arts or made public in any way you may think it merits.[6] The necessity of regulating and stopping the motion of the mill will no doubt occur to you; that part of it I have omitted at present from want of time, but it is very easy, nearly as much so as that of stopping a water mill and I shall have it fixed to another model I am preparing for the Philosophical Society here.[7] Your sentiments on this invention at a leisure moment will be very gratifying and esteemed a particular favor by your friend   THOMAS GILPIN.

P.S. I have an idea that this machine with some alterations would answer well in a current of water.

From [Samuel] Wharton   AL: American Philosophical Society

[Dated merely Friday; probably May 19, 1769. A note in the third person: is sorry to inform Franklin that the New York mail, according to Mr. Todd, was made up and dispatched on Wednesday

5. See the headnote of Gilpin to BF above, Jan. 29.

6. BF promised in July to exhibit the pump at the November meeting of the Society of Arts, but did not do so until the following spring, when he said he was about to meet with a committee to explain its workings. See his letters to Gilpin below, July 10, 1769, and March 18, 1770.

7. A short description of the machine was published in the APS *Trans.*, I (1771), 339.

night, when the letters for the governors were received from the various officers. The Captain sails for New York on Monday.[8]]

From James Parker

ALS: American Philosophical Society

Honoured Sir   Newyork, May 22[–24] 1769
    The 12th of this Month I wrote you per Packet, and sent the first Bill of a Set for £100 Sterling of which this incloses the second of the same: to that I refer for Particulars.

    You have never told me, whether you have received any of my Pay from the Custom-House.[9] As if you have, I should be glad if you would pay Mr. Potts for two years of the Chronicle.[1] It is possible the Want of the Pay makes him Slack in sending; for I have never but once got so late by the Packet, as other People have; perhaps when he gets the Pay, he may be willing to send the latest he can.

    As we were under strong Expectations of your Return home for some time past, I have not mentioned any Thing of the Books of Mecom's, which have now lain in Trunks and Boxes above five years.[2] I have never open'd or meddled with them; and tho' the place is dry where they lay, yet they may grow mouldy or worm-eaten by laying so long. There are not many of them very saleable at best, as I suppose Benny to have already sold those who were

8. We are assuming that Wharton referred to Hillsborough's circular letter to the colonial governors, and separate letters to Gov. Moore and Sir William Johnson, dated May 13 (1 *N.J. Arch.*, x, 109–10; *N.Y. Col. Docs.*, VIII, 164–6); if bureaucracy for once moved fast, they would have been ready for mailing by Wednesday, May 17. On the following weekend two ship captains sailed for New York: *N.-Y. Gaz., and Weekly Mercury*, July 17, 24, 1769. For Wharton's and William Trent's mission to England see the final note on WF to BF above, Jan. 31. Wharton had been scheduled to sail at the end of January (1 *N.J. Arch.*, x, 97), so that by this time he had presumably been in London for something over two months. Trent did not join him until the end of May: *PMHB*, LXXIV (1950), 48.

9. For Parker's efforts to collect his salary through BF see above, XIII, 474; XIV, 99 and subsequent references.

1. Since 1767 Samuel Potts, comptroller general of the Post Office, had been supplying Parker with the *Lond. Chron.* in exchange for the *N.-Y. Gazette*. See above, XIV, 10 n, 238.

2. The books were part of Mecom's estate that he lost at the time of his bankruptcy; see above, XI, 240–1, 332.

most so, and lying may make them worse. I remember some Dozen of Church of England Primers, which I have been frequently ask'd for lately, there being none here, but very little Demand for any other that I remember. I would only mention that I think, if you find yourself not likely to come home this Summer, that you should give Orders to have them open'd, and clean'd if Occasion, and if you should order them open'd for that Purpose, I would be desirous to take those Primers myself. I should not be fond of purchasing any others but if you chuse it, I would endeavour to sell them, or any of them, on Commission. I dare not involve myself further: I grow old and feeble, and I would not involve my Wife after I am gone more than Needs must; I shall not however, meddle with any Thing of them without your Orders.

I shall write again, God willing, by Mr. Robinson, who is preparing to go off for England; any Matters relating to the Post-Office I shall then treat of. Meanwhile I am with all Respect Your most obliged Servant   JAMES PARKER.

PS. May 24. Since writing the other Side, I this Day received the inclosed Bill from Mr. Courtenay[3] for £141 6s. 11d. Sterling which I chose to send along; the 2d Bill I shall send by a Vessel going in a Day or two after this.   JP

Addressed: For / Dr Benjamin Franklin / Craven-Street / London / per Capt. Haight

From Amelia Evans   ALS: American Philosophical Society

Dear Sir,   Tunis 23d May 1769
Your two very obliging favors by Mr. Stuart (who arrived a few weeks ago) I have received, and most sincerely thank you for the

3. Hercules Courtenay (1736–1816) was an Irish or Scottish immigrant who had become postmaster of Baltimore. He subsequently served in the American army, was twice court-martialed and finally dismissed, and after the war attained some prominence in Baltimore. John C. Fitzpatrick, ed., *The Writings of George Washington...* (39 vols., Washington, 1931–44), X, 258; XI, 19–20; Frederick A. Virkus, ed., *The Abridged Compendium of American Genealogy* (7 vols., Chicago, 1925–42), VII, 310; George W. McCreary, *The Ancient and Honorable Mechanical Company of Baltimore* (Baltimore, [ca. 1901]), pp. 14, 18–19; J. Thomas Scharf, *Chronicles of Baltimore...* (Baltimore, 1874), pp. 71, 130, 202, 239, 263, 281–2.

enquiries you was so obliging to make concerning him. Mr. Traill and his Lady have charged me with their compliments and warmest acknowledgements for the favor you have done them by it. You my dear Sir, who so much delight in acts of benevolence, can form to yourself an idea of the satisfaction Mr. and Mrs. Traill must experience on having an opportunity of supplying to a fatherless friendless young man, the long lost blessings of parental care.[4] How necessary is the extricating and restraining hand to inexperienced youth! Here permit me Sir, to mention with gratitude, the excellent advice my revered Godmama frequently favor'd me with, when I was too eagerly bent on the pursuit of new acquaintances and a life of dissipation: how often has she pointed out to me the ill consequences which would naturally result from them! And had not calamities of the heaviest kind, been my early portion, I might have experienced the truth of the dear Lady's predictions: but they effectually put a stop to my too earnest desire of pleasures; and I have reason to believe, that I am at present happier than I should have been, had uninterrupted prosperity been my lot.

About 6 or 8 months ago I heared of Miss Franklin's marriage, by a Gentleman from America;[5] and I did myself the pleasure of paying her my congratulatory compliments in a letter; and give me leave dear Sir, to felicitate you on the same happy event, and to wish that you may long be bless'd with a daughter so amiably dutiful; and may the relations this alliance has given you, be all equal objects of your regard, as you of their veneration, and respect. I am Dear Sir, Your most faithful and obliged Humble Servant

AMELIA EVANS.

Addressed: To / Benjamin Franklin Esqr. / Craven Street / London

[*Endorsed:*] Leghorn the 16th. June 1769—Received and forwarded by Sir Your Most Obdt. Servants per [*illegible*] & Orr

4. Amelia Evans, the daughter of the cartographer and DF's goddaughter, had gone to Tunis as governess in the family of the British Consul, James Traill; see above, XII, 64 n; XIII, 163–4. James Stuart was an indigent young man from Charleston, S.C., who reached Tunis by way of London with letter of recommendation from Peter Timothy; en route he delivered BF a letter from Timothy. Above, XV, 199. What Stuart intended to do in Tunis, and why the Traills so gladly agreed to act *in loco parentis*, remain a mystery.

5. The news of Sally Franklin's marriage to Richard Bache, on Oct. 29, 1767, took roughly a year to reach Tunis.

From Hannah Walker[6]

ALS: American Philosophical Society

Honoured Sir   Westbury May the 24, 1769

I hope you and Mrs. Stevenson are well and that She did not Dislike my Husbands Letter tho it was wrote as Short as Possible because the time would not allow for we did not receive it till 3 o clock in the Afternoon and he wrote that we agreed to Mrs. Stevensons Proposals in Every thing as She was so good as to go as far as a hundred and fifty Pounds we would be at the rest Expence and Pay her Six Pounds a year. The Reason of our having the Letter so Late was Mr. Payne went to see if there was any for him and saw it so took it to Save us the Expence of it being Sent over on Purpose and sent it by his man on Tuesday and then my Husband had the Letter to write and Carry a Mile and half to meet the post by half an Hour after four and tho it was Short his meaning was in the same manner and mr. Payne called upon me yesterday to see if we had had any Answer for he had not but he had sent to see Every Post since Sunday because he said if we wrote by the return of the Post as you Desired he thought on Sunday he Should have an Answer. I told him we wrote Immediatly but made himself Answer again and said you might be gone out.[7]

My Cousin Morris[8] is Suprizingly Hearty for one of her Agge I bless God and all my Family at Present are well which Blessing I hope God continues upon you and your good Family which is my continual Prayers. My cousin Morris and we joyn in begging the acceptance of our Humble Duty to you and your good Family and all our Humble Complements to mrs. Stevenson from your most Humble and most obdient Servant   HANNAH WALKER.

Addressed: To | Benjman Franklin Esqr | at Mrs Stevensons | in Craven Street | near the Strand | London

6. Mrs. Hannah Farrow Walker, BF's first cousin once removed; see above, XV, 142–4.

7. James Payne, a lawyer in Brackley, Northants., had long been trying to find a better house for the Walker family. In 1767 he had had two inspected, to judge by a bill in the Franklin Papers in the APS (Vol. LXVII, No. 7); they were at some distance from Westbury. Now he had apparently found one that was suitable but had to be obtained in haste, and Mrs. Stevenson had agreed to lend part of the money needed.

8. Eleanor Morris, BF's first cousin, who lived with the Walkers; see above, XV, 20.

From James Parker
ALS: American Philosophical Society

Honoured Sir   Newyork, May 30, 1769

You were so good a while ago, to Mention that if I chose to resign
the Custom House Business you would not be displeased. While I
had the Ability to do what I was taught was my Duty, I patiently
Submitted to any Unpopularity or Odium that might unjustly be
thrown upon me. But the Commissioners at Boston seem continually to be forming new Orders and Instructions, which if punctually
followed, enslaves the Officer and renders him despicable to the
Publick. I always conceived our Offices were designed to prevent
illicit Trade, and not to distress the fair Traders, whereas by their
new excessive Strictures the contrary will be the Case.[9] In particular some Instructions they have lately sent me, are so hard, rigid
and extraordinary, that were they but indifferently executed, my
whole Time must be taken up: By them I am constantly to attend
every Vessel that loads or unloads, and to render Accounts of every
particular, notwithstanding there may be other Officers attending;
and as such Attendance is quite inadequate to the Pay, as well
creating Trouble to the Merchants, without answering any End,
but to make the Officer odious, I find myself unable to perform it:
and tho' I have not had the most distant Hint of being faulted, yet
being conscious I am unequal to the Task, it is ungenerous to expect Pay without doing the Duty required. While I could do Justice
to the Employer, and not disgrace my Friends I was desirous to continue; for, as I at first was taught a Duty of daily walking to every
Vessel in a long extended Harbour, to see that every one made suitable Entries before they loaded or unloaded, which was conducive
to Health, and took up but part of the Day: I am now to be confined
often to one Vessel or perhaps two at a Time for whole Days together, and that probably in a cold wet Place which is very un-
wholsom. I own the Post may be some Profit in the Manner my
first Directions ordered it executed; which I did to the general

9. The Townshend Acts had established the American Board of Customs
Commissioners to curtail smuggling by a strict enforcement of the acts of trade.
The Board's activity—or in Parker's view, overactivity—was costly enough
to defeat its purpose; by the beginning of 1769, the Board reported, the ex-
pense of collection was almost a third greater than the net revenue. Gipson,
British Empire, XI, 241–2.

Satisfaction, till these new Regulations took Place. But a Man may buy Gold too dear: for not even a single Man could now live in this City (the dearest I really believe on the Continent) for £50 Sterling per Annum. And as it is to take up my whole Time, how could I do any other Business, or see it be done? On these Principles, I think you will not blame me, if I throw up; but I shall Struggle along till I hear from you; Our Collector telling me, the Commissioners at Boston could not turn me out, till they heard from England, if they had a Mind to, which he thinks is not the Case, and as my Appointment was by a Treasury Warrant, he thinks with me, it is best to acquaint you of it first, that you might possibly procure it for some younger Man or single Man, that you may wish to serve or oblige.[1] I don't doubt but Providence will provide for me otherways; I shall nevertheless always have a thankful Remembrance of your Favour in procuring it, of the Gentleman's Kindness who bestowed it, and of Mr. Strahan's Goodness in being one of my Securities.

Mr. Robinson, by whom I send this, has Hopes of obtaining, by Mr. Foxcroft's Friendship and Interest, some place in the Post-Office: If I may be permitted to give my Opinion, I would humbly observe, that no Officer appears to be wanting, unless it should be found expedient to appoint a Riding Surveyor of the Offices:[2] I think such a One has been mentioned from home: and it might be of general Service to the Cause: but it appears to me, that such an Officer and the Comptroller's are similar, or at least Assistant and Checks to each other. Now, I having often observed that moving about in good Weather does greatly relieve me, and conduce to my Health, so a long Confinement in one Place always impairs me, I would beg Leave to make the following Suggestions.

Suppose then, that an Officer is to be appointed to that Station, or the Comptroller's Commission taken from me, and given to One you shall think more-fitting for it than I am, as I am at your Will and Pleasure, if so I should be willing to take that of Riding Surveyor, as reasonable as any One: and be bound to visit every Office

1. If BF answered, the letter is not extant. In any case Parker resigned his position as land waiter in the customs service the following December; see his letters to BF below, Dec. 23, 1769; Jan. 4, 1770. For the collector who was advising him, Andrew Elliot, see above, XII, 228 n.

2. As early as 1763 Anthony Todd, the secretary of the Post Office, had suggested to BF and Foxcroft the creation of this office, and they had approved; no action was taken, however, until 1772. See above, X, 221.

on the Continent once a Year at least; but as there must be the Expence of a Horse also, and travelling you know is chargeable, I think it could not be done under £125 Sterling per Annum and Frugality must be used to make any Profit of that. Or, suppose such an Officer should be appointed, alternately to be Comptroller and travelling Surveyor, jointly with me, year and year about, would that be inconsistent? or would not thereby two Officers know the whole State of the Post-Office Affairs, ready to explain or set any Thing to Rights, if one of them should dye, &c. besides being a Cheque to each other? Or, if you appoint one to that Station, and let me remain as I am, I am thankful, or if I am displaced, I submit. For I would not pretend to dictate: I only mention these as Speculative Hints. The Business of the Post-Office, has greatly increased since my Time; and it is necessary I now throw up the Custom-House Business, that I may be able to do Justice to the Post-Office which I shall always endeavour to do, while I have the Honour to be continued in it.

Another Thing I would beg Leave to mention is, that if it should be thought expedient to have the Roads measured according to Act of Parliament, I have the Perambulator that was Lewis Evans's, and I would undertake to measure all the Post Roads with it, on my Qualification at a reasonable Rate.[3] I think about 20 or 25 Miles may be comfortably measured in a Day, when fair Weather, but there must be at least one Assistant, if not two: I would do it either at a Shilling Sterling a Mile, or a Guinea a Day, and that for two or three Hands would be not very high—but I have no Objection to another's doing it.

As to my printing Business, my Son being entirely averse to living in this City,[4] I don't think it will ever rise to any great Pitch: I am not able to work as usual myself: and the Dearness of the Place and the Deadness of the Times, renders Journey work subversive of the Profits: Also, there has just set up here, a Couple of young *smuggled* Scots Men, who have issued out a large Paper they call *the Chronicle*;

3. Almost immediately after the passage of the Post Office Act of 1765 (5 Geo. III, c. 25) Parker had suggested carrying out its provision for measuring the post roads in the colonies: above, XII, 309. His "perambulator" was the handiwork of the famous surveyor, draftsman, and geographer, for whom see above, III, 48 n.

4. Samuel Franklin Parker, to judge by his father's frequent complaints of him to BF in Vol. XV, was averse to work in general.

They are as bad Workmen as ever Bradford was, but from a large Portion of Impudence, and the National Biass of all Scotch Men in their Favour, I am told they have in three Weeks more Subscribers already than I have.[5] Gaine has enlarged his Paper; Holt always does a Supplement, and sometimes two whole Sheets; Only I keep Steady of one Size and Course: and I think they will all run themselves aground except Gaine, who has got the Lead so far, and so much ahead, there is little Danger but he'll overshoot us all.[6] On printing the American Whig, I had upwards of 200 new Subscribers constantly, but many of the high Churchmen left me, to the Number of about 70—and probably now many of the Whigs will leave me, as they are stopt.[7] I print about 30 Quire, and have not many left on Hand, and I hope so many will continue. Advertisements which are the Life of the Paper, I get a few of, about a 10th Part of what Gaine gets: and more than half of what Holt gets. Nevertheless I think to continue to push on with all the Vigour I can. I have young Hands coming up, and things may turn out better by-and-by, if it please God I live, if not His Will be done. Cloudy Weather may overshadow at present, but fair Weather may come again. Holts' Affairs stand with me just as they did, only I think I told you, I had got his Place at New Haven, which I will dispose of when I can.[8]

I think and fear I have been tedious in this; But the Occasion seem'd to oblige me to it. We all beg our humble Salutations may be accepted. With Respect to Mr. Foxcroft and self I am Your most obliged Servant   JAMES PARKER.

5. For the two Scots brothers, James and Alexander Robertson, see above, XV, 270 n. The Bradford with whom Parker compared them may have been Andrew, whose *American Weekly Mercury* BF had considered "a paltry thing" (*Autobiog.*, p. 119); but more probably he was William Bradford, to whom Parker had once been apprenticed, and whose *N.-Y. Gaz.* was badly printed and edited. Alexander J. Wall, Jr., "William Bradford, Colonial Printer; a Tercentenary Review," American Antiquarian Soc. *Proc.*, LXXIII (1963), 377; Charles R. Hildeburn, *Sketches of Printers and Printing in Colonial New York* (New York, 1895), p. 14.

6. For Hugh Gaine and John Holt, printers respectively of the *N.-Y. Mercury* and the *N.-Y. Jour., or General Advertiser*, see above, XIII, 344 n, 264 n.

7. In 1768 Parker had printed a series of articles in the *N.-Y. Gaz.* attacking the idea of establishing an American episcopate; see above, XV, 101.

8. For Parker's attachment of Holt's property in New Haven see his letter to BF above, March 29.

From James Parker

ALS: American Philosophical Society

Honoured Sir   New-York, 31 May [–June 10] 1769

The 22d and 24th Instant, I wrote you per Capt. Haight, inclosing you the 2d of a Bill for £100. Sterling and the first of a Bill from Mr. Hercules Courtenay, Post-Master of Baltimore, for £141 6s. 11d. Sterling drawn by Stevenson on Hervey of London, of which this has the 2d inclosed: Mr. Courtenay says it is the whole of the Ballance due from him. I hope this or the first will come safe to your Hands, and that it may have due Acceptance: By Mr. Foxcroft's Orders, I wrote to Mr. Courtenay about the Allowance he expected for collecting in Mr. Robinson's Money; he said, he should expect the usual Commissions for such Matters, but having paid in this Bill, all the Ballance due the Office, he would leave that to be settled with Mr. Foxcroft, &c.

(So far was wrote designing to go with Capt. Winn, but was told he would not sail in less than 10 Days, I waited, and now the Packet goes first.) June 10. 1769

Mr. Robinson sail'd the 2d Instant from this Port on board a Brig bound to Glasgow: by him I wrote a private Letter to you: Since that I have almost got all the Locks and Keys settled on the several Mails: tho' the Riders in many Places don't like it.

Mr. Luke Babcock, Post Master at New-Haven, writes me Word, he shall leave that Place in September next, recommends Mr. Christopher Kilby to succeed him.[9] I may possibly have your Opinion or Orders on it by that Time. I am a Stranger to him; nor is there one there, I would desire to prefer to another: I have such a Conception of them and their Chicanery that were you to shake them all in a Bag together, the first that comes out would be as good as any other; but you may possibly desire it to be given to some other; therefore wish to have your Orders before I send any Commission.

9. For Luke Babcock see above, XIV, 61 n, 238. He is said to have given up his position in order to go to England to be ordained. His successor, referred to as Capt. Christopher Kilby and not to be confused with the Boston merchant of the same name, apparently remained postmaster of New Haven until his death in 1774. *Journal Kept by Hugh Finlay* . . . (Brooklyn, 1867), pp. 40–1, 43; Edward A. Atwater, ed., *History of the City of New Haven to the Present Time* (New York, 1887), pp. 376–7.

By Mr. Robinson I wrote my Reasons for being desirous to throw up the Post, your Goodness procured me in the Custom-House; but I shall not do it, till I hear from you, unless I am turned out; which I don't apprehend likely to be the Case: If it be your Pleasure to promote Mr. Robinson, either with or without any Remove of me, I entirely Submit: Or, if it shall not be thought necessary to have any Additional Officer in the Post-Office, and your Favour still continues to me, in that Office, I shall always esteem it as such: And as the Commission I have in the Custom-House, is from the Treasury, by your Interest, perhaps the same Interest, if you espouse his Cause with Mr. Foxcroft's, might procure that Place for Mr. Robinson, as he has a very small Family, with the Help of some Clerkship, he might make a tolerable Livelihood: And indeed, the Business of the Post-Office increasing, One assistant Clerk would be advantageous to it, especially if the Letters relating to the Office Affairs are to [be] Copied; a Task I find myself almost unequal many Times to, and which I never practised till now; and even now many are sent without. I often find I want Help; but I strive with all my Powers to act uniform and right: and if he could at some times assist as such, whatever Allowance you should think proper to make would be acceptable I don't doubt to him, and at Times he might find other Chance writing to do: But this is all humbly submitted to your better Judgment. If an Office of a general Sort in the Post-Office is established here, such a Clerk will doubtless be thought necessary. In whatever Light you may View it, I have no Pretence to direct or advise, but to offer my Opinion I hope will not be thought impertinent, tho' it may not be agreeable or approved of.

I have endeavoured to obey Mr. Foxcroft's Directions, since he went. I have wrote to Halifax, and sent the Commission thither as he directed. Every thing else goes on nearly as usual.

I told you, my Son lives at Woodbridge, and if any printing Work offers, he has the Materials, he may Work if he will. I have not gave them to him; I keep them under my own Command, but he may use them.[1] He provides now for himself: If he betters himself he may do well, if not, he must suffer, while he has his Health; but he has hurt himself by his Folly, and had much Sickness. The last Intelligence that I have had of him, that he seems to reform a little;

1. See Parker to BF above, March 29, 1769.

We flatter ourselves, that it may be so, but perhaps we may be deceived. I find I every Day grow less able to encounter the Roughness of the World, but I keep up a good Heart. My Body is feeble and much weaken'd by the cruel Fits of the Gout; but I am about. We all are well at present, and we shall always be pleased to hear the Continuance of yours. Little Business of any kind in the printing Way, And hard Times in general. Publick Affairs you see from the publick prints. We beg our respectful Compliments to yourself, and to good Mr. Foxcroft, if he be arrived, as I hope he is. I am Your most obliged Servant JAMES PARKER.

Addressed: For / Dr Benjamin Franklin / Craven-Street / London / per Halifax Packet

From John Pownall[2]   ALS (copy): Public Record Office

Sir   Whitehall June 2d. 1769
I am directed by the Earl of Hillsborough to desire the Favor that he may see you at His House together with the Agents of some of the *other* North American Colonies on Wednesday next[3] at Eleven O'Clock in the forenoon, on the subject of some representations that have been made to his Lordship of irregularities committed by Masters of Bermuda Vessels raking Salt at Sal Tortuga[4] to the prejudice of Vessels from the other Colonies employ'd in that Traffick. If there are any Masters of Vessels now in England who have been in this Trade, their Information upon the Subject may perhaps be usefull, and therefore His Lordship wishes if you

2. For John Pownall, the secretary of the Board of Trade and brother of Thomas Pownall, see above, VIII, 315 n. This letter, as indicated below, was sent to BF and other agents.
3. June 7.
4. From an early period the Bermudians had sent their slaves to Tortuga, Grand Turk, and the other Caicos Islands for salt, which was stored in Bermuda during the winter and then taken to the continental colonies to be exchanged for food products and lumber. This profitable trade was jeopardized when the governor of the Bahamas laid claim to the Caicos Islands, and the Bermudians appealed to Whitehall. See Walter Brownell Hayward, *Bermuda Past and Present* (New York, 1923), pp. 32–4; Henry C. Wilkinson, *Bermuda in the Old Empire* (London, 1950), pp. 87, 237–41.

know any such you will be pleased to bring them with you. I am &c   J. POWNALL

[*In the margin:*] Dr Franklin Mr De Berdt Mr Charles Mr Sherwood Mr *Pigott*[5] leaving out the word *other*

To Deborah Franklin   ALS: American Philosophical Society

My dear Child,   London, June 3. 1769
　　Capt. Jefferies has so long talk'd of sailing, that People began to think he would never sail;[6] and now I am just told that he goes this Evening, so can only say that I am well, and that having receiv'd Sally's Letter by Capt. Falkner, I rejoice to hear you so soon got over your late Indisposition, but am impatient for the next Packet which I hope will bring me that good News under your own hand. My Love to Sally and thank her for the Seeds. I shall write to her and you by the Packet that goes next Wednesday, and to all my other Friends. I am Your ever loving Husband

B FRANKLIN

Mrs. Stevenson sends her Love talks of going with Falkner to make you a Visit. Mr. Foxcroft is arriv'd.[7]

5. Dennys DeBerdt (*c.* 1694–1770) was the agent for Massachusetts, Robert Charles for New York, Joseph Sherwood (d. 1773) for Rhode Island, and John Pigott, a London merchant, for Bermuda. For Pigott see *ibid.*, p. 232.

6. Capt. James Jeffries was master of the snow *Britannia*. He arrived in Philadelphia early in September; see *Pa. Chron.*, Sept. 4–11.

7. Foxcroft and Sally's letter had both come on the *Pennsylvania Packet*, Capt. Nathaniel Falconer, which had arrived a few days before BF wrote. See James Parker to BF below, July 22.

From John Shippen[8] ALS: American Philosophical Society

Skeleton-hall,[9] St. Thos. Street, Southwarke June 3d. 1769.
Most respected Sir

If after the Perusal of the inclosed Letters from my Father you will Venture to Assist Me, by accepting a Bill on the Man so Near and dear to Me,[1] Or in any other way you shall think more proper to Enable Me to Return to America with every requisite necessary to Accomplish my Scheme of reading Lectures on Natural History[2]—with your hearty recommendation and Advice—I shall ever Entertain a most gratefull remembrance of it in my Mind, Esteem it a most singular favor and ever remain inviolably your most Devoted Obliged and Obedient Humble Servant JOHN SHIPPEN

Dr. Franklin

Addressed: To / Doctor Franklin / Craven Street / present

Lightning Rods for St. Paul's Cathedral

Printed in The Royal Society, *Philosophical Transactions*, LIX (1769), 162–9.

Report from the Committee appointed to consider of the properest means to secure the Cathedral of St. Paul's from the Effects of Lightning. Addressed to James West,[3] Esquire, President of the Royal Society.

8. Dr. John Shippen (1741–70) was the son of BF's old Philadelphia associate, Dr. William Shippen (for whom see above, III, 428 n) and the younger brother of Dr. William Shippen, Jr. (above, IX, 219 n), of whom BF had seen a good deal during William's medical studies in Britain. John, after graduating from the College of New Jersey, had taken his medical degree at Rheims; he is said to have returned to America in March, 1768, but the date is clearly in error. Roberdeau Buchanan, *Genealogy of the Descendants of Dr. Wm. Shippen, the Elder* (Washington, 1877), p. 7.

9. Presumably a nickname for all or part of Guy's Hospital.

1. BF obliged, and accepted a bill on Dr. William Shippen for £25. It is among BF's papers in the APS, Vol. LXVII, No. 10; see also DF to BF below, Nov. 20.

2. He delivered a course of lectures on fossils in Philadelphia in 1770: *Pa. Gaz.*, April 5, 1770; Charles R. Hildeburn, "Descendants of William Shippen," *PMHB*, I (1877), 109.

3. James West (1704?–72), lawyer, politician, and antiquary, was president from 1768 until his death. *DNB*.

Sir,   7 June, 1769.

As, in consequence of a letter addressed to the Royal Society from the Dean and Chapter of St. Paul's,[4] the Society did us the honour to appoint us a Committee to examine that magnificent structure, and, as far as our experience would enable us, to prevent mischief thereto from lightning, by a properly disposed apparatus; we lay before you the following as our opinion thereupon, to be communicated, if you think proper, to the Royal Society. And here, Sir, you will permit us to take notice of, and acknowledge, the obligations we were under to Mr. Mylne,[5] a very worthy member of this Society, who is surveyor of St. Paul's, and attended several meetings of the Committee. This gentleman furnished us with a great variety of information, in relation to the structure of the several parts of this fabric, which, without his assistance, could not easily have been obtained.

As all metals are now known readily to conduct or transmit the electric fluid, or, which is the same thing, lightning, through them; the large quantity of lead, and some iron, disposed in different parts of St. Paul's church, will, by having its several parts connected, where there is at present no such connection, prevent the erecting a considerable part of the apparatus, which otherwise we should judge absolutely necessary.

We are of opinion that, *caeteris paribus*, all buildings upon the same level are liable to be injured by lightning in proportion to their height: and that the danger is increased by crosses, weather-cocks, or pieces of metal, in any form, placed upon or near their tops, unless there is a compleat metallic communication from these to the bottom of the building, which metal should terminate either in water, or moist ground.

In St. Paul's church, the objects of our more particular attention were the dome and its lanthern, and the two towers at the west end. The roof over the body of the church, being compleatly covered

4. The letter, dated March 6, 1769, requested the Society's help in determining the best way to protect the cathedral from lightning. Charles R. Weld, *A History of the Royal Society* (2 vols., London, 1848), II, 94; *Biographia Britannica: or, the Lives of the Most Eminent Persons Who Have Flourished in Great-Britain and Ireland*... (2d ed., 5 vols., London, 1778–93), III, 221.

5. Robert Mylne (1734–1811), architect and engineer, had been an F.R.S. since 1767; he was surveyor of the cathedral for forty-five years, from 1766 until his death. *DNB*.

with lead, will, we conceive, prevent mischief thereto from lightning; and the more so, as the lead on the roof joins to that of the
several leaden spouts, which come down the sides of the building,
and terminate in the ground at a considerable depth. For our more
certain information, one of these spouts was examined; and it
was found to descend perpendicularly about three feet under the
surface of the earth: and then, after being laid about seven feet
in an inclined direction, it ended in a brick drain, which communicates with the sewer. These circumstances induce us to
conclude, that what has been just now described is a sufficient
metallic communication between the roof of the church and the
ground.

No part of this whole fabric seems to be in so dangerous a situation of being injured by lightning, as the stone lanthern placed
above the dome. This danger arises not only from its height, but
from the diffcrent pieces of metal in different parts of it, being
at present detached and separated from each other. This stone
lanthern is supported by a truncated cone of brick-work, of no
more than eighteen inches, or two bricks, thick. To the honour,
however, of the architectural sagacity of Sir Christopher Wren,
who was formerly our President,[6] this support of the lanthern,
which has already stood much above half a century, has not in
the least given way in any of its parts. How far it would sustain
the violence of a stroke of lightning will, it is to be hoped, never
be tried: and what we have now to propose will, we flatter ourselves, lessen the probability of its being injured by it. The first
object of our attention, therefore, was to make a compleat
metallic communication between the cross, placed over this lanthern, and the leaden covering of the great dome; as from its height,
if any lightning was in its neighbourhood, it would most probably
affect the cross.

This cross with the ball, both composed of metal, are supported
by, and connected with, seven iron rods. These descend perpendicularly through the small leaden dome, which covers the lanthern, and are inserted into and pass through a strong frame of
timber, placed horizontally under that dome. The lower extremities

6. Wren (1632–1723), a gifted scientist as well as a great architect, was one
of the founders of the Royal Society; he was its president, however, for only
two years, 1680–82. *DNB*.

of these iron rods are fastened to the under surface of this timber frame with iron nuts and screws.

From this timber work, several large iron bars, placed at some distance from the ends of the above-mentioned iron rods, descend obliquely, and are fixed in the stone-work of the lanthern. The upper ends of each of these oblique iron bars pass through the frame of timber before mentioned, and are fastened to its upper surface with iron nuts and screws. Between these iron bars and the leaden covering of the great dome, there is at present no metallic communication. To this arrangement, therefore, is owing the danger from lightning, which the Committee apprehends that this part of the building is liable to. To obviate which, we are of opinion, that four additional iron bars, each not less than an inch square, should be securely placed over the frame of timber before mentioned in such a manner, that one end of each of these four additional iron bars may be in contact with one of the perpendicular iron rods, and the other end of each be in contact with one of the iron nuts and screws, which fasten the obliquely descending iron bars to this frame of timber. At the bottom of these oblique iron bars, just above where they are inserted into the stone-work, the Committee recommends, that a ring, made of bar iron, of about an inch square, should be placed so as to be fastened to, and be in contact with, these iron bars.

From this proposed ring to the upper part of the lead which covers the great cupola, the distance is about forty-eight feet. In this space, we are of opinion, that four iron bars should be placed, each not less than an inch square. These should be fixed within the lanthern in such a manner, that the upper end of each should be fastened to, and in contact with, the iron ring before mentioned, and their lower ends in contact with the lead on the upper part of the cupola; from which the metallic communication is compleat to the lower end of the pipes, that discharge the water from the circular part of the great cupola, upon the floor of the stone gallery.

From the bottoms of these pipes, which terminate with a shoe of lead within half a foot of the floor of the stone gallery, the metallic communication is again interrupted to the top of the leaden pipes, which convey the water from thence. Here it is proposed, that conductors of lead, not less than four inches in breadth and half an inch in thickness, should be placed so as to be in contact with the bottom of four of the pipes that come from above, and with the top of four of those that descend. Lead is recommended to be employed here, as more readily adapting itself to the various curvatures it must meet with in the now proposed arrangement.

These last pipes, after descending below the colonnade, near the circular stair-cases, make their appearance upon the outside of the drum-part of the cupola; where they are bent at obtuse angles, and discharge their water upon the roof of the church. From these angles to the roof the distance is about five feet. Here then is another interruption to the metallic communication. This is proposed to be compleated by conductors of lead, similar to those before mentioned, which should be so placed as to be in contact both with the bottom of the pipes and the adjoining roof.

From the roof, as has already been mentioned, the leaden pipes are continued below the surface of the earth, and terminate in a drain; and thus, by the method now directed, the metallic communication will be compleated from the cross on the top of St. Paul's church to some feet below the surface of the ground.

The Committee then turned their thoughts towards the two towers at the west end of the church; and here they beg leave to observe, that in one of these towers, between the pine apple and the leaden bell-shaped covering near it, placed at the top of each of these towers, there is no metallic communication deserving notice, till you come to the lead on the roof of the church. This distance is eighty-eight feet. To this tower, therefore, it is proposed to adapt a droor bar of iron, not less than an inch and a quarter square, in such a manner that one end of the bar should be in contact with the metal communicating with the pine apple on its top, which is of copper, and the other end with the lead on the roof of the church.

In the middle of the other tower, in which the great bell is hung, there is an iron stair-case of considerable height, which is placed in the middle of it, in order for the more conveniently coming at the clock-work. The top of this stair-case is at no great distance from the leaden covering upon the top of the tower: but from the bottom of this stair-case to the roof of the church, between which there is no metallic communication, the distance is considerable, not less than forty feet. The Committee recommend, therefore, that a bar of iron, of an inch and a quarter square, may be placed between the pine-apple, or the lead in contact with it, and the upper part of this stair-case; and that another iron bar, similar to this last, may be adjusted so, as to pass from the bottom of the stair-case to the lead on the roof of the church. The roof, as has been already mentioned, communicates with the leaden pipes, and these with the ground.

These towers, from their near situation to the cupola, which is a building so much higher, may possibly be less liable to mischiefs from lightning than if they were erected at a more considerable distance. As the direction of the lightning is, however, uncertain, from a variety of causes, as also to what extent one building will protect another, the Committee are of opinion, that this apparatus to the towers will be expedient.

It is to be remarked, that wherever iron is employed as a conductor of lightning, especial care must be taken to prevent its becoming rusty; as, from being long exposed to the moist atmosphere, it will be corroded to a considerable depth: and so much of the iron as is corroded ceases to be of use as a conductor; the Committee therefore have, in directing the size of these iron bars, made some allowance for the waste of the iron by rust.

The size, as well as number, of the iron bars recommended here by the Committee, are only to be considered as applicable to St. Paul's, and not as a standard for any church or building of less dimensions; as in these last, conductors of a smaller size, and fewer in number, may answer the purpose as securely as the larger. But St. Paul's church is particularly circumstanced: it is an edifice not only of great height, but its cupola, to say nothing of the lead on the body of the church, presents a large surface of metal to the clouds; on which account it is very liable to receive greater quantities of the electric fluid; and, from large quantities of such an elastic power, great mischiefs may arise to this magnificent building, in consequence of obstructions the fluid may meet with in passing through it. For these reasons we have recommended very large conductors, that it may pass through them into the ground, as readily as it enters.

These, Sir, are our sentiments in relation to the matter, referred to us by the Royal Society, upon the request of the Dean and Chapter of St. Paul's. If they should be acceptable to the Society, and by their means to the Dean and Chapter; and if, by being carried into execution, they should at all contribute to the preservation of that noble fabric, it will be a great satisfaction to us. We are, with very great respect, Sir, Your most obedient, humble servants,

W. WATSON.
B. FRANKLIN.
B. WILSON.
JOHN CANTON.
EDWARD DELAVAL.[7]

To Noble Wimberly Jones[8]

ALS: New York State Library, Albany

Sir,   London, June 7. 1769

I did myself the Honour of Writing to you on the 3d. of the last Month,[9] since when the Parliament has risen without repealing the Duties that have been so generally complain'd of. But we are now assured by the Ministry, that the Affairs of America have been lately considered in Council: that it was the unanimous Opinion no new Acts for the purpose of Raising a Revenue in America should be made here; and that it was the full Intention of his Majesty's Servants to propose early in the ensuing Session the Repeal of the Duties on Glass, Paper, and Painters Colours. Believing this News would be agreable to our Friends, I take the first Opportunity of communicating it to you; and hope that nothing will happen in the mean time, to change the favourable Sentiments towards us, which apparently begin to take place in the Minds of his Majesty and his Ministers. Possibly we may not at first obtain all we desire, or all that ought to be granted to us; but the giving Ground to us in some degree has a good Aspect, and affords room to hope that gradually every Obstruction to that cordial Amity so necessary for the Welfare of the whole Empire, will be removed.[1] Indeed I wish, as I

7. The other members of the committee, who varied widely in their professions but were all interested in electricity, have been identified above as follows: Watson, III, 457 n; Wilson, IV, 391 n; Canton, IV, 390 n; Delaval, VIII, 359 n. The work that the committee recommended was finished within the year; see BF to Winthrop below, June 6, 1770.

8. See above, XV, 94–6.

9. No such letter has been found; BF was doubtless referring to his letter above of April 3.

1. Parliament was prorogued on May 9 until June 14, and then again until July. *London Chron.*, May 9–11, June 13–15, 1769. In May rumors were rife that

think it would be best, that this could be done at once: But 'tis perhaps too much to expect, considering the Pride natural to so great a Nation, the Prejudices that have so universally prevail'd here with regard to the Point of Right, and the Resentment at our disputing it. I shall however remain here another Session, with a View to join in Endeavours with the other Agents, to obtain a Repeal as general as possible of all American Revenue Acts. If I can at the same time render any acceptable Service to your Province in particular, tho' you should not think proper to continue the Appointment, it will be a very great Pleasure to me. Be pleased to present my best Respects to the Assembly, and believe me to be, very respectfully, Sir, Your most obedient humble Servant   B FRANKLIN

N. Wimberly Jones Esqr

Endorsed: Dr. B. Franklin 7th. June 1769

From Thomas Bond[2]   LS: American Philosophical Society

My dear Sir,   Philada. June 7th 1769.

I receiv'd your Letter of the 9th of March with William Cowell's inclosed, at which I was much surprised, as his last to Bond & Byrn was in a very different Strain, it being only dubious Whether a Bill of Three hundred Pounds then in his Hands would be paid or not. That Bill was founded on a large Estate in his Neighbourhood, and on the Drawers Sister, who was unluckily dead, and the Estate got into bad Hands. Mr. Lister a Man of considerable Property in Leeds, wrote the Drawer he would pay the Bill if 'twas accompanyed with a Power of Attorney, which was done. A Merchant of the first Note in Hallifax wrote at the same Time he would give him a Credit of Fifteen hundred Pounds on the Estate, Mr. Cowell likewise solicited the Management of his Affairs. These Bond & Byrn thought sufficient to Authorise the Drawer to renew the Bill

---

all the differences between Britain and her colonies were now resolved to the satisfaction of both sides, and that all the acts levying taxes in America would be repealed at the beginning of the next session. *Ibid.*, May 13–16, 18–20, 1769. Although BF was clearly not taken in by these rumors, they may well have contributed to his guarded optimism.

2. For Dr. Bond, an original member of the APS and co-founder, with BF, of the Pennsylvania Hospital, see above, II, 240 n.

on Lister and which they make no doubt is payed, however T. Bond junior being in Maryland I immediately sent an £100 to Harford & Powell subject to Mr. Cowells Draught and you may depend I will take Care No Man shall suffer by your Recommendation of that House. They have a respectable Opinion of Mr. Cowell but think it ungenerous in him thus to complain when from a Blunder of his, the Goods were shipped for them by the way of New York, where they lay for near 12 Months, in the Hands of Larry Read, with Orders to sell them for the first Cost, which they would not fetch, and were afterwards taken by them, at the Request of Mr. Cowell (unseasonably and Pillaged) to their real Loss so that the Disappointments have been Mutual.[3]

Your good Mrs. Franklin was affected in the Winter with a partial Palsey in the Tongue, and a sudden Loss of Memory, which alarmed us much, but she soon recovered from them, tho her constitution in general appears impaired.[4] These are bad Symptoms in advanced Life and Augur Danger of further Injury on the nervous System. However you may depend every Relative of yours will engage my Particular Care and Attention.

I long Meditated a Revival of our American Philosophical Society and at length I thought I saw my Way clear in doing it, but the Old party Leven split us for a Time.[5] We are now united and with your Presence may make a Figure, but till that happy Event, I fear much will not be done. The Assembly have countenenced and encouraged us very generously, and kindly, and we are much obliged for your Care in procuring the Telliscope, which was used in the

3. Information about the principals in this complicated business is almost nonexistent. There were several William Cowells and several Listers in Leeds at the time, but none can be identified; nor can we guess what Dr. Thomas Bond, Jr., had to do with the affair. Harford and Powell, whom BF had recommended, were merchants of Mincing Lane, London. *Kent's Directory . . .* (London, 1770), p. 81. Lawrence Reade was, with Richard Yates, a New York importer of East Indian and European goods, with a store on Wall Street. James G. Wilson, *The Memorial History of the City of New York* (5 vols., New York, 1892–96), II, 468. But these are small details, and in the absence of BF's letter to Bond of March 9 the business as a whole remains even more obscure than the Doctor's syntax.

4. This was the "late Indisposition" to which BF referred in his letter to DF above, June 3.

5. See above, XV, 259–62.

late Observations of Venus's Transit, but the Micromiter did not move so well as it ought, from whence I fear their may be some defect in the Calculations.⁶ The Observations were made with four Glasses here, three at Norrington and one at the Cape,⁷ all which I hope to have the Pleasure of Transmiting to you in a fortnight.

The External and inturnal Contacts were taken with Accuracy. As to the other Parts I cannot form any Judgment at present, I know little of what passes out of my Own Sphere, but as far as I can Judge there is more Harmony amongst us than formerly. The Hospital flourishes much, the Old Managers stick to it steadily, the House of Employment⁸ is at present well regulated, the Colledge is as when you left it, The School of Physic,⁹ could we Streighten one or two Crooked Ribs amongst us, would soon make a considerable Figure, every Branch of Medicine is really well taught in it. There is the Appearance of a Plentiful Harvest. The Number of our Sheep Annually encrease and Manufactures of Necessity take place more and more. Maryland and Virginia both agreed to the Non Importation of all such Goods they can possibly do with out, and shew Examples of Industry and Patriotic Spirits.¹ If a Leisure Moment offers, a line or two from you would always give the greatest Pleasure to, Dear Sir, Your most Affectionate Humble Servant

THO BOND

Addressed: To / Doctr. Benja. Franklin / in / London / per Capt. Sparks

Endorsed: Dr Bond June 7. 1769

6. For the telescope and micrometer that Pennsylvania had commissioned BF to buy see *ibid.*, p. 228 n, and BF to Galloway above, Jan. 9.

7. The APS selected three sites for the observations: the State House square; an observatory erected by the mathematician and astronomer, David Rittenhouse (1732–96), at his farm in Norriton, Pa.; and Cape Henlopen at the entrance of Delaware Bay. Rittenhouse's observations, despite Bond's fears, were some of the best ever made. *DAB* under Rittenhouse. For other comments on matters alluded to in this paragraph see the next document and Evans to BF below, Sept. 7, Nov. 27.

8. The new almshouse or "Bettering House," for which see above, XIII, 262 n.

9. The medical school connected with the College of Philadelphia.

1. Baltimore merchants adopted a nonimportation agreement in March, and other merchants of the colony followed suit in May. Virginia, also in May, accepted a plan that was the work of the planters rather than of the merchants.

From Cadwalader Evans[2] ALS: American Philosophical Society

Dear Doctor   Philadelphia June 11th. 1769.

The late transit of Venus, has employ'd several of our Mathematicians, as well as others in several parts of the World. You will, probably, receive all the observations made by them, with full remarks; but in the mean time, I inclose those made by O: Biddle, and Joel Bayley, at Cape Henlopen. The former is a Son of John Biddle's; and the latter a young man from the forks of Brandywine, in Chester County: who was a considerable time with Dixon & Mason, running the line between Pensylvania, and Maryland. This is a simple relation how it appeared to them, and I beleive faithfull to the best of their abilities.[3] It was very hastily copied, which is some disadvantage.

I have not attended the meetings of the Philosophical Society, since the two were joined, and you elected. Mr. Wharton, knows why it has been so. It was my opinion then, that the eagerness, the Professors of the College shew'd for a Junction of the two Societies, was to avail themselves of the Labours of others, and filch reputation from their knowledge.[4] Several instances have occur'd to confirm it, particularly, the order of publishing the names of the observators, in the News Papers. They agreed at the State House, that each shoud say contact, as soon as they observ'd it, and those who

Pa. Chron., May 29–June 5, 1769; Arthur M. Schlesinger, *The Colonial Merchants and the American Revolution, 1763–1776* (New York, 1918), pp. 135–8.

2. For Dr. Evans, the Philadelphia physician, see above, VII, 287 n; BF had been in correspondence with him since 1765. BF replied to this letter on Sept. 7.

3. For another report of these observations see the preceding document. For Owen Biddle see above, XV, 262 n. The only meager information we have found about Joel Bailey (1732–97), aside from what Evans furnished, is in J. Smith Futhey and Gilbert Cope, *History of Chester County, Pennsylvania*... (Philadelphia, 1881), p. 467. Mason and Dixon, and the famous line that Bailey had helped to run, had engaged BF's attention in 1765: above, XII, 341–2.

4. For the rebirth of the APS in 1768 see above, XV, 259–62. Evans is referring BF for further information to Samuel Wharton, who was then in England. Members of the faculty of the College of Philadelphia were particularly prominent in the APS, and Provost William Smith and others were elected to office year after year. Brooke Hindle, *The Pursuit of Science in Revolutionary America, 1735–1789* (Chapel Hill, [1956]), p. 139. Whether the professors' purpose was to "filch reputation" is another question.

watch'd the time peice were immediately set down. Mr. Pryor called first, Mr. Shippen, next, in 2 seconds after. Mr. Ewing in 17 later. Dr. Williamson, without observing the agreement to call, set down for himself, and made it 2 seconds before Pryor—but as his veracity weighs little without vouchers, I am told no regard is paid to his observation. Nevertheless the Papers say, or insinuate that the observation was made by Mr. Ewing, Mr. Shippen, Dr. Williamson, Mr. Pryor &c. At Norriton, Mr. Ritt[enhouse] perceived the Transit first, Mr. Lucan, next, and Mr. Smith sometime after.[5] Here they were at some distance fr[om one an]other, not a word spoken, but Mr. Rittenhouse, and Mr. Smith without any knowlege of each other, communicated [torn] contact, by a signal to them that watched the time peice [torn] Mr. Smith, set down for himself.

Mr. Rittenhouse's, and Mr. Lucan's observations very nearly coincided, and are supposed to be accurate. Yet in the News papers, the order of the Names are, The Reverend Dr. Smith Mr. Lucan, Mr. Rittenhouse, tho the latter was incompareably the best Mathematician, and used the instrument with the utmost dexterity. At Cape Henlopen, one person called out the minutes, and another the seconds and the observator set down the contact, each without the privity of the other—so much for the Transit.

Last Month was a year, I inclosed to you, at the request of Wm. Henry of Lancaster, the draft of a register he had invented to regulate the heat in fire works.[6] I sent it by Capt. Faulkner, but have not heard whether you received it, or not.

By Capt. Sparks, I wrote to S: Wharton, that Mr. Galloway was

5. For the men mentioned who have already been identified see above, as follows: Joseph Shippen, XIII, 337n; the Rev. John Ewing, XI, 526n; Dr. Hugh Williamson, X, 266n; David Rittenhouse and his Norriton farm, the preceding document; the Rev. William Smith, IV, 467 n. Thomas Pryor or Prior (d. 1801) was an instrument-maker and member of the APS: Hindle, *op. cit.*, p. 153; Harrold E. Gillingham, "Some Early Philadelphia Instrument Makers, *PMHB*, LI (1927), 303. "Mr. Lucan" was John Lukens (d. 1789), the Surveyor General of Pennsylvania.

6. William Henry (1729–86) was a wealthy gunsmith and inventor, and the first man in the country to experiment with a steamship. He became a member of the APS in 1768, and his "Description of a Self-Moving or Sentinel Register" was published in its *Trans.*, I (1771), 286–9, and reprinted in Francis Jordan, Jr., *The Life of William Henry*... (Lancaster, Pa., 1910), pp. 43–7.

gone to Trevose,[7] for the recovery of his health——he returned last
night, not much better——he was so imprudent, out of complai-
sance to his Father,[8] to go out several hours in the heat of the day,
which was very hot, to level grass for watering a Meadow. I am not
apprehensive of danger but fear his recovery will be rather tedious.

Capt. Dowells Widdow, one of the Daughters of your old acquaintance Oswald Peel,[9] goes in this Vessel, to see her late Husband's Brother. It is probable she will go to London, and hopes to
have the pleasure of seeing you.

I came from Burlington 2 days agoe, when your son and daughter
were very well. Please to make my Compliments to Mr. Wharton,
and Mr. Trent and pray read a lecture to the former on temperance
as you know how small a quantity a man may live on, for I am af-
fraid the Luxuries of London will make another Bright of him. I am
told the Vessel is Just putting off. Adeiu. Your faithfull and Affectionate friend   C: EVANS

Addressed: To / Benjamin Franklin Esqr / Deputy Post Master of
North / America &c / Craven street / London / per the Chalkley /
Via Bristol

Endorsed: Dr Evans June 11. and July 15 1769

Notes on a Week's Diet and Poor Health

AD: Library of Congress

[Between June 12, 1769, and July 30, 1770[1]]
Monday—Din'd at Club[2]—Beef
Tuesday—at Mr. Foxcrofts—Fish

7. Joseph Galloway's country house in Bucks County; BF's papers were subsequently stored there, and most of them lost when the British sacked the house
during the War of Independence. See above, I, xxi.

8. His father-in-law, Lawrence Growden or Growdon (1694–1770), a
wealthy ironmaster and landowner.

9. Grace, the daughter of Oswald and Lydia Robinson Peel, had married
William Dowell in 1762. Geneal. Soc. of Pa. *Publications*, VIII (1933), 85.
Dowell, the former captain of a privateer and "a Man of great Integrity and
Benevolence," had died in 1768. *Pa. Gaz.*, June 16, 1768.

1. So dated because of the reference to dining at Mr. Foxcroft's. Although the
time bracket is unlikely to have much value, the means of establishing it may be

[*Notes 1 and 2 continued on next page*]

Wednesday—Dolly's[3] Beefstake
    Felt Symptoms of Cold Fullness
Thursday—Mr. Walker's[4]—Beef
    Predicted it
Friday at home   Mutton
    Little Soreness of Throat
Saturday   Club   Veal
    very bad at Night   Wine Whey
Sunday—no Dinner   continue bad[bed?]
    Monday morn. Had a good Night, am better
    U[rine] has deposited a reddish fine Sand.

From Anthony Tissington[5]

ALS: American Philosophical Society

Dear Sir   Alfreton 13th June 1769
    After two Months of Illness and Hurry, I cannot help inquiring if you and Mrs. Stevenson are well, and if you think of visiting Dirbyshire this Summer.

---

worth explaining to illustrate how such problems of dating can sometimes be narrowed when they cannot be solved. The *Pa. Packet*, on which Foxcroft came to England, arrived on May 30 or 31 (*Lloyd's Evening Post*, May 31–June 2, 1769), and by the following Tuesday he might conceivably have found lodgings in which to entertain BF; in that case the end of the week chronicled was Monday, June 12, and in accordance with our policy we are placing the notes there. As for the other end of the time bracket, BF would scarcely have referred to Foxcroft alone after the latter had been married, in a ceremony in which BF had given away the bride. The wedding was on Thursday, Aug. 2, 1770, and BF dined that day not with Mr. Walker but with Thomas Coombe (Coombe to his father, Aug. 4, Hist. Soc. of Pa.). Hence the latest date for BF's notes is the week ending on Monday, July 30.

2. Undoubtedly John Ellicott's Monday club at the George & Vulture, for which see Verner W. Crane, "The Club of Honest Whigs: Friends of Science and Liberty," *W&MQ*, 3d ser., XXIII (1966), 213–15.

3. Dorothea Blunt.

4. In all likelihood the same person who had invited him to dinner two years before: XIV, 93.

5. For Tissington, an owner or manager of mines in Derbyshire, see above, IX, 42 n, and subsequent volumes. This seems to have been his first letter to BF in more than two years.

For three weeks after I left London I lay Ill of its Smoak;[6] have been since in North Wales; and about the end of this month must go into Scotland, so shall have the benefit of change of Air.

Inclosed I send you a Letter from Richard Parkin the young man who din'd with you, to which You'l be so kind as to give such answer as you think proper, to me here, or to him at Middleton Tyas near Richmond Yorkshire. If I shou'd go too, you'd soon people America: but I've heared nothing of the mining scheme since I left London.[7]

My Wife is much better; can walk a mile or two; and now hopes a compleat recovery.[8] This She desires you'l tell Mrs. Stevenson—to whom and to your Self She joins in best wishes with Dear Sir Yours very affectionately ANTH TISSINGTON I'm very glad to learn that the American affairs will be settled to your wish.

Addressed: To / Benjamin Franklin Esqr / in Cravenstreet—Strand / London

From James Parker

ALS: American Philosophical Society

Honoured Sir   Newyork, June 18. 1769.

Eight Days ago, I wrote you per Packet, inclosing the 2d Bill from Mr. Courtney of Baltimore, the first of which I sent per Capt. Haight, for £141 6s. 11d. Sterling. Last Night I received the inclosed Bill for £10 1s. 3d. Sterling from Mr. Vernon of Rhode-Island; he says, it is good, and he is trying to get more for further Remittance. This is all I have received since my last; tho' I neglect no Methods I can think of, to press Payments from all Quarters.

6. He must have been singularly allergic to London smoke, for this had happened before. See above, XIII, 402.

7. Parkin has not been identified; his home, Middleton Tyas, a small town six miles from Richmond, was once famous for its copper mines. Thomas Allen, *A New and Complete History of the County of York* (6 vols., London, 1829–32), VI, 358. Tissington's mining scheme may have been related to his "farm" of 10,000 acres in East Florida, to which, two years before, he had thought of retiring: XIV, 163.

8. His wife, Margaret Bunting Tissington, had apparently been ill for the past two years. See above, XIII, 403; XIV, 162.

When Mr. Foxcroft left us, he knows, what Work we had with Mr. Chew in canvassing Matters with him; he was then a Bankrupt, and since confirmed. Besides a small Ballance due to the Office, he has omitted paying the Rider £33 9s. Lawful, which was due to him, and which Mr. Chew should have paid him:[9] but as Mr. Chew has intirely become insolvent, I apprehend the poor Rider must be paid, as he pleads he is hired by the Office, And indeed, it would be too hard to let him be ruined in the Service of the Office, for the Fault of one of the Officers, and as Mr. Chew makes a Plea or Pretence of the Office owing him for former Services, what can the poor Rider do? Therefore to prevent him from suffering, I have ordered Mr. Vernon to pay part of that Arrear, and shall lay the other part on some other Office. Whether I shall have done well or not, I cannot say, but I mean for the best, and hope your Approbation. The Rider says, the new Post-Master at New London[1] has hitherto paid him punctually, and we must take Care not to let such large Arrears run on for the future. But Mr. Chew has long equivocated much.

Both by Mr. Robinson and the Packet, I wrote about the Purpose, with your Consent, of resigning the Place in the Custom-House, from a Consciousness of my being unequal to the Task, and I would not bring my Sureties in Question: tho' I have yet had no Fault found with me, and I continue till I hear again from you; if peradventure you may either procure it for Mr. Robinson, or any one else, you may be desirous of assisting; which I leave to your own Discretion. It may possibly be in your Power, with Mr. Foxcroft, to procure it for Mr. Robinson, and I conceive, it would be of more advantage to him, than it ever could be to me, as he might possibly get promoted further in that Office, as his Capacity and youth may assist him therein: tho' I submit all to your better Judgment.

We have had a cold backward Spring, and now come on a hot, and very dry Summer hitherto: Every Thing in the Ground suffers for want of Rain, and if we have not some e'er long, we shall all

9. For the financial troubles of Joseph Chew, New London postmaster until his removal in 1769, and the controversy over whether he did or did not owe the Hartford postrider for services in 1755–56 see above, XI, 109 n; XIII, 59 n, 328, 395, 412; XIV, 232–3, 246; and Chew to BF below, Dec. 12.

1. John Still Miller, Chew's successor; see Jeremiah Miller to BF below, Dec. 11.

suffer. We shall perhaps be awaken'd at last, from our Sleep of Luxury and Extravagance. In general Things go on here as usual—only Times grow duller daily. We all join in our Respects to Mr. Foxcroft and self, from Your most obliged Servant

JAMES PARKER.

Addressed: For / Dr. Benjamin Franklin / Craven-Street / London / per Capt. Winn.

To Mary Stevenson

ALS: Library of Congress

Dear Polley   Tuesday morng. June 27 —69

Agreable to your Orders delivered to me very punctually per Temple,[2] I return you enclos'd Voltaire's Verses. The Translation I think full as good as the Original. Remember that I am to have them again.

I take this Opportunity to send you also a late Paper containing a melancholy Account of the Distresses of some Seamen. You will observe in it the Advantages they receiv'd from wearing their Clothes constantly wet with Salt Water, under the total Want of Fresh Water to drink. You may remember I recommended this Practice many Years ago.[3] Do you know Dr. *Len*, and did you communicate it to him? I fancy his Name is wrong spelt in this Paper, and that it should be *Lind*, having seen in the Reviews some Extracts from a Book on Sea Diseases published within these 2 or 3 Years, by one Dr. Lind;[4] but I have not seen the Book, and know not whether such a Passage be in it.

I need not point out to you an Observation in favour of our Doctrine that you will make on reading this Paper, that *having little to eat* these poor People in wet Clothes Day and Night, *caught no Cold.*

2. For WF's illegitimate son and BF's grandson, William Temple Franklin (D.1.1.), see above, XIII, 443–4.

3. See his letter to Polly in 1761 above, IX, 338–9.

4. Dr. James Lind (1716–94) is famous for his *Treatise on the Scurvy*, published in 1754, which first established conclusively the value of lemon juice as an antiscorbutic. *DNB*. BF is probably referring to the second edition of Lind's *An Essay on the Most Effectual Means of Preserving the Health of Seamen in the Royal Navy* (London, 1762).

My Respects to your Aunt, and Love to all that love you. Yours affectionately   B FRANKLIN

Return the Paper as it is Part of my Set.

Addressed: To | Miss Stevenson | at | K[ensington] | Tuesday 10 A.M.

Endorsed: June 27 ——69

From James Parker   ALS: American Philosophical Society

[New York, June 28, 1769. Encloses two bills of exchange, which he is sending by way of Bristol: one from Tuthill Hubbart of Boston for £122, drawn by Timothy Folger on Moses Allnutt of London,[5] dated June 19; the other from Thomas Vernon, the Newport postmaster, for £15, drawn by John Mawdsley on Messrs. Lane Son & Fraser of London,[6] dated June 16. Also encloses a second of Vernon's bill for £10 1s. 3d., and will forward the seconds of the others by the first good opportunity. No news yet of Foxcroft's arrival in England.]

From Sir John Pringle   AL: American Philosophical Society

[June?, 1769]

Sir John Pringle's Compliments to Dr. Franklin, and begs to introduce to his acquaintance the bearer Dr. Starck who has lately made the curious experiments on living on bread and water, and who wanting to make a pair of nice scales for weighing himself in this prosecution of those experiments[7] Sir J.P. has taken this liberty to address him to Dr. F. for his advice about the construction.

Addressed: To | Dr Franklin | Craven Street | at Mrs Stevenson's left hand as you go down 2/3 of the way

5. For Hubbart see above, v, 118 n. Moses Allnutt was an oil factor on Queen Street, listed in *Kent's Directory*... (London, 1770), p. 8.

6. John Mawdsley was a Rhode Island merchant, who subsequently became a loyalist; Sabine, *Loyalists*, II, 52. Lane, Son & Fraser was a merchant firm on Nicholas Lane, listed in *Kent's Directory*... (London, 1770), p. 106.

7. William Stark (1740–70) was a medical pioneer, whose research on himself brought him to an early grave. After finishing his studies at Edinburgh he came to London in 1765; in 1767 he took his M.D. at Leyden, then returned to

The Formation of the Grand Ohio Company

The two documents that follow are closely connected. Both were products of the obscure and complicated process by which a group, known as the "suffering traders," that claimed Indian lands west of the Alleghenies was transformed into an Anglo-American company with political influence and grandiose ambitions. Neither of the documents can be precisely dated. The first is a rough draft, in Franklin's hand, of the organization of the Company; the second is a petition from it, which is endorsed as having been read before the Privy Council on July 24, 1769. The two were presumably composed at almost the same time.

The treaty signed at Fort Stanwix in November, 1768, provided for a large cession by the Indians of land south of the Ohio River to compensate the "suffering traders" for their earlier losses.[8] The treaty was not valid until approved by the crown, and to secure approval William Trent and Samuel Wharton came to England early in 1769. Their consultations with Franklin and others soon convinced them that the best hope for the traders was to expand their group by including a number of Englishmen influential in politics, among them John Sargent and the Hon. Thomas Walpole.[9] The idea had obvious advantages for both sides: the politicians acquired land claims that might mean riches; the Americans acquired the political support that they needed in order to get the Fort Stanwix agreement confirmed. The next step was to block out the structure of the new organization, which was officially known as the Grand Ohio Company, but also went by the name of the Walpole Company and, somewhat later, the Vandalia Company.

Franklin's sketch of the articles of government reads as if they had

---

London to continue his studies. From observing patients at St. George's Hospital he amassed clinical notes, which were subsequently edited and published, on diseases of various parts of the body. In June, 1769, with the encouragement of Pringle and, it is said, BF, Stark began to experiment with living on different kinds of diet (of bread and another food added) which were all meager to a degree. He kept a journal with meticulous details of these experiments, including his weight each day to the dram, until Feb. 18, 1770. By then he was so seriously ill that he summoned Dr. Hewson, Polly Stevenson's husband-to-be, and five days later he died. James Carmichael Smyth, ed., *The Works of the Late William Stark, M.D., Consisting of Clinical and Anatomical Observations, with Experiments, Dietetical and Statical*... (London, 1788), pp. x–xi, 96–109; see also *DNB*.

8. See the letters from Thomas and Samuel Wharton to BF above, xv, 264–6, 275–9.

9. Sargent was a former M.P., a merchant, and an old friend of BF; Walpole, the nephew of Sir Robert, was a prominent London banker and military con-

been hammered out in a group discussion. Some of the marginal comments probably reflect his own ideas, some those of others at the meeting. In any case the articles were subject to further discussion through the rest of the year, and did not take final form until December.[1]

The petition to the King raises a number of questions. The first is whether it was the only petition from the Company, or one of several at approximately the same period. Samuel Wharton, writing some years later, twice referred to a petition in June, 1769, that was signed by a small committee; at one time he listed the members as Franklin, Walpole, Sargent, and himself; at another time he added Thomas Pownall.[2] Samuel Wharton and Franklin, writing in 1779, referred to a petition in June, 1769, that was signed by themselves on behalf of an Anglo-American group.[3] In both cases the aim was the same as that of the petition below, to secure for the Company the right to buy 2,400,000 acres of American land. This evidence could be read to mean that three petitions asking for the same thing, each with a somewhat different list of signers, were submitted within a period of a few weeks; but such redundancy would have been absurd. We are convinced that all these references are to a single document, the one we print, and that the signers were the numerous names that appear there, and not the small committee Wharton mentioned, or Wharton and Franklin alone. Those two agree on the June date, which we have no reason to question and which is reasonable for a petition that reached the Privy Council in late July.[4] The articles of organization preceded, as the first one makes clear, the drafting of the petition; and we believe that June was the most probable date for both.

---

tractor, and M.P. for King's Lynn. Namier and Brooke, *House of Commons*, III, 404–5, 598–600. Lewis asserts that the idea of expanding the company grew out of a conversation between Walpole and Wharton on June 14: *Indiana Co.*, p. 86 and n. 138. His citations, however, do not bear out his assertion; and we are convinced that the idea must have been born earlier. Otherwise there would scarcely have been time to organize the company, and draft and submit the petition that was before the Privy Council on July 24.

1. *Ibid.*, p. 88 and n. 141.

2. Samuel Wharton, *Plain Facts*... (London, 1774), p. 147, and *Facts and Observations*... (London, 1775), p. 137. These statements have led historians to assume, mistakenly in our opinion, that the committee members were the actual petitioners: Kenneth P. Bailey, *The Ohio Company of Virginia*... (Glendale, Cal., 1939), p. 239; Gipson, *British Empire*, XI, 465.

3. Bigelow, *Works*, XII, 342.

4. The date when the petition was received, July 24, has been confused by one historian with the date when it was composed, and by another with the date when the Grand Ohio Company was first organized. Lewis, *Indiana Co.*, p. 89; Jack M. Sosin, *Whitehall and the Wilderness*... (Lincoln, Neb., 1961), p. 186.

I. Heads of the Articles Relating to the Land Concern

AD: American Philosophical Society

Heads of Articles   [June?, 1769]

1. Apply to the King for a Grant of 2,400,000 Acres to be located in such Places as shall be hereafter agreed *by the Company*.
2. The Land to be divided *by the Company* into 60 Shares 40,000 each.
3. No Partner to hold less than a Share or [*in margin: and* no Person.] to have right to a Vote if he holds less.
4. Name of the Company.
5. A Majority in [*blank*] Days after Exec[uting] the Articles, to chuse a Committee and Treasurer for Management who are to keep Minutes to continue a year.
6. Election to be annual. Committee and Treasurer of preceding Year to deliver up the Books &c. to their Successors.
7. Committee and Treasurer to meet twice a Year, or oftner, and may call a general Meeting.
8. Quorum to consist of [*blank*] shall have full Power to order the Company's Affairs, *except such as are explicitly provided for* by these presents. [*In margin:* May they not chuse other Agents?]
9. Any of the Company may examine the Papers.
10. In Case of Death, Absence or Incapacity, surviving or remaining Members shall act for the whole Interest. Heirs, Ex[ecuto]rs Adm[inistrato]rs or Assigns *to have no vote*. [*In margin:* Their Interest however to be taken care of.]
11. Partnership to continue 10 Years.
12. Wm. Trent and S. Wharton constituted standing Agents in N America during the Continuance of the Partn[ershi]p with the sole and absolute Power of locating in such Manner as they shall think fit.
13. The Company shall furnish said Wharton and Trent with such Sum or Sums of Money or with full Power to draw, as shall be *sufficient* to pay all Charges and Expences which shall in any wise accrue in surveying, dividing, lotting &c and for all purposes relative thereto.
14. Said Tr. and Wh. with or *any three* [*in margin:* too few] of them to have full and absolute Power to sell the Lands in such Quan-

165

tities and for such Conditions, as they shall judge most for the Benefit of the Company.

A Quantity [*blank*] reserved, and not to be sold, unless directed by a Majority of the Company.

15. A Sum not exceeding [*blank*] Pounds per Share shall be advanced by each of the Parties unto Tr. and Wh. and others, to be disbursed in building Saw Mills Grist Mills and other Buildings on the Land, and in purchasing Waggons and Horses for the Use of the Company aforesaid. And the said Tr. and Wh. and [*blank*] shall every year send Accounts, and remit the Moneys, to be divided by the Committee and Treasurer.

16. That the said Tr. and Wh. and [*blank*] or a Majority of these Agents of the Company during the Continuance of the Copartnership shall have power to grant Lands for publick Uses.

17. That the said Tr. and Wh. and [*blank*] shall keep fair and regular Minutes of all their Transactions, and transmit them.

18. The said Tr. and Wh. shall not receive or be intitled to any Consider[ation] for their Trouble, the Company paying for 5 Shares or 200,000 Acres for them. [*In margin:* Query, is this intended the first Payment only, or all future Incidents?]

19. No one of the Company to be allowed any Comm[issio]n for his Trouble Expences to be borne equally by each Share.

20. Each Partner's Share liable to the Company's Demands against its Owner. Any Partner refusing or neglecting to pay his Part, shall have one 60th of his Share sold by Order of the Majority.

Lastly. At the End of the Term, all the Lands to be divided, and Lots to be drawn, to be held afterwards in severalty.

Endorsed: Heads of the Articles relating to the Land Concern.

II. Franklin, Thomas Walpole, *et al*: Petition to the King

DS (copy): Public Record Office

[June?, 1769]

To the Kings most Excellent Majesty in Council

The humble Petition of Thomas Walpole, Richard Walpole, Richard Jackson, Sir George Colebrooke, Thomas Pownall, Benjamin Franklin, Thomas Pitt, Lauchlin Macleane, Moses Franks,

Jacob Franks, Henry Dagge, Aaron Franks, Napthali Franks, Anthony Todd, John Foxcroft, James Dagge, John Dagge, and Robert Trevor,[5] on behalf of themselves and others their Associates.

Sheweth

That there is a large and extensive Tract of Land situate at the back of the British Settlements in Virginia in North America which the Sachems and Chiefs of the six Confederate Nations and of the Shawenesse Delawares Mingoes, of Ohio and other dependent Tribes have by Deed of Conveyance bearing date the 4th day of November 1768, granted bargained Sold released and confirmed to Your Majesty which said Tract of Land is at present vacant and unsettled by any of Your Majestys Subjects.

That your Petitioners are desirous to become Purchasers from Your Majesty of Two Million four hundred thousand acres part of the said Tract and will be ready to pay for the same such price and

5. The omission of John Sargent's name from this list is strange, and we cannot explain it. Richard Jackson, Thomas Pownall, John Foxcroft, and Anthony Todd have been too prominent in these volumes to need further introduction, and Thomas Walpole has been identified above. The Hon. Richard Walpole (1728–98), Thomas's brother, was a former merchant captain, a London banker, and M.P. for Great Yarmouth. Sir George Colebrooke (1729–1809), M.P. for Arundel, was the son of a London banker, from whom he had inherited a large fortune. Thomas Pitt, later first Baron Camelford (1737–93), M.P. for Okehampton, was a nephew of Chatham and a follower and close relative of George Grenville. Lauchlin Maclean (1727?–78) had been an army surgeon in America; he was, with Colebrooke, M.P. for Arundel, and was a business agent and close friend of Lord Shelburne. See Namier and Brooke, *House of Commons*, under the M.P.s listed. For Moses Franks and Henry Dagge, who was Wharton's and Trent's lawyer, see the former's note to BF above, Feb. 20. John Dagge, a lawyer, and James Dagge may have been relatives of Henry; John died in 1786 and James in 1793: *Gent. Mag.*, LVI (1786), 270; LXIII (1793), 677. Aaron Franks (1692–1777), Moses' father-in-law, was a wealthy London diamond merchant, and Napthali (1715–96), Moses' brother, was a London businessman. See Rachel Daiches-Dubens, "Eighteenth Century Anglo-Jewry in and around Richmond, Surrey," Jewish Hist. Soc. of England *Trans., Sessions 1953–55*, XVIII (1958), 150–2, 158–60. Jacob Franks we cannot identify. Three members of the clan had that name at about that time, but one was dead, one distant, and one dotty; see Israel Solomons, "The Genealogy of the Franks Family," American Jewish Hist. Soc. *Publications*, XVIII (1909), 213–14. For Robert Trevor, who like Foxcroft and Todd was an official of the Post Office, see above, X, 222 n.

to be subject to such Quit Rents as shall be thought reasonable so soon as the same shall be Surveyed and the boundary Line of the said Tract shall be finally settled between Your Majesty and the said six Nations.

That Your petitioners humbly propose that a Grant of the said Two Million Four hundred thousand Acres of Land under the Great Seal of Great Britain shall be made to Your petitioners and their Heirs and Assigns and that in such Grant shall be particularly specified the several and respective Boundaries and Limits within which the Lands thereby granted shall be located or set out so as to render the Description thereof fixed and certain.

That your petitioners are the first Adventurers who have proposed to purchase from Your Majesty Lands on the Continent of America and to make a Settlement there which it is apprehended will be of great Emolument to Government in point of Revenue and to Great Britain in point of Commerce as being a Frontier towards the Indians with whom Your petitioners promise themselves they shall be able to Cultivate and Secure in the most effectual manner a continuance of Peace and Harmony and by a more advanced situation be enabled to extend the Indian Trade to more numerous and remote Nations and they therefore humbly hope that this their undertaking will meet with Your Majesty's Royal Encouragement by making the Grant of the said Lands free from the payment of Quit Rents to be reserved thereon for the space of Twenty Years from the date of the Grant.

Your Petitioners therefore most humbly Pray that You would be pleased to take the promises into Your Royal Consideration and to Grant unto them such Lands as aforesaid in such manner and upon such Terms as are hereinbefore proposed.

Thomas Walpole	Jacob Franks
Richd. Walpole	Henry Dagge
Rd. Jackson	Aaron Franks
G. Colebrooke	N. Franks
T. Pownall	Anthony Todd
B. Franklin	John Foxcroft
Thos. Pitt	Jas. Dagge
L. Macleane	Jno. Dagge
Moses Franks	Rt. Trevor.

Endorsed: Copy

Petition of Thomas Walpole Esqr. and others, Praying for a Grant of a Tract of Land at the back of the Settlements in Virginia, with an Offer to become purchasors thereof from the Crown.

R 24th. July 1769.

14th. August 1769.

Referr'd to a Committee.

20th November 1769.

Referr'd to the Board of Trade.[6]

£1: 1*s*.

Board of Trade Read 24 July⎫ 1769
14 Aug ⎭

Referred   20 Nov. 1769.

To Samuel Wharton and William Trent

AL: American Philosophical Society

Monday July 3. 69

Dr. Franklin presents his Compliments to Messrs. Wharton and Trent, and acquaints them that on Thursday (or Friday) last, he had a good deal of Discourse with Mr. Mildred, and afterwards with Mr. Mildred and his Solicitor Mr. Lane,[7] when they concluded, on his Advice, to withdraw the Petition that had [been] presented to the King in Council, on Behalf of Messrs. Warder, Mitchel, &c.[8]

Addressed: To / Messrs Wharton and Trent

Endorsed: Dr Franklins Card July 3d. 1769

6. The Board, in its leisurely way, did not take up the matter until Dec. 13, 1769. *Board of Trade Jour.* 1768–1775, p. 152.

7. Daniel Mildred was a partner in the mercantile firm of Mildred & Roberts, which had extensive Philadelphia connections. See above, x, 108 n; XII, 100–1. Thomas Lane, the solicitor, lived in Boswell Court, Lincoln's Inn Fields: *Gent. Mag.*, XLIII (1773), 48.

8. Jeremiah Warder (1711–83) and Abraham Mitchel or Mitchell were both members of the group of Philadelphia merchants, the "suffering traders," whose interests Wharton and Trent were representing in London. We have found no other reference to this petition, and can only conjecture that it was withdrawn as part of the change in strategy, then under way, that produced the expansion of the "suffering traders" into the Grand Ohio or Walpole Company, for which see the preceding documents.

From James Elphinston: Bill for William Temple Franklin's Education.[9]

ADS: American Philosophical Society

[July 4. 1769]

Master William Temple
July 4. 1769

One half year's board and Education	15. ..	..
One half year's dancing	2.	2.
Education, a poem, bound		3. 6
Copybooks, paper, pens and ink &c		6. 6
Mending of cloaths		5. 6
Haircutting, twice		2.
Money		7. 6
An Apothecary's bill	1.	10. .
Extra's during ilness	1.	1.
Seat in Church		6
Servants		5

£21. 9. .

Received the above in full   JAMES ELPHINSTON

[*In another hand*]: Supposed to be paid in BF's Absence by Mrs. Stevenson[1]

Endorsed: Master William Temple / July 4. 1769 / No 19 Elphinston's Bill   Schooling for Mastr Temple pd July 4 1769

9. For young Temple's schooling under James Elphinston, William Strahan's brother-in-law, see above, XIII, 443; for further information about the schoolmaster see R. C. Dallas, "Biographical Memoir of James Elphinston, Esq.," *Gent. Mag.*, LXXIX (1809), 1057–63.

1. BF's Journal contains two payments to Elphinston, one on Jan. 30, 1769, of £20 11s. and the other on Jan. 23, 1770, of £19 13s.

To Deborah Franklin

ALS (facsimile) in John Jay Smith, *American Historical and Literary Curiosities; Consisting of Fac-Similes of Some Plates, &c. Relating to Columbus, and Original Documents of the Revolution...Second Series* (New York, 1860), pl. XLVI.[2]

My dear Child,   London July 5. 1769

By Capt. Falconer, I shall write to you fully; this only serves to acquaint you that I am as well as I can be without my usual Journey, but I begin to feel the want of it, and shall set out in a few days, for a Tour of a few Weeks.[3] I hope you are perfectly recovered.[4] My Love to Sally and all Friends. I am, as ever Your affectionate Husband

B FRANKLIN

To Charles Thomson and Thomas Mifflin

ALS (copy): Minutes of the Library Company of Philadelphia, November 29, 1769.

Gentlemen,   London July 7th. 1769.

I received your favour of the 3d. of May, and shall send you the Books you write for per Capt. Falconer. Seeing some Time since that other Libraries were about to be united with yours, I did for that Reason forbear buying any Books but Robinson's History, till I should have further Orders, lest I should purchase Duplicates. I think we should have, in some one of our public Libraries, all the Transactions of every Philosophical Society in Europe, vizt. The Memoirs of the Academy of Sciences at Paris; those of Petersburgh; of Haerlem in Holland; of Bononia in Italy &c. with the Continuations as they come out Yearly; and also the French Encyclopedia.[5] They would be extremely useful to us on many Ac-

2. The original, according to Smith, belonged in 1860 to Ferdinand J. Dreer. It seems to have vanished. It was not listed among the Dreer autographs sold on May 28–9, 1889, or in *A Catalogue of the Collection of Autographs Formed by Ferdinand Julius Dreer* (2 vols., Philadelphia, 1890–93), or in the sale of Dreer's library on April 11–12, 1913; and it has not been published in any edition of BF's works. The style, content, and handwriting of the note convince us, nevertheless, that it is genuine.

3. He set out for Paris on July 14 and returned on August 24.

4. See Thomas Bond to BF above, June 7.

5. The books in the order of their mention were William Robertson, *The History of the Reign of the Emperor Charles V...* (3 vols., London, 1769); the

counts, and are rather too heavy for private Collections. But as they are in different Languages, and the Majority of our Members are only acquainted with English, I have not ventured to buy them without Orders; and in general I wish to have express Directions, and that as little as possible may be left to my Judgment in laying out the Company's Money. With great Esteem, I am, Gentlemen, Your most obedient and humble Servant   B Franklin

Messrs. Thomson and Mifflin

To John Bartram   ALS: Stanford University Libraries[6]

Dear Friend,   London July 9, 1769
    It is with great Pleasure I understand by your Favour of April 10. that you continue to enjoy so good a Share of Health.[7] I hope it will long continue. And altho' it may not now be suitable for you [to make?] such wide Excursions as heretofore, you may yet be very useful to your Country and to Mankind, if you [sit?] down quietly at home, digest the Knowledge you [have] acquired, compile and publish the many Observations you have made, and point out the Advantages that may be drawn from the whole, in publick Under-takings or particular private Practice. It is true many People are fond of Accounts of old Buildings, Monuments, &c. but there is a Number who would be much better pleas'd with such Accounts as you could afford them: And for one I confess that if I could find in any Italian Travels a Receipt for making Parmesan Cheese, it would

---

Mémoires de l' Académie royale des sciences de Paris, first published in 1699; the *Commentarii* and *Novi commentarii Academiae scientiarum imperialis petropoli-tanae*, now the Akademiia Nauk SSSR; the *Verhandelingen, uitgeeven door de Hollandsche maatschappye der weetenschappen, te Haarlem*, first published in 1754; the *De Bononiensi scientiarum et artium Instituto atque Academia com-mentarii*, now the Accademia delle Scienze dell' Istituto Bologna; and the *Encyclopédie, ou Dictionnaire raisonnée des sciences des arts, et des métiers, par une société de gens de lettres* (17 vols., Paris, 1751–65).

    6. The Harwood Family Papers, Manuscripts Division, Department of Special Collections. For many years these MSS were on deposit with the Library of Congress; they were returned in 1969 to Mr. Wilson F. Harwood, from whom the Stanford Libraries acquired them.

    7. BF is responding to Bartram's letter above, April 10, where the references are explained.

give me more Satisfaction than a Transcript of any Inscription from any old Stone whatever.

I suppose Mr. Michael Collinson, or Dr. Fothergill have written to you what may be necessary for your Information relating to your Affairs here. I imagine there is no doubt but the King's Bounty to you will be continued; and that it will be proper for you to continue sending now and then a few such curious Seeds as you can procure to keep up your Claim. And now I mention Seeds, I wish you would send me a few of such as are least common, to the Value of a Guinea, which Mr. Foxcroft will pay you for me.[8] They are for a particular Friend who is very curious. If in any thing I can serve you here, command freely Your affectionate Friend

B FRANKLIN

P.S. Pray let me know whether you have had sent you any of the Seeds of the Rhubarb describ'd in the enclos'd Prints. It is said to be of the true kind [?]. If you have it not, I can procure some Seeds for you.[9]

To Humphry Marshall[1]   ALS: Mr. S. Hallock du Pont (1955)

Sir,   London, July 9. 1769

I received your obliging Favour of April 13. with Specimens of the several Colours suitable for Painting which you have found in different Parts of our Country. It gives me great Pleasure to see them, and I have shown them to many Persons of Distinction, to-

8. Presumably John Foxcroft's brother Thomas, the Philadelphia postmaster and a friend of the Franklin family; see above, XIV, 137. John Foxcroft did not return from England until the autumn of 1770, a fact that can be established from references to a loan BF made him; see BF, Journal, Aug. 17, 1770; Foxcroft to BF below, Jan. 14, 1771.

9. Bartram accepted the offer, and BF sent him the seeds the following January. See Bartram to BF below, Nov. 29, 1769, and BF to Bartram, Jan. 11, 1770.

1. Humphry Marshall (1722–1801), a cousin of John Bartram, was also a botanist. He corresponded with Peter Collinson until the latter's death, and for Dr. John Fothergill he collected plants, birds' eggs, and other specimens. In return Fothergill sent him books, a reflecting telescope, and through Franklin's good offices a microscope and thermometer. *DAB*. Marshall's letter to BF has not survived, but the tone of the latter's reply suggests that their correspondence was just beginning; it continued actively for the next six years.

gether with your Letter, which is allow'd to contain a great many sensible and shrewd Observations. There is at present an Appearance as if the Great Ones were about to change their Conduct towards us: I believe they begin to be a little sensible of their Error. It is perhaps too much to expect that they will become thoroughly wise at once. But a little Time, with a prudent steady Conduct on our side, will, I hope, set all right. I shall be oblig'd by a Continuance of your Correspondence, being, very respectfully, Sir, Your most obedient humble Servant   B FRANKLIN

Mr Humphrey Marshall

Addressed: To / Mr Humphrey Marshall / West Bradford / Chester County / Pennsylvania / B Free FRANKLIN

To the Philadelphia Merchants

Broadside: Yale University Library

Gentlemen,   London, July 9, 1769.
    I Received yours of the 18th of April, inclosing copies of the articles of your agreement, with respect to importation, and of your letter to the merchants here. The latter was published,[2] and universally spoken well of, as a well-written, sensible, manly and spirited performance; and I believe the publication has been of service to our cause. You are, in my opinion, perfectly right in your supposition, that "the redress of American grievances, like to be proposed by the Ministry, will at first only be partial; and that it is intended to retain some of the Revenue Duties, in order to establish a right of Parliament to tax the colonies." But I hope, that by persisting steadily in the measures you have so laudably entered into, you will, if back'd by the general honest resolution of the people, to buy British Goods of no others, but to manufacture for themselves, or use colony manufactures only, be the means, under GOD, of recovering and establishing the freedom of our country entire, and of handing it down compleat to our posterity. And in the mean time,

2. "A Genuine Copy of a Letter from a Committee of Merchants in Philadelphia, to the Committee of Merchants in London," *London Chron.*, June 8–10, 1769. The sentence that BF subsequently quotes is from the merchants' letter to him above, April 18.

the country will be enrich'd by its industry and frugality, those virtues will become habitual, farms will be more improved, better stock'd, and render'd more productive by the money that used to be spent in superfluities; our artificers of every kind will be enabled to carry on their business to more advantage; gold and silver will become plenty among us, and trade will revive after things shall be well settled, and become better and safer than it has lately been; for an industrious frugal people are best able to buy, and pay best for what they purchase. With great regard, I have the honour to be, Gentlemen, Your most obedient, And most humble Servant,

BENJAMIN FRANKLIN.

To the Committee of Merchants in Philadelphia.

To Thomas Gilpin   ALS: American Philosophical Society

Sir,   London July 10, 1769

I received your Favour per Capt. Osborne, with the Model of your Machine for raising Water.[3] The Manner in which you have apply'd a single Crank for the Working of three Pumps, wherein the whole Force is apply'd to each, and yet in such quick Succession that there is no Loss of Time, appears to me so extreamly ingenious, that I have scarce ever seen a new Invention that gave me greater Pleasure. And I am persuaded with you, that it may be of great Use in draining Mines, Quarries, &c. I intend to exhibit it to the Society of Arts, when they meet in November next, and believe it will meet with their Approbation. I am, Sir, Your most obedient humble Servant   B FRANKLIN

Mr. Gilpin

To Grey Cooper   ALS: Mr. Albert M. Greenfield (1955)

Dear Sir,   Craven Street, Tuesday July 11. 1769

An Application being about to be made for a Grant of Lands in the Territory on the Ohio lately purchased of the Indians, I cannot omit acquainting you with it, and giving you my Opinion, that they will very soon be settled by People from the neighbouring Pro-

3. See Gilpin to BF above, May 16.

vinces, and be of great Advantage in a few Years to the Undertakers.[4] As you have those fine Children, and are likely to have many more, I wish for their Sakes, you may incline to take this Opportunity of making a considerable Addition to their future Fortunes, as the Expence will be a Trifle.[5] If therefore you will give me leave, I shall put your Name down among us for a Share (40,000 Acres). Your Neighbour Mr. Dagge[6] will call upon you some Day and explain the Particulars more fully. I am to set out on Friday with Sir J. Pringle on a short Tour upon the Continent. Have you or Mrs. Cooper any little Commission that I can execute in France? With sincerest Esteem, and best Wishes for you and yours, I am, my dear Friend, Yours most affectionately   B FRANKLIN

Grey Cooper Esqr

To James Bowdoin   ALS: Massachusetts Historical Society

Dear Sir   London, July 13. 1769

I am honoured with yours of May 10. and agree with you perfectly in your Sentiments of publick Affairs. Government here seems now to be growing more moderate with regard to America,[7] and I am persuaded that by a steady prudent Conduct, we shall finally obtain all our important Points, and establish American Liberty on a clearer and firmer Foundation. The Folly of the late Measures begins to be seen and understood at Court, their Promoters grow out of Credit, and the Trading Part of the Nation with the Manufacturers are become sensible how necessary it is for their Welfare to be on good Terms with us. The Petitioners of Middlesex

4. BF is referring to the petition of the newly-formed Grand Ohio Company for permission to purchase 2,400,000 acres, for which see above, pp. 166-8.

5. By his second wife Sir Grey eventually had four children, two sons and two daughters; how many were born by this time we do not know. Neither do we know when he accepted BF's offer and paid £200 for a share, but he eventually did so; see Jack M. Sosin, *Whitehall and the Wilderness* . . . (Lincoln, Nebr., 1961), p. 200.

6. Presumably one of three men named Dagge who signed the petition to the crown; see above, p. 167 n.

7. The government had no intention of laying further taxes on America for revenue purposes, Hillsborough had assured the colonial governors in his circular letter of May 13, 1769, and intended to remove some duties at the next session of Parliament. 1 *Pa. Arch.* IV, 341.

and of London have numbered among their Grievances the *un-constitutional* Taxes on America,[8] and similar Petitions are expected from all Quarters: So that I think we need only be *quiet* and persevere in our Schemes of Frugality and Industry, and the rest will do itself. Your Governor is recall'd, and 'tis said the Commissioners will follow soon, or be new-modell'd with *some more* Men of Discretion among them.[9] I am just setting out on a Journey of 5 or 6 Weeks, and have now only time to add, that I am, with the greatest Esteem and Regard, Dear Sir, Your most obedient humble Servant

B FRANKLIN

My Respects and best Wishes attend Mrs. Bowdoin, Mr. Temple and your amiable Daughter.[1]

Honle James Bowdoin Esqr

From Smith, Wright, & Gray

ALS: American Philosophical Society

Esteemed F[riend:]   [Thursday, xiii of[2]] July, 1769

Pursuant to thy favour received yesterday afternoon we herewith send thee Forty Guineas to thy Debit in account. Shall pay our

8. The petition of the freeholders of Middlesex was presented to the King on May 24, and that of the livery of London on July 5. Both excoriated the ministry for unfair and illegal practices, largely connected with the Wilkes affair. The Middlesex petition accused the King's "evil counsellors" of creating the same grievances in America as at home, and the London petition spoke particularly of unconstitutional taxation of the colonies. *Annual Register*, XII (1769), 199, 202.

9. Francis Bernard had been called home, and left on Aug. 1; but BF's rumor about the Board of Customs Commissioners at Boston proved to be only wishful thinking. The one man of "discretion" then on the Board was John Temple, Bowdoin's son-in-law, for whom see above, x, 389 n. Temple's fellow commissioners were charging him with laxity, especially in regard to smuggling, and the next year he returned to England to defend himself. What BF is saying between the lines is that all the commissioners should be like him.

1. Bowdoin's wife was the former Elizabeth Erving, the daughter of a Boston merchant; and their only daughter, also Elizabeth, was John Temple's wife.

2. The date to this point is almost illegible, and our guess at it is influenced by outside evidence. The forty guineas in cash that the letter mentions were entered by BF under July 13 in his Journal. The corn mill and lottery tickets, on the other hand, were entered under July 11; but what remains legible of the date cannot be reconciled with "xi".

friends Freeths for the Corn Mill and forward it as directed for thy Son.[3] Shall also buy 2 Lottery Tickets and advise the Numbers to Jonathan Williams at Boston as order'd.[4] As thou art well known at Paris a Letter of Credit may be needless But thy drafts on us which thou'll please advise in Course shall be honoured with the Utmost punctuallity. We wish thee an agreable Tour and Shall be glad to see thee returnd well home being with great regard and Esteem Thy Respectful Friends SMITH WRIGHT & GRAY

To Benjamin Franklin Esqr

Addressed: To | Dr. Benjn. Franklin Esqre | Present

From Cadwalader Evans ALS: American Philosophical Society

Dear Sir, Philada July 15th. 1769.

By the Ship Chalkley, Capt. Volans I sent to you Owen Biddle's, and Joel Bailey's, observations, of the Transit of Venus, at Cape Henlopen; but as there was some error in that hasty copy, I am desired to inclose a more correct one. I have not got the observations made at the Statehouse, or at David Rittenhouse's, but woud if I had known time enough to procure copies.[5] I suppose the Secretarys have or will do it, if the rancour of party will permit them. It had not subsided when you were chosen President, for one of them did all in his power to prevent it.[6] I will not say the choice can reflect any honour on you, who have had so much from the most respectable Bodies in the World; but this I am sure of, the Votes given

3. See WF to BF above, March 2.

4. For Jonathan Williams see above, XIV, 288 n, and BF to Williams below, Oct. 4. The tickets cost £29 5s. (Jour., p. 21), but they apparently did not arrive in Boston, because BF inquired about them ten months later; see his note to Smith, Wright & Gray below, May 10, 1770.

5. See Evans to BF above, June 11. In his reply below, Sept. 7, BF acknowledged receipt of the corrected accounts.

6. The reorganized APS had four secretaries, two from each of the societies that had merged. The secretary who opposed BF's election was probably his old enemy, Provost William Smith of the College of Pennsylvania. See Peter S. DuPonceau, *An Historical Account of the Origin and Formation of the American Philosophical Society* (Philadelphia, 1914), p. 50; Brooke Hindle, *The Pursuit of Science in Revolutionary America, 1735–1789* (Chapel Hill, [1956]), p. 137.

for you, were not given from any influence employed, but from the Judgement of every voter.

I mentioned to Mr. Wharton, the spirit that seems rapidly increasing, among us, for the culture of Silk; and I think it a favourable oppertunity to make trial, whether it is worth while.[7] A small premium given by our Legislature, for every Pound of Cocoons, woud do much. The expence might be defray'd by a Tax upon dogs, whose great number is become a nusance. I desired S: W: to send me the mean value of a pound of Cocoons, and whether the Parliment has granted us any encouragement in the middle Colonies. I am in haste as much as any body, Your Affectionate friend

C: EVANS.

Addressed: To / Benjamin Franklin Esqr. / Deputy Post Master Genl. / for North America / in / Craven Street / London / Via Liverpool

From Hannah Walker

ALS: American Philosophcial Society

Most Honoured Sir   Westbury July th 17 1769

I Humbly beg your Pardon for giving you this Trouble but it is to let you know that I have been Extremely ill with an Intermiting Fever for about six wecks. I was fearfull I should never write again and In the Interim it afflicted my spirits very much to think of my offending you so much the Best Friend I Ever had.[8] I hope most Honoured Sir I may once more Beg your Humble Pardon and hope their is forgiveness to be found with so good a Person for my Grief is so great to think that Least I had[9] from your good hands I had so

---

7. Samuel Wharton, who was then in London. Pennsylvania, with the assistance of the APS, made a better organized effort to develop silk culture than any other northern colony, and BF in London did what he could to assist. *Ibid.*, pp. 201–3.

8. The offense was probably squandering money that BF had sent to the Walkers. For this the husband was more culpable than the wife, according to James Payne, the solicitor who had been trying to find them a better house (above, xv, 144 n); Hannah, he said, "heartily laments her imprudence," and he suggested that BF's annual contribution be sent in future to her without her husband's knowledge. "I wish the man felt more distress and the woman less." Payne to Mrs. Stevenson, Aug. 10, 1769, Franklin Papers, APS.

9. Our guess of her meaning is: "that [in return for even the] Least I had," etc.

offended you it Lies Heavier upon my spirits some times than I am well able to bear. Sir it is with tears I most Earnestly Intreat your forgiveness for it would be so Comfortable to me to know you had forgiven me and to know that you wisht me and my Family well most Honoured Sir I take the freedom hoping you will not take it ill to let you know that my goods was restored to me again on the 24 of may only a few odd things as I never used scarce since I came to westbury but f[e]ared to lay then in by Places because we had no room in the House.[1] I hope Sir that all your good Family in America are well and your self in good health which are my Daily Prayers for a Blessing upon you and your good Family my Children and I joyn in Begging the acceptance of all air [our] Humble Duties to you and all your Dear Family in America from your most Humble and most obdient Servant   HANNAH WALKER

Addressed: To / Dr Franklin / att mrs Stevensons in / craven Strait near the / Strand / London

From James Parker   ALS: American Philosophical Society

[New York, July 22, 1769. Repeats the substance of his letter of June 28. Encloses a bill of exchange for £50 from Luke & Prettyjohn, Barbados, drawn on Richard Gosling of London[2] and endorsed by Mrs. Moore of New York; bills are rising and now stand at 72½, and he bought this one for 70. Has received Franklin's letters by the packet and by Dr. Rush.[3] Captain Davis[4] has arrived; he

1. A by-place is a secluded spot, but we cannot unscramble her meaning. Were the "few odd things" the goods that were restored, or some that were not? And who restored them and why? A plausible conjecture is that a bailiff had distrained them, and BF had provided the money to get them released.

2. Director of the Royal Exchange Assurance and a member of Richard & John Gosling, merchants of Tower Street, listed in *Kent's Directory*... (London, 1768), p. 72. He was probably the Richard Gosling whose death on Dec. 14 was reported in the *Gent. Mag.*, XXXIX (1769), 609.

3. Young Dr. Rush, who has appeared in this and previous volumes, had finished his medical training at Edinburgh, made a trip to the Continent, and returned to New York on July 14. See Carl Binger, *Revolutionary Doctor: Benjamin Rush*... (New York [c. 1966]), p. 69.

4. Undoubtedly Capt. Benjamin Davies, master of the *Hope*, who arrived in New York on July 20: Gaine's *N.-Y. Gaz.*, July 24, 1769.

spoke Captain Falconer in the Downs on May 30, and brings word that Mr. Foxcroft has safely reached England.

Mr. McGruder has sent him the book of Mr. Scott, of Upper Marlboro, Md.; Scott owes a considerable balance, but McGruder fears none of it can be got out of him. Mr. Hubbart writes that nothing is yet done in Mr. Huske's affair,[5] and fears nothing will come of it. The same with Mr. Walker of Hartford, who is still in jail.[6] Parker also despairs of the arrears of Mr. Chace of Providence, who is almost bankrupt.[7] But a former apprentice of Parker's, now living in Providence, is in debt, and the father has asked Parker's help so that his son can come home to New York. The young man's Providence creditors have agreed to take forty Spanish dollars from what Chace owes the Post Office, and the father will turn over that amount to Parker in New York. Doubts that anything more can be extracted from Chace, but will do what he can.

The summer has been dry and warm. Struggles along though feeble in body; is delighted to hear from Dr. Rush that Franklin is well. Hopes that by now Mr. Robinson has returned home, and that Franklin and Foxcroft will help him in some way that will not injure Parker; still wants to resign from the customs house.]

From Thomas Hutchinson[8]

Letterbook copy: Massachusetts Archives, Office of the Secretary of State.

Dear Sir   Boston 29 July 1769
I cannot omit my complements to you by Sir Francis Bernard

5. Ellis Huske, the postmaster of Boston, had died bankrupt in 1755 and left his post office accounts unsettled. See above, XI, 338 n.

6. John Walker had been appointed postmaster of Hartford in 1764. Because of irregularities in his accounts he was displaced and jailed in 1767; see William DeL. Love, *The Colonial History of Hartford*... (Hartford, 1935), p. 230.

7. Samuel Chace, born in Newport in 1722, was the first postmaster of Providence (1754–64) and held various other local offices; he also served a term in the provincial assembly. Daniel Beckwith, "The Lippitt Family of Rhode Island," *New England Hist. and Geneal. Register*, XXVII (1873), 71; Thomas W. Bicknell, *The History of the State of Rhode Island and Providence Plantations* (3 vols., New York, 1920), II, 770.

8. Chief justice of Massachusetts since 1760, lieutenant governor since 1758, and about to be acting governor on Bernard's departure. He was appointed governor in 1770 and received his commission in 1771. See above, V, 367 n.

who embarks in the Rippon to report to His M[ajesty] the state of the Province which he is able to do in the fullest manner and is disposed to do in the most just and candid manner.[9] I know his esteem for you and that he will be ready to acquaint you with all our late occurences which renders it quite needless for me to do it. Only give me leave to remark upon them that the air of indecency and contempt which our publick proceedings carry with them can have no other tendency than further to provoke a power it cannot Reach. And yet I hope some allowances will be made for them. They are the artful performances of one or two designing men whose political existence depends upon keeping up a Clamour.[1] And the greatest part of the men who vote for them see neither the design or tendency of them. I shall be much obliged to you if you will communicate any occurences relative to the Colonies which may be of use to me in my critical situation. I am with the utmost sincerity and esteem

D Franklin

From Samuel Cooper
AL (draft): British Museum

Dear Sir, Aug: 3. —69

I am now to acknowledg the repeated Favor of your Letters, with the Notes of Mr. P.' Speech in Parliament, the arguments on the Dissenting Cause; and the Political Pamphlets, in which you have given me no small Entertainment. I could not forbear communicating what you wrote to some particular Friends, to whom I knew it would give great Pleasure, and to allow some Extracts to be circulated among the Merchants, which were of great Service in confirming their present truly public Spirit, tho I did not think myself at Liberty to give the Sanction of your Name.[2] I am persuaded that the prudent and legal Measure of Non-Importation, would have

9. Bernard had been governor since 1760, and was recalled because of charges made against him by the Massachusetts Assembly. He sailed from Boston on Aug. 1, 1769, carrying with him this letter to BF. The government had already shown its confidence in Bernard by creating him a baronet on April 5, 1769. See above, x, 353 n.

1. This sentence has a touch of irony in view of future developments. By 1772 BF was convinced that Hutchinson himself belonged in the category of "designing men" who stirred up trouble, and his conviction was a factor in his deciding to send the Hutchinson letters back to Massachusetts.

2. See BF's letters to Cooper above, Feb. 24 and April 27.

had an earlier and greater Effect but for the Hopes given to Administration from this Side the Water that it would not be adher'd to. These Hopes have hitherto been delusive; the Agreement is still persisted in with great Spirit; and the vague, indeterminate Promise of a Kind of Repeal,[3] which is generally regarded here as a Design to divide us and break this salutary Measure, has, as you will see by the Papers only serv'd to support and strengthen it. In the mean Time Industry and Manufactures are daily increasing among us: Many, even in our trading Towns, are fond of being clad in Homspun; and in the Country, People are ambitious to fabricate for themselves what they formerly bought from the Shops. Britain is not sensible what she has already lost by the late impolitic and severe Measures. Those that take only a superficial View of Things imagine the Mother Country is safe, because they do not see large Quantities of American Manufactures stor'd for Sale. They do not consider how greatly the Demand for British Goods is diminish'd, thro the Industry of Families privately supplying themselves, from what this Demand would have been from our increasing Numbers, had Mild and prudent Methods been pursu'd. I can however give a striking Instance that may be depended on, of a Manufacture that was formerly almost wholly imported, and now furnishes no inconsiderable Article of our Exportation. The single Town of Lynn, makes yearly not less than eighty thousand Pair of Womens Shoes, better and cheaper than any that we can import; and not only Supplies the maritime Towns around it with this Article, but sends large Quantities of it to the southern Colonies, and the West Indies. I could not believe this till upon particular Inquiry, I found it to be undoubtedly true.

What you predicted in your Letter is already in part verified. The greater Part of the Military, has lately been withdrawn from this Town; and it is said the Remainder will not tarry long among us; what Ground there is for this, and whether any effectual Measures will be taken to remove the Ground of our Uneasiness, and reduce Things to their old Channel, Time will discover.[4] I suspect, from

3. Probably a reference to Hillsborough's circular letter to the colonial governors, May 13, 1769, for which see 1 *Pa. Arch.* IV, 340–1. See also *Boston Chron.*, July 20–24, 1769.

4. BF's prediction was in his letter of April 27. During July the 64th Regiment was withdrawn from Boston to Halifax: *ibid.*, July 6–10 and 24–27, 1769.

what is past, whether there is yet Wisdom and Moderation enough in the British Councils, to produce an Event so happy to both Countries.

This Letter will be deliver'd to you by Mr. William Gray, a young Gentleman who goes to London, for the Prosecution of Medical Studies. He is of a respectable Family among us. His Father was a worthy Clergyman of this Town; One of his Uncles, is of the first Character among our Merchants, and another, the Treasurer of the Province: and the young Gentleman himself has acquir'd a good Reputation.[5] I am told you design to return to America this Year. Nothing could give greater Pleasure to me, and many Friends than to see you again in Boston. I am my dear Sir, with [rest missing]

To D. Franklin

From Joseph Galloway   ALS: American Philosophical Society

Dear Sir   [Phila]da. Augt. 12. 1769

Mr. James Adair, the Bearer of this Letter, intending to Publish Essays on the Origin, Language, Religion, Customs, Policy &c, of the American Indians, particularly of those residing to the Southward, has obtain Subscriptions and Encouragment from many Gentlemen of this and the other Provinces in America. He thinks he can better execute his Design in England than in this Country which is the Cause of his Present Voyage.[6] I am well assured from his long Residence among the Natives and many Observations he

5. William Gray (1747–72) was the son of the Rev. Ellis Gray (1715–53), pastor of the New Brick Church, Hanover Street, Boston, and his wife Sarah Tyler Gray. The uncle "of the first character" was Thomas Gray (d. 1774), a bachelor Boston merchant, who brought up young William and his brothers after their father's death; the other uncle was Harrison Gray (1711–94), who fled to England in 1776 and lost his American property. *Sibley's Harvard Graduates*, IX, 400–4; Sabine, *Loyalists*, I, 488–9.

6. James Adair (c. 1709–c. 1783) was one of the ablest of Indian traders, but little is known about him except what he tells of himself. He appears to have been an Irishman, who came to America in 1735 and engaged in trade with the Catawbas and Cherokees and later with the Chickasaws and Choctaws; he was a friend of Sir William Johnson and George Croghan, and may have been briefly in partnership with the latter. After he reached London in 1769 he spent years on his book, *The History of the American Indians, Particularly Those Nations Adjoining to the Mississippi, East and West Florida, Georgia, South and*

has already committed to writing, he is very capable of Executing his Design. But as he may stand in Need of the Assistance and Judgment of Men of Letters, I beg leave to recommend him to your Notice and Encouragment. I am Dear Sir your most Obedient humble Servant   JOS. GALLOWAY

Addressed: To / Benjamin Franklin Esqr. / Deputy Post Master General / of North America / in / Craven Street / London

Endorsed: Galloway Aug. 12 1769

From James Parker   ALS: American Philosophical Society

[New York, Aug. 12, 1769. Sent by the packet the seconds of two bills of exchange, Hubbart's for £122 and Vernon's for £15, and the first of a bill for £50 that Parker bought in New York; encloses the second of that, together with the first of a bill just received from Hubbart for £200, Folger upon Allnutt,[7] of which the second will follow shortly.

Mr. Stewart, the Annapolis postmaster, raises a difficult question: Lord Botetourt of Virginia franks his own letters, but they are nevertheless charged to Stewart's office. Governor Eden, to whom they are addressed, will not pay the postage, claiming Botetourt's privilege as a peer.[8] Stewart and Parker cannot contend with Eden; will Franklin please advise?

No confirmation yet of Foxcroft's arrival in England. Parker's own affairs much as usual; still no settlement, or likely to be, with Holt, who within a few years will be bankrupt. Will be lucky to avoid that fate himself. Can manage if his strength does not fail him, but it ebbs every day.]

North Carolina and Virginia (London, 1775). The book, despite its thesis that the Indians are descendants of the ancient Jews, has great value for the astuteness and accuracy of its observations. *DAB.*

7. See Parker to BF above, May 12 and June 28.

8. Norborne Berkeley, Baron de Botetourt, had been appointed governor of Virginia in 1768; see above, xv, 190 n, 195. Robert Eden (1741–84) had been appointed governor of Maryland at the same time, and had arrived in Annapolis in June, 1769; *DAB.* Since the founding of the Post Office under the Protectorate, all members of Parliament had had the privilege of franking letters; the Franking Act of 1764, which curtailed some abuses of the privilege, did not affect members. Hence Eden's position seems to have been correct, but why and by whom Botetourt's letters were charged to the Annapolis post office we cannot say.

From James Parker

ALS: American Philosophical Society

[New York, August 14, 1769. Repeats the substance of his letter of August 12, and encloses the second of Hubbart's £200 bill.]

Dates of Journeys Abroad, 1766–69[9]

AD: American Philosophical Society

[Memorandum of the dates of Franklin's departure from and return to England on his trips to Germany in 1766 (June 15 and Aug. 13),[1] to Paris in 1767 (Aug. 28 and Oct. 8), and to Paris in 1769 (July 14 and Aug. 24).]

To John Canton[2]

ALS: The Royal Society

Dear Sir   Craven street, Aug. 25. 1769

When I was at Paris about 10 Days since, I was told that a Comet was then visible with a Tail of considerable Length. If it has not been yet observed or heard of here, perhaps this little Notice may be agreable to you. I return'd but last Night, I hope you and yours are well; being very sincerely Your affectionate Friend and Servant   B FRANKLIN

I think it was said to be in some Part of the Bull,[3] and in its Progress towards the Sun. M. Monnier discover'd[4] and observ'd it.

9. Hitherto documents covering a span of years, such as accounts, have been printed under the first date entered. Hereafter they will be printed or résuméd under the final date, in this case Aug. 24, 1769, so that whatever light they throw on the period covered may be explained in terms of material already in print.

1. An error for Aug. 16; see above, XIII, 384.

2. See above, IV, 390 n.

3. *I.e.*, Taurus. The comet was also observed in late August in London and in Philadelphia: *London Chron.*, Aug. 29–31, 1769; DF to BF below, Aug. 31, and *Pa. Chron.*, Aug. 28–Sept. 4, 1769.

4. Pierre Charles LeMonnier (1715–99) was an eminent astronomer and member of the Académie des sciences. The discovery of the comet, however, is

To Jacques Barbeu-Dubourg

Extract printed from Jacques Barbeu-Dubourg, ed., *Œuvres de M. Franklin...* (Paris, 1773), p. 314.[5]

Londres, 30 Août 1769.

Cette lettre vous sera remise par le Docteur Lettsom, jeune Méde-cin Amériquain de beaucoup de mérite,[6] qui est de la paisible secte des Trembleurs, et que vous regarderiez conséquemment au moins comme une rareté à contempler, quand même vous auriez épousé toutes les préventions de la plupart de vos compatriotes sur le compte de ces bonnes-gens.

From Deborah Franklin   ALS: American Philosophical Society

My Deareste Child   Auguste the 31 1769

I have but time to tell you that yister day our Dear littel Boy was Caireyed to Christe Church and was baptised by the Name of Benj Franklin. His Unkill and Ante stood for him Mr. Banton as prock-sey for you and I was well aneuef to stand for my self.[7] I have the

---

generally attributed to another French astronomer, Charles Messier (1730–1817): *London Chron.*, Aug. 24–26, 1769; Joseph-Jérôme le Français de la Lande, "Mémoire sur la comète de 1769," *Histoire de l'Académie royale des sciences...*, LXXI (for 1769; Paris, 1772), 49–58 (2d pagination).

5. Barbeu-Dubourg entitled the extracts, of which this is the first, "Sur les Trembleurs ou Quakers," to which he appended the following note: "Je crois devoir à cette occasion assurer le Public que M. Franklin n'est point de cette Secte des Trembleurs, comme on l'a cru presque dans toute l'Europe."

6. John Coakley Lettsom (1744–1815), Quaker physician and philanthro-pist, was born at Little Vandyke, one of the Virgin Islands, and was sent to England for his education, where he came under the notice of Dr. John Fother-gill's brother Samuel, one of the leading Quakers of the day. Lettsom had just taken his M.D. at Leyden, in June, 1769. He set up practice the next year in London, and became an outstandingly successful physician. *DNB*.

7. Sally's first child and BF's first legitimate grandchild, Benjamin Franklin Bache, had been born on Aug. 12, 1769, and hence was not yet three weeks old. In addition to DF the godparents were WF and his wife (see the next document) and, as BF's surrogate, John Baynton of Baynton, Wharton & Morgan, for whom see above, VII, 37 n; XII, 272, 274. DF was still weak from her illness of the previous winter, for which see Thomas Bond to BF above, June 7, and DF to BF below, Nov. 20–7.

pleshuer to tell you that Salley is thank to god as well as we have resen to expeckte her to be and is in a way of makeing a fine nuerse. I thinke it wold be plesed to see houghe much plesher Billey takes in him and thinkes he is a verey fine child he is. I am much hurreyed at this time but this I muste to say. Mr. Petter proformed his offis[8] he was so verey kind to cole on us and saw Salley and is verey kinde to her. Mr. Beach had a fine tortol cume in but Sundays we dresed it to diner. The pason from Burlinton came with them.[9] Mr. Wharton the father[1] dined with us Mr. Banton and pason Petters. One Jentelman of Mr. Beaches maid the whole companey. Everey one semed much plesed and the younk Jentelman behaved verey well and gives everey bodey hapey that have seen him. I am in hope to write by the nexte Packit. Mr. Brenmer is a passaig[er] as is Capt. Elvess and his son is on Bord all so[2] the two Elves have seen your son and is to tell you aboute him. I donte say as it wold not be thoute possbel he is a fine lim[b]ed child but is verey spair and dilicat some thinke he is darke eyes sume sez blaik eyed but thay is verey prittey. He is verey good and quiet and if it shold plees god to spair him I think much in pleshuer of him. Be so kind as to give my love to good mrs. Stephenson and to Polley to Mr. and Mrs. Strahan to Mr. and Mrs. Weste Capte. Orrey Mr. Gombes.[3] I beleve all our children will write but thay air oute to dine to gather and tomorrow we air to dine tomorrow with Mr. Hopkinson[4] if I am well aneuef to dine abrod. So I write today leste I not write to morrow you will see hough in Conneckted staet I write. Have or had you seen Mr.

8. For the Rev. Richard Peters, rector of Christ Church, see above, III, 187 n.

9. *I.e.*, with WF and his wife. The "pason" was the Rev. Jonathan Odell, for whom see WF to BF above, March 2, and XIII, 508 n.

1. For Joseph Wharton, Sr., head of the Wharton clan and BF's "good old true Friend," see above, XI, 451 n.

2. For James Bremner, the music teacher, see above, XII, 64 n. His companions were probably Capt. Henry Elwes, of the 22nd Regiment of foot, and Henry Elwes, Jr., "of North America," who died in London in 1773. See Worthington C. Ford, comp., *British Officers Serving in America, 1754–1774* (Boston, 1894), pp. 5, 36; *Gent. Mag.*, XLIII (1773), 622. Capt. Elwes landed at Plymouth in October; see his letter to BF below, Oct. 22.

3. The Strahans and Wests and Capt. Lewis Ourry have appeared too often to need introduction. Mr. "Gombes" was Thomas Coombe, Jr., who had gone to England to receive Anglican ordination; see above, XV, 53 n.

4. Francis Hopkinson, who had returned from London two years before. See above, XII, 125 n; XIV, 227.

Foxcrofte I hope he is well supose you have seen the Commet that is seen in this plase.[5] I have not seen it but our children have seen it. I am your afeckshonet wife   D FRANKLIN

I shold a told you that he was dresed in his christening sute and looked verey well in them and will thanke you for them

[*In Sally Bache's Hand:*] Mama desires me to tell you that yesterday, she was well enough to dine abroad with us at Mr. F: Hopkinsons———and that yesterday also she recd. a few Lines from you by Capt. Keys, and that she knew nothing of Capt. Osborns sailing.

Addressed: To / Benjamin Franklin Esqr.

From William Franklin   ALS: American Philosophical Society

Honoured Father   Philade. Septr. 1, 1769
    I came to Town with Betsy on Monday last in order to stand for my little Nephew. He is not so fat and lusty as some Children at his Time are, but he is altogether a pretty little Fellow, and improves in his Looks every Day. Mr. Baynton stood as Proxy for you and named him Benjn Franklin, and my Mother and Betsy were the God Mothers.[6]
    I did not know that Friend[7] was to sail so soon or I should have wrote to you and Mr. Wharton before I left Home. Here it is not in my Power for I am not a Minute without Interruption, and am put under such a Course of Eating and Drinking that I am not able to do any Thing else.
    I had the Pleasure of receiving your Letter of the 28th. of June per Capt. Keays.[8] It was delivered to Mr. Galloway at Chester who brought it up last Night. I cannot answer any Part of it now, as I am in doubt whether this will be in Time; the Passengers being to leave Town this Morning; but I shall write soon. I sent you lately a Bill of

5. See BF to John Canton above, Aug. 25.
6. See the preceding document.
7. Captain James Friend of the *Carolina*, whose clearance for London was announced in the *Pa. Chron.*, Aug. 28–Sept. 4, 1769.
8. W. Keais of the *Nancy and Sukey*; *loc. cit.* BF's letter has not survived.

Mr. Odell's for £25 Sterling[9] and shall send you the 2d. by the next Packet.

Betsy wants a Pair of handsome fashionable Stone or Paste Buckles, and I shall be obliged to you if you would purchase a Pair and send them by the first safe Opportunity. She joins in Duty with, Honored Sir, Your ever affectionate and dutiful Son

WM. FRANKLIN

Neither the July Packet, nor Jefferies[1] yet arriv'd.

Addressed: To / Benjamin Franklin, Esqr. / Depy. Postmaster General / of N. America &c / Craven Street / London / per Favor / of Mr. Bremner[2]

Endorsed: Wm. Franklin

From Mary Stevenson ALS: Adinell S. Hewson, Bryn Mawr, Pa. (1957)

Margate Sept. 1. 1769

Welcome to England my dear, my honour'd Friend! Just as I began a Letter to my Mother I receiv'd the News of your Arrival.[3] I have the same Confidence in my Parent that the Iskimaux Woman had in hers, for if my Mother did not know "I always speak Truth" I could not venture to say what she might be apt to doubt. I confess she has some Reason to complain of me; I *must* not complain of her; I have written to her but once since I came hither, and she—A Blank will conclude that Sentence. I have had the Satisfaction to hear of her by several of my Correspondents. I hope you will intercede for me, that I may not be severely rebuk'd. Indeed my Expedition has afforded me so little Entertainment that I could not have given her any by my Letters, and I know she is not so well affected to the Government, as to wish to increase the Revenue without some Advantage to herself. She is a very good Subject not-

9. For the Rev. Jonathan Odell see the preceding document. His bill was drawn on the treasurer of the Society for the Propagation of the Gospel: "Memoranda" (vol. LXVII, no. 11), APS.

1. James Jeffries of the snow *Britannia*, who arrived soon afterward: *Pa. Chron.*, Sept. 4–11, 1769.

2. See the preceding document.

3. BF had been on a continental tour with Sir John Pringle, from which he returned on Aug. 24.

withstanding; and a faithful Disciple of yours in all Points but that of Tributes, there her Daughter exceeds her, for convinc'd by your Arguments I turn a deaf ear to all the Invitations to Smuggling,[4] and in such a Place as this, it is well to have one's Honesty guarded. As I have cast a Censure upon the Inhabitants of this Place I must for the Honour of my Landlord and his Family tell you that they condemn and avoid those illicit Practices which are too common here. Indeed the exemplary Conduct of these good people would make me join their Sect if Reason would qualify me for it, but they are happily got into the Flights of Enthusiasm, which I cannot reach.[5] They are certainly the happiest people, and I should be glad to be like them, but my Reason will not suffer me, and my Heart prevents my playing the Hypocrite, so your Polly must remain as she is, neither in the World nor out of it. How strangely I let my Pen run on to a Philosopher! I don't care, that Philosopher is my Friend and I may write what I please to him.

I met with a very sensible Physician yesterday, who prescribes Abstinence for the Cure of Consumption. He must be clever because he thinks as *we* do. I would not have you or my Mother surpris'd, if I should run off with this young man;[6] to be sure it would be an imprudent Step at the discreet Age of Thirty but there is no saying what one should do if sollicited by a Man of an insinuating Address and good Person, tho he may be too young for one, and not yet establish'd in his Profession. He engag'd me so deeply in Conversation and I was so much pleas'd with him, that I thought it necessary to give you Warning, tho' I assure you he has made no Proposal.

How I rattle! This Flight must be owing to this new Acquaintance or to the Joy of hearing my old one is return'd to this Country; I know which I attribute it to, for I can tell when my Spirits were

4. A reference to BF's essay on smuggling in 1767, for which see above, XIV 315–19.

5. Mrs. Tickell, Polly's elderly aunt, had taken her to Margate for the bathing; but the two had apparently fallen among Methodists.

6. William Hewson (1739–74) was not only a physician and surgeon but also a distinguished anatomist, physiologist, and writer on and teacher of medicine. He received the Copley Medal in 1769, and was elected to the Royal Society in the spring of the following year; shortly thereafter he and Polly were married. Four years later he died, as a result of a wound incurred during dissection. *DNB.*

enliven'd, but you may think as you please if you will believe me to be Dear Sir Your truly affectionate humble Servant

M STEVENSON

Can't you send me one little Letter directed for me at Mr. Coleman's Margate? where I shall be some days longer.

Addressed: To Dr Franklin / Craven Street / in the Strand / London

To George Whitefield

Reprinted from Joseph Belcher, *George Whitefield: a Biography, with Special Reference to His Labors in America* (New York, [1857]), pp. 414–15.

[Before Sept. 2, 1769[7]]

I am under continued apprehensions that we may have bad news from America. The sending soldiers to Boston always appeared to me a dangerous step; they could do no good, they might occasion mischief. When I consider the warm resentment of a people who think themselves injured and oppressed, and the common insolence of the soldiery, who are taught to consider that people as in rebellion, I cannot but fear the consequences of bringing them together. It seems like setting up a smith's forge in a magazine of gunpowder. I *see* with you that our affairs are not well managed by our rulers here below; I wish I could *believe* with you, that they are well attended to by those above; I rather suspect, from certain circumstances, that though the general government of the universe is well administered, our particular little affairs are perhaps below notice, and left to take the chance of human prudence or imprudence, as either may happen to be uppermost. It is, however, an uncomfortable thought, and I leave it.[8]

7. On that date Whitefield left London on his way to Charleston; *London Chron.*, Sept. 2–5, 1769. His final trip to America ended with his death in Massachusetts a year later. The wording of the letter strongly suggests that it was written while BF and Whitefield were both in England, and some time after news had reached London of the arrival of troops in Boston on October 1, 1768. If so, what was presumably BF's last communication with his old friend can be dated between January and August, 1769.

8. Whether or not BF intended to tease his friend into annoyance by these reflections, he certainly did so. "*Uncomfortable* indeed! and, blessed be God, *unscriptural,*" Whitefield wrote at the foot of the letter; "for we are fully assured that 'the Lord reigneth,' and are directed to cast *all* our own care on him, because he careth for us." Belcher, *op. cit.*, p. 415.

To Mary Stevenson ALS: Yale University Library

Saturday Evening, Sept 2. 1769

Just come home from a Venison Feast, where I have drank more than a Philosopher ought, I find my dear Polly's chearful chatty Letter that exhilarates me more than all the Wine.[9]

Your good Mother says there is no Occasion for any Intercession of mine in your behalf. She is sensible that she is more in fault than her Daughter. She received an affectionate tender Letter from you, and she has not answered it, tho' she intended to do it; but her Head, not her Heart, has been bad, and unfitted her for Writing. She owns that she is not so good a Subject as you are, and that she is more unwilling to pay Tribute to Cesar, and has less Objection to Smuggling; but 'tis not, she says, mere Selfishness or Avarice; 'tis rather an honest Resentment at the Waste of those Taxes in Pensions, Salaries, Perquisites, Contracts and other Emoluments for the Benefit of People she does not love, and who do not deserve such Advantages, because—I suppose because they are not of her Party. Present my Respects to your good Landlord and his Family: I honour them for their consciencious Aversion to illicit Trading. There are those in the World who would not wrong a Neighbour, but make no Scruple of cheating the King. The Reverse however does not hold; for whoever scruples cheating the King will certainly not wrong his Neighbour. You ought not to wish yourself an Enthusiast: They have indeed their imaginary Satisfactions and Pleasures; but those are often ballanc'd by imaginary Pains and Mortifications. You can continue to be a good Girl, and thereby lay a solid Foundation for expected future Happiness, without the Enthusiasm that may perhaps be necessary to some others. As those Beings who have a good sensible Instinct, have no need of Reason; so those who have Reason to regulate their Actions, have no Occasion for Enthusiasm. However there are certain Circumstances in Life sometimes, wherein 'tis perhaps best not to hearken to Reason. For instance; Possibly, if the Truth were known, I have Reason to be jealous of this same insinuating handsome young Physician: But as it flatters more my Vanity, and therefore gives me more Pleasure to suppose you were in Spirits on Account of my safe Return, I shall turn a deaf

9. See Polly's letter to BF above, Sept. 1; it explains the subjects to which he is alluding.

Ear to Reason in this Case, as I have done with Success in twenty others. But I am sure you will always give me Reason enough to continue ever Your affectionate Friend   B FRANKLIN

Our Love to Mrs. Tickell. We all long for your Return: Your Dolly was well last Tuesday, the Girls were there on a Visit to her: I mean at Bromley.[1] Adieu.

No Time now to give you any Account of my French Journey.

Endorsed: Sep 2 —69

From John Alleyne[2]   ALS: American Philosophical Society

Worthy Sir   Septr. 5th: 1769

I should not have broken in upon your Time in this Manner, if my Health wo'd have permitted Me, to have address'd You personally, but Confin'd, as I have been, and much weaken'd by the Gout I trust your Goodness will Excuse Me, if I ask the Favor of a Line from You, in Answer to the following Questions.

A Reverend Friend of Mine had an Offer, some few Months ago, of a Living in the Island of St. John[3] but having some Prospect, of being provided for in this Country, at that Time, he declin'd it. He has since found that his Hopes, were ill-founded, and is now desirous of going over to America, Apprehending no Danger, of [not] meeting with encouragement in that Part of the World; Having heard, of the Honor which I enjoy in being intimate with you he wish'd to have your Opinion on his Situation such as it wo'd be, was he to go over, immediately. You will therefore much Oblige Me,

1. Dorothea Blunt, Polly's old friend, was living at the time with the Hawkesworths at Bromley; see above, XIV, 153 n. The girls were probably Anne Johnson, BF's grandniece, who was then living at Craven Street (BF to Jonathan Williams below, Oct. 4), and Thomas Franklin's daughter Sarah, BF's first cousin twice removed.

2. For John Alleyne see above, XV, 182–3.

3. The island retained its French name, Anglicized, until it was renamed in 1799 Prince Edward Island in honor of the Duke of Kent. In the summer of 1769, when a separate government was created, £100 was set aside for an Anglican minister. Because the first incumbent was not named until 1774, however, he is unlikely to have been Alleyne's friend. See Duncan Campbell, *History of Prince Edward Island* (Charlottetown, Prince Edw. Is., 1875), p. 59; *Acts Privy Coun., Col.,* v, 80–5.

Sir, if you wo'd inform Me, what Encouragement, my Friend might expect—if Great Interest wo'd be necessary to procure Him an Establishment, If Merit, if great Merit wo'd not render it more easy to Him in your Rising Nation, than in his own.

Beleive Me, Sir, I do not ask this Favor in behalf of one, unworthy the Kindness of Dr. F. My Friend, is I beleive learned, Pious, and Diligent. Those who are better Judges, than myself, concur with Me in this Opinion of Him, and as He has Chosen the Sacred Office, I doubt not, but that he wo'd Answer, every Purpose, for which it was designed by a faithful Discharge of it.

You will permit Me to encroach yet fu[rther] on your Time that I may Express my hearty Sense of all Your Favors, and Join the Grateful Respects of my Wife, to my own, and beg they may be accepted by You, and that I may Assure You that I am never Happier than when I am Thought, what I really am Your much Obliged[4] and Faithful Friend   JOHN ALLEYNE

Addressed: To / Doctor Franklin / at / Mrs Stevenson's / Craven Street / Strand / Tuesday / Septr. 5th. 1769

Endorsed: Mr Alleyne Sept 5 1769 Budd

From John Winthrop   AL (extract): The Royal Society

The observations of the transit of Venus in 1761 had not fulfilled the widespread hope of establishing the solar parallax, and thereby the mean distance between the earth and the sun. The hope grew, however, as scientists of many countries prepared to improve and expand their observations of the transit of June, 1769. Although John Winthrop was no longer well enough to play the active part that he had in 1761, he was deeply concerned not only with the collection of data on the second transit but also with the interpretation of them.[5] In the letter below, sent

4. Alleyne was soon to be more obliged: on Nov. 11 BF lent him £10, and on Jan. 1, 1771, an additional £25; Alleyne repaid the debt in December, 1771. *Jour.*, pp. 22, 27, 38.

5. For the part he did play in attempting, unsuccessfully, to persuade Massachusetts to send an expedition see above, XV, 167. He also did what he could to arouse public interest: talks that he gave at Harvard subsequently appeared in print as *Two Lectures on the Parallax and Distance of the Sun as Deducible from the Transit of Venus... Published by the General Desire of the Students* (Boston, 1769), with an appendix in which the layman was shown how to make his own observation of the transit.

via Franklin to the Royal Society, Winthrop wrestled analogically with the problem of the relationship between three moving bodies: for the passage of light he substituted that of a cannon ball; for the sun and its two satellites, Venus and the earth, he substituted a fort and two ships under sail.

Sept. 6. 1769

Extract of a Letter from John Winthrop, Esqr. Hollisian Professor of Mathematics and Natural Philosophy, at Cambridge N. England, to B. Franklin, LL.D., F.R.S. Dated Sept. 6. 1769[6].

I find that Mr. Bliss and Mr. Hornsby in their calculations in the Philos. Transact.[7] suppose the phases of the Transit of Venus to be *accelerated* by the equation for the observation of light, which amounts to 55″ of time. According to my idea of aberration, I should think the Transit would be *retarded* by it. I can very easily suppose that I am in an error; and that I may more readily be led out of it, I beg leave to lay before you the several steps by which I have been led into it. And I think it will be best to take some similar instance, rather than to consider the thing in a general abstract manner.

1. Let the parallelogram E represent a vessel sailing in the line to R, from left hand to right; and S, a fix'd Station, e.g. a castle, discharging balls on the right line SM, perpendicular to the route of the vessel. If the vessel had been at rest, a ball arriving at the middle of it, M, would have gone right across it, to N. But as it is supposed to be sailing, the ball will not go right over from M to N, but will cross the deck obliquely, in another right line as MO, and so will be left behind toward the stern as much as the vessel had gone forward while the ball was crossing it; and MN will be to NO as the velocity of the ball to the velocity of the vessel. Thus to the people on board, the ball would seem to move obliquely across the deck, as if it came from some point T in the line OM produced, instead of coming from S. And a tube capable of receiving the ball would allow the

6. In BF's hand. The paper, read on April 5, 1770, was printed in *Phil. Trans.*, LX (1770), 358–62.

7. Nathaniel Bliss (1700–64) was Savilian Professor of Geometry at Oxford and became Astronomer Royal in 1762; the Rev. Thomas Hornsby (1733–1810) became Savilian Professor of Astronomy in 1763. *DNB*. Winthrop is probably referring to Bliss's paper on the transit of 1761 in *Phil. Trans.*, LII, pt. 1 (1761), 232–50, and to Hornsby's on that of 1769 in *ibid.*, LV (1766), 326–44.

ball to pass thro it without striking its sides, if it were inclined *forward* in the direction OM; which it would not do in any other situation. The angle OMN or SMT answers to the *aberration*; and supposing S to be the Sun; and E, the Earth, this angle is 20″; and the *general* effect is, to make the Sun or any fixed star to appear farther that way towards which the Earth is moving.

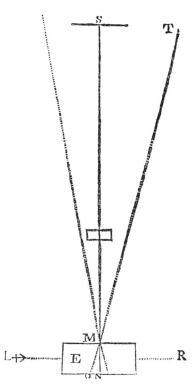

2. Let us suppose another vessel V, between S and E, sailing the same way as E in a parallel direction. If both the vessels sailed with the *same* velocity, a ball from V coming to M, would go right across to N, just as if both of them had been at rest; because the ball, which crossing the vessel E, would be carry'd just as far to the right hand as the points M and N are. And a tube to receive it must be held in the direction MN. So here would be no aberration of the vessel V.

3. Suppose V to move the same way, but *Slower*. A ball from V would now be *really carry'd forward*, that is, to the right hand, tho not so far as in the 2d. supposition; and therefore would be *left behind in respect of the vessel E*; and so, would come to the side of the vessel somewhere between O and N, but the greater its velocity towards the right, the nearer to N. So that if the velocity of V were to be continually increasing from nothing till it became equal to that of E, a tube to receive the ball must be held first in the direction OM looking *forward*, and afterwards, more and more inclined till it came into the perpendicular direction. From hence it is natural to conclude,

4. That if V move the same way, but *swifter*, a tube to receive the

ball must be reclined *backward*. For the ball would now be carried to the right hand farther than in the 2d supposition; and therefore would come to the other side of the vessel at some point P on the right hand of N, as if it proceded from some point Q on the left hand of S.

This last seems to be the case of the Transit, by supposing S to be the Sun, E the Earth, and V the planet Venus passing between them, from left to right, and with a greater velocity than the Earth; (greater, nearly as 24:20.). And it should seem that the aberration must make Venus appear farther to the left hand, or to the East from the Sun, and consequently retard the Transit, and make it happen later than it would otherwise do.

Thus, Sir, I have explain'd very particularly my apprehension of the matter, and I make no doubt you will immediately discover where the error lies; and shall take it as a great favor if you will please to point it out to me.

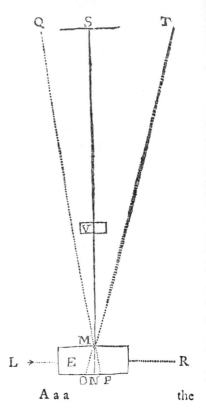

To Cadwalader Evans

Reprinted from Samuel Hazard, ed., *Hazard's Register of Pennsylvania*, XVI, no. 5 (August 1, 1835), 66–7; extract in American Philosophical Society Minutes.

Dear Sir: London, Sept. 7, 1769.

I have now before me your Favours of June 11, and July 15, I thank you for communicating to me the Observations of the Transit made by Messrs. Biddle & Bayley. I gave them Immediately to

Mr. Maskelyn, the Astronomer Royal, who will compare and digest the whole received from different Parts of the world, and report thereon to the Royal Society. They are the only ones I have received from our Society; those made by the others were sent to Mr. Penn. Being last week with Mr. Maskelyn at Flamstead House, I found he had got them.[8] I shall send him to-day the correct account which I have since received from you via Liverpool.

I should be very sorry that any thing of Party remained in the American Philosophical Society after the Union. Here the Royal Society is of all Parties, but Party is entirely out of the Question in all our Proceedings.[9]

It grieves me to hear that our Friend Galloway is in so bad a State of Health. He should make a long Journey, or take a Sea voyage. I wish he would come to London for the Winter.

Mr. Henry's Register, which you communicated to me last Year, is thought a very ingenious one, and will be published here tho' it has been long delay'd.

I have not seen Mrs. Dowell. I suppose she is not yet come to Town. At least I have not heard of her being here, tho' possibly she might while I was in France.

Our friend W[harton], who is always complaining of a constant Fever, looks nevertheless fresh and jolly and does not fall away in the least. He was saying the other day at Richmond (where we were together dining with Govern'r Pownall) that he had been pestered with a Fever almost continually for these three years past and that it gave away to no medicines, all he had taken advis'd by different Physicians having never any Effect towards removing it. On which I ask'd him, if it was not now time to enquire whether he

8. The Proprietary supporters in the APS brought faction into science: their reports on the transit of Venus went to the Proprietor, Thomas Penn, rather than to BF as president, and Penn passed them on to Maskelyne (for whom see above, XI, 482 n). Flamstead or Flamsteed House, named after the first Astronomer Royal, John Flamsteed (1646–1719), was the Greenwich Observatory; see Henry S. Richardson, *Greenwich: Its History, Antiquities, Improvements, and Public Buildings* (London, 1834), p. 73.

9. BF's optimism soon proved to be ill-founded. After 1772 the subject of lightning rods divided the Society, and the dispute had pro- and anti-American overtones. See Charles R. Weld, *A History of the Royal Society* (2 vols., London, 1848), II, 95–102; I. Bernard Cohen, *Franklin and Newton...* (Philadelphia, 1956), p. 417.

had really any Fever at all? He is indeed the only instance I ever knew of a Man's growing fat upon a Fever. But I see no Occasion for reading him the Lecture you desired, for he appears to be extreamly temperate in his Eating and Drinking. His affairs here are I think in a good Train, but every thing to be transacted in our great Offices, requires time. I suppose he will be hardly able to return before the Spring.[1]

By a ship just sailed from hence, the Captain, a Stranger whose name I have forgotten, I send you a late French Treatise on the management of Silk-worms. It is said to be the best hitherto published, being written in the Silk country by a Gentleman well acquainted with the whole affair. It seems to me to be (like many other French Writings) rather too much drawn out in Words; but some Extracts from it, of the principal Directions, might be of Use, if you would translate and publish them. I think the Bounty is offer'd for Silk from all the Colonies in general. I will send you the Act.[2] But I believe it must be wound from the Cocoons, and sent over in Skeins. The Cocoons would Spoil on the Passage, by the dead Worm corrupting and staining the Silk. A Public Filature should be set up, for winding them there: Or every Family should learn to wind their own. In Italy they are all brought to Market, from the the neighboring Country, and bought up by those that keep the Filatures. In Sicily each Family winds its own Silk, for the sake

1. For Evans' comments, to which BF is replying in this and the preceding paragraphs, see his letter to BF above, June 11. William Trent, writing to George Croghan in June, had reported that Wharton was "perfectly hearty," had met the most important people in the kingdom through BF and others, knew all that was going on at court, and was listened to on American affairs. "He has not the least sign of a Quaker about Him and wears his Sword &c. with as much ease, as if He had allways done it." *PMHB*, LXXIV (1950), 49.

2. BF had long been interested in silk-growing. Here he is responding to the request in Evans' letter above, July 15, by sending him Pierre Augustin Boissier de Sauvages, *Mémoires sur l'éducation des vers à soie* . . . (Nîmes, 1763), which Evans acknowledged below, Nov. 27. The Society of Arts had granted a bounty on silk cocoons from Georgia, Connecticut, and Pennsylvania from 1758 to 1767, when it was discontinued; see above, VII, 156 n; Brooke Hindle, *The Pursuit of Science in Revolutionary America* . . . (Chapel Hill, [1956]), p. 200. Georgia then lobbied for a parliamentary subsidy, and succeeded in obtaining a decreasing bounty, to be paid from 1770 to 1777, for colonial silk: 9 Geo. III, c. 38. Pennsylvania's efforts to obtain a similar bounty will appear in subsequent volumes.

of having the Remains to card and spin for Family use. If some Provision were made by the Assembly for promoting the growth of Mulberry Trees in all Parts of the Province, the Culture of Silk might afterwards follow easily. For the great Discouragement to breeding Worms at first, is, the Difficulty of getting Leaves, and the being obliged to go far for them. There is no doubt with me but that it might succeed in our Country. It is the happiest of all Inventions for Cloathing. Wooll uses a good deal of Land to produce it, which, if employed in raising Corn would afford much more Subsistance for Man, than the Mutton amounts to. Flax and Hemp require Land, impoverish it, and at the same time permit it to produce no Food at all. But Mulberry Trees may be planted in Hedge Rows, or Walks or Avenues, or for Shade, near a House, where nothing else is wanted to grow. The Food for the Worms which produce the Silk is in the Air, and the Ground under the Trees may still produce Grass, or some other Vegetable good for Man or Beast. Then the Wear of Silken Garments continues so much longer, from the Strength of the Materials, as to give it greatly the Preference. Hence it is that the most populous of all Countries, China, clothes its Inhabitants with Silk, while it feeds them plentifully and has besides a vast Quantity both of raw and manufactured to spare for Exportation. Raw Silk here, in Skeins well wound, sells from 20 to 25s. pr. lb. But if badly wound is not worth 5s. Well wound is where the Threads are made to cross each other every way in the Skein, and only touch where they cross. Badly wound is where they are laid parallel to each other; for so they are glu'd together, break in unwinding them, and take a vast deal of time more than the other, by losing the End every time the Thread breaks. When once you can raise plenty of Silk, you may have Manufactures enow from hence. With great Esteem, I am, my dear Friend, Yours affectionately,

B. FRANKLIN

To Cadwalader Evans   Copy: Historical Society of Pennsylvania

Dear Doctor,   London Sept. 8. 1769
    I am writing to you and all my friends by the packet that sails to morrow. This is only to cover the French work on Silk worms,[3]

3. See the preceding document.

said to be the best extant; which being too bulky to go per packet I send you by this ship. Some extracts may be made from it and published of the most useful directions; for it is like other French writings rather too wordy, &c. I have received yours per packet and via Liverpool, with the observations of the transit of which more in my next. I am, Yours affectionately   B. FRANKLIN.

Please let Mrs. Franklin know I am well.

To Dr Cadwalader Evans

From James Parker   ALS: American Philosophical Society

Honoured Sir   New-York, Sept. 12[-13]. 1769
    The Packet being detain'd two or three Days on the following Occasion, tho' I had wrote four Days ago, all that was then necessary, I could not dispence with writing again; And notwithstanding you will doubtless hear it, if I had not wrote: It pleased God to take our Governor Sir Henry Moore, Bart. out of this World, Yesterday half after 3 o'Clock in the Afternoon; he died of a Bloody Flux: and laid a great while very low, tho' on Monday Morning he seemed better than for some Time before, but it was only a little lightning before Death. He is to be buried this Afternoon. Tis said Old Mr. Colden will administer the Government again, he is at Flushing, but expected here this Day: He is but weakly and infirm, and Judge Horsmanden, the first Councillor lies almost dying also.[4] I had the same Flux a Fortnight ago but it is gone off in a Fit of the Gout: so that the manifold Infirmities that accompany me, induces me to think I ought to persevere in laying down the Custom-House Office, which I only Wait to hear from you.
    The Government of this Colony is esteemed the most lucrative of any on the Continent, exclusive of Virginia. I Would you had Interest and Inclination to procure it for yourself: A few years in it,

    4. Sir Henry Moore had been appointed to his post in 1765. But governors came and went, while Cadwallader Colden seemed to go on forever. The indomitable old man, who was now eighty, had been lieutenant governor since 1760 and intermittently acting governor; he now resumed this position and retained it until the arrival of Lord Dunmore in October, 1770. Daniel Horsmanden, who was seventy-five, recovered from his illness and continued as chief justice of the province.

would be of more Emolument to you, than any Thing you have yet had. I wish for your own Sake only, that could be the Case; far be it from me, to have any other View in this Wish. And as Wishing is all the Ability I have, I can only add, that I am as ever Your most obliged Servant   JAMES PARKER.

Honoured Sir   Nyork Sept. 13. 1769
   Yesterday Capt. Tingley arrived after a Passage of near 13 Weeks, by whom I've just received yours of June 14: I shall send it along this Day's Post, as ordered. I had sent my Letter of Yesterday to the Office, before I received yours, and I write this short note purposely to stick into it, if I can find it again. The Governor was buried last Night—Mr. Colden is governor. I am as ever Yours
                                              JAMES PARKER

Addressed: For / Dr Benjamin Franklin / Craven-Street / London / per Packet

Endorsed: J. Parker 1769–70

From Ephraim Brown[5]   ALS: American Philosophical Society

Respected Sir   Oxford, Sept 15. 1769
   Yours of the 13th lies before me. I am oblig'd to you for your offer of the loan of three Guineas, and have drawn on you payable to Wm. Jackson on order.[6] I don't know what to think of your excessive temperance in my case. I am of opinion if a hearty man get a bad cold, to drive it away by abstinance, is very right; but a person

   5. The adopted son of BF's dead brother, Peter; see above, XII, 78 n.
   6. Little is known about the closing years of Brown's life, which were spent in England. After BF had offered to find him work in London, and David Hall had given him letters to William Strahan, he sailed from America on Jan. 12, 1767, for Dublin, where he arrived in early March and was detained by illness; he reached London, nevertheless, in early April, and soon afterward entered Strahan's employ. XIII, 390; XIV, 5, 100. He later moved to Oxford, as this letter makes clear, and presumably worked for William Jackson. The latter was a printer in Oxford from 1753 to 1795: H. R. Plomer *et al.*, *A Dictionary of the Printers and Booksellers Who Were at Work in England, Scotland and Ireland from 1726 to 1775* (Oxford, 1932), p. 138. During Brown's illness at Oxford BF lent him money from time to time, to a total of £27 16s. 6d.: BF to W. J. Mickle below, Feb. 15, 1770.

in my Condition requires many nourishing things to keep Soul and Body together. I have lived very temperately myself all the Summer, and now taste hardly any thing but Spoon Meats; nor has it been (I believe) intemperance that has brought me in this way. In my last I told you I should be glad to get to London, as soon as I got a little better that I could travel; there I think I might be much better off, as perhaps I could get into a Hospital but here there is no such thing. Pray let me have your advice in that, and I would come even in a waggon if I could get one soft loaded, if it would be of service to me. If I do come it must be very soon, for my three Guineas wont last long when my Doctor's Bill is paid. [I forgot to mention when I wrote that I had not paid the Apothecary.][7] Dr. Fowlkes is reckoned a very skilful man, and they say he has performed many Cures in my way, and he tells me he has very little doubt but he will set me to rights soon. But I almost want faith.[8] I remain your very obliged humble Servant   E BROWN

N.B. I am better to-day than I have been this Week past.

Addressed: To | Dr Franklin | Craven-street | Strand | London

To Jacques Barbeu-Dubourg[9]

ALS (draft): American Philosophical Society

Dear Sir,   London, Sept. 22. 1769
    With this you will receive some Sheets of the Piece now printing, and which I am promis'd shall be finish'd in a few Days. I am afraid it is not so correct as it should be; But as I have been advis'd not to publish it till next Month, most of our Gentry being yet out of Town, there will be time for you to send me the Errata which may be printed at the End.[1]

7. Brackets are in the original. The apothecary's name was Stevens, and he tried hard to get full payment: *ibid.*
    8. He had reason to lack faith. Dr. Fowlkes (perhaps John Foulkes, M.D. Oxon., 1754) did not set him to rights, and he died late in the autumn; BF's Jour. has an entry under Dec. 3, 1769, of £2 5s. for Brown's funeral expenses.
    9. See above, XV, 112.
    1. What the piece was remains a mystery. Alfred O. Aldridge conjectures that it may have been the first English translation of Dubourg's "Code de l'humanité, ou Lois immuables qui servent de base aux devoirs, aux droits, et

I send you also Dr. Priestly's Essay on the first Principles of Government lately published,[2] in which you will find some [*missing*] and free Sentiments.

I wrote to you two or three Weeks since by M. Lettsom a Quaker Physician, recommending him to your Civilities.[3] I can now only add, (with my best Respects to good Madame Dubourg) that I am as ever, Dear Sir, Your affectionate Friend, and most obedient humble Servant.   B FRANKLIN

Be so good as to present my respectful Compliments to M. Beaumont, for whom I have the highest Esteem, and to Mr. Dupont.[4] Please to acquaint the latter, that Dr. Templeman had done nothing in the Subscriptions, the Society having been in *Vacance*; and the good Gentleman, is, I am afraid, now dying.[5]

M. Dubourg

To T[homas-François] Dalibard[6]

ALS (draft): American Philosophical Society

Dear Friend   London, Sept. 22. 1769
    Having this Opportunity by M. Le Roy,[7] I embrace it to thank

---

au bonheur de l'homme" (for which see above, xv, 115 n.), but admits that Dubourg did not receive copies of the translation until more than a year later. "Jacques Barbeu-Dubourg, a French Disciple of Benjamin Franklin," APS *Proc.*, xcv (1951), 341. This conjecture seems to us implausible, in the light of BF's phrasing and the subsequent lapse of time before the translation reached Paris; but we can offer no alternative conjecture.

2. The work was a year old: Joseph Priestley, *An Essay on the First Principles of Government; and on the Nature of Political, Civil, and Religious Liberty* (London, 1768).

3. See BF's letter above, Aug. 30.

4. Jean-Baptiste-Jacques Elie de Beaumont (1732–86) was a distinguished French jurist, friend of Voltaire, and author of a well-known memoir on the Calas case published in 1762. For Pierre Samuel Dupont de Nemours see above, xv, 118 n.

5. Dr. Peter Templeman had been secretary of the Society of Arts; see above, ix, 322 n. He had in fact died on Aug. 23, 1769. *DNB.*

6. The physicist and botanist, whom BF had met for the first time on his visit to Paris in September 1767. See above, iv, 302 n; xv, 35.

7. One of the several LeRoy brothers whom BF had met in Paris two years before. See above, xv, 83. It was not, however, Jean-Baptiste: see the next document.

you most heartily for the many Civilities and Marks of Friendship I received from you and Madame Dalibard while in Paris; and to express my sincere and cordial Wishes for your Health and Prosperity: in which I am join'd by my Friend Sir John Pringle.[8]

As I cannot soon again enjoy the Happiness of being personally in your Company, permit my Shadow to pay my Respects to you. 'Tis from a Plate my Son caus'd to be engrav'd some Years since.[9] With the greatest Esteem and Respect, I have the honour to be, Dear Sir, Your most obedient humble Servant   B FRANKLIN

Mr D[alibard]

To [Jean-Baptiste LeRoy[1]]

ALS (draft): American Philosophical Society

Dear Sir,   London, Sep[tember 22?,[2] 1769]

Soon after my Arrival in London, [I sent you] by Mr. Lettsom, a Quaker Physician, one of the [*torn*] Achromatic Glasses Compleat; which I hope you received safe.[3] By your good Brother I send you three of the Glasses we talk'd of, and which you will find describ'd in one of my Printed Letters.

Our Astronomers knew nothing before our Return of the Comet you first told us of at Paris.[4] They have since watch'd it pretty closely. But as yours saw it near three Weeks sooner, I suppose they

8. BF had returned on Aug. 24 from a second visit to Paris with his old friend Sir John.

9. The mezzotint by Edward Fisher, after Mason Chamberlain's portrait of BF, for which see above, X, frontispiece and illustration note.

1. "Your brother" of this letter is patently the LeRoy of the preceding document. It is a virtual certainty, therefore, that BF was writing to the only LeRoy with whom he corresponded.

2. This and the preceding document presumably went by M. LeRoy; we are therefore assuming that the two letters were of the same date.

3. For Dr. Lettsom see BF to Barbeu-Dubourg above, Aug. 30. An achromatic lens transmits light that is without color. BF may have sent one of the achromatic telescopes that John Dolland had invented a decade earlier, for which see XI, 22 n. LeRoy later acknowledged receiving a "lunette": below, April 22, [1770].

4. See BF to John Canton above, Aug. 25.

have been better able to determine its Orbit, &c. Some be[lieve?] [*torn*] the tail to be electrical.

Pray present my best [compliments to?] M. Malesherbes, whom I esteem infinitely.[5] I [am] [*torn*] [sen]sible of the many Civilities I received from [you and all of?] your Friends; be so good as to remember m[e to them? a]ll very respectfully. With the most sincere Esteem and Affection, I am, Dear Sir Your most obedient humble Servant,   B FRANKLIN

B[e so] good as to forward the Packets contained in the Box as directed. Pray send me word what Number of Paste Seals.

To Timothy Folger[6]

AL (incomplete): Yale University Library; extract printed in *The Boston Evening Post*, December 4, 1769.

Loving Kinsman,   London, Sept. 29. 1769

Since my Return from abroad, where I spent part of the Summer, I have received your Favours of June 10 and July 26. The Treasury Board is still under Adjournment, the Lords and Secretaries chiefly in the Country; but as soon as they meet again, you may depend on my making the Application you desire.[7]

5. This is a tantalizing reference. It appears to be to one of the outstanding liberals of the *ancien régime*, Chrétien Guillaume de Lamoignon de Malesherbes (1721–94), who was at the time president of the Cour des aides. He was of course not the only man of the name in France, but he was the natural one for BF to have met during his recent visit to Paris because of Malesherbes's literary and scientific interests and widespread acquaintance in the French intellectual world. Years later Malesherbes boasted that he had met and been complimented by BF during the latter's mission to France: John M. S. Allison, *Lamoignon de Malesherbes, Defender and Reformer of the French Monarchy . . .* (New Haven, 1938), p. 109. This seems to imply a first meeting, but Malesherbes by then may well have forgotten an earlier one.

6. Nantucket shipmaster and BF's distant cousin (B.1.4.6.1.3); see above, xv, 223, 246–7.

7. The application was undoubtedly connected with Folger's tangled affairs in Massachusetts. In 1764 John Temple, Surveyor General of the Customs, had appointed him to a post at Nantucket without consulting the collector at Boston. After the reorganization of the customs service in 1767, Temple's new colleagues in the Board of Customs Commissioners attacked him for the irregularity of the appointment. In March, 1768, they dismissed Folger as unfit; in August he sailed for England to appeal to the Treasury, which referred the

I shall enquire concerning the Affair of your two Townships settled under Massachusetts Grants, and let you know my Sentiments as soon as I can get proper Information. I should imagine that whatever may be determin'd here of the Massachusetts Rights to the Jurisdiction, the private Property of Settlers must remain secure.[8] In general I have no great Opinion of Applications to be made here in such Cases. It is so much the Practice to draw Matters into Length, put the Parties to immense Charge, and tire them out with Delays, that I would never come from America hither with any Affair I could possibly settle there.

Mrs. Stevenson sends her Love, and thanks you for remembring her. She is vex'd to hear that the Box of Spermaceti Candles[9] is seiz'd; and says, if ever she sees you again, she will put you in a way of making Reprisals. You know she is a Smuggler upon Principle; and she does not consider how averse you are to every thing of the kind. I thank you for your kind Intention. Your Son[1] grows a fine Youth; he is so obliging as to be with us a little when he has Holidays; and Temple is not the only one of the Family that is fond of his Company.

It[2] gives me great Pleasure to hear that our People are steady in their Resolutions of Non Importation, and in the Promoting of Industry among themselves. They will soon be sensible of the Benefit of such Conduct, tho' the Acts should never be repeal'd to

---

matter back to the Customs Commissioners. Folger recrossed the Atlantic, applied to them for reinstatement, and was refused in July, 1769. See L. Kinvin Wroth and Hiller B. Zobel, eds., *Legal Papers of John Adams* (3 vols., Cambridge, Mass., 1965), II, 147–57. Temple, who supported Folger throughout, suspected that his dismissal had been instigated by Thomas Hutchinson; and the resultant antagonism between the two men caused Temple, in turn, to be suspected three years later of stealing Hutchinson's letters and giving them to BF. See Peter O. Hutchinson, ed., *The Diary and Letters of His Excellency Thomas Hutchinson* (2 vols., London, 1883–86), I, 205–10.

8. Histories of Nantucket give no indication that "the affair of your two Townships" related to the island, and in any case the jurisdiction of Massachusetts would scarcely have been in question there as late as 1769. We assume that BF is referring to some land claimed by Folger in one of the many border areas that Massachusetts disputed with her neighbors.

9. Candles made from the oil of the sperm whale, a natural present from a Nantucketer.

1. Silvanus Folger, who was then almost fifteen.

2. The newspaper extract begins here and continues to the end.

their full Satisfaction. For their Earth and their Sea, the true Sources of Wealth and Plenty, will go on producing; and if they receive the annual Increase, and do not waste it as heretofore in the Gewgaws of this Country, but employ their spare time in manufacturing Necessaries for[3] themselves, they must soon be out of debt, they must soon be easy and comfortable in their circumstances, and even wealthy. I have been told, that in some of our County Courts heretofore, there were every quarter several hundred actions of debt, in which the people were sued by Shopkeepers for money due for British *goods* (as they are called, but in fact *evils*). What a loss of time this must occasion to the people, besides the expense. And how can Freeman bear the thought of subjecting themselves to the hazard of being deprived of their personal liberty at the caprice of every petty trader, for the paltry vanity of tricking out himself and family in the flimsy manufactures of Britain, when they might by their own industry and ingenuity, appear in *good substantial honourable homespun*! Could our folks but see what numbers of Merchants, and even Shopkeepers here, make great estates by American folly; how many shops of A, B, C and Co. with wares for *exportation to the Colonies*, maintain, each shop three or four partners and their families, every one with his country-house and equipage, where they live like Princes on the sweat of our brows; pretending indeed, *sometimes*, to wish well to our Privileges, but on the present important occasion *few* of them affording us any assistance: I am persuaded that indignation would supply our want of prudence, we should disdain the thraldom we have so long been held in by this mischievous commerce, reject it for ever, and seek our resources where God and Nature have placed them WITHIN OUR SELVES.

Your Merchants, on the other hand, have shown a noble *disinterestedness* and *love to their country*, unexampled among Traders in any other age or nation, and which does them infinite honour all over Europe. The corrupted part indeed of this people *here* can scarce believe such virtue possible. But perseverance will convince them, that there is still in the world such a thing as public spirit. I hope that, if the oppressive Acts are not repealed this winter, your Stocks, that us'd to be employed in the British Trade, will be turned to the employment of Manufactures among yourselves: For notwithstanding the former general opinion that manufactures were

3. The Yale MS breaks off here.

impracticable in America, on account of the dearness of labour, experience shows, in the success of the manufactures of paper and stockings in Pennsylvania, and of womens shoes *at Lynn* in your province, that labour is only dear *from the want of* CONSTANT *employment*; (he who is often out of work requiring necessarily as much for the time he does work, as will maintain him when he does not work:) and that where we do not *interrupt that employment* by importations, *the cheapness of our provisions* gives us such advantage over the Manufacturers in Britain, that (especially in bulky goods, whose freight would be considerable) *we may always* UNDERWORK THEM.

To Jane Mecom

ALS: American Philosophical Society

Dear Sister,   London, Sept. 29, 1769

When I returned lately from France, I found among other Letters for me that had been here sometime, yours of June 13.

It pleases me to hear you are at present relieved from the Weight, which lately lay so heavy on you that "all the Assistance of Reason and Religion were scarce sufficient to keep your Spirits up." It is well you had such Aids. Our Reason would still be of more Use to us, if it could enable us to *prevent* the Evils it can hardly enable us to *bear*. But in that it is so deficient, and in other things so often misleads us, that I have sometimes been almost tempted to wish we had been furnished with a good sensible Instinct instead of it.

The Sermon which you call mine, I know nothing of.[4] I have only heard of it: I never saw it. It was wrong to give me as the Author of it. Whether it be good or bad, I have no Right to the Reputation or the Censures it may deserve.

Mrs. Stevenson scarce ever can prevail on herself to write a Letter to any one; but she acknowledges the Receipt of yours, presents her best Respects, and holds herself always ready to serve you. My Love to Jenny,[5] and believe me ever Your affectionate Brother

B FRANKLIN

Addressed: To | Mrs Mecom | Hanover Street | Boston | Free | BF.

4. John Mein, the Boston printer, had attributed James Murray's *Sermons for Asses* to BF; see WF to BF above, Mar. 2.

5. Jane, later Jane Mecom Collas, BF's niece (C.17.9).

To Samuel Cooper

ALS: British Museum

Dear Sir,   London, Sept. 30 1769

Your Favour of Aug. 3 has given me great Pleasure. I have only time now to acknowledge the Receipt of it, but purpose to write fully by the next Opportunity. I am just returned from France, where I found our Dispute much attended to, several of our Pamphlets being translated and printed there, among the rest my Examination, and the Farmer's Letters with two of my Pieces annex'd,[6] of which last I send you a Copy. In short all Europe (except Britain) appears to be on our side the Question. But Europe has its Reasons. It fancies itself in some Danger from the Growth of British Power, and would be glad to see it divided against itself. Our Prudence will, I hope, long postpone the Satisfaction our Enemies expect from our Dissensions. With sincere and great Esteem, I am, Dear Sir, Your most obedient humble Servant

                                                                 B Franklin

Revd Dr Cooper.

Addressed: To / The Reverend Dr Cooper / Boston / Free / BF.

To Jonathan Williams[7]

ALS: American Philosophical Society

Loving Cousin,   London, Oct. 4. 1769

Before I went abroad this last Summer, I left Orders with my Banker to purchase two Tickets for you, and send you the Numbers. Since my Return I understand the Orders were executed. I hope you receiv'd the Banker's Letter; if not, this will inform you that the Numbers are 33m799 and 33m800. with which I wish you the best Success.[8]

I think I mention'd in a former Letter, that your Wife's youngest Sister, Martha, now the Widow Johnson, was here in England, and

6. *Des troubles qui divisent l'Angleterre et ses colonies, ou Réponses de M. Franklin, aux interrogations que lui a faites le Parlement d'Angleterre . . .* (London and Paris, 1768); John Dickinson, *Lettres d'un fermier de Pensylvanie, aux habitans de l'Amérique Septentrionale . . .* (Amsterdam [*i.e.* Paris], 1769).

7. The husband of BF's niece, Grace Harris Williams (C.5.3), and a Boston merchant who has appeared frequently in earlier volumes.

8. See Smith, Wright & Gray to BF above, July 13.

in a Way of doing well being settled in Business as a Shopkeeper in the Country. It has since turn'd out that her Husband's Relations, who had drawn her into a Partnership there, were too cunning for her, and in less than a year she return'd to London, stript of the greatest Part of the Money she had receiv'd as the Arrears of her Pension, and she is now to shift as well as she can, having only the future Pension to subsist upon. I have put her Son, who seems a well-disposed Boy, upon liking to a Philada. Merchant now here; her Daughter to learn Music in which she makes great Progress, and having a fine Voice, with a good Person and pleasing Behaviour, stands a Chance of advancing herself. They have all liv'd with me for some time past.[9]

My worthy old Friend Mr. Hughes I suppose has been in Boston before this time. In a Letter to Mr. Hubbard I recommended him to his and your Friendship.[1]

People's Minds at present seem in a State of Suspence concerning American Affairs. The great Officers of State are chiefly out of town, and it is not yet known what Measures will be taken when the Parliament meet. With Love to your good Wife and Children, I am, Your affectionate Uncle   B FRANKLIN

Jonathn Williams, Esqr

Addressed: To / Mr Jonathan Williams / Mercht. / Boston / Free / BF.

Endorsed: October 4, 1769

From Deborah Franklin   ALS: American Philosophical Society

The preceding letter from Deborah, written on August 31, suggests that she had recovered her mental powers after her previous illness. Her spelling, syntax, and punctuation (or rather lack of it) were as always *sui*

9. The three members of the family were Martha Harris Johnson, BF's niece, her son Samuel, and her daughter Anne, called Nancy. Martha, more than a year earlier, had asked BF's help in getting Samuel apprenticed, and in the previous September Mrs. Stevenson had paid a bill for his schooling: XV, 126; Franklin Papers (APS), Vol. LXVII, No. 4.

1. John Hughes had been appointed customs collector of Piscataqua, the region around Portsmouth, N.H.; Tuthill Hubbart, BF's step-nephew, was the postmaster of Boston.

generis, and she remarked on her "in Conneckted staet"; but the sequence of her ideas was no more confused than usual, and she talked of the christening and many virtues of Sally's baby as any fond grandmother might. The letter below, and a later one in November, indicate a change: her capacity for logical connections was becoming so weak that her husband must have been hard put to it to grasp her meaning. Her mind did not lapse into nonsense: she knew what she wanted to say, but apparently could not always concentrate for long enough to say it. Neither could she stay with one subject until she had finished it; she flitted from one to another and back again. The result is sometimes incomprehensible, just as her writing is sometimes illegible. Where we can guess at her meaning, we do so. Where we cannot, we print what she wrote or, at times, what we believe she wrote.

My Dear child   Ocktober the 4 1769

I have mised to write from this plase so I write a gen by the packit as I see in the paper that it donte saile tell nexte Satter day. I shall write by Capt. Folkner and tell you all I Can as to what you have asked. I forget wather had inquiered aboute my Nabor Sumaines Dafter thay have not heard from her senes you let them [know?] a boute her. Poor Mr. Sumain has Laid like one near his end he has deprived of his senes have in a number of fittes it is not thoute he Can recover. I am much trubled for her.[2] I have seen John Shippen and I have presented his drafte on his father he excepte it but ses he donte know how he shall get the money.[3] Mr. Beach is not returnd but by the end of this week we expeckte him. Salley is gon to see an old friend of hers who was broute to bed laste night and my Dear Benj Franklin has bin a talkeing a boute you[4] and is grone finely with in thees two weeks and is one of the beste temperd Child I ever saw and everey bodey ses he is much like you. I wish you but see him. This day Polley Standly is Cume to spend a day with her son a fine child as many munthes old as Salley['s] is weeks and a fine childe in dead.[5] This poste Salley had a letter he [Richard Bache]

2. Elizabeth Soumaine had married Thomas Empson and was living in England. Her father Samuel, a silversmith, had been ill for some time; see above, X, 135 n, XI, 190 n, XIII, 34 n.

3. See John Shippen to BF above, June 3, and DF to BF below, Nov. 20–27.

4. Only a fond grandmother could have understood what Benjamin Franklin Bache was talking about; he was not yet two months old.

5. The Standley family was in the pottery business for many years in Philadelphia. Polly Standley could have been Mary, the daughter of Valentine Stand-

was well and will be att home this week. I send this or the poste will leve it. I heard from Burlinton thay was well and full of Componey and when thay air gon the papey and mamey and the Child and his maid is to gon. Whair is Antey Macum is expeckted if shee donte Cume sooner then shee will Come down to your house firste. Mr. Beach is in hopes and keepe her Companey.⁶ I send the Newspaper for I Cante tell aney thing a boute the publick news. My love to everey bodey as thow I had menshoned them I am sumthing better than senes the wather is Coler then it was I am my Dear child your Loveing wife   D FRANKLIN

Addressed: Benjamin Franklin Esqr / in / Craven Street / London

From James Parker   ALS: American Philosophical Society

Honoured Sir   Nyork, Octob 5[–9]. 1769
   Ever since my last of the 11th Sept. have I been laid up, by the most excruciating Fit of the Gout, that ever I had: and I have now but scarce Ability to write a Line or two. Nothing worthy of Note has happen'd since in Relation to the Post-Office, except that Mr. Babcock has left New-Haven, and I sent a Commission to Mr. Kilby in his Stead, who has given Bond, and taken the Oath according to Law. I have received no Money or Bills since; altho' I have hinted to Mr. Colden, who is a good deal in Arrear again, that as Bills are low now, it would be agreeable to send, but he has not regarded it.⁷ I should have been glad to have heard from you about resigning my Place in the Custom-House, as I find myself every Day less able than other to execute that Office, and I suppose it is expected that I resign this Quarter Day, which is to-morrow: for

ley (d. 1781), or the wife of one of his sons. For the family, see Harold E. Gillingham, "Pottery, China, and Glass Making in Philadelphia," *PMHB*, LIV (1930), 107–12, and "Register of Baptisms, 1701–1746, First Presbyterian Church of Philadelphia," *Pa. Geneal. Mag.* XIX (1954), 303, 305–6.

6. DF's meaning seems to be that WF and his wife had house guests, after whose departure the Baches were to go to Burlington and meet Jane Mecom there if she arrived soon enough from Boston (as in fact she did); otherwise she would come directly to Philadelphia and visit the WF's on her return journey.

7. For Luke Babcock and Christopher Kilby see Parker to BF above, May 31. For Alexander Colden, the New York postmaster and eldest son of Cadwallader Colden, see above, VI, 113 n.

if I don't resign, now I can't do my Duty, it is probable they will suspend or turn me out, and should you be able to procure an Appointment for Mr. Robinson, it would not disappoint any other, so much as it would, were another actually appointed. I send the Book of Accounts, as copied exactly and examined by Mr. Robinson for the future, I keep a Day-Book, wish Heaven may give me more Health to enable me to be more exact. Mr. Foxcroft, has not given me his Direction, and I am also, so very poorly, that I hope you will make my Excuse to him, with my most respectful Complements, whilst I am Your most obliged Servant   JAMES PARKER

The Book goes by Capt. Th: Miller[8]

PS. Octob 9. This Letter I open'd again to inclose the 2d of each of two Bills just received from Mr. Hubbart—the first of which I sent per Packet Saturday Night: one is for £105 Sterling drawn by Hays & Polock, on Mr. David Milligan of London, dated Newyork, Aug 15. 1769—the other for £15 2s. 10d. drawn by Cary Mitchel, on Samuel Blythe,[9] dated Virginia 11 Octob. 1768. Wishing them safe to hand, not able to add more than Respect &c   JP

Addressed: For / Dr Benjamin Franklin / Craven-Street / London / per Capt. Miller

From James Parker   ALS: American Philosophical Society

[New York, October 6–7, 1769. Sent the Post Office account book with his letter of October 5. Confined to his room and can barely sit up. Has not touched Benjamin Mecom's books,[1] but will as soon as he is able to stir——if he ever is. Postscript of Sept. (*i.e.,* Oct.) 7:

8. The merchant captain who in 1767 had witnessed Parker's power of attorney to BF for collecting the former's salary: above, XIV, 284.

9. Baruch, or Barrak, Hays and Issachar Polock were partners in a mercantile firm of New York and Newport. J. Solis-Cohen, Jr., "Barrak Hays: Controversial Loyalist," American Jewish Hist. Soc. *Publications,* XLV (1955–56), 54–7. David Milligan & Co. were merchants and insurance brokers of Billiter Square and Samuel Blythe a merchant of Basinghall Street, London. *Kent's Directory*. . . (London, 1770), p. 123. Cary Michell, as he spelled his name, was apparently the son of the customs collector at Hampton, Va.; and by 1774 he was himself the collector. See *Tyler's Quarterly Hist. and Geneal. Mag.,* X (1929), 205; and a certificate signed by Michell, Jan. 2, 1774, APS.

1. See Parker to BF above, May 22.

encloses originals of Hubbart's two bills, of which seconds went by his letter of October 5–9.]

To William Franklin

Extract: reprinted from a quotation by William Franklin in a letter of January 1, 1770, Stan V. Henkels, *Catalogue*, No. 860 (April 9, 1901), p. 9.

[October 7, 1769]

It is very uncertain as yet what Turn American Affairs will take here on the Meeting of Parliament. The Friends of both Countries wish a reconciliation; the Enemies of either endeavour to widen the Breach, God knows how it will end.

From Thomas Gilpin

Reprinted from Joshua Gilpin, *A Memoir of the Rise, Progress, and Present State of the Chesapeake and Delaware Canal* (Wilmington, Del., 1821), pp. 15–17, with additions from Thomas Gilpin, Jr., "Memoir of Thomas Gilpin, "*Pennsylvania Magazine of History and Biography*, XLIX (1925), 305–7.

This letter from Franklin's new-found correspondent, Thomas Gilpin, is a minor but interesting contribution to the history of the canal age. The original letter has apparently been lost, and now exists only in two extracts printed a century apart. Both were edited with a *sang-froid* that the modern editor may envy but can scarcely emulate. We have chosen the fuller and earlier version, that of 1821, and have drawn upon the later version for words or passages (enclosed in brackets) that the original editor omitted.

Worthy Friend   Philadelphia Octr 10th 1769

By Capt. Falconer I had the pleasure of receiving your favor of 10th July. Your approbation and intention of exhibiting my machine to the Society of Arts gives me great pleasure and claims my sincere thanks and I hope it will meet with improvement and become beneficial to the public.[2] What I am now going to add fills me with doubt whether or not it may not prove more zealous than useful while your time is so much occupied with other objects; but as my intention is to promote public benefit I now communicate a few of the

2. For Gilpin's horizontal windmill see his letter to BF above, May 16.

216

outlines of the proceedings of the Committee, appointed to view the ground and investigate the practicability of a canal between the tide waters of the Chesapeake and Delaware bays.[3]

It is found that from Duck creek on the Delaware, to the Head of Chester river on the Chesapeake, the distance is about 12 miles, the extreme elevation 33 feet, the water high and the ground easy to dig.

From Appoquinimink creek on the Delaware, to the Head of Bohemia on the Chesapeake is 5 miles; the extreme height 66 feet, the streams small and they lie low, the ground easy to dig.

From the head of Christiana on the Delaware to Perch creek a branch of Elk river is about 12 miles; the ground has not yet been viewed by the committee, but they are appointed soon to go upon it.

The first of the above communications is too low down the Chesapeake and Delaware; the second is deep for digging and is very scant of water to supply locks; the third appears the best of all, as by a side canal or feeder, the water may be brought from the higher parts of Elk river, at the distance of six or seven miles to support the locks, as high as the extreme elevation of the middle ground, and as Elk river lies at the extremity of the Chesapeake, it renders it most convenient to every part of that bay.

It is said the inhabitants of Maryland will be averse to this canal, as it may lessen the profits of the carriage across the peninsula and prevent the growth of the [small] towns [at the head of the tide waters]; but in this I apprehend they are mistaken, and would doubtless be convinced of their error by many persons who understand the subject well, for it is evident that their trade at present is divided among so many small ports, that it is rendered weak for want of great leading markets. [The inhabitants of their back country are now compelled to resort to Philadelphia at great expence;] but, if this canal were open, boats would ply across and afford an option of a market in either bay, which would attract all produce to the head of the Chesapeake, and of course into Maryland itself, where its own ports if of sufficient importance, would have the first offer, and a second would occur by the opportunity of

3. For Gilpin's interest in canals and attempt to further their construction see APS *Trans.*, I (1771), 293–300; Brooke Hindle, *The Pursuit of Science in Revolutionary America*... (Chapel Hill, [1956]), pp. 210–12.

proceeding onward, but at all events, the certainty of one or the other and the choice of both markets, would unquestionably attract all produce to that quarter, instead of going round by sea as a great part of it now does; thus the western trade as well as that of all the waters of the Chesapeake, would be drawn to one great centre at its head and a depot formed for the sale of their own produce, and supplying them with every foreign article by the easy navigation of the Chesapeake, and by the ease also with which supplies might be obtained from the two markets of Baltimore and Philadelphia; I think that these undoubted objects which would open for the landed or agricultural interest, would give a decided preference to that of being confined to the markets of their own bay, and ensure their assent to the canal.

As to the Susquehanna, as it has been found navigable for boats of four and five tons nearly to its sources, which extend over a great part of Pennsylvania, and as the navigation may doubtless be improved by a canal, to its mouth, this would draw the produce of Pennsylvania to that quarter, and afford the double advantage of a market there, or proceeding to Philadelphia at a saving of 50 per cent. on carriage even from Lancaster, and the same saving in goods going backward, as they might be sent from Philadelphia to the Chesapeake and thence to the westward, at a considerable diminution of expence.

A great deal more might be said on the subject, but I know of no one who can perceive or appreciate the advantages I have pointed out, better than Doct. Franklin, to whom I submit these remarks, for him to correct and use them as he may think most beneficial to out country, [and remain most sincerely, his friend,

THOMAS GILPIN]

[P.S.] Barnet, who owns a furnace and forge on Octorara, a branch of Susquehanna, has in the driest part of this summer, when the water was remarkably low, gone with boats backward and forward from his works down the Susquehanna to the tide, and intends as I am informed, to pursue this navigation. This circumstance still further magnifies the importance of the navigation of the Susquehanna and the necessity of the canal.

From Grey Cooper ALS: American Philosophical Society

My dear Sir   Kew Cape[4]. Octr 13. 1769
  I Shall come to Town on Monday next, and will [with] great
pleasure carry you back with me, if you happen to be disengaged.
Yours ever very truly   GREY COOPER
Addressed: To / Dr. Francklin

Pennsylvania Assembly Committee of Correspondence to Benjamin Franklin and Richard Jackson

Printed in *Votes and Proceedings of the House of Representatives
of the Province of Pennsylvania,* 1769–1770 (Philadelphia, 1770),
p. 116.

Gentlemen,   Philadelphia, Oct. 17, 1769.
  By Order of Assembly we inclose you the Resolves appointing
you Agents for this Province, to transact the Affairs thereof in
Great-Britain, as well as that by which we are nominated a Committee of Correspondence, to whom you will communicate from
Time to Time all such Occurrences as may be necessary to be laid
before the Assembly.
  The present House have taken into their serious Consideration
the several Instructions which you have received from their Predecessors, and nothing of immediate Importance to the Province in
particular, or the Colonies in general, occurring to them, more than
what has been recommended in those Instructions,[5] to your Notice
and Attention, we are directed to desire you will refer yourselves
to them for the particular Matters relative to the Revenue Acts, the
Laws of Trade, Change of Government, the Restraint on American
Bills of Credit, and every other Thing therein mentioned, and that
you would act in Pursuance of those Instructions with all that Prudence and Caution so warmly recommended by former Assemblies,
and more especially while the present Administration continue to

---

4. Presumably Sir Grey's country house, where BF had written his essay on
smuggling. See above, XIV, 315.
5. See in particular above, XIV, 285–8; XV, 56–7.

be so unfavourably disposed towards the Colonies. We are, gentlemen, Your assured Friends,[6]

JOHN ROSS,	JOSEPH GALLOWAY, *Speaker*
ISAAC PEARSON,	JOSEPH FOX,
	JAMES PEMBERTON.

To Richard Jackson, and Ben- / jamin Franklin, Esquires, / Agents for the Province of / Pennsylvania, in London.

From Anthony Todd

ALS: American Philosophical Society

General Post Office Octr. 18, 1769.
Mr. Todd presents his Compliments to Dr. Franklin and begs the favour of his Company to Dinner on Friday next at four, to meet Mr. Foxcroft, Mr. Wharton and Major Trent. Mr. Todd will be very happy if this note should find the Dr. returned to Town.[7]

Addressed: To / Dr. Franklin / at Mrs. Stevenson's / Craven Street / Strand.

From William Small[8]

ALS: American Philosophical Society

Dear Sir,   Birmingham, 19. October 1769
I know not how to return the obligation you laid me under by making me acquainted with your respectable friend Mr. Pownall

6. For Ross, Pearson, Fox, and Pemberton see above, respectively, XI, 531 n; XV, 22 n; VI, 284 n; XIII, 260 n. Two other committee members, Thomas Livezey (above, XII, 290 n) and William Rodman (above, XV, 22 n), did not sign.

7. Sir Grey Cooper had offered to take BF into the country with him on the 16th, and the offer had apparently been accepted. See Cooper to BF above, Oct. 13. Todd repeated his invitation, with the same guests, a few weeks later; see his note below, Nov. 3. Whether or not BF missed the earlier dinner, the purpose behind Todd's hospitality was doubtless to work out plans for the Grand Ohio Company, in which the five were all involved.

8. A former professor of natural history at William and Mary, who had returned to England and settled in Birmingham, where he was one of a group that later became the Lunar Society. See above, XI, 480 n.

so properly as by introducing to you Dr. Roebuck.[9] The Dr. proposes to make but a short stay in London on this occasion, yet, as he will be in your part of the town, I am desirous you should have the pleasure of meeting each other, if it should be only for a few minutes. It is not necessary for me to say this is the gentleman so distinguished for successful applications of great philosophical abilities to important arts. His name will immediately suggest all that. I am with great respect Dear Sir Your most obedient humble Servant   W. SMALL.

Addressed: To Doctr Franklin

From Thomas Clifford[1]   ALS: American Philosophical Society

Philada. 21st Octobr. 1769.
The bearer hereof is Thomas Clifford junr.[2] just going to embark for Great Britain; I have desired him to wait on thee with my kind respects; Thy Friendly Notice of him as an Inhabitant of Pennsylvania, and my Son will be very obliging to Thy Respectful Friend
                                                                    THO CLIFFORD
Dr Benjamin Franklin

Addressed: To / Benjamin Franklin Esqr. / York Buildings / London / per favour of / T. Clifford junr

9. Pownall was probably BF's old friend Thomas, but might have been his brother John, secretary to the Board of Trade; both were members of the Society of Arts, in which Small was interested. John Roebuck, physician, inventor, and a founder of the Carron ironworks, had recently been associated with James Watt in developing the steam engine. See above, XIII, 166 n, and *DNB*.

1. See above, VIII, 86 n.

2. The writer's eldest son, who had just been given part ownership of his father's mercantile firm at the age of twenty-one. He was making his first trip to England on the firm's business; two years later he went again, met and married Sarah Dowell of Bristol, returned with her to America, and was promptly read out of the Philadelphia meeting for marrying a non-Quaker. He returned to Bristol in 1778, spent almost a decade there, then returned to a business partnership with his brother in Philadelphia. *PMHB*, v (1881), 25–6; Grace H. Larsen, "Profile of a Colonial Merchant: Thomas Clifford of Pre-Revolutionary Philadelphia" (unpublished doctoral dissertation, Columbia University, 1955), pp. 27 n, 28–30, 424.

From Henry Elwes[3]

ALS: American Philosophical Society

Dear Sir   Plimouth Octbr: 22d: 1769

We are just this moment come on shore; from on board Capt. Friend after a passage of seven weeks, very tedious Difficult weather; having a Number of Letters under my Care for You and Mr: Wharton which should have sent off by this Day post; But was Requested to Deliver them myself. If You judge it will be necessary to have them before I arrive in London; (for which place I beleive I shall be induced to sett off for by Land) advice to that purport will make me Dispatch them by the next post after Receivall of Yours; In the Interim I Can assure You Family where well as well as Mr: Wharton as I saw each of them the Day I Left Philada; Sir Your most Humble Servant   HENRY ELWES

Addressed: For | Doctr: Benjn: Franklin Esqr: | in Craven street, in the strand | London

From a Committee of the Town of Boston

LS[4]: American Philosophical Society

Sir   Boston October 23d. 1769

It is with the greatest Pleasure we obey the Orders of the Town of Boston in transmitting to you their Remarks upon the Letters from Governor Bernard, the Commissioners of his Majesty's Customs, General Gage and Commodore Hood Copies of which the Town have been furnished with by Mr. Bollan.[5]

3. See DF to BF above, Aug. 31.

4. Despite the fact that the letter is labeled a copy, the signatures are original.

5. After Parliament, late in 1768, had received damaging reports about riots and protests in Boston, the Selectmen had asked BF and other friends in England to counter the charges. See their letter to BF above under Feb. 18. William Bollan, agent for the Massachusetts Council, procured copies of unfriendly letters from Governor Bernard, from General Thomas Gage and Commodore Samuel Hood, commander in chief respectively of the King's land and sea forces, and from four members of the American Board of Customs Commissioners. The letters were published in three pamphlets in Boston during 1769, and the town meeting's "Remarks," written mostly by Samuel Adams, appeared as *An Appeal to the World; or a Vindication of the Town of Boston . . .* (Boston, 1769). The Massachusetts House petitioned for Bernard's removal, and the Boston

The Town of Boston are fully sensible of your extensive Influence and from your past Conduct have the strongest Reason to assure themselves that you will exert your great Abilities in promoting the united Interest of Great Britain and her Colonies.

The Happiness of British Subjects is founded on the Freedom of the Constitution. And in behalf of the Town of Boston we beg you would always and particularly at this Time defend this injured Town against the injurious Calumnies of those who wish the total Abolition of Liberty both in Great Britain and America. We are with strict Truth, Sir Your most obedient and very humble Servants[6]

THOMAS CUSHING	R. DANA
SAML ADAMS	JOSHUA HENSHAW
JOHN ADAMS	JOSEPH JACKSON
JAMES OTIS	BENJA KENT
JOS WARREN	

Committee of the
Town of Boston

Benjamin Franklin Esq (Copy)

P: S:[7] We have wrote to Dennys DeBerdt Esq. to whom we had before transmitted Papers and Evidences respecting the Affairs of the Town and have desired him to communicate them to you, if you

---

town meeting sued the letter-writers for libel; see Francis G. Wallet, "Governor Bernard's Undoing: an Earlier Hutchinson Letters Affair", *New England Quarterly*, XXXVIII (1965), 217–26; G. B. Warden, *Boston, 1689–1776* (Boston, 1970), p. 223.

6. For Thomas Cushing (1725–1788), Speaker of the Massachusetts House, see *DAB*. Samuel and John Adams, James Otis, Jr., and Dr. Joseph Warren are too familiar to need an introduction. Richard Dana (1700–1772) achieved notoriety in 1770 as a Justice of the Peace investigating the Boston Massacre; see *Sibley's Harvard Graduates*, VI, 236–9. For Benjamin Kent see above, XI, 80 n, and, for Joshua Henshaw and Joseph Jackson, the letter to BF cited in the previous note.

7. The postscript had become separated, but we are convinced that it belongs with the letter. The handwriting, although smaller, is the same. The town meeting of Oct. 18, furthermore, had instructed the committee to transmit copies of its report to, among others, Bollan, Pownall, and Trecothick: W. H. Whitmore *et al.*, eds., *Reports of the Record Commissioners of the City of Boston* (30 vols., Boston, 1881–1909), [XVI] (1886), 297, 299–300.

shall think it necessary to apply to him for the same. Have also wrote William Bollan, Thomas Pownal and Barlow Trecothick Esquires Letters of the same tenor with this.

From [William?] Curtis[8]   AL: American Philosophical Society

[Monday, October 23, (1769?).[9] An invitation to dine on Thursday in Martin's Lane with Dr. Price, Mr. Canton, and Dr. Jeffries.[1]]

To James Lind[2]

ALS (facsimile): reprinted from Rowfant Club *Program*, November 27, 1901

Dear Sir,   London, Oct. 25. 1769

After the many Civilities I have received from you, I am ashamed that you have not yet received from me one of my Books, which was done up to be sent you last Winter,[3] and I thought it had gone with others to Edinburg, till a few days since it was found to have been left behind and unaccountably mislaid. Mr. Bancroft is so good as to undertake to deliver it to you; and I beg Leave at the same time to recommend him to your Civilities, as an ingenious young American, who visits Edinburgh, with a View of prosecuting his Medical Studies in your School of Physic now the most celebrated of the kind in the known World.[4] With sincere Esteem and best Wishes

8. William Curtis (1746–99) was a Quaker physician and botanist, who later acquired considerable fame as the translator of Linnaeus and an expert on the flora of London. *DNB*. If our conjectural date is correct he was scarcely twenty-three at the time, and his youth perhaps makes him an implausible host for such eminent men. He was, however, precocious, and by 1771 he seems to have been moving in the circle of BF's friends; see Whitfield J. Bell, Jr., "Thomas Parke's Student Life in England and Scotland, 1771–1773," *PMHB*, LXXV (1951), 241, 243, 246.

9. 1769 was the only year during BF's second mission when Oct. 23 fell on a Monday.

1. Only one of these guests needs introduction: Dr. Joseph Jeffries was a dissenting clergyman and a member of the Club of Honest Whigs. See Van Doren, *Franklin*, p. 402; Verner W. Crane, "The Club of Honest Whigs: Friends of Science and Liberty," *WM&Q*, 3d ser., XXIII (1966), 217 n, 218.

2. For this Scottish physician see BF to Mary Stevenson above, June 27.

3. Probably the fourth edition of *Exper. and Obser.* (London, 1769), which had been advertised in the *London Chron.* on June 7–10.

4. This is BF's first known mention of Dr. Edward Bancroft (1745–1821),

for your Prosperity, I am, Dear Sir, Your most obedient humble Servant, B FRANKLIN

Dr Lind.

From Anthony Tissington   ALS: American Philosophical Society

Dear Sir   Hercules Pillars[5] 27th Octor 1769

I got here last Wednesday Evening, am at present closely engag'd in what brought me to Town, but in a day or two, hope to wait upon you, in the Interim, let the penny Post tell me if you and Mrs. Stevenson are well.

My Wife is much recover'd, and talk'd of sending Mrs. Stevenson, a Stubble Goose[6] by this Weeks Carrier, which I hope will get safe and sweet tomorrow. My Compliments to Mrs. Stevenson, and I am Dear Sir Your most oblig'd   ANTH TISSINGTON

Mr Franklin

Addressed: To / Benjamin Franklin Esqr / at Mrs Stevensons in Craven Street / Strand

---

physician, scientist, novelist, pamphleteer, and subsequently BF's secretary in Paris and one of the most successful double agents in the history of espionage. Bancroft, born in Westfield, Mass., was apprenticed for a time to a physician, ran away to sea at an early age, practiced medicine in South America, and then belatedly came to Britain to study it. He arrived in London about 1767 and worked at St. Bartholomew's; in 1770 he made a second and brief visit to South America, apparently for scientific purposes. If he seriously intended to study at Edinburgh, he must have soon abandoned the idea. BF took him under his wing, introduced him to Priestley, Pringle, and others, and was instrumental in his election to the Royal Society in 1773. In the following year Bancroft received his M.D. from Aberdeen. By then he had become not only a distinguished physician but also one of the leading experts of his day on vegetable dyes. Sir Arthur S. MacNally, "Edward Bancroft, M.D., F.R.S., and the War of American Independence," Royal Society of Medicine *Proc.*, XXXVIII (1944), 7–10; Julian P. Boyd, "Silas Deane: Death by a Kindly Teacher of Treason?," *W&MQ*, 3d ser., XVI (1959), 176–82. For his later life see *ibid.*, pp. 182–7, 319–42, 515–50; MacNally, *op. cit.*, pp. 10–15; *DAB*; *DNB*.

5. A small inn or public house at Hyde Park Corner, a little west of Hamilton Place, which acquired literary fame when Squire Weston put up his horses there while pursuing Tom Jones. Henry B. Wheatley, *London Past and Present...* (3 vols., London, 1891), II, 211.

6. For his wife and her illness see his letter to BF above, June 13. A stubble goose is one that is full-grown: it has lived long enough to feed on the stubble.

From James Parker
ALS: American Philosophical Society

[New York October 30, 1769. Is recovering after six weeks from the worst fit of gout he has ever had. Pain is gone, but he is so weak he can scarcely stand; "so have only Patience and Flannel." Has heard nothing from Franklin, and nothing has happened in the Post Office since he last wrote.]

From Anthony Todd
ALS: American Philosophical Society

Gen. Post Office Nov. 3. 1769.
Mr. Todd presents his Compliments to Dr. Franklin and begs the favour of his Company to Dinner on Monday next at ½ past three to meet Major Trent, Mr. Wharton and Mr. Foxcroft.[7]
Addressed: To | Dr. Franklin | Craven Street.

From John Hawkesworth[8]
ALS: Haverford College Library

Dear Sir   Bromley Kent Wed: night 8 Novr 1769.
    These few Lines comes hopping that you may not forget your promise of putting me in the way of getting a pensylvanian Stove time enough to enjoy the benefit of it this Winter: have you spoken to the Man to whose Eyes you addressed a proof that could not reach his Understanding? Will you fix a time for him to come hither, and will you fix such a time as will be convenient for you to meet him?[9] Perhaps he may make some part of the Machine before he comes, and so save time, which is very valueable, for time is Life. A few Lines would have come hopping on this Subject before, but I was unwilling to solicit the favour of your Company here while Miss Dolly[1] was absent; she is probably with you now, if so remember me most affectionately to her, and consult her upon the

7. Presumably to discuss the affairs of the Grand Ohio Company, of which Todd and his guests were members. See his earlier invitation above, Oct. 18.
8. The author and schoolmaster, for whom see above, IX, 265 n.
9. BF had demonstrated to a stove-maker, we conjecture, that a Franklin stove would work, and had persuaded the man to build one without understanding its principles.
1. Dorothea Blunt, Polly Stevenson's friend.

Expedition, perhaps you and she may come together. I have just received a Line from the Virgin Mary,[2] and I dine with her at Kensington on Fryday; I hope there will be no Jealousy in Heaven for my wife will be of the Party.

My kindest respects attend Mrs. Stevensone. I am Dear Sir Affectionately and faithfully Yours   JNO HAWKESWORTH

Addressed: To / Dr. Franklyn / at Mrs. Stevenson's / Craven Street / Charing Cross,

Endorsed: Hawkesworth

From Samuel Wharton   AL: American Philosophical Society

[Dated merely Thursday night; probably November 9, 1769.[3] A note in the third person to inform Franklin that Wharton has just received via Bristol a letter from the latter's wife, dated Sept. 20, 1769, saying that the Franklin family was well.]

From Samuel Wharton   AL: American Philosophical Society

[Dated merely Friday afternoon; probably November 10, 1769.[4] A note in the third person, to send Franklin the American newspapers received that day in the New York mail. Has heard nothing by the packet; expects a letter from "his Friend" by Capt. Jeffries, who was to sail from Philadelphia on Oct. 7.]

2. Polly Stevenson was soon to escape from her nickname by marrying William Hewson.

3. The brigantine *Concord* cleared from Philadelphia for Bristol at the right time to have carried a letter written on Sept. 20, and arrived in early November. *Pa. Chron.*, Sept. 18–25; *London Chron.*, Nov. 9–11, 1769. Nov. 9 was a Thursday, and it seems reasonable that Mrs. Wharton's letter reached London at the same time as news of the *Concord's* arrival.

4. A New York mail reached London on Nov. 10; *London Chron.*, Nov. 9–11, 1769. The snow *Britannia*, Capt. James Jeffries master, cleared Philadelphia on Oct. 5; *Pa. Gaz.*, Oct. 5, 1769.

From Richard Huck[5]   AL: American Philosophical Society

[November 15, 1769.[6] An invitation to dine with Sir John Pringle on Friday next.]

From [Samuel] Wharton   AL: American Philosophical Society

Thursday Morning. [November 16?,[1] 1769]

Mr. Wharton presents his Compliments to Dr. Franklin and will be much obliged to Him, If He will be so good as to take an early Opportunity of explaining to Governor Pownall, Abraham Mitchel's[2] base Conduct; As Mr. Wharton finds the Governor and his Brother[3] have read the Affidavit in the Gazeeteer[4] and He is afraid, it may make an injurious Impression on Them, Unless They are soon acquainted by the Doctor, with the Falsity of it.

5. The noted physician, for whom see above, xv, 172 n.

6. The note is merely dated Wednesday, but the invitation is for Friday, Nov. 17; between the knighting of Pringle and BF's departure from England Friday fell on the 17th only in 1769.

1. The affidavit mentioned below was published on Friday, Nov. 10; we are assigning this note to the first Thursday thereafter.

2. Abraham Mitchel or Mitchell (1710–88) was a Quaker, apparently the son of Thomas and Sarah Densey Mitchell: William W. Hinshaw, *Encyclopedia of Amer. Quaker Genealogy* (6 vols., Ann Arbor, Mich., 1936–50), II, 599. He is described both as a hatter and as an eastern capitalist in Nicholas B. Wainwright, *George Croghan, Wilderness Diplomat* (Chapel Hill, [1929]), pp. 12, 176. He was one of those included in the land grant that the Six Nations made at Fort Stanwix in November, 1768: Kenneth B. Bailey, ed., *The Ohio Company Papers, 1753–1817* (Arcata, Cal., 1947), pp. 190–5; his name appears frequently but incidentally in much of the literature on the Grand Ohio Company.

3. Former Governor Thomas Pownall and his brother John, secretary of the Board of Trade. Thomas was a signer of the petition to the King from the Grand Ohio Company printed above, end of June.

4. The published affidavit, taken by a Philadelphia justice of the peace on Feb. 27, 1769, dealt with the alleged skulduggery of Samuel Wharton and William Trent. Late in 1763, Mitchell deposed, a group of "suffering traders" —those who had sustained heavy losses from Indian depredations in that year and earlier—met at Philadelphia at the instance of Wharton and others, to lay plans for obtaining compensation. They decided to apply to the crown, and appointed Wharton to correspond with a London agent. Some time later Mitchell was approached by Trent, who asked him to make over his claims for 1763; his earlier losses, Trent told him, could never be recouped. The value of the assigned claims might readily be inflated, Trent suggested, and Mitchell

Mr. Wharton hopes the Doctor may yet find Mitchel's Letters; As They are of so much Consequence to Mr. W.'s Reputation.[5]

[*In the margin:*] I send the three last Boston News Papers for your Amusement.

Addressed: To | Doctor Franklin | Craven Street.

From William Strahan   AL: American Philosophical Society

Sunday Noon [November 19, 1769?][6]

Mr. Strahan presents his Compliments to Dr. Franklin, and begs to know if he is to be at home and at Leisure this Afternoon, as he wants much to have a Conference with him; If the Dr. is not engaged (which Mr. S. is afraid he is by this time) would be very glad of the favour of his Company to eat a Bit of Beef with him at 1/2 after two.

P.S. Intended to have waited on the Dr. this forenoon but was preventd.

Addressed: To | Dr. Franklin | at Mrs Stevenson's | Craven Street

---

would be paid thirty percent of whatever was received. Wharton urged him to accept Trent's proposal, pointed out that he and others had already done so, and assured him that the traders in their desperate position had no other hope of recovering a penny. Mitchell reluctantly agreed, although he refused to inflate his losses. Only later did he learn that Wharton had known that prospects of compensation were improving, and had been hand in glove with Trent in purchasing the traders' claims. *The Gazetteer and New Daily Advertiser*, Nov. 10, 1769. For further information about Trent's activities in buying up the claims see 4 Mass. Hist. Soc. *Collections*, X (1871), 605–6; Sewell E. Slick, *William Trent and the West* (Harrisburg, Pa., 1947), pp. 128, 130–1.

5. The Doctor either did not find the letters or, if he did, turned them over to Wharton; they are not among BF's papers, which contain no other mention of Mitchell in this period. Wharton was presumably worried about the affair because it touched a more immediate concern than his reputation: the petition from the Grand Ohio Company (above, end of June) came before the Privy Council Committee for Plantation Affairs on Nov. 20, and was referred to the Board of Trade. *Acts Privy Coun., Col.*, V, 202.

6. This note could of course have been written at any time when BF was in London. Our guess, based largely on Strahan's tone, is that he was writing to initiate the collaboration between the two that produced his queries on the American question and BF's reply, for which see below, Nov. [21–]22, 29. If our guess is correct, the most likely Sunday would have been Nov. 19.

From Deborah Franklin ALS: American Philosophical Society

November the 20[-27] 1769

yisterday I reseved yours dated September the 9 whare in you was so kind as to sende me Sir John Pringels advise to me[7] all I am much obliged to you and to so worthey a good man as Sir John but I muste tell you as well as I Can my disordor was for this reson my distres for my dear Debbeys misforten and hers being removed so far from her friend and such a helpeles famely and before I had got the better of that our Cusin Betsey macum was taken ill and so much distrest so soon that aded to my one dis satisfid distresed att your staying so much longer that I loste all my resey lushon and the verey dismall winter bouth Salley and my self live so verey lonley that I had got in so verey low a Staite and got into so unhapey a way that I Cold not sleep a long time.[8] Good old Mr. Whorton[9] did Cume sumtimes to aske how we did and asked us to Cume to spend a day att his house when we got up to the street I was sirprised att seing a croud and was told sum pepel to be whiped and such things all way distresed me but we wente on our visit and while thair I loste all my memerey I Cold not tell aney thing but stayed all day but verey sleepey and as soon I got to bed I sleep all night and semed quite hapey and esey and I shold a got better but Salley was surprised att my sleeping so [?] as I did and you know that I had aney Complaintes I yousd to live verey spairing but on know to me for Dr. Bond to cume and supmited to be Bleeded and took sumthing againste my one Judgment (to oblige Salley as shee was in such a Condison as shee was) I had no head ake or fever the Dr. sed my blood was verey good but sed he wold sende to you[1] I beged him not but it gave me much onesey nes aboute it or I wold not a lett you to aknowe aboute it. I still sleep verey well and sleep as soon a night but did loos my apeytite and loosing memerey grew verey week no paine tell one day I had one of a sever pain in my sid and stomick I

7. Probably on how to take care of herself after her serious illness of the previous winter.
8. The Rev. William Dunlap and his wife Debby, DF's niece, had both been ill in 1768; see above, XV, 23. "Cusin Betsey" was Benny Mecom's long-suffering wife. Sally, like her mother, was lonely because her husband was away; Richard Bache had recently left town on business. See DB to BF above, Oct. 4.
9. Joseph Wharton, Sr.; see above, XI, 451 n.
1. See Thomas Bond to BF above, June 7.

yousd to have and then wold be better agen for sume time after but this time I was verey ill for few days verey mortely and thanke god while I semed to recover my memerey and thanke god I have my memerey in sume meshaer returnd, I donte remember I have had one fitt of the head ake excepte while Salley was ill as I loste my sleep I donte taste molleyses for severel mounthes and I Cold verey eseyley to for bair aney thing of drinke or aney thing to eate I did grow verey thin so much that Billey sed he had never seen so much chainges in me and senes the wather I have grone better and recoverd my Coller agen. I am in hopes I shall get better agen to see you I ofen tell my frindes I was not sick I was only more to bair aney more and so I fell down and cold [*illegible*] not get up agen indead it was not aney sicknes but two much disquiit of mind but I had taken up a resey lushon never to make aney Complainte to you or give you aney disquiet to you. About 5 or 6 days after I reseved your leter Dr. Evens sente me his letter[2] to let me know that you was well for which I am thankfull. I have to tell you sum thing of my self what I believe you wold not beleve of me oney I tell you my selve. I have bin to a play with Sister.[3] I expeckte that sumbodey to speek to me but I have bin to twise to the prispatreiny [Presbyterian] metin which will be worse to sume folkes.[4] I did no more on that side. I have wrote to send Pitt have Laid on sid[5] but I shall Send by the packit but this is to saile to morrow in Capt. Sparkes. On bord is a small caske Indin meel and sume buck wheit flower and 2 Bowels of Appills which I hope will prove good. I am to tell you Dr.

2. *I.e.*, BF's letter to him above, Sept. 8.

3. In November a theatrical company had presented *Hamlet* and *Romeo and Juliet*, and such lighter fare as *Love à la Mode*, *The Musical Lady*, and *The Constant Couple*; see Thomas C. Pollock, *The Philadelphia Theatre in the Eighteenth Century* (Philadelphia, 1933), pp. 107–8, 112. The city had become a refuge for players, despite efforts of "sober and religious" Philadelphians to ban them; see above, XIV, 29–30. DF had clearly been in low spirits since her illness, and her sister-in-law had been depressed before coming to Philadelphia (see BF to Jane Mecom above, Sept. 29); they may well have sought relief in the deviltry of an evening at the theatre.

4. BF and the Presbyterians had been enemies for years; see above, XI, 125, 434. Jane Mecom, a Congregationalist, may have lured DF into her Presbyterian aberration, but they also attended Christ Church, DF's regular parish; see Carl Van Doren, *Jane Mecom*... (New York, 1950), p. 96.

5. The meaning is apparently that she had written a letter to send by the *Pitt*, but had laid it aside for this one.

Rush came and paid to me 32 pounds this currentsy he told me you had borrowed of you in London the Exchange is a hundred and fiveftey pounds but he thoughte at the time he had aboute the same sum.[6] Dr. Shipen has paid to me in cash 30 and he has a demand of Brother Petters.[7] I shall by the packit to send you word. Benj Franklin dos grow finely indead and Sister is as happey as I am he is a fine child.

In an ower Sparkes leves town the poste is Cum in no packit arived I continew to get better [each?] day. Sister is verey well and as happey as shee Can all things Considered. Laste night [James Parker[8]] Come hear but hardly abel to stir. His Son come a long to helpe him to dres and on dres he had Come to Burlinton and was obliged to waite to Come down to see us. I donte know wather aney one writes tell the packit arives. Our Children and Sister Joyne with me my beste Compley ments to good mrs. Stephenson and Dear polley and all our friends my Love to Salley Franklin it is so darke as it raines I Can hardly see I hope to write to your satis fackshon by the packit I am your afeckshonet wife

D FRANKLIN

November the 27 1769

Addressed: To | Benjamin Franklin Esqr. | on | Craven Street | London

6. We cannot guess what DF meant, if indeed she completed the sentence at all, and we are not confident that our reading is correct; the writing is obscure even by DF's standards, and punctuation is nonexistent. BF recorded the loan as £20 sterling (Jour., July 30, 1769), to which £32 Pennsylvanian would be roughly equivalent. Rush himself, writing years later, said he had borrowed 30 guineas: George W. Corner, ed., *The Autobiography of Benjamin Rush* . . . ([Princeton], 1948), p. 74.

7. Dr. William Shippen had managed to get together enough to repay part of the £25 sterling that BF had lent to his son; see above, John Shippen to BF, June 3, and DF to BF, Oct. 4. The Rev. Richard Peters presumably owed the senior Shippen enough to provide the remainder in Pennsylvania currency.

8. DF omitted a subject for the verb, but it was clearly Parker; see his letter to BF below, Nov. 30.

From William Strahan

ALS (copy): British Museum

Although early in 1769 Parliament had favored strong measures against the colonies, by the time the session ended in May Lord Hillsborough made a guarded promise that some of the Townshend duties would be repealed when the new session opened the following January. William Strahan, Franklin's old friend, took much credit for the American Secretary's change of position; but it was actually forced upon Hillsborough by his colleagues in the Cabinet, and it fell far short of the total repeal for which Franklin and other friends of America were working. The Duke of Grafton, for once, was more in agreement with the latter than with the other ministers, who voted down his proposal to repeal the Townshend duty on tea. As the year wore on, Grafton became more and more isolated in his own ministry, alienated from the King and from Chatham, and subject to assaults in the press; he had decided in May to resign as soon as opportunity offered, and the only question was when. The prospect of a new and unknown administration stimulated Franklin and Strahan to mobilize such support for repeal as they could before the old ministry broke up. Strahan accordingly composed these queries in order to elicit Franklin's reply, which appears below under November 29. The two documents were originally intended for the eyes of Grafton and other members of the Cabinet, but copies were sent to America for private circulation.[9]

Dear Sir   Newstreet Nov. [21–]22. 1769[1]

In the many Conversations we have had together about our present Disputes with North America, we perfectly agree in wishing they may be brought to a speedy and happy Conclusion. How this is to be done is not so easily ascertained.

9. The documents, according to Strahan, were given to Grafton and other ministers, but had no effect on the governmental policy outlined soon afterward in the King's speech at the opening of Parliament. Strahan sent copies of the documents to David Hall in Philadelphia, apparently with strict injunctions not to let them out of his hands: "Correspondence between William Strahan and David Hall, 1763–1777," *PMHB*, XI (1887), 224, 349. BF later sent copies to Samuel Cooper in Boston for his private use; see the postscript of BF's letter to him below, June 8, 1770. See also Crane, *Letters to the Press*, pp. 165–6, and for the political background sketched in the headnote Gipson, *British Empire*, XII, 242–7.

1. The following document makes clear that the queries were written, at least in draft, by the 21st, and they bore that date when first published years later: *Public Advertiser*, Feb. 19, 1774. But BF, when he replied below on Nov. 29, dated them the 22nd. It seems probable to us that Strahan drafted them on one day and reworked them the next.

Two[2] Objects, I humbly apprehend, his Majestys Servants have now in Contemplation. 1st. To relieve the Colonies from the Taxes complained of, which they certainly had no hand in imposing. 2dly. To preserve the Honour, the Dignity, and Supremacy of the British Legislature over all his Majestys Dominions.

As I know your Singular Knowledge of the Subject in Question, and am as fully convinced of your Attachment to his Majesty, and your sincere Desire to promote the Happiness, equally of all his Subjects, I beg you would in your own clear, brief and explicite Manner, send me an answer to the following Questions. I make this request now, because this matter is of the utmost Importance, and must very quickly be agitated. And I do it with the more freedom, as you know me and my motives to well to entertain the most remote Suspicion, that I will make an improper Use of any Information you shall thereby convey to me.

1. Will not a Repeal of all the Duties (that on Tea excepted which was before paid here on exportation, of course no new Imposition) fully satisfy the Colonists? If you answer in the Negative

2. Your Reasons for that Opinion?

3. Do you think the only efectual Way of composing present Differences, is to put the Americans precisely in the Situation they were in before the passing of the Late Stamp Act? [*In Franklin's hand:* If that is your Opinion,]

4 Your Reasons for that Opinion?

5 If this last Method is deemed by the Legislature and Majisty's Ministers, to be repugnant to their Duty as Guardians of the Just Rights of the Crown, and of their fellow Subjects, can you suggest any other Way of terminating these Disputes, consistent with the Ideas of Justice and Propriety conceived by the Kings Subjects on both Sides of the Atlantick?

6 And if this Method was actually followed, do you think it would encourage the Violent and Factious part of the Colonists to aim at Still farther Concessions from the Mother Country.

7 If they are relieved in part only, what do you, as a reasonable and dispassionate Man, and an equal Friend to both Sides imagine will be the probable Consequences?

The Answers to these Questions, I humbly concieve, will include

2. "Five" in MS; the copyist's slip was corrected in the published version cited above.

all the information I want; and I beg you will favour me with them as soon as may be. Every Well wisher to the peace and Prosperity of the British Empire, and every Friend to our truly happy Constitution, must be desirous of seeing even the most trival Causes of Dissention amongst our Fellow-Subjects removed. Our Domestic Squabbles, in my Mind, are nothing to what I am speaking of. This you know much better than I do, and therefore I need add nothing farther to recommend this Subject to your serious Consideration. I am, with the most cordial Esteem and Attachment, Dear Sir, Your faithful and affectionate humble Servant

WILLIAM STRAHAN.

Dr Franklin

Copy

From William Strahan
ALS: American Philosophical Society

New Street Wednesday noon Novr. 22 [1769³]
Dear Sir

I shewed the inclosed last night, after I saw you, to Mr. B.⁴ who highly approves of the Way in which I have stated the Matter, which he says is precisely as it ought to be. I hope you will therefore let me have your Answer as soon as you conveniently can. I am Ever Your most obedient
W. S.

Addressed: To / Dr. Benjamin Franklin / at Mrs Stevenson's / Craven Street

From Michael Hillegas⁵
ALS: American Philosophical Society

Dear Sir
Philada: Novr. 25th. 1769
Your kind Letter to the Nova Scotia Adventurers dated the 13th. July last came safe to hand, and for which am in behalf of Self and all Concerned very much Obliged to you. Such of the Proprietors

3. Aside from the fact that Nov. 22, during BF's second British mission, fell on a Wednesday only in 1769, this was obviously a covering note for the preceding document.
4. Probably William Bollan, agent for the Massachusetts Council.
5. See BF's letter to him above, Jan. 5, and his reply, April 15.

who I have from Time to Time mett with, has seen it, and are much pleased; I shall however endeavour to get them together some time this Winter, in order That they may take what Steps may be thought necessary, when perhaps they may think of Subscribing the Sum for the taking out of the Office, The Copy of the Indulgencies and ease of terms of Settlement granted to Alexr. McNutt and his Associates. As soon as this is effected you shall hear from us.[6]

Am well satisfied that nothing in this World affords you more pleasure Than when you can render service to the Community, be it in whatsoever way Possible. Know then, That many among us have frequently been very uneasy on Account of the Roofs of our Houses, not only on Account of their short duration, but on Account of the Shingling taking Fire, and Understanding That many Houses in Europe are Covered with Copper, Should be glad to be Informed, How That mode is like to Answer, How Thick the Sheets of Copper are, and how much the Expence may amount on an Average when done, per Squard Yard or so? If you can Conveniently obtain an Account from a good hand, I no way doubt your Chearfulness of Transmitting the same hence.[7]

Before I conclude Permitt me of reminding you of my old troublesome Commission, to wit, the Glasses for my Armonica beg you'll send them under particular care if Possible per Capt. N. Falconer.[8]

I have the honour of Subscribing my Self Dear Sir Your already much Obliged and most Obedient humble Servant M HILLEGAS

Addressed: To / Doctr: Benjamin Franklin Esqr / Craven Street / London / per Capt: Sparks

Endorsed: Hillegas Nov. 25. 1769

6. For Col. Alexander McNutt and BF's interest in Nova Scotia, see above, XI, 470 n; XII, 345–50.

7. For BF's answer to these questions see below, March 17, 1770. For Philadelphians' concern with the danger of fire see George C. Gillespie, "Early Fire Protection and the Use of Fire Marks," *PMHB*, XLVI (1922), 244–54; Harold E. Cunningham, "Philadelphia's First Fire Defences," *ibid.*, LVI (1932), 355–77.

8. For BF's difficulty in getting armonicas made in London see above, XIII, 253.

From Charles Thomson

Printed in *The London Chronicle*, March 1–3, 1770

Sir, Phila, Nov. 26, 1769.

As Capt. Sparks sails sooner than was expected, the Committee of Merchants here have not time to write to you, they have therefore desired me to enclose you a copy of their letter to the Committee of Merchants in London.[9] As the Parliament will no doubt at their meeting take under consideration the affairs of America, it is necessary you should be fully acquainted with the temper and disposition of the Colonies.

Though the Merchants of this place and New York[1] have agreed to confine their non-importation to the repeal of the act laying duties on tea, paper, glass, and paint: yet this does not arise from any alteration of sentiment in the minds of the people in general, nor from a conviction that this is the only act that affects the liberty of America. It was necessary therefore that the conduct of the Merchants might not affect the general cause, and prevent such a redress of grievances as would give general satisfaction, to explain those wrongs of which the people complain, and inform them of what alone can put a full and final end to the unhappy dispute which has arisen between Great Britain and the Colonies; a partial redress will little avail to allay the heats and quiet the minds of the people. The Colonies see plainly that the Ministry have adopted a settled plan to subjugate America to arbitrary power; that all the late acts made respecting them tend to this purpose. First, the Parliament claims a right to levy taxes on the Americans, without their consent; and, to shew the extent of the authority which they mean to exercise, they declare that they have a power to make laws to bind them in all cases whatever: By another act they suspend the legislative authority of an American Assembly for daring to dispute their commands, and for not implicitly obeying their dictates. Nay, to

9. The letter from a group of Philadelphia merchants that included Thomson, dated Nov. 25, 1769, was published in the same issue of the *London Chron.* that carried this letter.

1. New York led the way: its merchants entered into their agreement on Aug. 27, 1768, whereas those of Philadelphia did not take the final step until March 10, 1769. Arthur M. Schlesinger, *The Colonial Merchants and the American Revolution, 1763–1776* (New York, 1918), pp. 124, 129.

convince the Americans that no act of their legislatures, however solemnly passed and ratified, can screen them from the power of Parliament, they, by another act, order a certain sum to be paid as a fee to one of the petty Officers of the Customs, with these words annexed, "*Any law, bye-law, or act of Assembly in any of the Colonies to the contrary notwithstanding.*"[2] But as the raising revenue, and taking the purse-strings into their own hands, is their main end and view, knowing that every other power must follow this, they impower the King to erect a board of Commissioners here with unlimited powers, and that the courts of common law may not obstruct them in their proceedings, they extend the jurisdiction of the Admiralty Court, and grant the Officers of the Customs, and every informer, the option of commencing every suit, relative to the revenue, in that Court.[3] The army which was left in America after the late war, under pretence of securing and defending it, is now publicly declared to be for the purpose of enforcing obedience to the authority of Parliament. The remonstrances and petitions of the Assemblies in favour of their rights, and against these claims of Parliament, are treated as seditious; and the attempts of individuals to procure a redress of grievances, are deemed rebellion and treason: And, in order to intimidate the Colonies, an antique obsolete law is revived, and the Crown addressed to send for persons accused of treasonable practices in America, and try them in England.[4] How much farther they may proceed, is uncertain; but, from what they have already done, the Colonies see that their property is precarious, and their liberty insecure. It is true, the impositions already laid are not very grievous; but if the principle is established, and the authority by which they are laid is admitted, there is no security for what remains. The very nature of freedom supposes that no tax can be levied on a people without their consent given personally, or by their Representatives. It was not on account of the largeness of the sum demanded by Charles I that ship money was so odious to the

2. The three statutes to which Thomson refers were 6 Geo. III, c. 12, the Declaratory Act; 7 Geo. III, c. 49, the act suspending the New York Assembly; and 5 Geo. III, c. 45, para. 27, which he slightly misquotes.

3. The Townshend Acts.

4. For the attempt to revive the statute of Henry VIII relating to treason see BF to Strahan below, Nov. 29. This attempt, originating late in 1768, had been reported in the *Pa. Chron.*, March 20–27, 1769.

Commons of Britain, but because the principle upon which it was demanded left them nothing they could call their own.[5]

The continuation of this claim of the Parliament will certainly be productive of ill consequences, as it will tend to alienate the affections of the Colonies from the Mother Country.[6] Already it has awakened a spirit of enquiry. The people by examining have gained a fuller knowledge of their rights, and are become more attentive and watchful against the encroachments of power: at the same time they are become more sensible of the resources they have among themselves for supplying their real wants. Resentment as well as necessity will drive them to improve these to the utmost. And from the genius of the people, and the fertility of the soil, it is easy to foresee, that, in the course of a few years, they will find at home an ample supply of all their wants. In the mean while their strength, power, and numbers, are daily increasing. And as the property of land is parcelled out among the inhabitants, and almost every Farmer is a Freeholder, the spirit of liberty will be kept awake, and the love of freedom deeply rooted. And when strength and liberty combine, it is easy to foresee that a people will not long submit to arbitrary sway. Thus, by a blind infatuation and madness of politics, a weak, short-sighted Ministry, have been ruining their country, and hastening a period they seemed to dread, by the very means which they intended to prevent it.

I have often viewed, with infinite satisfaction, the prodigious growth and power of the British Empire; and have pleased myself with the hopes that in a century or two the British Colonies would overspread this immense territory added to the Crown of Britain, carrying with them the religion of Protestants, and the laws, customs, manners, and language of the country from whence they sprung; while England placed at the head of the Empire superintended the whole, and by the wisdom of her councils prevented

5. Thomson uses "commons" in the broad sense; the crucial years of ship money, 1634–38, were those when the House of Commons was not in session. The levy was extended from ports to the country at large, and threatened to become a regular form of taxation by prerogative. If it had succeeded, it would have eliminated the need for Parliament in future; it failed because of popular resistance. Thomson's analogy with the threat to the colonial assemblies is clear if unexpressed.

6. The remainder of the letter echoes BF's views, many of which were expressed in the Canada pamphlet almost a decade before; see above, IX, 59–100.

the jarring interests of the several inferior states, united their strength for the general good, and guarded them from the attacks of foreign powers. In such a situation she might have laughed at the compacts of the Bourbon family, and defied the united powers of Europe. But alas! the folly of a weak administration has darkened the prospect. And what the issue will be must be left to Providence; while we with humble adoration pray the supreme Governor of the Universe to over-rule events for the general good.

From Cadwalader Evans   ALS: American Philosophical Society

[Dear] Doctor   Philadia Novr. 27th. 1769.
    Your letters of the 8th. and 9th. of Sepr., together with the four French memoirs on the *Education* of Silk worms, and culture of Mulbery trees, came safe to hand; for which I cordially thank you.[7]
    As I do not read French with ease, and have not leisure enough to consult Boyer,[8] I have got my worthy friend Mr. Odell, to take the memoirs, and make such extracts as his Judgement may dictate; which shall be published.[9] I have wrote to Mr. Wharton, and Mr. James[1] on this subject, which they will communicate to you, if worth your notice.
    I am pleased that Messrs. Biddle, and Bayley's, observations of the Transit of Venus, was agreeable to you.
    I have not attended the Meetings of our Society for 10 months past; because I must have been a solemn witness to transactions,

7. See BF to Evans above, Sept. 7, 8; Evans' slightly different dates are presumably a slip.

8. Abel Boyer (1667–1729) published a French-English dictionary in 1702, which was a standard reference work of the period. *DNB*.

9. The Rev. Jonathan Odell published *Directions for the Breeding and Encouragement of Silk-Worms . . .* (Philadelphia, 1770), which included translations from the French treatise that BF had sent; it also contained the plan for a society to encourage silk-manufacturing.

1. We have no indication that Abel James (*c.* 1726–90), a Philadelphia merchant then in London, consulted with BF on silk culture at this time; Wharton did touch on it as a possibility in applying for a land grant for the Grand Ohio Co.: *Acts Privy Coun., Col.*, V, 206.

inconsistent with my Judgement or perpetually engaged in party, and disputation; both of which were irksome to me. On this account, I cannot of my own knowledge, give the reasons, why the other observations were not sent to you. But Dr. Bond can, and probably will; but lest something shoud prevent him I will give his state of the matter, which I beleive is very near the truth. Soon after the Transit Biddle carried his observation to the Society; but Smith and Ewing, who were, or assumed the credit of being at the head of the other observations, delayed bringing in their accompts, under colour, that many Calculations and adjustments were previously to be made. About the time they were brought in, Dr. Bond moved that a copy of all the observations shoud be transmitted to the President by the first Oppertunity. Dr. Smith opposed it for this reason—that as the papers of the Society were shortly to be printed, partial publications woud lessen the curiosity of the publick, and diminish the demand for the work. At that very time, we had great reason to beleive, he had sent all the observations to the Proprietor. So far as I know, and have been informed, all who voted for you resent very highly the impotent indignity intended; but I think the consequence will be, divesting him of his Secretaryship at next Election.

When Dr. Bond proposed to me the plan of the last Society, with Smith and Ewing for Secretaries I told him I coud not join them; because I considered the objects or purposes of the institution were enquieries after things as they really are, with the uses they are capable of being applied to, for general benefit but that such real facts, or truths coud not possibly pass thro such tainted conduits, without contracting a tang—A tang that woud so disguise them, as to deceive the world, and eventually do discredit to every member of the Society.

I was, further, of opinion, that the earnestness of some members for an union of the two Societies was only to have a greater range, for filching of reputation from the labours of others. This was obvious in the observations of the Transit. Smith, Ewing, Williamson got themselves named in the Committee's of observation, but neither of their observations, were in the least counted upon; Nevertheless, they were named first in the Newspapers, and as professors of the Colledge, woud be thought by such as did not know them, entitled to most if not all the merit. A Pirate, and a Highwayman, I [feel?] some charity for; but a lyar and filcher of reputation, are to me, the most detestable scunks in human society.[2]

I am in hopes you will have the pleasure of taking Mr. James by the hand, in better health than he left us. I have wrote preety fully to him and Mr. Wharton, and if anything in their letters are worth your notice, they will undoubtedly communicate it to you. Mrs. Franklin was here two days agoe, in preety good health. I was up at Burlington 2 weeks agoe, to see Chas. Read's wife, Just before she died.[3] The Governor and Mrs. Franklin were in high health, and as much beloved and esteemed, as your Paternal affections can desire. Adeiu, Dear Doctor, and be assured I am, most affectionately Your friend   C: EVANS

Addressed: To / Benjamin Franklin Esqr. / Deputy Postmaster General, for / North America in / Craven street / London / per Capt. Sparks

Endorsed: Dr. Cad. Evans Nov. 27. 1769   BF

Put in the Genl. post Without A penny

From William Strahan   AL: American Philosophical Society

Monday 11 o'Clock [November 27, 1769?[4]]
Mr. Strahan's best Respects to Dr. Franklin and begs, if the Letter is now ready, that he will send it by the Bearer.

Addressed: To / Dr. Franklin / Craven Street

2. For the transit of Venus and the factions in the APS see above, Bond to BF, June 7, Evans to BF, June 11, and BF to Evans, Sept. 7, where most of the participants are identified.

3. Alice Thibou Read, wife of New Jersey's former deputy secretary, died on Nov. 13, 1769, aged 51; Carl R. Woodward, *Ploughs and Politicks: Charles Read of New Jersey and His Notes on Agriculture, 1715–1774* (New Brunswick, 1941), p. 213.

4. This note could of course have been written at any time during BF's years in England. But the queries that Strahan sent him on Nov. 22 had a hint of urgency in them, and BF was out of town and did not answer for a week. Our guess—and it can be nothing more—is that Strahan grew increasingly impatient to have the reply: that he first sent a man with this note and then, when it produced no result, sent again two days later with the note printed under Nov. 29.

To William Strahan

ALS (copy): British Museum[5]

This letter, one of Franklin's major statements on colonial affairs, was in response to the queries Strahan had sent him a week before, which are printed above under November 21–22. As explained there, the queries and the reply were not designed for publication, and were not in fact published until 1774; they were intended for private circulation, in order to mobilize support for total repeal of the Townshend Acts at the next session of Parliament. Franklin here condensed and organized some of the arguments that he had been working out for himself, in letters and in the marginalia printed at the end of this volume, and applied them to specific issues that the queries had raised—to the duty on tea, for example, which soon proved to be momentous. He dealt mildly with the dangers of partial repeal, and then left Strahan's queries in order to prophesy about the greater, underlying danger: that repression would provoke resistance and more repression, in a vicious circle wherein both sides were caught. The effect of his letter must have been slight. Perhaps it engendered some support for partial repeal, on which he set no store at all, when that measure came before Parliament the following spring; but it certainly did nothing to deflect the government from a course that fulfilled his pessimistic prophecy.

Dear Sir,   Craven Street, Nov. 29. 69

Being just return'd to Town from a little Excursion I find yours of the 22d, containing a Number of Queries that would require a Pamphlet to answer them fully. You however desire only brief Answers, which I shall endeavour to give you. Previous to your Queries, You tell me, that "you apprehend his Majesty's Servants have now in Contemplation; 1st. to relieve the Colonists from the Taxes complained of: and 2dly to preserve the Honour, the Dignity, and the Supremacy of the British Legislature over all his Majesty's Dominions." I hope your Information is good, and that what you suppose to be in Contemplation will be carried into Execution, by repealing *all the Laws* that have been made for raising a Revenue in America by Authority of Parliament, without the consent of the People there. The *Honour* and *Dignity* of the British Legislature will not be hurt by such an Act of Justice and Wisdom: The wisest Councils are liable to be misled, especially in Matters remote from their

5. The copy has numerous small errors and omissions, which have been silently corrected and supplied from the first printing of the letter in the *Public Advertiser*, Feb. 19, 1774.

Inspection. It is the persisting in an Error, not the Correcting it that lessens the Honour of any Man or body of Men. The *Supremacy* of that Legislature, I believe will be best preserv'd by making a very sparing use of it, never but for the Evident Good of the Colonies themselves, or of the whole British Empire; never for the Partial Advantage of Britain to their Prejudice; by such Prudent Conduct I imagine that Supremacy may be gradually strengthened and in time fully Established; but otherwise I apprehend it will be disputed, and lost in the Dispute. At present the Colonies consent and Submit to it for the regulation of General Commerce: But a Submission to Acts of Parliament was no part of their original Constitution. Our former Kings Governed their Colonies, as they Governed their Dominions in France, without the Participation of British Parliaments. The Parliament of England never presum'd to interfere with that prerogative till the Time of the Great Rebellion, when they usurp'd the Government of all the King's other Dominions, Ireland, Scotland &c. The Colonies that held for the King, they conquered by Force of Arms, and Governed afterward as Conquered Countries. But New England having not oppos'd the Parliament, was considered and treated as a Sister Kingdom in Amity with England; as appears by the Journals, Mar. 10. 1642.[6]

Your first Question is,

1. "Will not a Repeal of all the Duties (that on Tea excepted, which was before paid here on Exportation, and of Course no new Imposition) fully satisfy the Colonists?"

I think not.

"2 Your Reasons for that Opinion?"

Because it is not *the Sum* paid in that Duty on Tea that is Com-

6. Virginia, Bermuda, and Barbados resisted Parliamentary authority until brought to heel by Cromwell. On March 10, 1643 (new style), the House of Commons resolved to free from duty any goods that were exported from the mother country to New England and anything grown in "that kingdom" that was imported into England. But this concession was to remain in force, as BF fails to mention, only until the House took further action, which the Rump Parliament did in 1651: it reasserted legislative control in the economic sphere by passing the first Navigation Act. See Leo F. Stock, ed., *Proceedings and Debates of the British Parliaments Respecting North America* (5 vols. to date, Washington, 1924 —), I, 141–2, 155, 225. A copy of the resolution of 1643 is in BF's papers, APS; and it was referred to again in a memorial that he helped to draft from the Continental Congress to Parliament in 1775, for which see Smyth, *Writings*, VI, 414.

plain'd of as a Burthen, but the Principle of the Act express'd in the Preamble, viz. that those Duties were laid for the Better Support of Government and the Administration of Justice in the Colonies. This the Colonists think *unnecessary*, *unjust*, and *dangerous* to their Most Important Rights. *Unnecessary*, because in all the Colonies (two or three new ones excepted) Government and the Administration of Justice were and always had been well supported without any Charge to Britain; *Unjust* as it made such Colonies liable to pay such Charge for other Colonies, in which they had no Concern or Interest; *dangerous*, as such a Mode of raising Money for these Purposes, tended to render their Assemblies useless: For if a Revenue could be rais'd in the Colonies for all the purposes of Government, by Act of Parliament, without Grants from the People there, Governors, who do not generally love Assemblies, would never call them, they would be laid aside; and when nothing Should depend upon the People's good will to Government, their Rights would be trampled on, they would be treated with Contempt. Another Reason why I think they would not be satisfy'd with such a partial repeal, is, that their Agreements not to import till the Repeal takes place, include the whole, which shows that they object to the whole; and those Agreements will continue binding on them if the whole is not repealed.

"3. Do you think the only effectual Way of composing the present Differences, is, to put the Americans precisely in the Situation they were in before the passing of the late Stamp Act?"

I think so.

"4. Your Reasons for that Opinion?"

Other Methods have been tryed. They have been rebuked in angry Letters. Their Petitions have been refused or rejected by Parliament. They have been threatened with the Punishments of Treason by Resolves of both Houses. Their Assemblies have been dissolv'd, and Troops have been sent among them; but all these Ways have only exasperated their Minds and widen'd the Breach; their Agreements to use no more British Manufactures have been Strengthen'd, and these Measures instead of composing Differences and promoting a good Correspondence, have almost annihilated your Commerce with those Countries, and greatly endanger'd the National Peace and general Welfare.

"5. If this last Method is deemed by the Legislature and his

Majisty's Ministers to be repugnant to their Duty as Guardians of the just Rights of the Crown, and of their Fellow Subjects, can you suggest any other Way of terminating these Disputes, consistent with the Ideas of Justice and propriety conceived by the Kings Subjects on both Sides the Atlantick?

A. I do not see how that Method can be deemed repugnant *to the Rights of the Crown*. If the Americans are put into their former Situation, it must be by an Act of Parliament, in the Passing of which by the King the Rights of the Crown are exercised not infringed. It is indifferent to the Crown whether the Aids received from America are Granted by Parliament here, or by the Assemblies there, provided the Quantum be the same; and it is my Opinion more will generally be Granted there Voluntarily than can ever be exacted and collected from thence by Authority of parliament. As to the rights of *Fellow Subjects* (I suppose you mean the People of Britain) I cannot conceive how they will be infringed by that method. They will still enjoy the Right of Granting their own money; and may still, if it pleases them, keep up their Claim to the Right of granting ours; a Right they can never exercise properly, for want of a sufficient Knowledge of us, our Circumstances and Abilities (to say nothing of the little likelihood there is that we should ever submit to it) therefore a Right that can be of no good use to them. And we shall continue to enjoy, *in fact*, the Right of granting our own Money; with the Opinion now universally prevailing among us that we are free Subjects of the King, and that *Fellow Subjects* of one Part of his Dominions are not Sovereign over *Fellow Subjects* in any other Part. If the Subjects on the different Sides of the Atlantic, have different and opposite Ideas of Justice or Propriety, no one Method can possibly be consistent with both. The best will be to let each enjoy their own Opinions, without disturbing them when they do not interfere with the common Good.

"6. And if this Method were actually followed do you not think it would encourage the Violent and Factious Part of the Colonists to aim at still farther Concessions from the Mother Country?"

A. I do not think it would. There may be a few among them that deserve the Name of factious and Violent, as there are in all Countries, but these would have little influence if the great Majority of Sober reasonable People were satisfy'd. If any Colony should happen to think that some of your regulations of Trade are inconvenient to the general Interest of the Empire, or prejudicial to them without being beneficial to you, they will state these Matters to the Parliament in Petitions as heretofore, but will, I believe, take no violent steps to obtain, what they may hope for in time from the Wisdom of Government here. I know of nothing else they can have in View. The Notion that prevails here of their being desirous of setting up a Kingdom or Common Wealth of their own, is to my certain Knowledge entirely groundless. I therefore think that on a total Repeal of all Duties laid expressly for the purpose of raising a Revenue on the People of America, without their Consent, the present Uneasiness would subside; the Agreements not to import would be dissolved, and the Commerce flourish as heretofore. And I am confirm'd in this Sentiment by all the Letters I have received from America, and by the Opinion of all the Sensible People who have lately come from thence, Crown Officers excepted. I know indeed that the people of Boston are grievously offended by the Quartering of Troops among them, as they think, contrary to Law; and are very angry with the Board of Commissioners to have calumniated them to Government; but as I suppose withdrawing of those Troops may be a Consequence of Reconciliating Measures taking Place; and that the Commission also will either be dissolv'd if found useless, or fill'd with more temperate and prudent Men if still deemed useful and necessary, I do not imagine these Particulars will prevent a return of the Harmony so much to be wished.

"7. If they are relieved in Part only, what [do] you, as a reasonable and dispassionate Man, and an equal Friend to both sides, imagine will be the probable Consequence?"

A. I imagine that repealing the offensive Duties in part will answer no End to this Country; the Commerce will remain obstructed, and the Americans go on with their Schemes of Frugality, Industry and Manufactures, to their own great Advantage. How much that may tend to the prejudice of Britain I cannot say; perhaps not so much as some apprehend, since she may in time find New Markets. But I think (if the Union of the two Countries continues to subsist) it will not hurt the *general* interest; for whatever Wealth Britain loses by the Failure of its Trade with the Colonies, America will gain; and the Crown will receive equal Aids from its Subjects upon the whole, if not greater.

And now I have answered your Questions as to what *may be* in my Opinion the Consequences of this or that *supposed* Measure, I will go a little farther, and tell you what I fear is more likely to come to pass *in Reality*.

I apprehend, that the Ministry, at least the American part of it, being fully persuaded of the Right of Parliament, think it ought to be enforc'd whatever may be the Consequences; and at the same time do not believe there is even now any Abatement of the Trade between the two Countries on account of these Disputes; or that if there is, it is small and cannot long Continue; they are assured by the Crown officers in America that Manufactures are impossible there; that the Discontented are few, and Persons of little Consequence; that almost all the People of Property and Importance are satisfyd, and disposed to submit quietly to the Taxing-Power of Parliament; and that if the Revenue Acts are continued, those Duties only that are called anti-commercial being repealed, and others perhaps laid in their stead, that Power will ere long be patiently submitted to, and the Agreements not to import be broken when they are found to produce no Change of Measures here. From these and similar Misinformations, which seem to be credited, I think it likely that no thorough redress of Grievances will be afforded to America this Session. This may inflame Matters still more in that Country; farther rash Measures there may create more Resentment here, that may Produce not merely ill-advis'd and useless Dissolutions of their Assemblies, as last Year; but Attempts to Dissolve their Constitutions; more Troops may be sent over, which will create more Uneasiness; to justify the Measures of Government your Ministerial Writers will revile the Americans in your Newspapers, as they have already began to do, treating them as Miscreants, Rogues, Dastards, Rebels, &c. which will tend farther to alienate the Minds of the People here from them, and diminish their Affections to this Country. Possibly too, some of their warm patriots may be distracted enough to expose themselves by some mad Action, to [be] sent for Hither, and Government here be indiscreet enough to Hang them on the Act of H. 8.[7] Mutual Provocations will thus go on to complete the Separation; and instead of that

7. 35 Hen. VIII, c. 2. In December, 1768, a resolution of the House of Lords had urged the King to proceed under this statute, if need be, against offenders in Massachusetts; and two months later the House of Commons had concurred. Gipson, *British Empire*, XI, 234–8.

cordial Affection that once and so long existed, and that Harmony so suitable to the Circumstances, and so Necessary to the Happiness, Strength Safety and Welfare of both Countries; an implacable Malice and Mutual Hatred, (such as we now see subsisting between the Spaniards and Portuguese, the Genoese and Corsicans,[8] from the same Original Misconduct in the Superior Government) will take place; the Sameness of Nation, the Similarity of Religion, Manners and Language not in the least Preventing in our Case, more than it did in theirs. I hope however that this may all prove false Prophecy: And that you and I may live to see as sincere and Perfect a friendship establish'd between our respective Countries as has so many years Subsisted between Mr. Strahan and his truly affectionate Friend   B. FRANKLIN

Copy

Endorsed: Copy BF's Answer to Mr Strahan's Letter

From John Bartram   ALS: American Philosophical Society

Dear worthy Friend   November the 29th 1769
   Yesterday I had the pleasure of takeing Mrs. Franklin by the hand in her own house as allso thy daughter and grandson a fine boy. Likewise thy sister from Boston all whome I expect at my house according to promise.[9] I have now before me thy dear affectionate letter of July the 9th 1769. My health and familys still continueth: (God allmight be praised and adored) I sent my Journal of No. and So. Carolina Georgia and florida to Peter Collinson who approved of it.[1] I dont doubt but Michal Collinson if thee desireth it would readyly lend it to thee and if thee should think it worth printing I have nothing against it with proper correction which I know thee is very capable to do.
   I have received doctor Fothergills and Michael Collinsons letters

8. For Portugal and Corsica see above, respectively, pp. 23 n and 18, headnote.
   9. For Sally's baby see DF to BF above, Aug. 31. Jane Mecom had recently arrived in Philadelphia after visiting WF and his family at Burlington. Van Doren, *Franklin–Mecom*, p. 111; DF to BF above under Nov. 20.
   1. See Bartram to BF above, April 10, 1769.

the latter declines haveing any thing to do in the seeds affair. The doctor recommends his nephew as a very honest person to supply our dear Peters place with relation to disposeing of the seeds and receiveing and remiting the money.[2] I have thoughts of giveing him orders for the same purpose if he pleas to accept it. This is one of the worst seed year I ever knowed the excesive dry summer [and] terible storm hath demolished most: I have collected what I could but cant assure them all to vegitate such as thay are I offer freely to my dear friend.

I have not any of that rhubarb growing of which thee kindly sent me a draught, if thee please to send me a few seeds it would much oblige thy sincear friend[3]   JOHN BARTRAM

I have a couple of Bull frogs in a Barrel with Colocasia roots[4] to Doctor Fothergill for the King. I wish thay may come safe and be the first.

Benjamin Franklin

Addressed: To | Mr Benjamin Franklin

From Seth Paddack[5] ALS: American Philosophical Society

Sir   London November: 29th: 1769

I arivd here The 15th Inst: from Nantucket and Being an Intimate acquaintance of Capt. Timo: Folger, he Put on Board a Quintal of Salted Cod fish Cured: Directed To You But The Letter was omited: and if youll Send a Line to me with an order on Board

2. Collinson's letter has not survived, but Dr. Fothergill's is printed in William Darlington, *Memorials of John Bartram and Humphry Marshall...* (Philadelphia, 1849), pp. 339–41. The Doctor's nephew, James Freeman, was a mercer, who was living in the house in Gracechurch Street that Peter Collinson had occupied.

3. The offer of seed and request for rhubarb were responses to BF's letter of July 9.

4. *Nelumbium luteum*, a rare water plant that grew in the Delaware below Philadelphia. Bartram was responding to a request that Dr. Fothergill had made of his cousin, Humphry Marshall, a year before; the Doctor had asked for roots rather than seeds because the latter germinated and then died. Darlington, *op. cit.*, pp. 497–8.

5. One of a large Nantucket clan, but which one we cannot say. The Paddacks (or Paddocks) and Folgers frequently intermarried, so that BF was related

The Yarmouth Laying off with Iron Gate or at Mrs. Fossick,[6] The Fish is at your Service: I am Sir with Respect your's To Serve.

SETH PADDACK

P S: The Reason I Gave you No Notice Before was: I Knew Capt. Folger Sent a Letter To Mrs. Stevenson and Perhaps might advise her of the above.

S P

Mr. Franklin

Addressed: To / Benjamin Franklin / Esqr. at Mrs Stevensons / Craven Street / London

From William Strahan

AL: American Philosophical Society

New Street Wednesday past 8 [November 29, 1769?[7]] Mr. Strahan presents his kindest Respects to Dr. Franklin, expected to have had the Pleasure of his Company to day to Dinner, and to have seen His Paper he knows of. If it is now done, he will please send it by the Bearer; if not, will be obliged to him to let him know when he may expect it.

Addressed: To / Dr. Franklin / at Mrs Stevenson's / Craven Street

---

to both families. Seth Paddack may well have been the relation who called on him in London in 1773 (Van Doren, *Franklin–Mecom*, p. 139), for he signed his last surviving letter to him, in 1777, "your most Effectianate Kinsman." During the French and Indian War, that letter makes clear, Paddack served as a naval officer; he then became a merchant captain, and during the War of Independence he was on a privateer in the Mediterranean. Paddack to BF, Aug. 2, 1777, APS.

6. The *Yarmouth*, of which Paddack was master, arrived at Dover from Boston: *Public Advertiser*, Nov. 14, 1769. She then sailed to London and anchored off Irongate Stairs, a wharf near the Tower. Samuel and Daniel Fossick, metalworkers, had shops on Cannon Street, also near the Tower. Henry B. Wheatley, *London Past and Present* . . . (3 vols., London, 1891), II, 263; *Kent's Directory* . . . (London, 1770), p. 67.

7. This note refers to a paper of BF's, perhaps not yet finished, which Strahan is eager to have at the earliest moment. The strong probability, we believe, is that that paper was BF's reply to his queries, printed above under Nov. 29, in which case it and this note may have crossed.

From James Parker   ALS: American Philosophical Society

[Woodbridge, N.J., November 30, 1769. Has taken the journey from New York in the hope that it would help his recovery from the gout. Just back from a trip by waggon to Burlington, where the Assembly is sitting, and finds on his return Franklin's letter of September 9 with its remarks about Mr. Robinson and Parker's office in the customs. Is resigning that office, and so informing the Commissioners within a few days. Has pressed Mr. Colden to send a bill, first by this packet and then, when he delayed, by the next one; Colden is considerably in arrears, and if he does nothing will deserve reproof. Will send Franklin another power of attorney, but cannot tell when, because he walks little and is carried almost every where he goes. Visited the Franklin family four days ago and found every one well.]

To Adolf Benzelius[8]   AL: University of Uppsala Library

Saturday Evening [November or December, 1769[9]]
Dr. Franklin presents his best Respects to Mr. Benzel, and will be glad to see him and his Friend[1] tomorrow morning at Eleven a

8. Adolf Benzelius or Benzelstierna (1715–75) came of a distinguished Swedish family; his father and grandfather were archbishops of Uppsala. He served in the Swedish, Hessian, and French armies before coming to America in 1749; three years later he married a Swedish-American, the daughter of the pastor of Holy Trinity Church, Wilmington. During the French and Indian War Benzelius was a lieutenant of engineers in a British regiment; he remained in America, apparently for the most part on a tract of land that he had surveyed for himself near Crown Point, until he returned to England early in 1769. Gustaf M. Elgenstierna, *Den introducerade svenska adelns ättartavlor med tilläggoch rättelser* (9 vols., Stockholm, [1925–36]), I, 302; Horace Burr, tr., *The Records of Holy Trinity (Old Swedes) Church*... ([Wilmington, Del.], 1890), p. 691; Carter, ed., *Gage Correspondence*, II, 498; *N.Y. Col. Docs.*, VIII, 140; *Board of Trade Jour.*, 1768–75, p. 200. Benzelius retired from the army in 1770, was appointed a surveyor of the royal forests in North America at £300 a year, and on this stipend settled down, according to one informant, to drink himself to death. G. D. Scull, ed., "The Montresor Journals...," N.-Y. Hist. Soc. *Collections*, XIV (1882), 135; *Johnson Papers*, VII, 946; VIII, 209–10.
9. So dated from information furnished by Dr. Åke Davidsson, Keeper of Manuscripts in the University of Uppsala Library.
1. This was Johan Henrik Lidén (1741–93), a Swedish literary historian who

Clock, if that time will suit them, and they think fit to do him the Honour of a Visit in Craven street.

Addressed: To / Mr Benzel / at Mrs Philips's / Jeweller. / St Martin's Court

From the New Jersey Assembly Committee of Correspondence
LS: American Philosophical Society

Sir   Burlington Decemr. 7th. 1769

The House of Representatives of this Colony on the 8th of last mo. unanimously chose you their Agent in London and appointed us to correspond with you on the affairs of the Colony.[2] The Resolve of the House by which you are appointed Agent, his Excellency will transmit to you properly attested.

To a Gentleman whose inclination to serve these Colonies, we believe equal to his knowledge of their true Interests much need not be said to induce an attention to American concerns, in the ensuing Sessions of Parliament; and the confidence the House have in the assurances of his Majestys Ministers, that they will use their endeavours for the Repeal of the Revenue Acts,[3] and that those endeavours will be successful, renders any particular direction to you on this head unnecessary, but we cou'd wish his Majesty's faithful American Subjects to stand in their true point of light before him, that no doubt may remain of their Loyalty and firm attachment to his Royal Person and Government.

We are directed by the House to desire you will apply to the

---

was visiting England during a tour of the continent; he subsequently published the correspondence between Benzelius' father and uncle. *Svenska män och kvinnor, biografisk uppslagsbok* (8 vols., Stockholm, 1942–55) IV, 557–8. For the identification of Lidén we are also indebted to Dr. Davidsson.

2. BF was succeeding a London solicitor, Henry Wilmot, who was secretary to Lord Chancellor Camden, and agent for the Penn family and the East Jersey Proprietors, and had been agent for the New Jersey Assembly since 1766. The Assembly had been inveigled into appointing him, and soon afterward WF had asked BF if he knew of anyone better; in 1767 Wilmot had increased his unpopularity by doing nothing. See above, XIII, 498; XIV, 176; *Votes, N.J.* (Oct.–Dec., 1769), p. 47.

3. For the New Jersey petition against the Townshend Acts see 1 *N.J. Arch.*, X, 18–21.

proper Offices, and sollicit his Majesty's Assent to the Bill for Septennial Election of Representatives, and the Bill for giving the Counties of Morris, Cumberland and Sussex a right to choose Representatives in Assembly, transmitted in 1768, the Province is very sollicitous for a confirmation of these Laws,[4] and we must desire you will use your influence to Obtain the Royal Assent to them as soon as possible, another Bill in 1765 was transmitted for amending of the practice of the Law, which the House woud rather choose shoud not have the Royal Assent, as a Bill they like better has been passed by the House this Session, which, altho' the Governor coud not pass, yet he has, upon a message from the House, promised to ask his Majestys Permission to give his Assent at a future session.[5]

His Excellency our Governor will transmit for his Majestys Royal approbation, An Act of Assembly, passd this Session, for making current One hundred thousand pounds in Bills of Credit, to be let on Loan at five per Cent, the particular distress of this Province for want of a Currency, and the little prospect of being able to obtain a Bill very soon, to make the Bills a legal tender, was what induced the Assembly to comply with this method; and, as the funds for the redemption of the Bills are good beyond a doubt, we are under no apprehension of any difficulty, as to the Bills obtaining a Credit and passing in lieu of money. We refer to the preamble to the Bill, and to your own knowledge of the propriety of the measure and it gives us particular pleasure to entrust to your care a matter, so generally desird by the People of this Colony, because you so well understand the subject, and can so readily answer any objections that may be made against it.[6]

4. For the two acts mentioned see *ibid.*, p. 142; XVII, 478, 497–8; *Votes, N.J.* (April–May, 1768), p. 13; *Board of Trade Jour.*, 1768–1775, p. 203; *Acts Privy Coun., Col.* v, 283–4.

5. The Assembly was attempting to reduce high fees and costs in debtors' suits. The bill passed in 1765 was disallowed in 1770. That passed in 1769 had no clause for suspending its operation until royal assent was given; hence WF refused to approve it until the crown permitted him to do so. Early in 1770, however, riots by debtors and other violence forced his hand, and a similar bill was enacted. *Votes, N.J.* (May–June, 1765), p. 74; (Oct.–Dec., 1769), pp. 54, 76, 83, 87, 89; (March, 1770), pp. 5, 6, 23; 1 *N.J. Arch.*, XVII, 430, 435; XVIII, 101–2, 170; *Board of Trade Jour.*, 1768–75, p. 203; *Acts Privy Coun., Col.*, v, 284; Edgar J. Fisher, *New Jersey as a Royal Province, 1738 to 1776* (New York, 1911), pp. 256–62.

6. This bill was one of many colonial expedients to provide a much-needed

The House have orderd a sum of money to pay the expence that may attend the getting of the Royal Assent to these Bills, and we inclose a Bill of Exchange for two hundred pounds sterling for that purpose.

The House have also pass'd a Bill for lending a sum of money to the General Proprietary of the Eastern Division of this Province, and have by a Message to the Governor inform'd him, that they woud direct their Agent by a Memorial to support the claim of this Colony before his Majesty in Council.[7] You will, from the Agents appointed by Law to manage the controversy between the Colonies, receive a state of the controversy, and every paper necessary for you to inspect before drawing your Memorial. The House have therefore directed us to inform you, that the principal motives of the House for your application to his Majesty are

1st. That Justice may be done to individuals, as well as the Colony in general, and altho' the House does not pretend to direct where the said Line ought to be fixed, yet, as the settlement of said Line will in its consequences affect the Colony very sensibly, especially shoud any station be fixed Southward of the line solemnly settled in the Year 1719, in consequence of which great numbers of people settled up to said Line, and have ever since done Duty and paid their Taxes in this Government, should that Line be alterd and brought Southward, many honest and *bona fide* purchasers will be involvd in ruin, unless his Majesty shoud think proper to interpose.

2. The Injustice to this Colony will appear very great, when its consider'd that the line of 1719 has constantly been deem'd the Line of Division between the Governments, and the Settlers and lands up to that line have ever been estimated in the Taxes; hence, shoud the line be removd Southward this Colony that has incurrd a Debt of one hundred and ninety thousand pounds in the late war, yet undischargd will be deprivd of the aid of valuable Settlements in paying off this Debt, and the Burthen increasd on the remainder of the Colony. From this Sketch of the Sentiments of the House, and the

currency within the limits of the Currency Act. Despite BF's efforts the Board of Trade, in the following spring, recommended disallowing the provincial bill: *Board of Trade Jour.*, 1768–75, p. 184.

7. For the complicated boundary dispute between New Jersey and New York see above, XIV, 196–201; *Votes, N.J.* (Oct.–Dec., 1769), pp. 49, 58–9, 88; 1 *N.J. Arch.*, XVIII, 102–4; Fisher, *op. cit.*, pp. 210–39.

papers that will be laid before you by the Agents appointed by Law to manage the Controversy between the Colonies, you will be able to frame a memorial to his Majesty, but as no appeal is yet made and only threatend, no application from you to his Majesty will be necessary untill such appeal is actually made by the Agents for New York. We are, Sir, with great Sincerity and respect Your humble servants[8]

> CORTD. SKINNER
> AARON LEAMING
> ABRM. HEWLINGS
> HENRY PAXSON
> EBENEZ MILLER
> JOSEPH SMITH.

P.S. When you write by way of New York please to direct to Cortland Skinner Esqr. Speaker of the Assembly of New Jersey and by way of Philada. to Abraham Hewlings or Jos: Smith Esqrs at Burlington.

Bill inclosd Garrat and Geo Meade on James Dormer Esq[9]

Endorsed: Committee of N Jersey Assembly Dec 7. 1769.

8. For Cortlandt Skinner, Speaker of the Assembly, see above, XIII, 335 n. The other representatives who signed the letter were Aaron Leaming, Jr. (Cape May County); Abraham Hewlings (town of Burlington), the president of the West Jersey Proprietors; Henry Paxson (Burlington County); Ebenezer Miller (1702–74; Salem County), a Quaker and surveyor; and Joseph Smith (town of Burlington), another Quaker. Smith (1742–1822) acted as secretary of the committee; see his letter to BF below, Dec. 19. He was the son of Samuel Smith, the historian of New Jersey, and had been a member of the Assembly for less than two months; he served until the end of 1771. He subsequently succeeded his father as treasurer of the West Jersey Proprietors. Two other committee members did not sign: Hendrick Fisher (1697–1779; Somerset County) and John Wetherill (Middlesex County). See 1 *N.J. Arch.*, XVIII, 37, 519, 537; XIX, 390–4; Fisher, *op. cit.*, pp. 84–100; and in addition, for Smith, Evan M. Woodward and John F. Hageman, *History of Burlington and Mercer Counties, New Jersey . . .* (Philadelphia, 1883); p. 171; William W. Hinshaw, *Encyclopedia of American Quaker Genealogy* (6 vols., Ann Arbor, Mich., 1936–50), II, 184, 203; N.J. Hist. Soc. *Proc.*, V (1851), 23, 32.

9. Garrat and George Meade were brothers and partners in a Philadelphia mercantile firm; see *DAB* under George Meade. James Dormer was a London merchant with offices in Throgmorton Street: *Kent's Directory . . .* (London, 1770), p. 55.

From Nevil Maskelyne   ALS:[1] American Philosophical Society

[Greenwich, December 11, 1769. The Astronomer Royal asks Franklin, when he next writes to Philadelphia, to inquire of Owen Biddle about the exact distances between the observation points for the transit of Venus. Maskelyne cannot make Biddle's two accounts agree with each other, or with the distances given by Mason and Dixon in their survey.[2] He is also uncertain about the exact location of the Norriton observatory in relation to the southernmost point of the city of Philadelphia, and wants more exact data. The Pennsylvania observers will likewise send him, he hopes, their observations on the transit of Mercury on November 9, 1769, along with any other observations that will help to establish the difference of longitudes.[3]

He cannot, until his questions are answered, transmit Biddle's report to the Royal Society.[4] He has transmitted the report from John Winthrop that Franklin sent him, and also Winthrop's observation of the transit of Mercury in 1743, which had been read to the Society but for some reason was not yet in print.[5]]

1. The letter is so badly mutilated that even the gist of some passages cannot be conjectured. An abridged version, which omits most of these passages, is in APS *Trans.*, I (1771), 90. Maskelyne repeated much of what he asked in this letter, but without the technical details, in his note to BF below, Dec. 27.

2. For this famous survey, which precisely located points near Philadelphia, see above, XII, 341 and the references there given. Precision was necessary to calculate the times and angles by which the sun's distance from the earth might be determined.

3. William Smith reported on the location of Norriton in APS *Trans.*, I, app., 5–11, but this report does not seem to have reached the Royal Society; Smith, Biddle, and their colleagues reported on the transit of Mercury in *ibid.*, app., pp. 50–4, and their observations also appeared in *Phil. Trans.*, LX (1771), 504–7.

4. He changed his mind, as indicated by his note to BF below, Dec. 27. Biddle's first account was read before the Royal Society and printed, with Maskelyne's comments, in *Phil. Trans.*, LIX (1770), 414–21. Biddle's corrected account appeared in APS *Trans.*, I, 89–96, but like Smith's report on Norriton did not, apparently, reach the Royal Society.

5. The report from Winthrop on his own observations of the transit of Venus, rather than his query above about earlier observations, Sept. 6. The report was in the form of a letter to Maskelyne, who must have forwarded it some weeks earlier, because it was read on Dec. 7; it was subsequently printed in *Phil. Trans.*, LIX (1770), 351–8. Winthrop's observations of the transit of

From Jeremiah Miller

ALS: American Philosophical Society

Much respected Sir,   New London 11 Decemr. 1769.

It is not a want of the higest regard and Esteem for you (an old Friend and Auquaintance of my Dear Fathers[6]) that is the Cause of my not troubling you with a line, but your Correspondence and Connections with the greatest men and Geniuses of the present age; and the Sense I have of your Superiour Merrit, which Induces me to think any literary Efforts of mine would be Impertinent.

Duty now Excites me (if you are not auquainted with it) to thank you on my Sons Behalf who is now in the Post Office in this Town; on Mr. Chews throwing it up, he was much urged by Most of the Gentlemen in Town to take the Care of it upon him,[7] (if agreable to Mr. Foxcroft) and as I knew he had quite enough in the writing way on his hands, I advised him not to undertake it; but as he has done it, if agreable to you and Mr. Foxcroft would have him Continue therein, but as there is Considerable writing necessary to keep the accounts regular, and the Office rent and Fire wood &c Costs at Least £5 per annum, and the whole Profitts but about £20 per annum, whether you would not think it reasonable the Comptroller should alow him that Charge; Especially as its Impossible to avoid trusting Out the Letters Quarterly, which money can never be Seasonably Enough Collected to Pay the Post, and this he advances punctually, and I hope his Conduct will be to acceptance. I have sent two Pamphlets to Dr. Johnson on the Susquehanah disputes,[8]

Mercury in 1743 were not reported until twenty years later, were read on Nov. 10, 1763, and were not printed until 1770: *ibid.*, pp. 505–6.

6. The younger Jeremiah Miller succeeded his father, who died in 1756, as naval officer at New London; see above, XII, 238 n.

7. For the troubles of Joseph Chew, who was removed as New London postmaster in 1769, see Parker to BF above, June 18, and the references there cited. Miller's son, John Still Miller, did replace Chew and proved to be an excellent choice. See *Journal Kept by Hugh Finlay . . .* (Brooklyn, 1867), pp. 34–5.

8. William S. Johnson (1727–1819; hon. LL.D., Oxon., 1766) was in London as agent for Connecticut and the Susquehannah Co.; he was the son of the Rev. Samuel Johnson, BF's old friend and the President of King's College (now Columbia). *DAB*. The pamphlets that Miller sent him were presumably Benjamin Gale, *Doctor Gale's Letter to J.W., Esquire . . .* (Hartford, 1769), and Eliphalet Dyer, *Remarks on Dr. Gale's Letter to J.W., Esq.* ([Hartford], 1769), both of which are reprinted in Julian P. Boyd et al., eds., *The Susquehannah Company Papers* (9 vols. to date, Wilkes-Barre, Pa. and Ithaca, N.Y., 1930—),

and herewith Inclose you a Petition printed with types made in this Colony, they are not correct for want of proper [*in margin:* verte] Conveniency which the Inventor Expects to get as the Assembly have lent him some money to Carry it on.[9] It would be a pleasure I could wish, to be able to furnish you with any American Matters that were new or Entertaining; the most of which we talk of, or know, is Transported from one End of the Continent to the Other, in the News Papers there are things you have a thorough knowledge of, (American Greiveances) and I beleive theres no American whose heart has not a most gratefull Sense of your Assiduity and Important Services in this Critical Era. That the Almighty may reward you with Unceassing Felicity hereafter is the real wish of your Most Obliged and Affectionate Humble Servant

JER. MILLER

P.S. Should have returned my thanks to Mr. Foxcroft (to whome I am unknown) for my Son, but soon after he received his Deputation I heard Mr. Foxcroft went to Maryland and thence to England, may I be allowed to do it by you. I am with Supra

To Benjamin Franklin Esqr

Endorsed: Mr Miller New London, Decemr 11. 1769

From [Joseph Chew]

AL (incomplete): American Philosophical Society

Dear Sir   New London Decr. 12th. 1769
    Having wrote you so many Letters without being Favoured with an Answer, I should not now have presumed to trouble you, was their not some Dispute or Reather Misunderstanding between Mr. Parker and me about the settlement of my Post office Accounts.[1]
    In the years 1755 and 1756 agreable to your directions their was a

---

III, 224–68. BF was interested in the Company because it challenged the vested interests of the Penn family; see above, X, 420–2.

9. Abel Buell petitioned the Connecticut General Assembly to support his projected type-foundry; he received £100 but did not make good use of it. *DAB.*

1. See the preceding document.

Cross Post from New London to Hartford Middletown &c, all the Letters Brought by this Post was Received into the Post Office and Every advantage by it went to the Emolument of the General Post office, I paid the Rider and never directly or indirectly had one Farthing allowed me for it.

The multiplicity of Bussiness and affairs that I transacted during the war, not only hinder'd me from having my Post office Accounts made out in due time (as you know) but prevented my looking into and taking that Care of my own Bussiness I ought to have done which has since Occasioned my having many Mallonchaly hours, together with the most Cruel and severe Reflections. To the above mentioned Cause it was owing that I omitted Charging the General Post office with the money paid the Hartford Rider as well as the Expence of Books (which were more to me then to many larger Offices as I the whole time I keep the Office followed the Instructoins by Entring every mans name who Recieved a Letter or who one Came for which may now be seen by the Books) and money paid the printers in this town for post masters bills &c. When I settled the General Account with you in Octr. 1763, I never had but one Book from the General post office which was in Octr. 1765 and Great part of the time was without post masters Bills they being omitted by Mr. Parker owing I suppose to his hurry of Bussiness. Mr. Parker says he never was allowed anything for what he paid Brooker for Riding from New Haven to Hartford. I don't think it a similar Case, Brooker was I suppose imploy'd by him to Carry his papers at least he made use of him for that purpose, and perhaps his imployments have been such in the post office that he Can afford to loose something, which mine never were on the Contrary I lost a great deal of money which I Could make appear to you if had the pleasure of seing you.

However I have no Inclynation or will I Enter into any dispute with Mr. Parker about this affair but will leave it intirely to you sir and Can safely say I want and desire no more then the money I have paid out of my Pocket which I omitted to Charge in my Account when I made the General Settlement and for which I was Very Negligent.

Mr. Foxcroft says the Transaction was before his time and that he was Content to leave it to be settled by you to which I most Readily Consented being well assured you never in your Life de-

sired any Person Employ'd under you to pay money for the publick
service out of his own Pocket or was it Ever your Principle to take
advantage of a Mistake or Omission in an Account.

To the Best of my memory I mentioned this matter to you in the
year 1764 at your house in Phila. but as I had omitted to take the
Account with me from N London nothing Could be done without
it and as the Balance on my two Quarters Accounts were so small I
then paid them to you soon after my Return to New London. Before I had Occasion to send my Next Account you went to England
and so the matter has lain untill the time I quitted the post office, and
I have delayed troubling you as I was told by my good friend the
Governor of the Jerseys that you Expected to be at home last
Spring. There is as the Matter now stands a Balance due from me
to the General post office if my Account of the money paid as above
is allow'd there will be one due to me, which my unfortunute situation will make Very Acceptable—be it more or Less when I Remit-
ted you the Money from N Y [*torn*] which you lent me at Philadelphia there was a [*torn*] over which with a Little Left in your
hands [*torn*] 36s. Pensilvania Currency. I then askt the Favor of you
to [*torn*] to send for a pair of Cast steel Razors and a Little [*torn*]
shaving Powder for me. This I immagine the [*torn*] affairs you have
had on hand has Occasioned to slip your Memmory, if it is not two
Much trouble I should be particularly Oblidged to you for the
Razors and if the money Comes to more a Very Neat good strong
knive of two Blades, and two pair of scizars for my Little woman
and Daughter both of whome desire me to give their sincere Respects and best Compliments to you.

The Rhubbarb seed you were so kind as to give me Flourishes
Extreemly well. I wish I knew the proper season for Digging and
Curing of it. I send you a small piece by Capt. Cummins which was
taken up about the first of November last, dipt in Boiling water the
outside Bark or skin pealed of and then hung up in a Dry warm
place I have put a few seeds with [*remainder too badly torn to be
intelligible*]

Endorsed: Dec. 12. 1769 answer'd by Mr Babcock[2]

2. Undoubtedly Luke Babcock, former New Haven postmaster, who was
then in England for Anglican ordination; see above, IX, 397 n.

From Deborah Franklin ALS: American Philosophical Society

My Dear child   Desember the 13 1769
  this day mr. Foxcrofte[3] tells me that this poste is to take the letters in the 2d packites which I did not get my letter that I ansers your qustons I can only say that I had not one line in the Ocktober packit nor have not heard only mr. Comes[4] that he heard that you was well in ocktober for wich I was verey glad.

  I am to tell you that I am much better then I was when I wrote to you the laste letter I Can find my self Stronger and my culler and look as yous all [usual]. Sister is verey a greabel to me and makes everey thing verey plesant to me and we air as hapey as we Cold expeckte to as in your absenes[5] but we hope you will be as soon in the Spring. You asked me who Cumes to see us as to nabors. I muste tell you that verey few Cumes to see us my verey kind Nabor Thomson has bin gon ever senes the begining of the summer and my worthey mrs. Thomson has labered under a verey maloncoley disordor[6] so as not to be abel to take aney notes of her famely nor aney thing but yit I mis her verey much I loved her much indead the youngest of the Cliftons is all moste Dead.[7] Salley is with her Sister shee is thair now I beleve shee donte know the packit sailes so soon shee sed shee shold write. Our Dear king bird[8] is verey well he is seting by me and is as fine a dear Lad and sendes his Dutey to you and his allso to good mrs. Stephenson and miss Polley my beste Compley mentes to Sir John Pringill for his goodness for his advise to me[9] (if you thinke it proper) the poste cume in the night and I am up to finish this nobodey but my Dear Benj

3. For Thomas Foxcroft, the Philadelphia postmaster and brother of BF's colleague John, see above, XII, 77 n.
   4. Presumably by a letter from Thomas Coombe, then in London for ordination, to his father of the same name (c. 1721–99) in Philadelphia.
   5. For Jane Mecom's visit see DF to BF above under Nov. 20.
   6. Charles Thomson had been busy with the APS observations of Venus and the nonimportation movement. The illness of his wife, Ruth Mather Thomson, soon proved fatal. *DAB*.
   7. Probably a child of DF's and BF's old friends, John and Eleanor Clifton, and a sibling of Anna Maria Clifton, for whom see *PMHB*, XXXIX (1915), 320–1. Anna Maria later corresponded with BF in France.
   8. The four-month old baby, Benjamin Franklin Bache.
   9. See DF to BF above under Nov. 20.

Franklin with me. Sister desiers her Love to you. I am your Afeck-shon Wife

D FRANKLIN

Desembe the 14

Addressed: To / Benjamin Franklin Esqr / Craven Street / London

Bond: William and Mary Catharine Goddard[1] to Benjamin Franklin

Printed form with MS insertions: Historical Society of Pennsylvania

[Dated December 15, 1769. A bond in the sum of one hundred and twenty pounds, Pennsylvania currency, to be paid to Franklin or his attorney, heirs, assigns, etc. If a payment of sixty pounds, plus interest, is made on June 15, 1770, the bond will be void; otherwise it will remain in force.[2]]

1. For William Goddard, printer and journalist, see above, XII, 287 n; XIV, 9 n. Mary Katherine Goddard (1738–1816) was his sister; she had learned the printing trade in his Providence shop and had, with her mother, joined him in Philadelphia in 1768.

2. Goddard had been postmaster at Providence, and his biographer conjectures that the bond represented a debt he owed the Post Office, despite the fact that BF left the unpaid bond in his will to Richard Bache. Ward L. Miner, *William Goddard, Newspaperman* (Durham, N.C., 1962), pp. 91–2. An obligation to the royal Post Office could scarcely have been treated as a legacy in 1790; in BF's last years, furthermore, both he and Goddard wrote of it as if it were a private debt. Goddard to David Lenox, Jan. 23, 1787, Hist. Soc. of Pa.; BF to Goddard, Jan. 6, 1789, APS. Our conjecture is that the bond had something to do with the murky financial affairs of Benjamin Mecom. A complete inventory of Mecom's printing equipment was sent to BF in London, for the benefit of creditors there; and Goddard was subsequently involved in evaluating some of this equipment. James Parker to Goddard, June 16, 1770, Hist. Soc. of Pa. The letter is tantalizingly obscure, but it raises the possibility that Goddard had acquired at least part of the equipment he needed by giving this bond to BF six months earlier.

From James Parker   ALS: American Philosophical Society

[New York, December 16, 1769. Crept back from Woodbridge two days ago, in order to send by packet anything of interest. Mr. Colden has applied for a bill for £200, which was promised him today; but he was disappointed because Mr. Watts, who signs the bills together with Mr. McEvers, was out of town.[3] Will send the bill by Captain Davis, eight or ten days hence; will also send a new power of attorney, witnessed by Davis,[4] so that Franklin can get Parker's wages and reimburse himself for whatever he has paid or may pay on the other's account. Weather is bad. Continues to creep about but thinks he grows stronger. Has received nothing of consequence on the Post Office accounts since he last wrote.]

From Joseph Smith[5]   ALS: American Philosophical Society

[Burlington, December 19, 1769. Encloses a copy of the letter from the New Jersey Assembly Committee of Correspondence; the original was sent by way of Bristol. Also encloses a second bill for £200, Garrat and George Meade on James Dormer.]

3. Colden wrote Parker a note of explanation, dated Thursday (*i.e.*, Dec. 14) and saying that he expected the bill the next day. Franklin Papers, APS. Mr. Watts was unquestionably John Watts (1715–89), one of the wealthiest landed proprietors of the province, for many years a representative of New York City in the Assembly, and subsequently a member of the Provincial Council; he had in the past had numerous business dealings with Parker. James G. Wilson and John Fiske, eds., *Appleton's Cyclopaedia of American Biography* . . . (rev. ed., 7 vols., New York, 1899–1900), VI, 395; *Letter Book of John Watts, Merchant and Councillor of New York, January 1, 1762–December 22, 1765*, N.-Y. Hist. Soc. *Collections*, LXI (New York, 1928), 256–7, 269, 272. Mr. McEvers was in all probability Charles McEvers (1739?–1808), who succeeded to his brother's importing business on the latter's death in 1768. See John A. Stevens, ed., *Colonial Records of the New York Chamber of Commerce, 1768–1784* (New York, 1867), pt. 2, p. 149.

4. Benjamin Davies, the master of the *Hope*, for whom see Parker to BF above, July 22. Davies sailed for London on Dec. 24: Gaine's *N.-Y. Gaz.*, Dec. 25, 1769.

5. For Smith, and the letter and bill he enclosed, see N.J. Assembly Committee of Correspondence to BF above, Dec. 7.

From Richard Stockton[6]

LS: American Philosophical Society

Dear Sir   Princeton Decr. 22. 1769

You will give me leave to congratulate you or at least the province of New Jersey, upon your late appointment to be our Agent also.[7] Such an event cannot fail of promoting the best interests of the Colony, while it may suit you to remain on the other side of the water; and even after you retire to your native country (if that should ever happen) the connection thus formed, I doubt not, will be of service to us. The object I confess is very inconsiderable in point of advantage to yourself, but I hope the prospect of advancing the good of the Province, will not withstanding induce you to accept it. Upon this presumption, I must take the liberty of begging your particular attention to an Act of Assembly which passed in our late Sessions, intitled "A Supplementary Act to an Act entituled An Act appointing Commissioners for finally settling and determining the several rights, titles and claims to the Common Lands of the Township of Bergen, and for making partition thereof in just and equitable proportions among those who shall be adjudged by the said Commissioners to be intitled to the same."[8] You will have this, no doubt, with the other Acts, sent over to you, as soon as printed, with the Assembly's directions to sollicit the royal allowance of such as require it, before they can have operation: but this Act having no suspending clause, you will not advert to the necessity of solliciting it, unless you are informed of the particular circumstances with which it is attended; whereof the Committee of Correspondence, may not perhaps sufficiently advise you. The several branches of the Legislature have the Bill much at heart, as being very necessary and important; and the Governor, with my Brethren of the Council agree in the propriety of my furnishing you with all the

6. An attorney and member of the New Jersey Council, for whom see above, XII, 78 n.

7. See New Jersey Assembly Committee of Correspondence to BF above, Dec. 7, 1769.

8. The initial act appointing commissioners was passed in 1763, and the supplementary act on Nov. 16, 1769; the latter was disallowed by the Privy Council on June 6, 1770. Ownership of the Bergen lands was not finally settled until after the passage of a New Jersey statute in 1784. Charles H. Winfield, *History of the Land Titles in Hudson County, N.J., 1609–1871* (New York, 1872), pp. 18–24, 285–8; 1 *N.J. Arch.*, X, 152 n.

information in my power. You must know then, Sir, that the Freeholders of the Township of Bergen in East Jersey, in the year 1668
having been incorporated, and a much greater quantity of land included within the bounds of the Corporation than had been before
granted or patented; all such excess was by the Charter directed to
be divided among the Freeholders (patentees) in proportion to
their allotments; that is, every person who before the Charter had
become a Freeholder, within the bounds of the Corporation, and
owned patented lands, should, in proportion to such patented lands,
share in the other lands, now included within the said Corporation
which excess or other lands, were and still are called the Commons
of Bergen. In process of time, it became very difficult, and finally
impossible, to make the Allotments and Dividends of the Common
Lands to the various persons who became Freeholders; which induced them in the year 1763 to apply to the Legislature for an Act
for that purpose. A certified Copy of the petition exhibited on that
occasion, I send you herewith; from which you'll see the state of
this matter more fully. An Act was obtained, and the Commissioners therein appointed, proceeded to determine the right and
make partition of the Common Lands among the owners; and did
settle the whole thereof, excepting the Commons belonging to a
certain tract within the Township called *Sekakus*—in this single
instance, the Commissioners being equally divided in opinion (only
six attending) no determination could be had. This made it necessary, in order to carry the design of the Act into execution, to obtain the Supplementary Act now recommended to your care. It
would seem strange that any of the Freeholders, who petitioned
for the first Act, should have opposed the Supplementary Act—
but so it is, that Mr. William Bayard a considerable Merchant of
New York and Freeholder of Bergen,[9] whose name appears at the
head of the petitioners, and by whose zeal and sollicitation, principally, the first Act was obtained having by the determination of the
Commissioners under that Act recovered his full proportion of
Common Lands for all the patented lands he holds; and very justly
apprehending that no future Commissioners would allow him any
portion of Common Lands belonging to the patented lands of Sekakus (his Ancestor having sold and conveyed all his right to that
tract in the year 1676) petitioned against and violently opposed the

9. For Col. William Bayard see above, XV, 125 n.

passing of this Supplementary Act:[1] alledging that it was proper to have a trial at Law upon the operation of his Ancestor's Deed; that it might be determined [?] as a legal question, whether by the words thereof it did or did not convey the proportion of Common Lands which belonged to Sekakus; all of which is patented land, and which (quoad[2] the patented Lands) he agrees did pass by this same Deed; but denies that the Commons thereunto belonging did pass. One principal design of the Legislature in passing the first Act was to put a stop to the Law-Suits which had been agitated for thirty or forty years before, about these lands (very much you'll suppose to the loss of the inhabitants) and no sooner had the Commissioners finished what they could do, but suits were immediately recommenced respecting Sekakus, which they had unhappily left undetermined, for the prevention whereof, and that the most equitable and just determination upon the rights to the only remaining Tract might be had, this Supplementary Act was passed.

My Interest as a practising Lawyer is opposed to the Bill; but my duty as a member of the Legislature makes it proper for me to urge its establishment. Opposition from Mr. Bayard certainly comes with a very ill grace: for he not only was a principal in obtaining the first Act; but, upon the Commissioners having, in one instance, determined against Captn. Kennedy, and it seems offended him (by judging for themselves) in such a manner that he made representations to the Board of Trade against the Act, and the Governor, for having passed it, without a suspending clause;[3] Mr. Bayard very properly stood forth on this occasion, as Captn. Kennedy's Antagonist, and used his utmost influence on your side the water to preserve the Bill; alledging it was a most important and necessary Act, and that it might well have been passed without a suspending clause, as it was, in fact, not a *private* but *public* Bill, and affected the peace and interest of the whole province. You may perhaps recollect something of this last transaction, as I presume the Governor wrote you at that time upon the occasion; and if necessary, I presume you may be able to furnish yourself with the papers he sent over.

1. For Bayard's petition to the Board of Trade see 1 *N.J. Arch.*, x, 168–72.
2. As to.
3. For Capt. Archibald Kennedy, R.N., a large landowner in New Jersey, see above, xiv, 293n; for documents relating to his complaint see 1 *N.J. Arch.*, IX, 459–75.

My letter is swelling to an undue extent, and yet all the facts which peradventure may be expedient for you to be acquainted with have not been mentioned: but upon a perusal of the former Bill; of the Supplementary Act, when it shall come to your hands; and other papers perhaps in your own hands and the plantation office; together with the Copy of the petition herewith sent, and this letter, I hope you will have facts sufficient to defeat any attempts which Mr. Bayard may make against the Bill. He is now in England—went over as he pretended, to sollicit an Adjudication of the King and Council against the late determination of the Commissioners respecting the New Jersey and New York line:[4] but it is not doubted will, at the same time use every method in his power to get this Supplementary Act condemned.

The Council advised the Governor to pass the present Act without a suspending clause, as it was only supplementary, and the original Bill had no such clause: yet they thought it proper to give Mr. Bayard full opportunity of spending his fire against it; and therefore by a Clause which *they* added, the Act is not to take effect till some time next September, if I recollect right. It is probable I think that all the noise Mr. Bayard may make about it, will not induce the Lords of Trade to take the Bill into consideration, as it is only to carry into execution what remained to be done under the former Act: but if he should, I must beg you'll please to take it very particularly under your protection, and if any extra expence shall attend your care in opposing Mr. Bayard, I engage in behalf of the proprietors of Sekakus to make full compensation.

Mrs. Stockton[5] remembers you with great respect, and desires me to present her compliments. I am, with much esteem, Dear Sir Your most obedient and very humble Servant

RICHD STOCKTON

B. Franklin Esqr;

Endorsed: Mr Stockton Dec. 22. 1769

4. The recent fixing of the boundary by a royal commission had dissatisfied both colonies; see above, XIV, 196–7.

5. Annis Boudinot Stockton, the daughter of BF's former neighbor, Elias Boudinot. See above, X, 174 n.

From James Parker   ALS: American Philosophical Society

[Woodbridge, December 23, 1769. Has crept back here to print the
New Jersey laws.[6] The enclosures will show (1) why the bill of exchange that Colden had promised is not sent; and (2) that Franklin
has power of attorney, witnessed by the captain and mate of the
ship, to recover the wages due Parker.[7] Has written the Board of
Customs Commissioners at Boston to resign from the customs
house, and expects his wages only until January 6. His strength
is somewhat recovered, but the weather is bitter cold; unless it
warms the Delaware will soon be frozen.]

From James Parker   ALS: American Philosophical Society

[Woodbridge, N.J., December 26, 1769. Had intended this to go
by Captain Davis, but he sailed before it reached New York. Has
received since then the enclosed bill from Mr. Colden for £200,
drawn by Watts and McEvers on Harley & Drummond,[8] "cost 65
per Cent the Exchange at this Time."]

From Nevil Maskelyne   ALS: American Philosophical Society

Dear Sir,   Greenwich Dec. 27th. 1769
    I think I desired the favor of you lately by letter, that when you
wrote to Philadelphia you would desire Mr. Owen Biddle and Mr.
Joel Bayley to take the trouble to determine the difference of
meridians of Philadelphia and Norriton, in order to connect all the
observations made by the three setts of observers together.[9] I
should be glad if you would also desire of your correspondents to

6. Since 1758 Parker had been the province's official printer.
    7. For these two matters see Parker to BF above, Dec. 16. The note from
Colden, mentioned there in a footnote, was presumably one of the enclosures
in this letter, because it is endorsed in an unidentified hand "J. Parker Dec. 23.
1769."
    8. John Drummond (1723–74), of Drummond's Bank, and the Hon.
Thomas Harley (1730–1804) were contractors for remitting money to the
army in America. Namier and Brooke, *House of Commons*, II, 343–4, 586–7. For
Capt. Davies and Colden's financial affairs see Parker to BF above, July 22,
Oct. 5–9, Nov. 30, and Dec. 16, 1769.
    9. See Maskelyne to BF above, Dec. 11, 1769; the annotation there deals with
most of the points in this letter. For the Astronomer Royal see above, XI, 482 n.

obtain their observations of the transit of Venus &c. made at Philadelphia, in the State house square from the observers,[1] and that they describe the telescopes made use of, and all circumstances of the observations, particularly in what manner they observed the contacts of the limbs[2] of the Sun and Venus. I have delivered Mr. Biddle's and Mr. Bayley's observations to the Royal Society in your name. I am Dear Sir, Your most Obedient Servant

N. MASKELYNE

Turn over for the P.S.

P.S. I shall also be obliged to you to forward a request to the Philadelphia observers, that they would favor me with their observations of the late transit of Mercury Nov. 9th. and the eclipse of the moon Dec. 12th. if they observed them. I have wrote an answer to Mr. Winthrop's letter to me which will bring with me when I come to town, and if you have any opportunity of sending [for] it soon will beg leave to trouble you with it, otherwise will dispatch it by the usual conveyance. I have communicated Mr. Winthrop's letter, and also his observation of the transit of Mercury in 1743, to the Royal Society.

Addressed: To | Dr. Benj: Franklin | at Mrs. Stephensons | In Craven Street | In the Strand.

Endorsed: Mr. Maskelyne to Dr Franklin

From Ezra Stiles

ALS (draft): Yale University Library

Dear Sir   Newport Dec 27. 1769

This acknowledges the Receipt of your Collection of philosophical Letters, and Dissertations in a quarto Volume which with your Letter came safe to hand last Summer.[3] For which please to accept my Thanks. They have given me great Pleasure and Instruction.

---

1. See Evans to BF above, June 11; *Pa. Chron.*, May 29–June 5, 1769.
2. *I.e.*, outer edges. The reference is to the black-drop effect, which baffled eighteenth-century observers: Venus, after it had moved inside the limb of the sun, appeared to be still connected with it by a band or drop of planetary matter. See Harry Woolf, *The Transits of Venus*... (Princeton, 1959), pp. 148–9, 193, 195.
3. The book was *Exper. and Obser.* (4th ed., London, 1769); the letter has not been found.

I have desired Capt. Peck,[4] by whom you receive this, to procure me in London

Relands Collection from the Rabbinical Writings showing the Jewish Manner of initiating Proselytes by Baptism &c. I forget the true Title of the Book.[5]

Zohar. With the latin Translation if to be had: else in Hebrew alone

Acta Pilati: a Book considered as spurious by Divines and Antiquarians; but which I have a Curiosity to see.[6]

Will you be so kind Sir as to procure them and deliver them to Peck, who will pay for them. I should not give you this Trouble, but that it may be difficult for him to find, especially the two last. The Rev. Samuel Lock of Sherburn is lately elected President of Harvard College in the Room of the late President Holyoke.[7] Wishing you every Blessing I am Sir Your obliged Friend and most obedient Servant   EZRA STILES

Dr. B. Franklin London

4. William Augustus Peck, a Newport sea captain and member of Stiles's church.

5. Because he forgot the title we have been unable to find it; and so was BF. Adriaan Reland, the Dutch orientalist, was prolific enough to provide a wide choice of titles. In the following September Stiles received from BF "Reland's Introduction to the Rabbinical Literature": Franklin B. Dexter, ed., *The Literary Diary of Ezra Stiles* ... (3 vols., New York, 1901), I, 70. This was the *Analecta Rabbinica* ..., perhaps the second edition (Utrecht, 1723). It was not what Stiles wanted; at least one of the tracts he was looking for, he decided, was in Reland's "Hist. Hebraea," presumably the *Antiquitates Sacrae Veterum Hebraeorum* (Utrecht, 1708): Stiles to BF below, Sept. 28, 1770. Whether BF eventually located the "collection" before his patience wore out we do not know.

6. Zohar was a cabalistic work, introduced into Spain in the 13th century, which appears to have been the product of many hands and many epochs; Stiles received a copy in 1772 of an edition published in Nuremberg in 1768: F. B. Dexter, *op. cit.*, I, 298. The *Acta Pilati* cannot be identified from such a meager reference. What now goes by that name is usually included in the apocryphal Gospel of Nicodemus; but the eighteenth century abounded in writings about Pilate, and Stiles may have had any one of a number of books in mind. Whichever he was curious about, we have no indication that his curiosity was satisfied.

7. Edward Holyoke (1689–1769) had died on June 1; on Dec. 18 Samuel Locke (1732–78) was elected to succeed him as president. *Sibley's Harvard Graduates*, XIII, 620–7.

From a Committee of Boston Merchants

ALS (copy): American Philosophical Society

Sir   Boston 29th December 1769

The Merchants and Traders of the Town of Boston having on the 1st. August 1768 Enter'd into an agreement not to send for or import any Goods from Great Britain (Some few Articles except) from the 1st. January 1769 to the 1st. January 1770 and as this agreement was near expiring on the 17th. October Last they enter'd into an other agreement not to write for any Goods to be ship'd them from Great Britain untill all the revenue Acts imposing Duties for the purpose of Raising a revenue in America shou'd be totally repealed, at the Signing of which agreement it was expected that the merchants at New York, Philadelphia, and other Colonies, would Come into a Similar Agreement. They were accordingly wrote to upon the Subject, but as they had already orderd their goods to be shipp'd in Case the Act imposing Duties on Tea, Glass & ca. was repealed, for this and other reasons mention'd in their Letters declin'd Concurring with us at present, but have proposed to join us in any plan that may be thought prudent to pursue for Obtaining the repeal of the Acts of the 4th. and 6th. of George the third. The Merchants Here being fully Convinced that it is of the Utmost importance that the Traders in all the Colonies shoud act upon one and the Same plan have agreed to Conform to the Agreement enter'd into at New york and Philadelphia and to write their Correspondents that the Goods they have and may send for should be shipp'd on this Express Condition, that the Act imposing Duties on Tea, Glass paper and Colors be totally repealed and not other ways and have directed their Committee to Confer with the Committee of the other Colonies relative to their proposal abovemention'd.[8] In the mean time as the Acts of the 4th. and 6th. George the third Contain many Greivous and unreasonable restrictions upon Trade and are by far the most Exceptionable, the Merchants here have

8. The Philadelphia and New York merchants, in other words, refused to support Boston's extension of total nonimportation; and the Bostonians were modifying their demands for the sake of unity. Their committee was presumably an organ of the Merchants' Club, a loosely-knit association of the merchants of the city. See Charles M. Andrews, *The Boston Merchants and the Non-Importation Movement* (New York reprint, [1968]), pp. 72–4.

tho't it necessary to make some Observations upon these Acts as also upon the Conduct of the Custom House Officers here that our Friends in Parliament may be acquainted with the Difficulties the Trade labor under by means of these Acts, A number of which they now inclose you which we doubt not you will make the best improvement of.[9] We are with Great Respect your most Obedient and humble Servants[1]

ISAAC SMITH	EDWARD PAYNE
EBENEZER STORER	WM. PHILLIPS
WM. GREENLEAF	JOSEPH WALDO
THOMAS CUSHING	JONA. MASON

Committee of Merchants

P.S. The Pamplets are Committed to the Care of Capt. Hall.

To Benjamin Franklin Esqr

Addressed: To / Benjamin Franklin Esqr / At / London / per Capt: Hall

Endorsed: Boston

9. John Almon published *Observations on Several Acts of Parliament...by the Merchants of Boston* (London, 1770). The pamphlet may have appeared while Parliament was considering repeal in March, but was not noted until April in *Gent. Mag.*, XL (1770), 192.

1. Isaac Smith (1719–87) was a justice of the peace and an uncle of Abigail Adams; Ebenezer Storer, Jr. (1730–1807) was a former selectman; William Greenleaf (1725–1803) later served on the Boston Committee of Correspondence, as did Thomas Cushing (1725–88), who became a representative and Speaker of the House and, after 1770, corresponded regularly with BF. Edward Payne (1722–88), secretary of the Merchants' Club, was later wounded during the Boston Massacre; William Phillips (1722–1804), deacon of the Old South Church and selectman, often served as moderator of the Club meetings. Joseph Waldo (1722–1806), an overseer of the poor, later came under suspicion as a loyalist and spent most of the 1770s in England. Jonathan Mason (1725–98), another deacon of the Old South, was a member of the Sons of Liberty, an overseer of the poor, and selectman. *Sibley's Harvard Graduates,* VII, 188; XI, 91–4, 377–95; 208–14; Mass. Hist. Soc. *Procs.,* XIII (1875), 410, 415, 417–19; XVI (1879), 280; XXIV (1889), 85; XXXII (1899), 140–1; L (1917), 195; *An Historical Catalogue of the Old South Church...* (Boston, 1883), pp. 46, 51, 343; *The Manifesto Church, Records of the Church in Brattle Square* (Boston, 1902), p. 41; *New England Historic and Geneal. Record,* XXXV (1881), 194; XXXIX (1885), 109–18; James E. Greenleaf, comp., *Genealogy of the Greenleaf Family* (Boston, 1896), pp. 68, 90–1.

From Mary Stevenson[2]

AD: American Philosophical Society

To Dr. Franklin with a pair of Ruffles Decr / 69

These flowers Dear Sir, can boast no lively bloom,
Nor can regale you with a sweet perfume,
This dreary season no such present yeild's,
The Trees are naked, unadorn'd the fields,
The Gardens have their sweets and beauty lost
But Love and Gratitude, unchill'd by frost;
Put forth this foliage—poor indeed I own
Yet trust th'intent will for the faults atone.
   Altho' my produce not with nature vies,
I hope to please a friend's indulgent eye's,
For you my fancy and my skill I tried
For you my needle with delight I plied
Proud even to add a triffling grace to you
From whom Philosophy and Virtue too
I've gain'd—If either can be counted mine
In you they with the clearest lustre shine
   My noble Friend this artless line excuse
Nor blame the weakness of your Polly's muse
The humble gift with kind compliance take
And wear it for the grateful givers sake

NB Dr Franklin to whom these verses

From [Richard Henry Alexander?] Bennet[3]

AL: American Philosophical Society

St. James's Street Tuesday night [1769?]

Mr. Bennet presents his Comp[limen]ts to Doctor Franklin and returns him many thanks for the Honor of his very obliging Present which he esteems infinitely.

2. Verses which accompanied her Christmas gift to BF.
3. The writer and date are equally conjectural. The Bennet to whom we have assigned the note was an F.R.S. and a co-sponsor, with BF, of the nomination of William Hewson to the Society in December, 1769; Bennet's signature on becoming an F.R.S. is much like the handwriting of the note; he lived on the way from London to Bromley, where BF frequently visited the Hawkesworths.

From [John] Foxcroft[4] AL: American Philosophical Society

[1769? A note in the third person, dated only Friday, asking Franklin to visit him for a game of chess "on his New Invented Table." A very bad cold has prevented Foxcroft from calling, and the visit would be an act of charity.]

From W. Masters[5] LS: American Philosophical Society

Sir   [1769?[6]]

Though I have not the honour of an intimate acquaintance with you, yet your character of humanity and benevolence, and the in-

---

Notes and Queries, 11th ser., 1 (1910), 198, 238, 311, 370–2; *The Signatures in the First Journal-Book and the Charter-Book of the Royal Society* (London, 1912), p. 30. These slender clues are the only grounds for our ascription. As for the date, we are guessing that Bennet is acknowledging BF's gift of a copy of the fourth edition of *Exper. and Obscr.,* published early in 1769.

4. So identified by the handwriting. But his brother Thomas, the Philadelphia postmaster, wrote a closely similar hand, and visited England briefly in 1771. Thomas, unlike John, is known to have been a chess-player: see John Foxcroft to BF below, Jan. 14, 1771. Hence it is possible, though in our opinion unlikely, that the invitation was from Thomas in 1771. John arrived from America in the late spring of 1769; see Parker to BF above, July 22. He stayed late into the following year, and the invitation could of course have been at any time during his stay.

5. We believe that this was William Masters (*c.* 1735–88), and that he was the same person as the W. Masters who was elected one of the managers of the Bettering House in 1766, and served as a justice of the Philadelphia Court of Common Pleas and of the Orphans' Court. Above, XIII, 284; John T. Scharf and Thompson Westcott, *History of Philadelphia* (5 vols., Philadelphia, 1884), II, 1565, 1570. He died in Philadelphia on Aug. 5, 1788, and was buried in Christ Church cemetery: above, XIV, 282 n. His reference in this letter to his father suggests that he was the son of the William Masters who, when he died in 1760, left BF as an executor of his will. Samuel H. Needles, "The Governor's Mill, and the Glove Mills, Philadelphia," *PMHB,* VIII (1884), 293 n; see also above, IV, 193 n, 214; VI, 312 n. In that case the father must have had a son by an earlier wife, of whom we do not know, before he married Mary Lawrence (1725–99) in 1754; she bore him only daughters. Charles P. Keith, *The Provincial Councillors of Pennsylvania...* (Philadelphia, 1883), pp. 453–4.

6. So dated by I. Minis Hays, *Calendar of the Papers of Benjamin Franklin* (5 vols., Philadelphia, 1908), I, 104. The presumable reason is that Masters, in a second letter below, July 17, 1770, thanked BF for his kind reply but repeated the request in this letter.

timacy that subsisted between you and my Father, and especially the desire of contributing to the Peace and Happiness of an old Neighbour whom for several Years I have found an honest worthy industrious Man, imboldens me to give you the trouble of a Letter.

A Soldier in the Train[7] has married his Daughter. The Army you know is far from being a School of Virtue. Besides the Miseries and Fatigues to which his Daughter will be exposed by following the Camp or living in Garrison, the old Man is exceedingly distressed at the prospect of his grand Children being brought up in the midst of vice and debauchery. His Son in law is desirous of quiting the Army, but can only be discharged by applying to the Marquis of Granby who is Capt. General.[8] He has got a Petition drawn up but does not know to whom to send it. The Father in law being a poor Man has no acquaintance with Men in Trade; as notwithstanding his poverty I know him to be a deserving Man, I have at his earnest intreaty presumed to inclose the Petition to you, and to request the favour that you would get it presented; which shall be ever acknowledged by Your Friend and humble Servant   W MASTERS

Addressed: To / Doctor Benjamin Franklin / Craven Street / London

Endorsed: Mr Masters with Petition of Thos Truck

Marginalia in *Good Humour*, an Anonymous Pamphlet

MS notations in the margins of a copy in the Historical Society of Pennsylvania of *Good Humour: or, a Way with the Colonies, Wherein Is Occasionally Enquired into Mr. P———t's Claim of Popularity; and the Principles of Virtuous Liberty, as Taught in the School of Mr. Wilkes, and Other Peripatetics* (London, 1766).

This is the first of a series of marginal comments by Franklin on pamphlets that are, at least for the modern reader, of much less interest than the comments themselves. The pamphlets are thus in a different category from the protests in 1766 by members of the House of Lords against the

7. Thomas Truck: see *ibid.* He was probably with the artillery train of the army.

8. John Manners, Marquis of Granby (1721–70), was a brilliant soldier who had commanded the British contingent in Germany during the Seven Years' War; in 1769 he was master general of the ordnance and commander in chief of the army. *DNB.*

and such they would necessarily continue, *This Necessity is merely imaginary.*
though perhaps in a much lower degree,
under some other powerful European state,
in case their more safe and honourable tie,
with what they are still pleased to call,
their *Mother Country*,† should happen to be
dissolved.

† They used to call her by that endearing Appellation; but her late Conduct entitles rather to the Name of Step-mother.

I shall therefore conclude with saying,
that the separation of Great Britain from her
American appertinencies would be destructive of the prosperity and liberty of both. If
so, it seems to follow that till such time as
New England is strong enough to protect
Old England, and the seat of the British
empire is transferred from London to Boston,
there is an absolute necessity that the right
of giving law to America, *should continue
to be vested in Great Britain. That it is the
interest of Great Britain to protect and che-
rish her American provinces instead of oppressing them, is an undeniable truth;† and
it is, perhaps, no less true, that some farther
attention, and some farther means of

The Protection is mutual and equal in Proportion to Number & Wealth, as present.

✗ Not the least Necessity for this.

† Stick then to that Truth.

5   communication, ✗

✗ *Consider then what those should be?*

A Page of Franklin's Marginalia

repeal of the Stamp Act,[9] and consequently receive different treatment. The printed original is paraphrased and drastically condensed in the right-hand column, with direct quotation only of words or passages on which Franklin specifically remarked. All italics in this column represent his underlining; the author's italics and other emphasis have been removed. Gaps in the column, to accommodate the marginalia, do not indicate any break in the paraphrase. Franklin's comments are printed verbatim in the left-hand column, where italics again are his emphasis.

The importance of these and subsequent marginalia is that they reveal, as nothing else does, Franklin's private views on the developing Anglo-American controversy, and particularly on its constitutional aspect. He was guarded about expressing himself in letters, which might get into the wrong hands, and even more guarded about what he wrote for the press. In writing for his own eyes the guard was down: he was free to develop his idea that the King's British subjects had no authority over his other subjects, and that the Parliamentary claim to legislate for Americans was sheer usurpation. This idea was not a new one: it had been growing on him since at least the beginning of 1766.[1] He had hinted at it in his examination before the House of Commons that February, and had touched on it lightly in an article he published two years later.[2] But its implications he preferred to keep to himself, for he knew that they would be utterly unacceptable to the British and even to many Americans. He could not avoid them, however, when he encountered in the pamphlets

9. See above, XIII, 207–32.

1. The earliest expression of it that we have discovered is BF's comments on a copy in the New York Public Library of an anonymous pamphlet, *The Claim of the Colonies to an Exemption from Internal Taxes Imposed by Authority of Parliament, Examined . . .* (London 1765). These brief marginalia were inadvertently omitted from XIII and will in due course be published in a volume of addenda. BF attributed the pamphlet to "Knox, Esq. Agent for Georgia"; William Knox was ousted as agent in November, 1765, and the news must have reached London at least by early 1766, which is therefore the latest date for the comments. In them BF denies not only Parliament's right to tax the colonies but also asserts flatly that its legislating for them is an unjust and wicked usurpation of power. For a valuable study of the evolution of BF's ideas, as revealed in his marginalia, see Verner W. Crane, "Franklin's Marginalia, and the Lost 'Treatise' on Empire," *Papers* of the Mich. Academy of Science, Arts, and Letters, XLII (1957), 163–76.

2. In his examination BF had remarked in passing that the colonies were not within the realm and had parliaments of their own, and had hinted that they might in future come to deny Parliament's right to legislate for them. Above, XIII, 153, 156. In 1768 he had asserted, again in passing, that the colonial assemblies were coequal with Parliament. Above, XV, 36–7.

he was reading the smug and repeated assertion of Parliamentary supremacy. The smugness angered him into responses which, even if equally repetitive, hammered out his opposing assertion.

The dates of his marginalia can be established only conjecturally and by internal evidence. In the present case the most important bit of evidence is his reference to the letters of Governor Bernard. These were first printed in Boston in the spring of 1769, and were reprinted in England by December of that year.[3] We are therefore assigning these comments, according to our usual practice, to the earliest likely date, which is the close of 1769.

The colonial question engages every one's attention. Demagogues who wish to bring government into contempt accuse Parliament of exerting lawless power; the colonists deny its right to tax them when they are not represented in it, and they are supported in this by their great champion, who is also the false idol of the British populace, William Pitt. Any well-wisher to the country must regret Pitt's popularity, for he has used it to fan the flame of sedition.

In the colonies trade and commerce are at a standstill, government is defied, and anarchy prevails. In They knew the Massachusetts Governor Bernard, faithful to the Governor to be, crown and the rights of Parliament, has shown as it afterwards spirit, understanding, and integrity in dealing with turn'd out, their a rancorous Assembly and a furious people.

Enemy and Colonial resentment of Britain is passionate and Calumniator in irrational. Even assuming that Parliament exercised private Letters an illegal authority in passing the Stamp Act, what to Govt. here. then? "Must the Colonies in *the first instance*, and

How many of without waiting the issue of one humble remon-their Petitions strance,...proceed to an extreme, which nothing were rejected but the most contemptuous neglect, and the most on the most resolved tyranny can excuse?" Does such resent-trivial Pre- ment imply subordination? It would have been more tences?

3. See Dennys DeBerdt to the Boston Selectmen, Dec. 5, 1769, Colonial Soc. of Mass. *Publications*, XIII (1912), 389; *Gent. Mag.*, XXXIX (1769), 84, 502, 549.

How ignorant
is this Writer of
Facts! How
many of their
Remonstrances
were rejected!

becoming to have remonstrated in terms of filial duty, trusting for relief to the world-famous justice and equity of Parliament.

Parliamentary authority to tax the colonies is in doubt, though not clearly illegal. If it cannot be asserted to the satisfaction of the Americans, "they

There never
was any Occa-
sion of legal
Exemption
from what they
never had been
subject to.

must give us leave in our turn to except against their demonstrations of *legal exemption* from it." The legal question may then be discarded, and the issue settled on the basis of reason and utility.

Here appears
some Sense.

The colonies have a natural right, stronger than any legal one, to be treated fairly. This right derives from the natural right of all men to equity and justice, and it is indefeasible. Whatever the basis for the authority of a government, it has no right to oppress; for a right to do wrong is a logical absurdity. Hence the colonies are entitled to all the equity and indulgence that Britain can show them.

Here is the old
Mistake of all
these Writers.
The People of
the Mother
Country are
Subjects not
Governors.
The King only
is sovereign in
both Countries.

This argument, however, applies as much "to *the Mother Country* as to the Colonies; for it would be ridiculous to suppose, that a people should have a claim to whatever happiness their situation will admit, and that Princes and Governors should be excluded from it.... Great Britain and her Colonies then are to be consider'd as *mutually bound to promote*

Right.

Why not, if
they have a
Right to them?

one another's interests.... If this reasoning be just (and I think it cannot be disproved) the Colonies will no longer think it equitable to *insist upon Immunities which the people of Great Britain do not enjoy.* To claim

It is a Right however, and what signifies what Air it has?

a *right of being taxed by their Assemblies only*, appears to have too much the air of Independence; and though they are not represented here. . . would

The Inhabitants being Free-holders ought to have the same. If they have it not, they are injured. Then rectify what is amiss among yourselves, and do not make it a Justification of more Wrong.

give them an *Immunity beyond the inhabitants of this Island.*"

Representation does not depend upon geography: worthy and honorable gentlemen elected from any part of the kingdom can secure the rights to liberty and property of citizens in any other part.

Why not? As well as Scotland from 45? or rather 61?[4]

Hence the fact that the colonists do not have their own members of Parliament is immaterial. "Could they hope to procure any advantages from 100

Common Sense, on the contrary, says, that a Body of 100 Votes in Parliament will always be worth the At-

Representatives? *Common Sense answers* all this in the Negative." Some sensible Americans insist that their compatriots want no such thing.

4. By the Act of Union of 1707 Scotland acquired forty-five members in the House of Commons of the new British Parliament, and in the House of Lords sixteen representatives elected by the Scottish peers.

tention of any Ministry; and the Fear of offending them, will make every Minister cautious of injuring the Rights of their Country, lest they join with his Opposers in Parlt.

The colonists have virtual representation in Parliament, because its members are concerned with preserving colonial freedom and immunities insofar as these can be reconciled with dependence on the mother country. British and colonial interests are interdependent; Parliament is therefore as solicitous of the second as of the first, because in furthering one it is furthering the other. "The interests of Great Britain and her colonies are the same." She will always have a parental regard for the Americans, and lay no unnecessary burdens upon them.

All this Argument of the Interest of Britain and the Colonies being *the same* is fallacious and unsatisfactory. Partners in Trade have a *common* Interest, which is the same, the Flourishing of the Partnership Business: But they may moreover have each a *separate* Interest; and in pursuit of that *separate* Interest, one of them may endeavour to impose on the other, may cheat him in the Accounts, may draw to himself more than his Share of the Profits, may put upon the other more than an equal Share of the Burthen. Their having a common Interest is no Security against such Injustice. The Landholders of G. Britain have a common Interest, and yet they injure one another in the Inequality of the Land Tax. The Majority in Parliament being favoured in the Proportion will never Consent to do Justice to the Minority, by a more equal Assessment.

The colonists fear to submit to what they regard as an exercise of arbitrary power, lest it become a precedent. They fear, that is, either that the British government is ignorant of colonial interests and hence liable to injure them and, unintentionally, British interests as well, or that the government is in essence arbitrary. But Parliament cannot fail to recognize the identity of interest. If it is acting against both Britain and America, the danger should be as apparent to one as to the other; and it is not apparent.

If the Parliament is so knowing and so just, how comes it to restrain Ireland in its Manufactures; America in its Trade? Why may not an Irishman or an American make the same Manufactures and carry them to the same Ports with an Englishman? In many Instances, Britain [has] a selfish Regard to her own Interest in prejudice of the Colonies. America therefore has no Confidence in her Equity.

The same is true of arbitrary power. "But I can conceive no earthly security better, none indeed so good, as that which depends upon the wisdom and integrity of a British King and Parliament."

Suppose Seats in your House of Commons hereditary, as those of the House of Lords; or suppose the Commons to be nominated by the King, or chosen by the Lords; Could you then rely upon them? If your Members were to be chosen by the People of Ireland, could you then rely upon them? Could you depend upon their Wisdom and Integrity as a Security, the best possible, for your Rights? And wherein is our Case different if the People of Britain chuse Legislators for the People of America?

Whether or not the Stamp Act is a suitable and fair method of taxation may confidently be left to the wisdom of Parliament, which will study the issue and devise a remedy, if needed, for colonial grievances. If the colonists have any virtue left, "they

There was no
Posture of
Hostility in
America. But
Britain put her-
self in a Posture
of Hostility
against Amer-
ica; Witness the
Landing of
Troops in
Boston, 1768.

will blush to be found *in a posture of hostility* against Great Britain, and will recover from it as expeditiously as they can; there being nothing so inexcusable as enmity to one's country, no name of infamy half so reproachful, as that of a base and ungrateful Parricide."

The colonists' real fear seems to be that they will be saddled with a part of the British national debt. Why not absolve them from this threat in return for an annual contribution of raw materials or manu-

They want no
British troops
for that pur-
pose, nor ever
did.

factures, or a grant of money to maintain troops for colonial defense?

[The remainder of the pamphlet deals largely with John Wilkes, and has no marginal comments.]

Marginalia in *The True Constitutional Means*, an Anonymous Pamphlet

MS notations in the margins of a copy in the New York Public Library of *The True Constitutional Means for Putting an End to the Disputes between Great-Britain and the American Colonies* (London, 1769).

[*On the title
page:*] Query,
Could this be
written by Mr.
Jackson? from
some Expres-
sions and Argu-
ments it should

The Americans are discontented principally because they have a false idea that their privileges are being infringed and because they fear oppression. The idea has been refuted; I shall deal with the fear by proposing a system of taxation that they cannot consider oppressive. They must admit their obligation to contribute to the common defense of the state. But who compose the state? Only landholders,

seem so;[5] but others are so unlike his Precision that I rather think he is not the Author.

because land is what invaders covet. From earliest times the landholders of England have borne the burden of defense, either in person or later through taxes and, in many cases, through military service as well.

A very unnecessary Purpose.

The government has recently stationed part of the army in America, "not for *the sole purpose of defending the colonists against the Indians*" but also to guard against European invasion. The Americans might reasonably have been expected to support these troops, but have refused to do so or to pay taxes for the purpose. I propose a tax on all land held by British subjects in America, "*ad valorem of their rents,*" to be imposed at the same time and rate as the land tax in Great Britain.

Not one American Tract of Land or Farm in 500 are or ever were rented. How then is this *ad valorem* to be found? This shows the Folly of thinking to make Laws for a Country so unknown.

The British State is only the Island of G. Britain. The British Legislature are undoubtedly the only proper

In every state one part must have the direction of the whole, and every British subject must acknowledge "that the directive influence of the *British state* remains with the British legislature, who are the only proper judges of what concerns the general welfare of the *whole empire.*" Every part must submit to the burdens imposed for the common defense, provided that these burdens are equitably proportioned among the parts. "But the land-tax which I have proposed, is in its very nature unoppressive,

5. Presumably a reference to Richard Jackson's essay on population in 1755: above, VI, 75–82.

Judges of what concerns the Welfare of that State: But the Irish Legislature are the proper Judges of what concerns the Irish State, and the American Legislatures of what concerns the American States respectively. By *the whole* Empire, does this Writer mean all the King's Dominions? if so, the British Parliament should also govern the Isles of Jersey and Guernsey, Hanover, &c. but it is not so.

This Writer seems ignorant that every Colony has its own civil and military Establishment to provide for, new Roads and Bridges to make, Churches and all other public Edifices to erect, and would he separately tax them moreover with a Tax on Lands equal to what is paid in Britain?

and is equally well suited to the poorest, as to the richest province of the British empire; for, supposing the rents of the lands near the capital to be five pounds an acre, in other places five shillings, and in others five pence; it is demonstrably plain, that a tax of a fifth or a tenth upon the lowest sum, is not more burdensome than a tax of the same rate upon the highest sum. A fifth of the lowest would be a penny, while a fifth of the highest would be a pound." Parliament is the sole judge of the necessity of such a tax, and could not discriminate against any taxpayer because each would be assessed according

---

It is only plain that you know nothing of the matter.

to his means. "*It is plain*" that the Americans would have no cause to complain of unfairness. They double their population every twenty-five or thirty years. To do this they must have "*a luxuriant*

How does this appear? Is not a mere Compe-

abundance" of produce and manufactures, and is it unreasonable to require "a part of this *luxuriant*

tence sufficient
for this pur-
pose?

If America will *abundance* to be paid *as taxes to support the general*
consent to pay *establishment"* of imperial defense, leaving the
thus its Propor- colonial legislatures to take care of the other needs
tion of British of their provinces?
Taxes, will
Britain pay out
of the whole all
the American
Taxes? Or is
America to pay
both?

The shortage of gold and silver among them can
be balanced by a regulated paper currency, and
taxes paid in paper might readily be converted into
First advanced sterling. Ireland is an example of "a *new doctrine*, that
by B. Franklin.[6] a nation may prosper and become opulent, with the
balance of trade annually against her, which in
truth is always the case with almost every distant
province in regard to the capital." Any kind of currency that circulates freely quickens industry. If too
much is issued by any one colony, that colony will
be most hurt and first compelled to take corrective
measures. Prohibiting the colonists from issuing
paper for fear that they will print too much is as silly
as limiting their food and drink for fear that they will
The foregoing overeat. The old emphasis on gold and silver as the
Observations means of national power is outdated. What breeds
on a Paper cur- industry is industry, and to discourage it by sup-
rency seem pressing paper currency is an intolerable grievance
just. It is further for the colonists.
true that such
Currency in

6. See, for example, above, XIV, 78–9. BF is there arguing, however, that the
colonies have thrived, with the balance of trade against them, only because of
their use of paper money.

America was of greater Advantage to Britain than to the Colonies, as it facilitated the Purchase and Consumption of British Commodities, and discouraged American Manufactures.

Aside from the Floridas, Georgia, and Nova Scotia, the poorest of the colonies is Canada. Yet, to

The greatest Part of this was in Goods for the Indian Trade, and not for the Consumption of the Colonists. Therefore no Consequence of the Opulence of the Canadians can be drawn from it.

judge by the customs house receipts, even Canada takes annually some £300,000 worth of British commodities. Before the war it must have been far more prosperous than it is now. Yet even then, to judge by Charlevoix's account,[7] its wealth could not compare with that of New England, where the inhabitants had more opulence than they knew how

It is strange that this Writer should recur to Charlevoix, a Foreigner, for Information of

to enjoy, whereas in New France the appearance of prosperity concealed an underlying poverty.

7. Pierre François Xavier de Charlevoix, *Histoire et description générale de la Nouvelle France, avec le journal historique d'un voyage fait par ordre du roi dans l'Amérique Septentrionnale* (3 vols., Paris, 1744).

287

the State of the
N. England
Colonies. In
fact those
Colonies are
very poor.
There are only
some few rich
Men in the
capital Towns.

More recently New England seems to have acquired so much money that the inhabitants complain of it. At the end of the last war the Governor of Massachusetts told the legislature that it would be necessary "'to revive and *promote a spirit of industry*, frugality, and oeconomy, all of which have of late been but too much *relaxed* by an unusual flow of money, much exceeding what would naturally *arise from the produce* and manufactures of the country.'[8] This *declaration of the legislature*, as it may be justly called, shews the good sense of that colony...." This superabundance of money indicates either that the balance of trade during the war was favorable to the colony, or that its produce had an

Nonsence! It
could only
arise from
thence, as they
took very few
Prizes from the
Enemy.
  A foolish
Expression of a
Governor in
his Speech is
not a Declaration of the
Legislature.

How could a
Consumption
of the Produce

unusually favorable market, for when "the flow of money is more than what would naturally arise from the produce and manufactures of the country,

8. From Gov. Bernard's speech to both Houses, May 26, 1763: Malcolm Freiberg, ed., *Journals of the House of Representatives of Massachusetts, 1763–1764* (Boston, 1970), p. 9.

288

and Manufactures increase without an Increase of the Produce and Manufactures and how could they increase without an Increase of the Spirit of Industry, which he says has been relax'd? This is all Stuff.

it can hardly mean anything else than that the common and usual consumption of the *produce* and *manufactures* of the country was greatly increased." The war clearly bettered their circumstances, whereupon the circulation of too much money encouraged idleness and discouraged industry; the colony then, apparently, drained off the excess in improving agriculture, trade, and fishing.

Are not the poor Negro Slaves who are past their Labour, sick or lame, as great a Burthen to the Colonists?

In other colonies, where agriculture is based on slavery, there are no indigent. How happy the British would be were there "no *parish-poor* nor *common beggars*"! The great planters use their produce to buy goods for which others need cash, but even small landholders have been known to buy

Was not the Gold first purchased by the Produce of his Land, obtained by hard Labour? Does Gold drop from the Clouds in Virginia, into the Laps of the Indolent?

slaves "*with gold.*"

Their very purchasing Plate and other Superfluities from England is one Means of disabling them from paying Taxes to England. Would you have it

In Virginia, I have been assured, few families are "without some *plate*," and the servants at some entertainments are almost as numerous as the guests.

both in Meal and Malt? It has been a great Folly in the Americans, to entertain English Gentlemen with a splendid Hospitality ill suited to their Circumstances; by which they excited no other grateful Sentiment in their Guests, than that of a Desire to tax the *Landlord*.

This is arguing the Riches of a People from their Extravagance, the very Thing that keeps them poor!

We may judge the wealth of the colonies by the value of their imports, which from Britain alone amounts to three million pounds a year. Another million may be added for imports from the West Indies and elsewhere, bringing the total to four million. But they produce for themselves many of the articles that they consume, and manufacture a great deal of what they wear. The value of these products must be double the value of their imports, which means that their annual consumption amounts to twelve million sterling. The British pay about thirteen million a year in taxes, including

A Turnpike Tax is no Burthen, as the Turnpike gives more Benefit than it takes. And ought the Rich in Britain, who have made such Numbers of Poor by engrossing all the small Divisions of Land: and

turnpikes and poor rates, from which the colonists are exempted. It is reasonable that the colonists should pay taxes for the general defense, and there

who keep Labourers and working People Poor by limiting their Wages; Ought these Gentry to complain of the Burthen of maintaining the Poor that have work'd for them at unreasonably low Rates all their Lives? As well might the Planter complain of his being oblig'd to maintain his poor Negroes, when they grow old, are sick or lame and unable to provide for themselves.

290

The Colonies are almost always considered by these ignorant, flimsey Writers as unwilling to contribute to the general Exigencies of the State which is not true. They are always willing, but will have the granting of their own Money themselves; in which they are right for various Reasons.

What Land have they ever taken from you?

Climate and soil worse in New England.

He should have said more than 500,000.

False! The Lands did not

is no fairer way to do so than by a general land tax that falls as equitably on the most sparsely inhabited colony as on the most populous county in Great Britain.

The colonists complain of the high prices they must pay for British commodities, and some argue that these prices are the equivalent of bearing public burdens. In other words "they would be content *to take land from us* gratuitously," but are aggrieved at having to buy from Britain whatever they do not manufacture themselves. They should realize that, if manufactures are somewhat dearer for them than for the British, land is cheaper and more fertile. Cultivated land in America is already more exten-

sive than in Great Britain, "and *fewer than 100,000* freeholders possess all this extent among them,

generally *by the bounty of the crown*, the greatest number having paid no pecuniary equivalent for them.

291

belong to the
Crown but to
the Indians, of
whom the Col-
onists either
purchased
them at their
own Expence,
or conquer'd
them without
Assistance from
Britain.

The lands in Great-Britain and Ireland, on the other hand, are divided among a million of freeholders,

Equivalent.
The Engage-
ment to settle
the American
Lands, and the
Expence of
Settlement, are
more than
an Equivalent,
for what was of
no Value to
Britain without
such Settle-
ment.

most of whom have given *a very high equivalent* for them; an equivalent which would have procured them land any where on the surface of the globe." Most of the land in Britain and Ireland is rented, and the rent is reckoned at a third of the value of the produce; this amounts to a 33% tax on the farmer, and makes provisions 33% dearer than they would

How then is
your Tax to be
found? How
will you know
the Rate of
Rent of Lands
that never were
rented?

otherwise be. In America "*the farmer and the proprietor are generally the same person*," who consequently can sell his produce more cheaply. Rents in Great Britain total about twenty-two million, "but

What signifies Extent of unsettled Lands that produce nothing?[9]

the rental of the *same extent* of lands in America is not probably one million sterling." The British have

Should the Landlords who receive those high Rents, complain of the high Price, such Rents oblige the Farmer to sell his Provision at?

as many difficulties "in the *purchase of provisions*, as the Americans in the purchase of manufactures." In consequence the cost of living in Britain is so high

This among genteel People is owing more to expensive Modes of Living than to the Difficulty of procuring Subsistance. Among the Poor it may be otherwise; but they are kept Poor by Law.

that "*the island is crowded with old Batchelors and old maids*," which has cut down the growth of population and prosperity in the past thirty years. "The Americans on the other hand, in the same space of time, have doubled their number of inhabitants by procreation alone; which is certainly not owing to any particular fecundity in the females, but to the great easiness of procuring a subsistence, which is

9. The extent of such lands in Pennsylvania had meant a great deal. During the French and Indian War and the subsequent disturbances in the Province in 1764 BF had been involved in the attempt of the Assembly to have taxes laid on the Penns' located but uncultivated lands. The quarrel with the Proprietors and Governor that this attempt engendered was a theme of earlier volumes, and was never finally settled. See in particular above, VI, 523–7; VII, 107; XI, 203–13.

B.F.[10]

They never refused. Cultivate it then.

an inducement to the establishment of new families." The Americans should acknowledge that their burdens are lighter than the British and "*chearfully contribute* their share to the public charges of the state. Were but *harmony and good correspondence firmly established* between European and American Britons," the burdens of both would soon be diminished, prices would fall, public revenues would swell, and the share of each taxpayer would shrink.

But the Americans should shun manufacturing until their rising population forces them into it. For agriculture is more profitable: "I beg to know if the returns of any traffic on earth ever produced so many per cent as the returns of agriculture in a fertile soil, and favourable climate." Have as many fortunes been made in the past century by manufacturing in Britain, or by trading in Holland, as in America by improving land and opening new settle-

How little this Politician knows of Agriculture! Is there any Country where 10 Bushels of Grain are generally got in for one sown? And are all the Charges and Advances for Labour, &c., nothing? No Farmer of America, in fact, makes 5 per cent of his Money. His Profit is only being paid for his own Labour and that of his Children.

10. Presumably a notation that the author's argument here parallels BF's in two essays, on the increase of mankind in 1751 and on Canada in 1760, for which see above, respectively, IV, 228, 233; IX, 77.

The Opulence of one English or Dutch Merchant would make the Opulence of 100 American Planters.

m ents? "For one person that has risen to *opulence* by *manufactures*, there are ten planters who have, from almost nothing, acquired not only independence, but lordly possessions, or at least what will become lordly possessions to their sons or grandsons...."

There is no Necessity for their leaving their Plantations: they can manufacture in their Families at spare Times.

Their riches would not increase so fast if they leave the land "and *run eagerly upon manufactures.*"

The wages of a farm laborer are much less than his value to the state, because he is creating wealth out of the earth and thereby augmenting the national wealth, whereas manufacturing brings merely an exchange of wealth, not its augmentation. Wherever agriculture is profitable, therefore, it

Depend upon it, the Americans are not so impolitic, as to neglect profitable Settlements for unprofitable Manufactures: But some Manufactures may be more advantageous to some Persons than the Cultivation of Land, and these will prosecute such Manufactures notwithstanding your Oratory.

would be "a great *impolicy*" to neglect it. City dwellers prey on each other and live on the edge of poverty; country dwellers, enjoying a favorable

How then are   climate and *"having no rents to pay,"* seem out of the
you, as I said   reach of poverty. The planter and his family are
before, to find   better off than the manufacturer and his. If, then,
the Proportion   the legislature secures the planter in his estate, may
you propose to   it not fairly ask of him to contribute to the public
take for their
Tax?

If he must pay   defense, *"when no greater proportion* is demanded of
his Colony   him, than is demanded of every other land pro-
Taxes as well as   prietor?"
your propos'd
Land Tax, he
will pay a much
greater Pro-
portion.

Marginalia in a Pamphlet by Israel Mauduit[1]

MS notations in the margins of a copy in the New York Public Library
of [Israel Mauduit,] *A Short View of the History of the Colony of Massachusetts Bay, with Respect to Their Original Charter and Constitution*
(London, 1769).

The Virginians   "In all the late American Disturbances, and in every
claim the Hon-   Attempt against the Authority of the British Gov-
our of having   ernment, the People of Massachusetts Bay have
taken this   taken the Lead. Every new Move towards Inde-
Lead.[2] But, as   pendence has been theirs: And in every fresh Mode
they are Episco-   of Resistance against the Laws, they have first set
palians, and the   the Example, and then issued their admonitory
N E. People   Letters to the other Colonies to follow it."
Dissenters, of   The colony prides itself on having been one of the
whom Sedi-   first charter governments, and harps upon its char-

1. Israel Mauduit (1708–87) was a prolific pamphleteer. He and his brother
Jasper had been agents for Massachusetts, and Israel was sufficiently close to
Gov. Hutchinson and Lieut. Gov. Oliver so that he subsequently acted as their
representative in the hearings before the Privy Council in 1774.

2. See Edmund S. and Helen M. Morgan, *The Stamp Act Crisis* (Chapel Hill,
[1953]), pp. 88–98.

tion, Republic-
anism and
Rebellion are
more easily
believ'd, and
against whom
an Accusation
of any sort is
more readily
believ'd, there-
fore the *Ton*
here is to as-
cribe the Lead
to them.

ter rights. What are they, and how much authority
do they confer? The charter is a crown grant, and
"no Grant of the Crown can supersede the Authority of

Pray what Act
of Parliament
was there that
forbid those
Grants?

an Act of Parliament."

This [the
paragraph] is
good Sense.

During the Stuart era the power of the crown was
undefined, and men were more concerned with
getting grants from it than with disputing their
validity. If the colonists put mistaken confidence in
privileges accorded them by charter, and settled the
country upon that basis, only the most urgent necessity can justify abrogating those privileges. "Though
wrongly given, they are rightly established, and it
would be much more wrong to take them away."

[The remainder of the pamphlet, which attempts
at great length to demonstrate that Massachusetts
has no claim under its charter to be exempt from
parliamentary taxation, contains no marginalia.]

Observations upon [Thomas Pownall,] *State of the Constitution of the Colonies* [London, 1769?]

MS (copy): American Philosophical Society

In December, 1769, or possibly in the following month,[3] Thomas Pownall attempted to formulate general principles of law that applied to the issues in dispute between Britain and her colonies. He composed a short document in two parts; the first set forth six principles, and the second adduced corollaries from them. This document he had printed but not published: twenty copies were struck off, which he circulated to his friends for their comments;[4] his presumable purpose was to make sure of his legal arguments before speaking further on the American question in the House of Commons. He presented Franklin with a copy.[5] The latter annotated it at considerable length but not, as with most of his marginalia, for his eyes alone; his comments were returned to Pownall, who replied in writing to one of them.

The pamphlet that Franklin annotated has not survived. The earliest extant version of his observations is a manuscript copy of them, in an unidentifiable hand and without Pownall's text, that is among Franklin's papers. The comments and text were first published by Benjamin Vaughan in 1779.[6] We print them in parallel columns, as Vaughan did not, but necessarily follow his placing of the former in relation to the latter. Where the text is quoted verbatim, it is from a copy of the original pamphlet in the Library Company of Philadelphia. We have paraphrased and abridged those parts of it on which Franklin

3. Vaughan gives December: *Miscellaneous Pieces*, p. 537 n. Charles A. W. Pownall gives January: *Thomas Pownall, M.P., F.R.S., Governor of Massachusetts Bay...* (London, [1908]), p. 224. Neither offers evidence; but BF, who collaborated with Vaughan in his edition, may have provided the date.

4. Franklin to unknown, below, April 12, 1770; see also William S. Johnson to Jonathan Trumbull, Feb. 3, 1770, Mass. Hist. Soc. *Collections*, 5th ser., IX, 407.

5. Pownall, in giving it to him, remarked that the principles and their application "'were intended to remedy the prejudice indigestion indecision and errors then prevailing either in opinions or conduct; he [Pownall] adds, 'The very attention to the investigation may lead to the discovery of *some truths respecting the whole British Empire*, then little thought of and scarce even suspected; and which perhaps it would not be *prudent* at this time to mark and point out.'" Vaughan, *Miscellaneous Pieces*, p. 547 n. The authority for this remark can only have been BF, but Pownall's words—as was often the case—obscured his meaning.

6. *Ibid.*, pp. 537–47.

did not specifically comment, and with two exceptions have omitted Pownall's footnotes, which may be found in Vaughan. Our aim is to reproduce only enough of Pownall to make Franklin comprehensible.

1. The Settlers of Colonies in America did not carry with them the *Laws of the Land*, as being bound by them wherever they should settle. They left the Realm to avoid the inconveniences and hardships they were under, where some of those Laws were in Force; particularly ecclesiastical Laws, those for payment of Tythes and others. Had it been understood that they

"I. Whenever any *Englishmen* go forth *without the Realm*, and make Settlements *in Partibus exteris*, 'These Settlements, as *English* Settlements, and these Inhabitants, as *English* Subjects, *carrying with them the Laws of the Land*,[7] wherever they form Colonies, and receiving his Majesty's Protection by virtue of his Royal Charter...have and enjoy all Liberties and Immunities of Free and Natural Subjects, to all Intents, Constructions, and Purposes whatsoever, as if they and every of them were born within the Realm;'[8] and are bound by the like Allegiance as every other Subject of the Realm.

were to carry these Laws with them, They had better have staid at home among their friends,[9] unexposed to the risques and toils of a new settlement. They carried with them, a

Right to *such Parts* of the *Laws of the Land*, as they should judge advantageous or usefull to them: a Right to be Free from those they thought hurtfull: And a Right to make

such others, as They should think necessary, not infringing the general Rights of Englishmen. And such *new* Laws they were to form, as agreeable as might be to the Laws of England. B:F

"II. Therefore the Common Law of *England*, (except as hereafter excepted) and all such Statutes as

7. The pamphlet in the Library Co. of Philadelphia has here a note in BF's hand: "Query. Did they carry any Laws with them, or only a Power of Making Laws?" This was apparently a first jotting for his later and fuller observation.

8. [*Pownall's note:*] General Words in all Charters.

9. BF repeated this argument in 1770 in his marginalia on *An Inquiry into the Nature and Causes of the Present Disputes* . . ., printed below at the end of XVII.

were Enacted and in Force at the Time in which such Settlers went forth, and such Colonies and Plantations were established, together with all such Alterations and Amendments as the said Common Law may have received, is from Time to Time, and at all Times, the Law of those Colonies and Plantations.

2. So farr as they adopt It; by express Laws or by Practise.   B:F

---

3. It is doubted whether any Settlement of the Crown by Parliament takes place in the Colonies, otherwise than by Consent of the Assemblies there. Had the Rebellion in 1745 succeeded so far as to settle the Stewart Family again on the Throne, by Act of Parliament,

"III. Therefore all Statutes touching the Right of the Succession, and Settlement of the Crown, with the Statutes of Treason relating thereto; all Statutes regulating or limiting the general Powers and Authority of the Crown, and the Exercise of the Jurisdiction thereof; All Statutes declaratory of the Rights and Liberty of the Subject; do extend to all *British* subjects in the Colonies and Plantations, as of common Right, and as if they and every of them were born within the Realm.

I think the Colonies would not have thought themselves bound by such an Act. They would still have ad-

hered to the present Family, as long as they could.   B:F
[Obs. in Reply. They are bound to

the King and his Successors, and We know no Succession but by Act of Parliament.
                T:P.][1]

---

4. It is doubted whether any Act of Parliament should *of right* operate in the Colonies: *in fact* [how-

"IV. All Statutes enacted since the Establishment of Colonies and Plantations do extend to and operate within the said Colonies and Plantations in which Statutes the same are specially named.

---

1. Brackets in the original.

ever]² several of
them have and
do operate.

5. These Laws   "V. Statutes and Customs which respect only the
have no Force   special and local Circumstances of the Realm do not
in America; not extend to and operate within said Colonies and
merely because   Plantations where no such special and local Cir-
local circum-   cumstances are found."
stances differs; Examples are laws relating to ecclesiastical and
but because   manorial courts, copyholds, tithes, the poor, and
they have never particular localities.
been adopted,
or brought
over by Acts of
Assembly or by
Practice in the
Courts.   B:F:

                 VI. No statute made since the establishment of the
                 colonies, except as described in Articles III and IV
                 above, operates within the colonies.
6. Answer. No.   Query: Would such a statute be operative if it abro-
The Parliament   gated the colonial charters when they were not
has no such   contrary to law or otherwise forfeited, or if it took
Power. The   away the colonists' rights and privileges as British
Charters can-   subjects?
not be alter'd   Assuming that matters of fact, right, and law have
but by Consent   been correctly stated above, it follows that British
of Both
Partīes; the
King and the
Colonies.   B:F:

                 subjects outside the realm, as long as they are not
                 included in a union with it, have a right to civil
7. Right.   B:F: governments of their own, which exercise the same

2. Brackets in the original; Vaughan omitted this word.

power over them as the British government does over subjects within the realm.

8. Several of these Rights are established by special Colony Laws. If any are not yet so established, the Colonies have Right to such Laws: And the Covenant having been made in the Charters by the King, for himself and his Successors, Such Laws ought to receive the Royal Assent *as of Right*.   B:F:

It follows, secondly, that the rights of the subject as declared in the Petition of Right, the act abolishing Star Chamber, the Habeas Corpus Act, the Bill of Rights, etc., extend to the colonists of common right.

It follows, thirdly, that freeholders in the colonies share in the power of making the laws by which they are governed, through sending representatives to an assembly which has, with the crown, the same jurisdiction in the colony that parliament has in Britain.

It follows, fourthly, that executive and judicial officers and courts have the same power and jurisdiction as their British equivalents, and that no court outside a colony has legal authority over any citizen of that colony.

9. The King has *the Command* of all military Force in his Dominions. But in every distinct

It follows, lastly, that the command of all military forces resides in the King or his vicegerent, "so that the King cannot by any Commission of Regency[3] ... separate or withdraw the supreme Command of the Military from the Office of supreme Civil Magistrate, either by reserving this Command in his own Hands, to be exercised and executed independent

---

3. [*Pownall's note:*] If the King was to absent himself, for a Time, from the Realm, and did, as usual, leave a Regency in his Place, his Locum Tenens as supreme Civil Magistrate, Could he authorize and commission any Military Commander in Chief to command the Militia, Forts, and Forces, independent of such Regency? Could he do this in *Ireland*? Could he do this in the Colonies and Plantations, where the Governor is already by Commission, or Charter,

State of his Dominions there should be the Consent of the Parliament or Assembly (the Representative Body) to *the Raising and Keeping up* such Military Force. He cannot even raise Troops and Quarter them in another, without the Consent of that Other. He cannot *of Right* bring Troops raised in Ireland and quarter them in Britain, but with the Consent of the Parliament of Britain: Nor carry to Ireland and quarter there, Soldiers raised in Britain, without the Consent of the Irish Parliament; unless in Time of Warr and Cases of extreme Exigency. In 1756 when the Speaker went up to present the Money-Bills, He said among other things, that "England was capable of Fighting her own Battles and defending herself; And although ever attached to your Majestys Person, ever at ease under your just Government; They

of the Civil Power, nor by granting a distinct Commission to any Military Commander in Chief,—so to be exercised and executed—But more especially not within such Jurisdictions where such supreme Military Power (so far as the Constitution knows and will justify the same) is already annexed and granted to the Office of supreme Civil Magistrate. And hence it is that the King cannot erect or establish any law martial or military command, by any commission which may supersede and not be subject to the supreme civil magistrate, within the respective precincts of the civil jurisdiction of said colonies and plantations; otherwise than in such manner as the said law martial and military commissions are annexed or subject to the supreme civil jurisdiction within his Majesty's realms and dominions of *Great Britain* and *Ireland*. And hence it is that the establishment and exercise of such commands and commissions would be illegal."[4]

or both, under the Great Seal, Military Commander in Chief, as Part of (and inseparably annexed to) the Office of supreme Civil Magistrate, his Majesty's Locum Tenens within said Jurisdictions? If he could—Then while openly, by Patent, according to Law, he appeared to establish a free *British* Constitution —he might, by a Fallacy, establish a Military Power and Government.

4. Pownall elaborated upon this point in his speech in the House of Commons on May 8, 1770: he argued that the Secretary of State had had no legal right to order Gage's occupation of Castle William in Boston harbor, because this constituted an infringement of the military power granted to the Governor in his commission under the great seal. *Cavendish's Debates*, II, 5-7.

cannot forbear taking Notice of some Circumstances in the present Situation of Affaires, which nothing but the Confidence in your Justice, could hinder from alarming their most serious Apprehensions. Subsidies to foreign Princes, when already burthened with a Debt scarce to be borne, cannot but be severely felt. An *Army of* FOREIGN TROOPS, *a thing unprecedented, unheard of, unknown,* BROUGHT INTO ENGLAND; cannot but alarm &c. &c." (See the Speech.)[5] N.B. these FOREIGN TROOPS were part of the Kings Subjects, Hanoverians, and all in *his* Service; which the same thing as *****. B:F:

Marginalia in a Pamphlet by Allan Ramsay

MS notations in the margins of a copy in the Library of Congress of [Allan Ramsay,] *Thoughts on the Origin and Nature of Government, Occasioned by the Late Disputes between Great Britain and Her American Colonies: Written in the Year 1766* (London, 1769).

Allan Ramsay (1713–84), the son of the Scottish poet of the same name, was one of the most fashionable artists of the period, and in 1767 became portrait-painter to the King. He was also a political theorist of more boldness of mind than logical rigor, as this pamphlet indicates. It is the first of four on governmental subjects that he published between 1769 and 1783, and it covers a wide range of subjects. Franklin's comments, in consequence, have an equal range. Some of them, such as those on the Americans' independence of Parliament, are repetitious; but others explore new ground or old ground in new ways—the freedom of men in a state of nature, the principle of representation, the role of land in taxation. Although the comments are at times fragmentary and always unpolished, they reveal in sum Franklin's interests and outlook as fully as, if more informally than, his other writings of the time. The date of the marginalia, as usual, cannot be precisely determined. Our guess is that they were written shortly after the pamphlet appeared; in any case we are assigning them, according to our practice, to the earliest likely date.

5. The emphases are of course BF's. He condenses the part of the speech that he quotes, and omits a pertinent point that Speaker Onslow made at the end: the Commons hope "that the sword of these foreigners should not be entrusted a moment out of your hand, to any other person whatsoever." Cobbett, *Parliamentary History*, XV, 770.

The question of Parliament's right to tax America is the most important that has ever been debated in Britain, because it raises the issue of supreme authority and therefore of Britain's existence as a state. Although I support the rights of government, I blame the administration for the way in which American claims have been advanced; "I cannot help considering *those claims*, and the *indecent manner in* which they have *been urged*, as something very much to their disadvantage." Once the government is attacked, it must be defended by every one who supports the empire, "the prosperity, the *very existence* of which depend upon *the union of all its parts under one head*."

Almost any calamity in a nation will be advantageous to some one in it. Caesar, who preferred to be first in a village to being second in Rome, would

Margin: By whom?

Margin: If such an Union be necessary to G.B. let her endeavour to obtain it by fair Means. It cannot be forced.

---

doubtless have reduced Rome to a village rather than let another be superior to him there. I am not addressing my arguments to such ambitious men.

The principle is frequently advanced that all men in their natural state are free and independent, but in practice this is untrue. "*No history of the past, no observation of the present time, can be brought to countenance such a natural state.*" The principle of an equal right to liberty, which is inseparable from an equal right to property, has never in fact been acknowledged by any but the lowest classes, who use it to cut the throats and seize the goods of their betters.

From the principle, nevertheless, has been derived the conclusion that government exists by virtue of a social contract, whereby each individual surrenders a portion of his natural independence in order to form a sovereign power for the protection

Margin: A bad Account of Cesar.

Margin: This Writer is ignorant that all the Indians of North America not under the Dominion of the Spaniards, are in that *Natural State*, being restrain'd by no Laws, having no Courts or Ministers of Justice, no

Suits, no
Prisons, no
Governors
vested with any
legal Authority.
The Persuasion
of Men distin-
guish[ed] by
Reputation of
Wisdom is the
only Means by
which others
are govern'd or
rather led. And
the State of
these Indians
was probably
the first State of
all Nations.

This is an As-   of all. But, because "*no such state of independence was*
sertion contrary *ever known to exist*," the social contract is equally
to Fact, as I   mythical. If the legality of a government depended
have shown   on contract, there never was a legal government.
above, and
therefore all
Inferences from
it are un-
founded.

This is only   "Such are the idle dreams of metaphysicians."
your Dream.

     The rights of government derive, not from a vol-
untary human contract, but from human weakness
and necessities. A solitary individual flies for pro-
May not Equals   tection to whoever is strong enough to provide it,
unite with   and offers that person his service in return for sec-
Equals for   urity. This is the true social contract, a relation of

common Pur- | weaker and stronger. Society is composed of the
poses? | ruling and the ruled, "*all equality* and *independence*

being by the law of nature *strictly forbidden:* and it is

I do not find
this strange
Law among
those of Nat-
ure. I doubt it
is forged, and
not in the
Book.

being by the law of nature *strictly forbidden:* and it is
farther declared by the same authority, that whoso-
ever is not able to command, nor *willing to obey,*
shall *forfeit his living or his life."*

The relationship of master and servant clearly has
natural and divine sanction; what is not so clear is the
limits of the master's right. The whole basis of my
argument is "that *the sole determination of that right*

That is, He that
is strongest
may do what
he pleases with
those that are
weaker. A most
Equitable Law
of Nature in-
deed.

rests with the superior; because, if that is not allowed,
it cannot under God reside any where; and so the

No Man would
unite in Society
on such Terms.

union, which we suppose so *necessary in society*,...
must of course be dissolved."

Is it, has it been
always so?

Any viable society, then, is divided into two parts,
of which the governing is "*always the least numerous*" and acts as a single mind. This is the ruling

Is there then no
such thing as a
Society in
which the Ru-
ling Power is
circumscrib'd
by previous
Laws or Agree-
ments?

power, "*whose will*...must be allowed *the measure
of its own rights*, and of those of its subjects." Such a
power has no right to do wrong, but it alone can
determine right and wrong; and against it private
judgment has no standing. Conflicts between indi-

307

One may easily imagine then how the Decisions will turn.

viduals may be left to ordinary judges, but in whatever concerns the safety of the whole *"the governing part must, of necessity, be both judge and party."* This is the price of having government.

Natural rights and natural laws are the framework within which the ruler must legislate. Any act of power that is unnecessary, or that does not promote the safety of the whole, is a breach of the natural compact between ruler and ruled. Sacrifices made in war, even when pointless, do not impair that

But then you say the *Ruler* and not the *Ruled* are to judge whether any Exertion of Power is illegal.

This seems extravagant on the other side. Does he expect ever to see Rulers incapable of Mistakes, even the smallest?

compact; yet *"the smallest injury done by Government to the meanest peasant,* where no necessity of state can be rationally alledged, is sufficient to throw the whole into confusion."

It appears here [that?] He does not expect such Impeccability but the Contrary: What then can hinder the whole (as he says above) going into Confusion?

God seems to have said to those in authority, take power and use it for the good of all. "'The task I impose is difficult,...and *you will commit many errors in the performance of it:* but go on boldly, be not discouraged, for *none of those errors shall be imputed*

How so?

to you as crimes, if you can forgive yourself, all men shall forgive you." Power must be used only for maintaining authority and preserving order; use for any other purpose will be punished.

No wonder these Commands were not attended to, as perhaps they never were before heard of.

"From an *inattention to these great commands* have arisen all the disorders and revolutions in government with which history acquaints us." Forcing men to profess religious opinions, for instance, that

And yet King Lords and Commons of England have supposed this, as well as other Kings and Governments. France still supposes it, and Spain and Portugal.

were contrary to their consciences "could *never be supposed by any but ideots*, necessary for the support of government." Yet we all know what happened to the Spaniards when they tried this in the Low Countries, or to the Stuarts in Britain.

Nobody; but Every body.

If you ask who has the right to judge which acts of power are or are not contrary to nature, "I answer, *no body.* The immediate impulse of *every man's* feelings *stands in the stead of all judgment* in such cases." For men rise together against the government, and it falls.

What do these laws of nature have to do with the controversy between Britain and America? The original compact, it is alleged, has been broken; but when and how? By our being taxed without our consent, say the Americans, which is contrary to the law of nature. "*When you ask them to quote the page*; or shew them some law of nature which speaks the very reverse, it is then by the constitution of Britain.

Does not *every Man's Feelings*, as he says, Declare that his

Property is not
to be taken
from him with-
out his Con-
sent?

The Solemn
Declaration of
the Petition of
Right &c., is
that no Man
shall be taxed
but by common
Consent in
Parliament.

There when they are shewn that the *solemn declarations* of the legislature, and the constant practice,....
speak against them, they declare themselves against
all those solemn declarations and practices, telling

Very true.

Probably he
here means
Lock, Sidney,
&c.

us, that what has been done, if wrongfully done,
confers no right to repeat it, and back again they go
to their laws of nature, or to the *flimsy hypothesis of
some scholastic writer* to new-model nature and the
constitution of England...."

What is the nature of the taxing power, and does
it differ, as the Americans contend, from other forms
of legislation? Not all subjects can be employed in
the public service, but all should contribute to the
support of those who are. A tax is itself a form of
service, and such a vital one that only the supreme
power may determine it. A subject who determines
his own service is no longer a subject. The English

This is a quib-
bling Argu-
ment. If I
appoint a Rep-
resentative for
the express
purpose of

people have no right of consent to taxation: once
they elect a House of Commons, they surrender to
it the absolute control of their purse strings. If their
confidence is abused, it is true, they may oust their
representatives at the end of seven years; but this
has nothing to do with the freedom of the Commons
to do as it pleases while it holds power.[6] Although

6. The "quibbling Argument" with which BF takes issue is, even more
clearly than other parts of the pamphlet, straight Rousseau. Ramsay is para-

doing a Business for me that is for MY SERVICE and that of others, and to consider what I am to pay as my Proportion of the Expence necessary for accomplishing that Business, I am then tax'd by my own Consent. A Number of Persons

its composition may change with elections, its right as part of the government is perpetual. A manifestation of this right is the Parliamentary rule that with

unite to form a Company for Trade, Expences are necessary, Directors are chosen to do the Business and proportion those Expences. They are paid a Reasonable Consideration for their

Trouble. There is nothing of weak and strong, Protection on one hand, and Service on the other. The Directors are the Servants, not the Masters; their Duty

is prescrib'd, the Power they have is from the Members and returns to them. The Directors are also accountable. The Money paid is for the Benefit of the Payers.

No Petition is admitted against a Money Bill because the Representatives are sent expressly to make such Bills, among other Business to be done for the People.[7]

a money bill, unlike almost any other form of legislation, a petition against it is not admitted while the bill is under consideration.

---

phrasing the following passage from *The Social Contract*: "The English imagine they are a free people; they are however mistaken: they are such only during the election of members of parliament. When these are chosen, they become slaves again...." *The Miscellaneous Works of Mr. J. J. Rousseau...* (5 vols., London, 1767), V, 125.

7. BF's explanation is correct but incomplete. For the reasons behind the formulation of this relatively new rule of the House see P. D. G. Thomas, *The House of Commons in the Eighteenth Century* (Oxford, 1971), pp. 68–71.

To show "the frivolousness of the vulgar notion that the people of England keep the possession of their own purses, and give their consent to their own taxation by their representatives," suppose that the Commons, Lords, and even the King were elected every seven years by all the men of England: still *"they would be taxed without their own consent,* as much as if they lived under the great Turk.... This supposed representation, even with regard to the House of Commons, is very far from being true, and... the word *Virtual,* which has been clapped in, to supply this defect, has no meaning at all." The history of the evolution of Parliament proves that an elected member represents only his own constituency. He votes, however, to tax people all over the country who had no part in choosing him; *"yet*

All mere quibbling!

This Author seems to like a Paradox.

Thus the English change their Ground as well as the American! We were once told much of this virtual *Representation.*[8]

it never came into any bodies head to fancy that the money levied from them for the publick service, was illegally and unconstitutionally levied."

Freeholders either sat or were represented in Parliament because they were powerful. When they lost their power through becoming impoverished, they lost their vote: the act of 8 Henry VI limited the franchise to those among them who

When Money was levied from the Principality of Chester by Act of a Parliament in which they had no Representative, it came into the Heads of all the Bishops, Abbots, Barons, Knights, and other Free holders and Inhabitants,

8. For the earlier controversy on this point see Edmund S. and Helen M. Morgan, *The Stamp Act Crisis* (Chapel Hill, [1953]), pp. 76–81.

Clergy and
Laity, that the
Money was
levied from
them *illegally*.
They told the

King so, and he
owned it. They
told the Parlia-
ment so, and it
came into the

Parliaments
Heads to con-
fess it, make
the Remon-
strance of that

County a Pre-
amble to the
Bill by which
Redress was
given them.[9]

This Act was
an infamous
Breach of
Trust and viola-
tion of the
Rights of the
Freeholders,
who certainly
never by their
Choice intend-
ed to impower
their Repre-
sentatives to
deprive them of
their Right of
Voting for
Representatives
thereafter. The
very next Act

possessed at least 40 shillings a year, on the ground that elections would otherwise become dangerously tumultuous.

This act was intended to stabilize the constitution by halting the increase in the number of voters. The intention has been thwarted, however, by the changing value of money. There are now ten 40-shilling freeholders for one in the time of Henry VI. "But although these are legal voters by the letter of

arbitrarily
limits the
Wages of
Working
People, and
provides for
compelling
them to work
at the Rates pre-

scribed, which
seems to show,
that Tumults
were only
the Pretence,
and that the
true Intention
was to put it

out of the
Power of the
Populace [to]
obstruct the
Election of
those who thus
oppress'd
them.[1]

9. Medieval Chester, as a palatinate, was immune to national taxation. When a Parliament in 1450 attempted to levy a subsidy on the city and county, they petitioned on the ground that they had their own parliament; and Henry VI agreed that they should remain free from outside levies. For their petition and the King's answer see Joseph Hemingway, *History of the City of Chester from Its Foundation to the Present Time*... (2 vols., Chester, 1831), I, 107–9.

1. The famous statute of 1430 (8 Hen. VI, c. 7), which determined the property qualification for county voters until 1832, was only one in a series of acts intended to regularize elections. The purpose was not so much to disenfranchise freeholders on principle as to prevent local magnates from swamping the county courts with retainers in order to secure the election of their own men to the House of Commons. "The very next Act" (8 Hen. VI, c. 8) set no new policy, as BF implies, but merely continued an act of two years before that had expired, whereby local magistrates were empowered to set workmen's wages by proclamation. These acts also were parts of a long series, beginning with the Statute of Laborers of 1351.

313

The ancient
Constitution
was previous to
this Act: and
by that all had
a Right to
vote.[2]

the law, they are not so by the spirit of *the ancient constitution*, which plainly intended to lop off nine out of ten of them...." In addition there are "the

Why have not
the Copy-
holders a Vote?
As to those
who hold no
Lands, they in
fact never pay
any Taxes in
reality, but in
appearance
only. You may
if you please
make a Law
that all the
Taxes necessary
for the Service
of the State
shall be paid by

labourers, the farmers, and even the copy-holders of land, who have no vote in chusing those who impose taxes on them."

the Labourers
only. This
would not
affect the La-
bourers. Sup-
pose by such a
Law each
Labourer who
receives but
12*d.* a Day
should be
taxed £5. The
Effect would
only be that he

must thence-
forth have
£5 1*s.* for a
Days Labour
paid by his
Employer.
Taxes must be
paid out of the
Produce of the
Land. There is
no other pos-
sible Fund.
Therefore the

Consent of
Landholders is
only necessary.
Merchants,
Manufacturers,
&c. pay no
taxes really, but
only appar-
ently: For they
rate their Goods
in Proportion
to the Con-
sumers.

All Quibble.
If the Grand
Seignior is sole
Landlord he
pays all Taxes
out of his

Virtual representation, as a principle of government, means that those elected, whatever their number, represent the whole. But suppose that all the land is held by a single freeholder, as in Turkey. "Then is the Grand Signor virtual representative of all the people of Turkey, their universal knight of the shire, and, in a most parliamentary manner, levies what taxes he pleases upon them, by their own consent."

2. This is of course untrue: members of the House of Commons in the Middle Ages, whether burgesses or knights of the shire, were in fact often chosen by small oligarchies and sometimes even by individuals.

Rents, for the greater his Tax the less he can otherwise receive of his Tenants, Since the Produce of the Earth is the only Source of Revenue. So it is by *his own Consent* that he *taxes himself.*

I have begun by showing that the idea of a

A most impudent Assertion!

people's consenting to be taxed "is *contrary to the nature of government,* and *unsupported by any fact.*

A Scotchman by this Phrase.

I have been *at pains* to shew that the notion of the legislative power acting by virtue of representation,

How comes it then, that the Commons *only,* who are chosen by the People, grant Money, and lay Taxes?

is no principle in the British constitution; and I have

They would once have us Americans satisfy'd with this Notion of *virtual Representation:* But having made them asham'd of it, they now tell us there is

finished by shewing that the words *virtual representation,* either mean nothing at all, or mean a great deal more than those who use them would be willing to admit: and yet, after all my pains, my American antagonists are as much out of my reach as before."

Their claiming the right of Englishmen to be taxed by their own consent misled me into thinking that they wanted to be represented in Parliament. They say instead that each colony has a parliament, which alone has the power of raising money. The question at issue, for all its importance, is so simple

315

[marginal note] no such thing in the British Constitution as Representation at all!

[marginal note] Yours does not seem to be such.

as to be "within the compass of a *plain and sound understanding*. The *principles* upon which it is to be

[marginal note] This excellent Principle is, that Power gives Right. A Right to judge, think and act as it pleases.

discussed are *universal, comprehensive*, and applicable to every possible case; and *every opposition* to

[marginal note] Mere Assertion without the least Proof.

them is immediately *reducible to a falsity* in point of fact, or *an absurdity in point of reasoning.*" The only difficulty in applying them arises from the Americans' inability or unwillingness to say what they want. First they apparently want the rights of

[marginal note] A Falsity! They were always taxed like British Subjects by their own Representatives, and are willing to continue so to be taxed.

When an American says he has a Right to all the Privileges of a British Subject, he does not call

British subjects; then "*they refuse to be taxed like other British subjects*, and each colony requires a parliament of its own.

himself a British Subject, he is an American Subject of the King; the Charters say they shall be entitled to all the Privileges of Englishmen as if *they had been* born *within* the Realm. But they were and are *without* the Realm, therefore not British Subjects; and tho' within the King's Dominions, because they voluntarily agreed to be his Subjects when they took his Charters, and have created those Dominions for him, yet they are not within the Dominion of Parliament which has no Authority but *within* the Realm.

Only to the King.

This is an invidious Turn. *They have indeed equal Right.*

"At one time they acknowledge their *subjection to Great Britain*; and almost in the same breath, endeavour to prove that each petty colony has *a right to be her equal.* One moment *they* bar all considerations of force... in deciding the rights of sovereigns

Here the Acti[ons] of one or two Mobs are ascribed to the whole People of America. If this is so then ascribe the Actions of Wilkes' Mob to the whole People of Britain.

and subjects, and the next *endeavour to establish what they call their rights by a variety of outrages, such as were never imputed to any established government of the most arbitrary kind.* At one time an American claims the rights of an Englishman; if these are not suffi-

When did he ever drop them? He has undoubtedly this Right both of an Irishman and a Hano verian, to be govern'd by his own Prince and the Laws of his own Country, and not by the Parliament of Britain.

Who has ever

cient, *he drops them,* and claims the rights of an *Irishman*; and, when these do not fully answer his purpose, he expects to be put upon the footing of a *Hanoverian....*

"First they try to found the extraordinary privileges they claim upon birth-right; but when *they are shewn that by birth they had no right to desert their native*

shewn them this? Does not all History show the con-trary? Have not all Mankind in all Ages had the Right of deserting their Native Country when made un-easy in it? Did not the Saxons desert their Native Country when they came to Brit-ain? Is it not Tyranny in any Government to make Prisoners of its Subjects, and is it not contrary to their Rights? Will a Scotch-man tell us this, whose Com-patriots are to be found in every Country upon Earth? Could there possibly be more than one legal Govern-ment in the World at this Time if this Doctrine is true? Must not all Nations but the first be Deserters?

An impudent Falsity! When did they ever drop their Birth right? When were they shewn this? Are Charters exempting the Receivers from the Laws in being, empowering them to make new Laws and different, to make War, punish with Death, &c. given to every common Corporation?

country, they drop the birthright, and bring forth their charters. When they *are shewn* that *these charters* are *no other* than *what are given to every common corporation and trading company*, they then cease to be char-

And Compacts they are and ever were.

ters and become all at once *compacts*. At one time *it is the love of liberty* that made them take shelter in

Another Mis-

those distant climes, from the tyranny of preroga-

318

representation. It was to enjoy *Liberty* of Conscience, and Freedom from tyrannical Acts of Parliament, that they went to a Country where neither

tive; yet when we ask them with whom they made those compacts just mentioned, they tell us, with a King James or a King Charles. How must the *great*

| the Power of Parliament nor of Prerogative had any Existence, and where the King, | on the Condition that they would continue to own him as their Sovereign, was contented | to limit the Pretensions of his Prerogative by solemn Charters. |

These great Men he treats with great Contempt in a former Part of this Pamphlet, calling their Opinions *the idle Dreams of Metaphysicians*, and *the flimsey Hypotheses of scholastic Writers.*3 It is the Character of the Scotch to be contemptuous.

shades of Algernon Sidney and John Lock exclaim, how must they rage... to hear that there should be Englishmen who pretend to read and admire their writings, and yet understand them so little as *to own that they had entered into a compact,* or as these patriots would call it, a conspiracy, with a King, in order to obtain a dispensation from the laws of the land, and the authority of parliament!

He does not know that both Sidney and Locke were concerned in drawing up two of those

"The assertion that these charters are not charters, but Pacta conventa, is brim-full of absurdity. For, passing over the manifest illegality already

3. See above, pp. 306, 310. BF is now asserting as fact his earlier supposition about the writers whom Ramsay had in mind.

Charters, viz.
that for Caro-
lina, and that
for Pensilvania.[4]
This Paragraph
is all mere
Banter.

The whole had   hinted, of one part of the sovereign power *dispensing*
[no] Authority   *with the authority of the whole*; the *whole sovereign*
in America and
so the Absurd-
ity vanishes.

This is a most   power *could not*, by the nature of things, enter into
extravagant   any indefeasible compact of that sort." For sover-
Assertion.   eignty by its nature has no degrees but is always
Would the   supreme, and cannot be destroyed, whereas a com-
Author per-   pact is between independent sovereignties. If such
suade us that   a compact is to be anything more than a treaty, to be
the *whole Sov-*   observed only as long as it suits the convenience of
ereign Power   both parties, the agreement itself must recognize
cannot stipulate   some superior power that will enforce its terms and
with a Part of   amend them as the need arises. Otherwise, "in case
the People that   of any misunderstanding, there lies no appeal but to
are gone into   the God of battles, whose decision only suspends
a foreign
Country, that   were t[rue?]   to Colonists as   Writer imports
for their   not only Char-   something to be   that there is no
Encouragement   ters but Acts of   depended on.   Right but
they shall have   Parliament are   Indeed the   Power, and that
certain Advant-   mere Vanity   whole Doctrine   nothing is
ages? If this   when propos'd   of t[his?]   wrong which

4. Sidney is supposed to have assisted William Penn in drawing up the
Frames of Government of Pennsylvania, but whether he did so is doubtful.
DNB. John Locke's famous Fundamental Constitutions of 1669 provided for
a quasi-feudal system in Carolina, which never became operative but contributed to the friction between colonists and proprietors that eventually ended
proprietary government.

you are able to
do; and conse-
quently, when-
ever the Colo-
nies are strong
enough, they
may dissolve
their Charters,
and set up Kings
of their own.

And so it seems   the suit till a future term, when the party that was
that whoever   cast may find the means of entering a new action."
has [a] Decision The classic example of such a superior power is in
in his Favour,
is really in the
Right; and thus
successful Vil-
lainy is never
wrong, and the
Cesar he con-
demns p. 6 [p.
305 above] was
as good a Man
as Marcus
Antoninus.

                  the Act of Union between England and Scotland.
A Phrase of the   In "this *solemn paction*" one article empowers the
Scottish Law.   new British Parliament to interpret all the other
                  articles of the union so created. In 1725 many Scots
                  objected to a newly enacted tax on malt as an un-
                  constitutional exercise of Parliament's authority,
Would you   and rioted against the tax-collectors and those who
charge these   had supported the act. The government recognized
Riots to the   that the dignity of Parliament required obedience.
Account of all
Scotland, as
you do those in

Boston to all
the Americans?
P. 51 [p. 317
above].

Troops have
also been sent
to Boston; but
with what Ef-
fect? They have
made the mat-
ter worse.

"There were sent to Glasgow, where the pretended standard of liberty was set up, some companies of foot, and some troops of dragoons," who soon brought the rioters to understand the rights of the

This is telling
us, We will not
reason with
you, but we will
cut your
Throats.

legislature.[5] This the Americans will call "club law, . . . but there never was a question of supremacy decided by any other sort of law." Force and law are inseparable. "Is it to *argument* or club law, to which the *respectable populace* of Boston and Rhode-island

Is it fair to put
this Charge
upon the Pub-
lic, and intro-
duce the Mobs
and their Ac-
tions instead of
the Assemblies
and their Peti-
tions Remon-
strances and
solemn Resolu-
tions?

trust the justice of their cause? Is it *argument* to demolish the houses or destroy the goods of those who differ from them in opinion; or is it argument to carry them to the *tree of liberty*, and there oblige them to take God to witness to sentiments not their own,

5. A knotty constitutional question was implicit in the Act of Union: did or did not the Parliament of Great Britain have the power to amend the statute that had called it into existence? Two early Parliamentary attempts to tax Scottish malt, one in 1713 and one in 1725, brought this question to the fore. Both attempts were denounced as violations, on different grounds, of the Act of Union. The first was abandoned in face of a threat to repeal that act, and the second led to the Glasgow riots.

for fear of being immediately put to death? *These are*

What is all this *outrages* which none but the most ignorant and dis-
to the Purpose? tempered imaginations could ever dread from any
Have not the kind of established government, and yet are com-
Assemblies mitted by those, who...complain of cruel and ar-
condemn'd bitrary exertions of power in the mild government
these Actions, of Great Britain, under the most just and humane of
and made good Kings."
all Damages to
the Sufferers?
How wicked it
is then, thus to
misrepresent a
Country, in
order to irritate
Government
against it?

I have used the word "colony" in conformance

The Term of with present usage. But falsehood is promoted by
British Subjects "the admission of *improper terms*," which in this case
he might have has led to an analogue with Greek colonies, "*which,*
given as an
Instance.

Well acknow- *indeed, had little other relation to their mother-country,*
ledg'd. *than a sort of cousinship.*" In fact the American pro-

A Mistake then vinces "are not properly *colonies* either in word or
in the Acts of deed. Their most ancient name is plantations, and
Parliament that
call them so.

A Province, they have always been, in fact, *provinces*, governed
strictly speak- by a lieutenant or governor, sent by the King...."
ing, is a *Country* The inhabitants are entitled to their rights, not by
conquered,[6] virtue of descent, but from

6. BF is right about the derivation, if not the meaning, of the word: a province
in Roman history was an area outside Italy conquered and administered by
Rome.

therefore not so
applicable to
the Settlements
in America, no
conquered
People living
in them.

Here the Author   "their being faithful *subjects of Great Britain*; since
(and most of
these Writers
do the same)
bewilders him-
self by admit-
ting an
improper Term.
See P. 60 [p. 323
above]. They
are Subjects of
the King. The
People of G. B.
are Subjects
themselves.
They are not
Sovereigns.
They have no
Subjects.

But what signi-   the same advantages are *by law* expressly com-
fies this Law,   municated to such of them as were born in West-
since you tell   phalia and the Palatinate, and who never set foot
us, p. 53 [p. 320 upon
above], That
the whole
Sovereign
Power can-
not make such
a Compact?

No British Ground out of Britain.

British ground till they meet with it on the other side

Names are of little Importance in this Question.

of the Atlantic." The Americans prefer "colony" to any other term because it gives them a degree of independence. But, whatever name is used, "the

Here is the Authors great Mistake repeated. Britain is not an Emperor. They are Parts of the King's Dominions, as the Provinces in France were, as

plain truth is, that those countries...are, from their nature and situation, *only subordinate parts in the empire of Britain,* and such they would

Scotland was before the Union, as Jersey, Guernsey, and Hanover are still; to be	Governed by the King according to their own Laws and Constitutions, and not by	Acts of the British Parl[ia-men]t, which has Power only *within* the Realm.

This Necessity is merely imaginary.

necessarily continue...under some other powerful European state, in case their...tie, with what they are still pleased

They us'd to call her by that endearing Appellation; but her late Conduct entitles rather to the Name of Stepmother.

to call their Mother Country, should happen to be dissolved."

The separation of Britain and her "American appertinencies" would destroy the prosperity and liberty of both. Until "New England is strong enough to *protect Old England,* and the seat of the British empire is transferred from London to Bos-

The Protection is mutual and

325

equal in Pro-
portion to
Numbers and
Wealth, at
present.

Not the least   ton, there is an *absolute necessity that the right of*
Necessity for   *giving law to America* should continue to be vested
this.   in Great Britain. That it is the interest of Great
                    Britain to protect and *cherish her American provinces*
Stick then to   *instead of oppressing them, is an undeniable truth*; and
that Truth.   it is, perhaps, no less true, that some farther atten-

Consider then   tion, and some *farther means of communication*, are
what those   still wanting to that desirable end: but let every true
should be.   friend to Britain and to all her connexions stand
                    forth in defence of her great legislative uncoun-
                    troulable power, without which no union, and of
                    course no safety, can be expected."

This Writer is concise, lively, and elegant in his Language, but his reasonings
are too refin'd and Paradoxical to make Impression on the Understanding or
convince the Minds of his Readers. And his main Fact on which they are founded is a Mistake.

Index

Compiled by Mary L. Hart

Botetourt, Lord, franked mail of, 185
Boudinot, Elias, mentioned, 268 n
Boundary, N.Y.–N.J. dispute on, 255–6, 268
Bourbon kings, mentioned, 240
Bowdoin, Elizabeth Erving, mentioned, 177
Bowdoin, James: BF's book for, 52 n, 66; work in *Exper. and Obser.*, 4th ed., 66; mentioned, 53; letter to, 176–7
Boyer, Abel, French-English dictionary, 240 n
Bradford, Andrew, prints *Amer. Weekly Mercury*, 140 n
Bradford, William (1663–1752), prints *N.Y. Gaz.*, 140 n
Bradford, William (1721?–91): enmity to BF, 35; prints BF pieces, 35; prints *Pa. Jour.*, 35
Brakenridge, William, on London population, 91, 92, 93 n, 94
Brattle Square Church, Boston, mentioned, 52 n
Bremner, James, trip to England, 188, 190
Breslau, life expectancy in, 87–8, 90, 92, 94, 96, 99, 101
Bridges, Gilpin interest in, 32
Britannia (snow), arrives, leaves Phila., 144 n, 190 n, 227 n
British Empire: importance of Anglo-American unity in, 79–80, 305, 325–6; commercial policies as danger to, 107; England's role in, 239–40; growth of, 239; Parliament's role in, 244; constitution of, 284–5; defense of, 284, 286, 290, 296; Jersey, Guernsey, Hanover role in, 325; colonies' role in, 325; mentioned, 235, 298 n
"Briton, A," (BF's pseudonym): arguments on American claims, printed, 35 n; mentioned, 17 n
British Zoology... (Pennant), for Lib. Co., 8
Brooker (postrider), mentioned, 260
Brown, Ephraim: BF's loan to, 203–4; illness, death, 203–4; letter from, 203–4
Buckles, for Elizabeth Franklin, 190
Budden, Capt. William: detained in London, 29; accident to, 29 n
Buell, Abel: petitions Conn. Assembly, 259 n; type foundry of, 259 n
Burgesses, House of, Va., petition on Townshend Acts, 15–16, 19 n; agents' petition on Townshend Acts, 54–5
Burgoyne, Gen. John, Saratoga campaign, 131 n
Burial statistics. *See* Statistics, vital.
Burke, Edmund: opposes Hillsborough's Mass. resolves, 79 n; *Observations on a Late State of the Nation...* mentioned, 120 n
Burton, Daniel: Drage recommended to, 71–2; letter to, 70–2
Bush, Gervase Parker, pamphlet attributed to, 17 n, 120 n
Bust: of BF proposed, 4; of Lords Halifax, Chatham, 4, 4 n, 6–7
Bute, Lord, mentioned, 9
Butler, George P., pamphlet attributed to, 17 n, 120 n

Cabinet, British, and efforts to repeal Townshend Acts, 233
Caesar, Julius, mentioned, 305, 321
Caicos Islands, Bahamas claims, 143 n
Caiger, Mr., recommended to BF, 128
Camden, Lord, mentioned, 253 n
Camden, S. C., Drage pastor in, 71
Canada: wealth of, compared to New England, 287; trade with Indians, Britain, 287
Canada Pamphlet. *See* Interest of Great Britain Considered....
Canals: BF's, Gilpin's interest in, [xxv], 32; possible Chesapeake–Delaware, 216–18
Candles, spermaceti, seized, defined, 208, 208 n
Canton, John: electrical phenomenon of, 112 n; on lightning rod committee for St. Paul's, 151; advised of comet (1769), 186; to dine with BF, Curtis, 224; letter to, 186
Cape Henlopen, Del., Venus' transit observed from, 154, 155, 156, 178
Carolina. *See* North Carolina; South Carolina.
Carolina (ship), leaves Phila., 189 n
Carron Ironworks, mentioned, 221 n
Carver, Jonathan: biog. note, 117 n; BF meets, 117; *Travels through the Interior of North America...* mentioned, 117 n
Case of Great-Britain and America...: BF distributes, 17; printed, 17, 17 n; Otis' ideas in, 17 n; attribution of, 17 n, 120 n; mentioned, 80 n
Castle William, Gage occupies, 303 n
Catholics, birth, burial records on, 90 n
Cattle, use of, in colonies, 46
Caudle, defined, 69 n
Census: of London, 93 n; need for, 106
Chace, Samuel, Providence postmaster, 181
Chalkley (ship), carries mail, 157, 178
Chamberlain, Mason, portrait of BF, 5 n, 206 n
Charles I: and demand for ship money, 238; and colonial charters, 319

Colonies (*cont.*)
tram, 9; BF's satirical plan for British reconciliation with, 17–18; alleged British plan to subdue, 18–19, 19–20, 237; royal placeholders, defended, 20–2; satirical estimate of cost to Britain, of subduing, 25–6; attitude toward Britain, 32, 118, 239, 245, 248–9, 278, 282, 283; use of farm animals in, 46; British, European support for, 52–3, 70 n, 120, 211; loyalty to Crown, Hanoverian kings, 118, 253, 300; Anglican bishop proposed for, 140 n; labor scarce in, 210; and efforts to revive Treason Act, 238, 245, 248; British troops in, 238, 245, 248, 283, 284; Protestantism in, 239; dominions of king, not Parliament, 244, 246, 316–17, 319, 324, 325; ignorance of, in Britain, 246, 284, 285, 291; and supposed common interest with Britain, 279, 281, 282; and British national debt, 283; supposed wealth of, 285–6, 290; and opulent entertainment of British, 290; annual value of goods consumed, 290; settlement of, 292; farm expenses, profits, 294; Mass., Va. as leaders, in anti-British agitation, 296; causes of immigration to, 317–18, 319; misrepresented, 323; Germans naturalized in, 324; as "provinces," 323–4; Britain as "step-mother," 325. *See also* Agents, colonial; Assemblies, colonial; Authority, civil; Charters, colonial; Constitution, British; Courts; Currency Act, 1764; Currency, paper; Customs Offices, Colonies; Declaratory Act; Governors; Independence; Land; Law; Manufactures; Middle colonies; New England; Nonimportation movement; Petitions and remonstrances; Post Office, North American; Queries on Townshend Act Repeal; Representation, Parliamentary; Requisition, royal; Rights; Riots and disturbances; Southern colonies; Specie; Subjects, British; Taxation; Townshend Acts; Trade, colonial, *and individual colonies by name.*
"Colonist's Advocate" series, mentioned, xxiv n
Columbia University. *See* King's College.
Comet, viewed in Paris, London, Phila. (1769), 186, 186 n, 189, 206–7
Commerce: Parliamentary regulatory acts on, 34; in labor theory of value, 108. *See also* Trade.
Commission on N.Y.–N.J. Boundary, mentioned, 268
Committee of Correspondence, N.J.: ap-

pointed, 253; instructs BF, 253–6; members of, 256, 256 n; letter from, mentioned, 264; letter from, 253–6
Committee of Correspondence, Pa.: and efforts to repeal Townshend Acts, 12; Hillsborough's Mass. resolves sent to, 12; letter to, mentioned, 35; on Phila. riot, 113–14; instructs agents, 114, 219–20; members of, 114, 220, 220 n; mentioned, 30; letters from, 113–14, 219–20
Committee of Merchants, Phila. *See* Merchants, Phila.
Committee on Lightning Rods for St. Paul's: report from, 145–51; members of, 151
Commons, House of: expels Wilkes, xxiii, 40; Hillsborough's Mass. resolves, address to king, xxiii–xxiv, 13–14, 29–30, 32 n, 35, 40 n, 64 n, 79, 245: passed, 14 n; attack on Hillsborough, 12; presentation of petitions in, 14–15; Pa., Va. petitions, 14–17; Declaratory Act read, 15; ministerial influence in, 30; T. Pownall's speeches, motion in, 30 n, 51 n, 64, 67, 79 n, 80 n, 119, 182, 298, 303 n; Grenville, R. Jackson speeches, 40, 64 n; colonial agents' petition, 54–5, 62–4; and efforts to repeal Townshend Acts, 64, 70, 80–1; efforts to amend Quartering Act, 69, 80; BF's examination before, 124, 277; and ship money demands, 239; and duties on New England goods (1643), 244 n; resolves on Treason Act, 248; Scottish representation in, 280 n; and quartering of Hanoverians' troops in England, 304; and established religion, 309; taxing power of, 310–11, 315; elections of, 313 n, 314 n; mentioned, 282, 312. *See also* Long Parliament; Representation, Parliamentary; Rump Parliament.
Compacts: colonial charters as, 318–19, 320; and sovereignty, 320
Concord (brig), leaves Phila., arrives Bristol, 227 n
"Concurrence," (trading term), defined, 34 n
Conestoga Manor Indians. *See* Indians, Indian affairs.
Congregationalists: BF raised as, 123; BF's alleged efforts to please, 125. *See also* Dissenters.
Connecticut: type made in, 259; bounty on silk cocoons, 200 n. *See also* Assembly, Conn., Charter, Conn., New England.
Connecticut Gazette, Mecom prints, 76 n
Connecticut Journal, Green brothers print, 76 n